Lecture Notes in Computer Science   1048

Edited by G. Goos, J. Hartmanis and J. van Leeuwen

Advisory Board: W. Brauer   D. Gries   J. Stoer

Springer

Berlin
Heidelberg
New York
Barcelona
Budapest
Hong Kong
London
Milan
Paris
Santa Clara
Singapore
Tokyo

Maurizio Proietti (Ed.)

Logic Program Synthesis and Transformation

5th International Workshop, LOPSTR'95
Utrecht, The Netherlands
September 20-22, 1995
Proceedings

 Springer

Series Editors

Gerhard Goos, Karlsruhe University, Germany

Juris Hartmanis, Cornell University, NY, USA

Jan van Leeuwen, Utrecht University, The Netherlands

Volume Editor

Maurizio Proietti
IASI-CNR
Viale Manzoni 30, I-00185 Rome, Italy

Cataloging-in-Publication data applied for

Die Deutsche Bibliothek - CIP-Einheitsaufnahme

Logic program synthesis and transformation : 5th international
workshop ; proceedings / LOPSTR '95, Utrecht, The
Netherlands, September 20 - 22, 1995. Maurizio Proietti (ed.). -
Berlin ; Heidelberg ; New York ; Barcelona ; Budapest ; Hong
Kong ; London ; Milan ; Paris ; Santa Clara ; Singapore ;
Tokyo : Springer, 1996
  (Lecture notes in computer science ; Vol. 1048)
  ISBN 3-540-60939-3
NE: Proietti, Maurizio [Hrsg.]; LOPSTR <5, 1995, Utrecht>; GT

CR Subject Classification (1991): D.1.2, I.2.2, D.1.6,F.4.1, F.3.1

ISBN 3-540-60939-3 Springer-Verlag Berlin Heidelberg New York

Typesetting: Camera-ready by author
SPIN 10512651   06/3142 – 5 4 3 2 1 0   Printed on acid-free paper

Foreword

Program transformation is a very powerful methodology for the development of correct and efficient programs. In applying this methodology one usually assumes that an initial program version (or a program specification) is given and it is required to derive a new program (or an implementation of the given specification). Since program specifications are often given as formulas in a logical theory, it is particularly important to study the transformation methodology in the case of logic programming.

The field of program derivation by transformation is very closely related to the field of program synthesis. In these fields, in fact, similar techniques of formula manipulation are used. For this reason it is appropriate to study the techniques for Logic Program Synthesis and Transformation as a single set of related methodologies. This is the aim of the LoPSTr workshops. During the past years, these workshops have been very fruitful and stimulating. Their success also shows the importance and the relevance of the synthesis and transformation of logic programs within the area of theoretical computer science and its practical applications.

Other areas of artificial intelligence and programming methodologies are connected to logic program synthesis and transformation. Papers from these areas have been presented and discussed in previous LoPSTr workshops and in LoP-STr'95 as well.

Among these areas I would like to mention: i) Constructive type theory, by which one may synthesize programs from a constructive proof of the existence of an element of a given type, ii) Inductive logic programming, which studies the problem of synthesizing logic programs from examples and counterexamples, iii) Abstract interpretation and program analysis, which aims at proving properties of programs by interpreting the concrete operations of the programs in some given abstract domains, iv) Partial evaluation (or partial deduction), by which one derives new and more efficient programs by exploiting some information on the values of the input variables, and v) Theorem proving, which studies the different techniques of making proofs within various logical theories.

Now I would like to list some desirable properties of the derivation steps which support the development of logic programs. These properties should be taken into account when designing a system for logic program synthesis and/or transformation. I will list those properties with reference to the program transformation process, but I think that they are of great importance also in the case of program synthesis.

1. First of all, it is desirable that every derivation step be *constructive*, that is, program P_{i+1} should be derived from program P_i by the application of a constructive transformation rule. I will not formally specify here the notion of *constructive rule*. It will be enough to say that rewriting rules of the kind one uses in rewriting systems, that is, rules which are based on: i) syntactic matching, and ii) rewriting of old expressions by new expressions, are

constructive. Thus, for instance, the usual schema-based program transformation rules are considered to be constructive. By contrast, non-constructive rules are, for instance, those whose application needs the solution of a problem which is undecidable.

2. Some derivation steps can be *lemmatic*. The meaning of this property is that when performing transformation steps, we allow ourselves to use lemmas, and these lemmas can be proved off-line (possibly, by taking advantage of some ad hoc theorem provers). This feature of the program derivation process is of major importance, because it is often the case that only by the use of lemmas can one derive very efficient programs. Indeed, for instance, linear running time algorithms for the evaluation of linear recurrence relations can be derived from given exponential running time algorithms, only if the functionality of some relevant predicates is proved.

3. Some derivation steps should allow *substitutivity*. The meaning of this property is that when a subformula, say φ, of a given program, say P_i, is shown (using program P_i) to be equivalent to a formula ψ, then we may get a new program P_{i+1} by replacing φ by ψ within P_i. This substitution should preserve the semantics of P_i, and it is performed for changing the behaviour of P_i so that, for instance, the computations evoked by P_{i+1} are more efficient than those evoked by P_i. (Here we assume that new programs are derived from old programs with the aim of improving efficiency.)

   Notice also that, although the equivalence of φ and ψ is derived from P_i, the replacement of φ by ψ within P_i may change the semantics of P_i. For instance, from the simple formula (or program) $a \leftrightarrow b$, obviously one may derive the equivalence $a \leftrightarrow b$. Thus, by replacing within $a \leftrightarrow b$ the expression b by the equivalent expression a, we get the new program $a \leftrightarrow a$ which is not equivalent to the original program.

Finally, the reader should notice that constructive, lemmatic, and substitutive derivation steps allow for machine assistance. This is important, in particular, when the size of the programs to be derived becomes considerably large, and indeed, such mechanization makes it possible to propose the derivation methodology as a valuable technique for real-life programming.

Rome
January 1996

Alberto Pettorossi

Preface

This volume contains the 19 papers presented at the *Fifth International Workshop on Logic Program Synthesis and Transformation*, LoPSTr'95, held near Utrecht (The Netherlands), September 20–22, 1995. Previous LoPSTr workshops were held in Manchester, U.K. (1991 and 1992), Louvain-la-Neuve, Belgium (1993), and Pisa, Italy (1994).

The aim of the LoPSTr workshops is to stimulate new ideas and research in the field of machine-assisted development of logic programs. The main topics of interest are: program synthesis, program transformation, and program specialization. The papers presented at LoPSTr'95 give an up-to-date overview of the current research on these topics, as well as related topics in the field of program development, such as: automated deduction, constructive type theory, implementation techniques, inductive logic programming, meta-languages, program analysis, program specification, program verification, and software engineering.

LoPSTr'95 was organized in parallel with PLILP'95 (*Seventh Symposium on Programming Languages: Implementations, Logics, and Programs*). The overall attendance at the two meetings was about 110 people from 21 countries.

Out of 40 submissions, the Program Committee selected 19 papers for presentation. After the workshop, 17 papers were submitted in their revised versions which took into account the discussion at the workshop and the comments by the referees. These papers underwent a second refereeing process and they were further revised. The two remaining presentations are recorded in these proceedings as abstracts. Most submissions, the referee reports, and the discussion among the members of the Program Committee were done by electronic mail. Several hundred electronic mail messages concerning LoPSTr'95 have been delivered to my mailbox.

LoPSTr'95 and PLILP'95 shared three invited lectures which were given by Mark Jones (Nottingham, U.K.), Oege de Moor (Oxford, U.K.), and Kim Marriott (Melbourne, Australia). The papers presented by the invited lecturers appear in the PLILP'95 proceedings (Lecture Notes in Computer Science, Vol. 982, Springer-Verlag).

I would like to thank all those who contributed to making LoPSTr'95 a successful and fruitful event. In particular, my gratitude goes to the researchers who submitted the papers, the referees, the members of the Program Committee, and the various agencies which provided financial support. Special thanks go to Prof. Doaitse Swierstra and his colleagues of Utrecht University for their invaluable work which allowed the workshop to run very smoothly and in a pleasant environment. I also would like to thank Alberto Pettorossi for his continuous advice and help. Finally, I would like to give my warmest thanks to all participants who contributed, by means of lively discussions, to making LoPSTr'95 a very stimulating event.

Rome   Maurizio Proietti
January 1996

Program Committee

A. Bossi   (Università della Calabria, Rende, Italy)
D. Boulanger   (Katholieke Universiteit Leuven, Belgium)
S. Debray   (University of Arizona, Tucson, USA)
Y. Deville   (Université Catholique de Louvain, Belgium)
L. Fribourg   (LIENS-CNRS, Paris, France)
N. Fuchs   (University of Zurich, Switzerland)
J. Gallagher   (University of Bristol, U.K.)
T. Mogensen   (University of Copenhagen, Denmark)
M. Proietti   (IASI-CNR, Roma, Italy, chair)
H. Seki   (NIT, Nagoya, Japan)
P. Tarau   (University of Moncton, Canada)
G. Wiggins   (University of Edinburgh, U.K.)

Organizing Committee

Jeroen Fokker, Erik Meijer, Margje Punt, Doaitse Swierstra

Sponsors (of LoPSTr'95 and PLILP'95)

European Commission - ESPRIT Basic Research (CompuLog-Net)
Royal Dutch Academy of Sciences (KNAW)
The Netherlands Computer Science Research Foundation (SION)
The Association of Logic Programming
IASI-CNR (National Research Council of Italy)
Universiteit Utrecht

List of Referees

The following people helped the Program Committee in refereeing the papers submitted to LoPSTr'95:

Michel Bidoit, Michele Bugliesi, Nicoletta Cocco, Livio Colussi, Sandro Etalle, Gilberto Filé, Robert Glück, Neil Jones, Vincent Lombart, Tadashi Kawamura, Alberto Pettorossi, Jakob Rehof, Taisuke Sato, Morten Heine Sorensen, Wamberto Vasconcelos.

Table of Contents

Ecological Partial Deduction: Preserving Characteristic Trees Without Constraints

Michael Leuschel

K.U. Leuven, Department of Computer Science
Celestijnenlaan 200A, B-3001 Heverlee, Belgium
e-mail: michael@cs.kuleuven.ac.be

Abstract. A partial deduction strategy for logic programs usually uses an abstraction operation to guarantee the finiteness of the set of atoms for which partial deductions are produced. Finding an abstraction operation which guarantees finiteness and does not loose relevant information is a difficult problem. In earlier work Gallagher and Bruynooghe proposed to base the abstraction operation on characteristic paths and trees. A characteristic tree captures the relevant structure of the generated partial SLDNF-tree for a given goal. Unfortunately the abstraction operations proposed in the earlier work do not always produce more general atoms and do not always preserve the characteristic trees. This problem has been solved for purely determinate unfolding rules and definite programs in [12, 13] by using constraints inside the partial deduction process.

In this paper we propose an alternate solution which achieves the preservation of characteristic trees for *any* unfolding rule, *normal* logic programs (it can even handle some built-in's if so desired) and *without* adding constraints to the partial deduction process (making the re-use of existing unfolding techniques very simple). We thus provide a powerful, generally applicable and elegant abstraction operation for partial deduction providing a fine-grained and terminating control of polyvariance.

1 Introduction

Partial evaluation has received considerable attention in logic programming (e.g. [5, 8, 22, 24]). In the context of pure logic programs, partial evaluation is often referred to as *partial deduction*, a convention we will also adhere to in this paper. An important milestone is [17], where firm theoretical foundations for partial deduction are established. It introduces the notions of *independence* and *closedness*, which are properties of the set of atoms for which the partial deduction is performed. Under these conditions, soundness and completeness of the transformed program are guaranteed. In the light of these conditions, a key problem in partial deduction is: given a set of atoms of interest, $\mathcal{A}$, provide a *terminating* procedure that computes a new set of atoms, $\mathcal{A}'$, and a partial deduction for the atoms in $\mathcal{A}'$, such that:

- every atom in $\mathcal{A}$ is an instance of an atom in $\mathcal{A}'$, and
- the closedness and independence conditions are satisfied.

Moving from the initial set $\mathcal{A}$ to the new set $\mathcal{A}'$ requires the (repeated) application of an abstraction operation. The problem of finding a proper abstraction operation is closely related to the problem of *polyvariance*, i.e. controlling how many different specialised versions of a given predicate should be generated. A good abstraction operation should, while guaranteeing termination, produce enough polyvariance to ensure satisfactory specialisation.

An approach which aims at achieving all these goals in a refined way is that of Gallagher and Bruynooghe ([7, 4]). Its abstraction operation is based on the notions of *characteristic paths* and *characteristic trees*. Intuitively, two atoms of $\mathcal{A}$ are replaced by their msg^1 in $\mathcal{A}'$, if their (incomplete) SLDNF-trees have an identical structure (this structure is referred to as the characteristic tree). Unfortunately, although the approach is conceptually appealing, several errors turn up in arguments provided in [7, 4]. These errors invalidate the termination proofs as well as the arguments regarding precision and preservation of specialisation under the abstraction operation.

In [12, 13], Leuschel and De Schreye have significantly adapted the approach to overcome these problems. An alternative abstraction operation has been introduced, which is based on so called *negative binding constraints*. The partial deduction procedure is then formulated in terms of a special purpose constraint logic programming language. The adapted approach allows to solve all problems with the original formulations in [7, 4], without loosing the claimed termination and precision properties. Unfortunately the approach is (exactly like [7]) limited to purely determinate unfolding rules (i.e. without lookahead for detecting determinacy) and is restricted to definite logic programs. These restrictions limit the practical applicability of the method.

In this paper we will present an alternate technique for *normal* logic programs (with built-in's if so desired) which is valid for *any* unfolding rule and which preserves characteristic trees *without* using constraints. As such we use the central ideas of [12, 13, 7, 4] in a novel way to provide a practically useful system which can make use of existing unfolding technology (e.g. [3, 19, 18]) in a straightforward way. The overview of the paper is as follows. In Sect. 2 we introduce the concept of a characteristic tree and give some motivations. In Sect. 3 we present the new technique of partial deduction working on characteristic atoms. In Sect. 4 we put this idea in practice and present an algorithm for partial deduction. Some examples and results are also presented. We provide some concluding remarks in Sect. 5.

2 Preliminaries and Motivations

Throughout this paper, we suppose familiarity with basic notions in logic programming ([16]) and partial deduction ([17]). Notational conventions are standard and self-evident. In particular, in programs, we denote variables through strings starting with (or usually just consisting of) an upper-case symbol, while

---

[1] The *most specific generalisation*, also known as anti-unification or least general generalisation, see for instance [10].

the notations of constants, functions and predicates begin with a lower-case character. Unless stated explicitly otherwise, the terms "(logic) program" and "goal" will refer to a *normal* logic program and goal, respectively.

Given a program P and a goal G, partial deduction produces a new program P' which is P "specialised" to the goal G. The underlying technique is to construct "incomplete" SLDNF-trees for a set of atoms A to be specialised and extract the program P' from these incomplete search trees. An *incomplete* SLDNF-tree is an SLDNF-tree which, in addition to success and failure leaves, may also contain leaves where no literal has been selected for a further derivation step. Leaves of the latter kind will be called *dangling*. Under the conditions stated in [17], namely closedness and independence, correctness of the specialised program is guaranteed. In the context of partial deduction, incomplete SLDNF-trees are obtained by applying an unfolding rule, defined as follows:

Definition 1. An *unfolding rule* U is a function which given a program P and a goal G returns a finite, possibly incomplete and non-trivial[2] SLDNF-tree for $P \cup \{G\}$.

Definition 2. Let P be a program and A an atom. Let τ be a finite, incomplete SLDNF-tree for $P \cup \{\leftarrow A\}$ in which A has been selected in the root node.[3] Let $\leftarrow G_1, \ldots, \leftarrow G_n$ be the goals in the (non-root) leaves of the non-failing branches of τ. Let $\theta_1, \ldots, \theta_n$ be the computed answers of the derivations from $\leftarrow A$ to $\leftarrow G_1, \ldots, \leftarrow G_n$ respectively. Then the set of resultants *resultants*(τ) is defined to be $\{A\theta_1 \leftarrow G_1, \ldots, A\theta_n \leftarrow G_n\}$.

Partial deduction, as defined e.g. in [17, 2], uses the resultants for a given set of atoms A to construct the specialised program (and for each atom in A a different specialised predicate definition is generated). Under the conditions stated in [17], namely closedness and independence, correctness of the specialised program is guaranteed. The problem of *control of polyvariance* of partial deduction consists in coming up with a *terminating* procedure to produce a *finite* set of atoms A which satisfies the *correctness* conditions of [17] while at the same time providing as much potential for *specialisation* as possible (usually the more instantiated[4] the set A is, the more specialisation can be performed). Most approaches to the control of polyvariance in the literature so far are based on the syntactic structure of the atoms to be specialised (like e.g. the 1 *msg* per predicate approach in [19] or dynamic renaming of [1], the latter not guaranteeing termination). The following example shows that the syntactic structure alone does not provide enough details for a satisfactory control of polyvariance.

Example 1. Let P be the append program (where clauses have been numbered):

(1) $append([], Z, Z) \leftarrow$
(2) $append([H|X], Y, [H|Z]) \leftarrow append(X, Y, Z)$

---

[2] A trivial SLDNF-tree is one whose root is a dangling leaf. See also Definition 2.
[3] If this is not the case we will get the problematic resultant $A \leftarrow A$.
[4] A is more instantiated than A', iff every atom in A is an instance of an atom in A'.

Also let $B = append([a], X, Y)$, $C = append(X, [a], Y)$ and $\mathcal{A} = \{B, C\}$. Typically a partial deducer will unfold the atoms of $\mathcal{A}$ as depicted in Fig. 1, yielding the SLDNF-trees τ_B and τ_C. These two SLDNF-trees, as well as their resultants, have a very different structure. For $append([a], X, Y)$ we obtain for $resultants(\tau_B)$ the single fact:

$$append([a], X, [a|X]) \leftarrow$$

while for $append(X, [a], Y)$ we obtain the recursive $resultants(\tau_C)$:

$$append([], [a], [a]) \leftarrow$$
$$append([H|X], [a], [H|Z]) \leftarrow append(X, [a], Z)$$

So in this case it is vital for precision to produce separate specialised versions for the dependent atoms B and C. However it is very easy to come up with another predicate definition of $append$ (which then no longer appends two lists but for instance, as in the program below, finds common elements at common positions) such that the incomplete SLDNF-trees τ_B and τ_C for B and C are almost fully identical:

(1') $append^*([X|T_X], [X|T_Y], [X]) \leftarrow$
(2') $append^*([X|T_X], [Y|T_Y], E) \leftarrow append^*(T_X, T_Y, E)$

In that case it is not useful to keep different specialised versions for B and C because one more general version can be used without loss of specialisation:

$$append^*([a|T_1], [a|T_2], [a]) \leftarrow$$

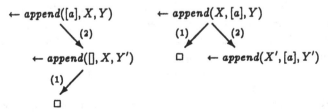

Fig. 1. SLDNF-trees τ_B and τ_C for example 1

This illustrates that the syntactic structures of B and C alone provide insufficient information for a satisfactory control of polyvariance. It is much more important to know how the syntactic structure behaves in the context of the program to be specialised. This information can be obtained by using the following characterisation of the associated incomplete SLDNF-trees (and as such also of the resultants they represent). The definitions are adapted from [4, 12, 13].

Definition 3. Let G_1 be a goal and let P be a program whose clauses are numbered. Let $G_1, \ldots, G_n$ be a finite, incomplete SLDNF-derivation of $P \cup \{G_1\}$. The *characteristic path* of the derivation is the sequence $(l_1, c_1), \ldots, (l_{n-1}, c_{n-1})$, where l_i is the position of the selected literal in G_i, and c_i is defined as:

- if the selected literal is an atom, then c_i is the number of the clause chosen to resolve with G_i.
- if the selected literal is $\neg p(\bar{t})$, then c_i is the predicate p.

The set of all characteristic paths for a given program P and a given goal G will be denoted by $chpaths(G, P)$.

Note that if two non-failing derivations for two goals with the same number of literals (and for the same program P) have the same characteristic path then they are either both successful or both incomplete (for a proof see [13]). This justifies the fact that the leaves of derivations are not registered in characteristic paths.

Definition 4. Let G be a goal, P a program and U an unfolding rule. Then *the characteristic tree τ of G (in P) via U* is the set of characteristic paths of the non-failing derivations of the incomplete SLDNF-tree obtained by applying U to G (in P). We introduce the notation $chtree(G, P, U) = \tau$. We also say that τ is *a characteristic tree of G (in P)* if it is *the* characteristic tree for some unfolding rule U. Also τ is *a characteristic tree* if it is *a* characteristic tree of some G in some P.

Although a characteristic tree only contains a collection of characteristic paths the actual tree structure can be reconstructed without ambiguity. The "glue" is provided by the clause numbers inside the characteristic paths (branching in the tree is indicated by differing clause numbers).

Characteristic trees are a very interesting abstraction because there is a close link between characteristic trees and the specialisation performed locally by partial deduction. If two atomic goals have the same characteristic tree then:

- the same branches have been pruned by partial deduction. The pruning of branches at partial deduction time is one important aspect of the specialisation. For instance in Example 1 and Fig. 1 we can see that two branches have been pruned for B (thereby removing recursion) whereas no pruning could be performed for C.
- the atoms have been unfolded in exactly the same way, e.g. the same clauses have been resolved with literals in the same position in that process. This captures the computation steps that have already been performed at partial deduction time, which is another important aspect of specialisation.
- the resultants have the same structure, differing only by the particular instantiations. For instance this captures that, in Example 1, a single fact will be generated for B whereas a potentially recursive predicate definition with two clauses will be generated for C.

As such a characteristic tree is an almost perfect characterisation of the specialisation that has been performed *locally* on an atom. When two atoms have the same characteristic tree then a single predicate definition can in principle be used without local specialisation loss.[5] For more details about the interest of characteristic trees and local and global precision aspects, we refer to [13, 7, 4].

---

[5] Sometimes atoms with different characteristic trees have (almost) identical resultants (due to independence of the computation rule) and could therefore also be replaced

The approach to partial deduction in [4] (see also [5]) uses characteristic trees to classify the atoms to be specialised according to their characteristic tree. The basic idea is to have only one specialised version for each characteristic tree. If the number of characteristic trees is finite[6] we get a control of polyvariance which ensures termination and correctness of the specialised program while at the same time (hopefully) ensuring that different specialised version are produced if the associated predicate definitions have a different form. The basic outline of the algorithm in [4, 5] is as follows:

1. For a set of atoms $\mathcal{A}$ to be specialised: apply an unfolding rule to obtain a set of incomplete SLDNF-trees.
2. Add the atoms occurring in the bodies of the resultants of these SLDNF-trees to $\mathcal{A}$.
3. Apply an *abstraction operation* which, based on characteristic trees, will produce a new set $\mathcal{A}'$ such that every atom in $\mathcal{A}$ is an instance of an atom in $\mathcal{A}'$.[7]
4. If $\mathcal{A}'$ is different from $\mathcal{A}$ restart the procedure, otherwise apply a renaming transformation (to ensure independence) and generate the specialised program by taking the resultants of the incomplete SLDNF-trees.

The following example illustrates the above procedure.

Example 2. Let P be the following program:

(1) $member(X, [X|T]) \leftarrow$
(2) $member(X, [Y|T]) \leftarrow member(X, T)$

Let $\mathcal{A} = \{member(a, [a, b]), member(a, [a])\}$. As can be seen in Fig. 2 both these atoms have the same characteristic tree $\tau = \{((1, 1))\}$ (given an unfolding rule which unfolds deep enough to detect the failing branches). The method of [4, 5] would thus decide to abstract both atoms producing the generalisation $\mathcal{A}' = \{member(a, [a|T])\}$ (the *msg* has been calculated). Unfortunately (as already pointed out for other examples in [12, 13]) the generalisation has a different characteristic tree τ' (depending on the unfolding rule: $\{((1, 1)), ((1, 2))\}$ or $\{((1, 1)), ((1, 2), (1, 1)), ((1, 2), (1, 2))\}$ or something even deeper).

This loss of precision leads to sub-optimal specialised programs. In this case the atom $member(a, T)$ would be added to $\mathcal{A}$ at the following step of the algorithm. This atom (usually) also has τ' as characteristic tree. Hence the final set $\mathcal{A}'$ is $\{member(a, L)\}$ (the *msg* of $\{member(a, [a|T]), member(a, T)\}$) and we obtain the following sub-optimal specialisation:

---

by a single predicate definition. Normalising characteristic trees (after unfolding) by imposing e.g. a left-to-right ordering of selected literals and delaying the selection of negative literals to the end solves this problem (see also [13]). Thanks to Maurice Bruynooghe for pointing this out.

[6] In [4] this is ensured by using a depth bound on characteristic trees.

[7] Note that without an abstraction operation the procedure is not guaranteed to terminate.

(1') $member(a, [a|T]) \leftarrow$
(2') $member(a, [X|T]) \leftarrow member(a, T)$

So although partial deduction was able to conclude that both $member(a, [a, b])$ and $member(a, [a])$ have only one non-failing resolvent and are determinate, this information has been lost due to an imprecision of the abstraction operator leading to a sub-optimal program in which the determinacy is not explicit (and redundant computation steps will occur at run-time). Note that, for the set of atoms $\mathcal{A} = \{member(a, [a, b]), member(a, [a])\}$, an "optimal" program would just consist of the clause (1').

Unfortunately imprecision is not the only problem. The fact that the generalisation does not preserve the characteristic trees can also lead to non-termination of the partial deduction process. An example can be found in [13]. So it is vital, as well for precision and termination, that the abstraction operation preserves characteristic trees.

To remedy this problem (while still ensuring termination of partial deduction in general) we would have to replace the atoms in $\mathcal{A}$ by a more general atom having the same characteristic tree. Unfortunately in a general context this is impossible, no such generalisation exists. Also notice that the unfoldings in Fig. 2 are not "purely" determinate (because a lookahead has been used to decide about determinacy, see [4, 12, 13]). Hence the method of [12, 13] cannot be applied (unless failing branches are incorporated into the characteristic trees and a post-processing phase is added which removes the unnecessary polyvariance).

In the following sections we will present an elegant solution to this problem in general and this example in particular.

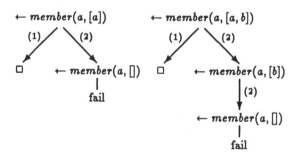

Fig. 2. Incomplete SLDNF-trees for example 2

3   Partial Deduction with Characteristic Atoms

The basic idea of the solution proposed in this paper is to simply *impose* characteristic trees on the generalised atoms. This amounts to associating characteristic trees with the atoms to be specialised. This will allow the preservation of characteristic trees in a straightforward way without having to construct intricate generalisations. Let us provide the definitions.

Definition 5. A *P-characteristic atom*, for a given program P, is a pair (A, τ) consisting of an atom A and a characteristic tree τ with $\tau \subseteq chpaths(P, \leftarrow A)$.

Often, when the context allows it, we will drop the P annotation and simply refer to *characteristic* atoms. Also note that τ is not necessarily a characteristic tree of $\leftarrow A$ in P. The following definition associates a set of concretisations with each characteristic atom.

Definition 6. An atom A is a *precise concretisation* of a P-characteristic atom (A', τ') iff A is an instance of A' and for some unfolding rule U we have that $chtree(\leftarrow A, P, U) = \tau'$. An atom B is a *concretisation* of (A', τ') iff it is an instance of a precise concretisation of (A', τ').

A P-characteristic atom can thus be seen as standing for a (possibly infinite) set of atoms, namely the concretisations according to the above definition.

E.g. both $member(a, [a])$ and $member(a, [a, b])$ of Example 2 are precise concretisations of $(member(a, [a|T]), \{((1, 1))\})$. This already hints at a possible solution for Example 2. Also note that it is decidable whether or not an atom is a (precise) concretisation of a characteristic atom.

Definition 7. Let (A, τ) be a P-characteristic atom. Then $\delta(P, (A, \tau))$ is the set of all (necessarily non-failing) SLDNF-derivations for $P \cup \{\leftarrow A\}$ such that their characteristic paths are in τ.

A characteristic atom (A, τ) uniquely determines a set of resultants (which in the definite case is a subset of the resultants for A and some properly chosen unfolding rule):

Definition 8. Let (A, τ) be a characteristic atom and P be a normal program. Let $\{\delta_1, \ldots, \delta_n\}$ be the SLDNF-derivations in $\delta(P, (A, \tau))$ and let $\leftarrow G_1, \ldots, \leftarrow G_n$ be the goals in the leaves of these derivations. Let $\theta_1, \ldots, \theta_n$ be the computed answers of the derivations from $\leftarrow A$ to $\leftarrow G_1, \ldots, \leftarrow G_n$ respectively. Then the set of resultants $\{A\theta_1 \leftarrow G_1, \ldots, A\theta_n \leftarrow G_n\}$ is called the *partial deduction of* (A, τ) *in* P. Every atom occurring in some of the G_i will be called a *body atom* (in P) of (A, τ). We will denote the set of such body atoms by $BA_P(A, \tau)$.

For example the partial deduction of $(member(a, [a|T]), \{((1, 1))\})$ in the program P of Example 2 will be $\{member(a, [a|T]) \leftarrow\}$. Note that it is different from any set of resultants that can be obtained for incomplete SLDNF-trees of the normal atom $member(a, [a|T])$. However the partial deduction is valid for any concretisation (as defined in Definition 6) of the characteristic atom $(member(a, [a|T]), \{((1, 1))\})$.

As can already be guessed from the above definition the main idea pursued in this paper will be to generate a partial deduction not for a set of atoms but for a set of *characteristic* atoms. As such the same atom A might occur in several characteristic atoms with entirely different characteristic trees. For instance $member(a, L)$ might occur as well in $c_1 = (member(a, L), \{((1,1))\})$, $c_2 = (member(a, L), \{((1,2))\})$ as in $c_3 = (member(a, L), \{((1,1)), ((1,2))\})$. The set of precise concretisations of these characteristic atoms is disjoint for a fixed unfolding rule and the partial deductions will be completely different. In order to guarantee correctness of the specialised program we have to handle some form of renaming to ensure that the correct partial deductions are called. For example (for any unfolding rule) $member(a, [a])$ is a precise concretisation of c_1 and the call $\leftarrow member(a, [a])$ has to be mapped to the resultants of c_1 (and never to c_2). Similarly (for an unfolding rule which unfolds deep enough) $\leftarrow member(a, [b, a])$ has to be mapped to the resultants of c_2 (and never to c_1).

In addition to renaming we will also incorporate argument filtering (which often greatly improves the efficiency of the specialised program, see for instance [6] or also [23] where filtering is obtained automatically when using folding to simulate partial evaluation).

Definition 9. Let A, B be atoms such that $A = B\theta$ and let the list of distinct variables of B (ordered according to the first occurrence in B) be $(X_1, \ldots, X_n)$. Let p be a predicate symbol with arity n. Then $A[B \mapsto p] = p(X_1, \ldots, X_n)\theta$.

For example $q(a, f(b))[q(a, f(Y)) \mapsto p] = p(Y)\{Y/b\} = p(b)$. Let us now define a renaming (and filtering) operation adapted for characteristic atoms.

Definition 10. Let $\mathcal{A} = \{(A_1, \tau_1), \ldots, (A_n, \tau_n)\}$ be a finite set of characteristic atoms and F a set of first-order formulas. A *renaming function for $\mathcal{A}$ wrt F* is a function ρ which assigns a distinct predicate symbol not occuring in F to each element in $\mathcal{A}$ such that the arity of $\rho((A_j, \tau_j))$ is equal to the number of distinct variables in A_j.

Definition 11. Let $\mathcal{A} = \{(A_1, \tau_1), \ldots, (A_n, \tau_n)\}$ be a finite set of characteristic atoms and F a set of first-order formulas. Let ρ be a renaming function for $\mathcal{A}$ wrt F. Let F' be obtained from F by replacing each atom A occuring in F which is a concretisation of some (A_j, τ_j) (and possibly some other elements of $\mathcal{A}$ as well, preference should normally be given to precise concretisations) by $A[A_j \mapsto \rho((A_j, \tau_j))]$. Then F' is a *renaming of F wrt $\mathcal{A}$ and ρ*.

Notice that in order for A to be a precise concretisation of (A_j, τ_j) the characteristic tree of A has to be τ_j for some U (see Definition 6). This ensures that all the unfolding steps in τ_j (also the ones selecting negative literals) are valid (and sufficient) for A and instances of A. We are now in a position to generate a partial deduction for a set of characteristic atoms.

Definition 12. Let $\mathcal{A} = \{(A_1, \tau_1), \ldots, (A_n, \tau_n)\}$ be a finite set of characteristic atoms, P be a program, U an unfolding rule and let ρ be a renaming function for $\mathcal{A}$ wrt P. For each $i \in \{1, \ldots, n\}$ let $R_i = \{A_i\theta_{1,i} \leftarrow G_{1,i}, \ldots, A_i\theta_{n,i} \leftarrow G_{n,i}\}$ be the partial deduction of (A_i, τ_i) in P. We define $R_i^\rho = \{F_{1,i} \leftarrow G_{1,i}, \ldots, F_{n,i} \leftarrow$

$G_{n,i}\}$ where $F_{j,i} = A_i\theta_{j,i}[A_i \mapsto \rho((A_i, \tau_i))]$. We also define the intermediate program $P' = \{R_i^\rho \mid i \in \{1, \ldots, n\}\}$. A *partial deduction of P wrt A (and ρ)* is obtained by generating a renaming of P' wrt A and ρ.

Example 3. Let P be the following program

    (1) $t \leftarrow member(a, [a]), member(a, [a, b])$
    (2) $member(X, [X|T]) \leftarrow$
    (3) $member(X, [Y|T]) \leftarrow member(X, T)$

Let U be an unfolding rule such that: $\tau = chtree(\leftarrow member(a, [a]), P, U) = chtree(\leftarrow member(a, [a, b]), P, U) = \{((1, 2))\}$ and $\tau' = chtree(\leftarrow t, P, U) = \{((1, 1))\}$. Let $A = \{(member(a, [a|T]), \tau), (t, \tau')\}$, $\rho((member(a, [a|T]), \tau)) = m_1$ and $\rho((t, \tau')) = t$. Then a partial deduction of P wrt A and ρ is:

    (1') $t \leftarrow m_1([]), m_1([b])$
    (2') $m_1(X) \leftarrow$

We will now adapt the standard correctness result for partial deduction of ordinary atoms for partial deduction of characteristic atoms.

Definition 13. Let P be a program and A a set of P-characteristic atoms. Then A is called *covered* iff for every characteristic atom in A each of its body atoms (in P) is a concretisation of a characteristic atom in A.

Theorem 14. *Let U be an unfolding rule. Let P be a normal program, A a set of characteristic atoms and P' a partial deduction of P wrt A and some ρ. Let G be a goal and G' be a renaming of G wrt A and ρ.*

If A is covered and if the atoms of G are all concretisations of at least one characteristic atom in A then the following hold:

1. *$P' \cup \{\leftarrow G'\}$ has an SLDNF-refutation with computed answer θ iff $P \cup \{\leftarrow G\}$ does.*
2. *$P' \cup \{\leftarrow G'\}$ has a finitely failed SLDNF-tree iff $P \cup \{\leftarrow G\}$ does.*

PROOF SKETCH. In the definite case, each set of resultants for $(A, \tau) \in A$ is a subset of a set of standard resultants (as defined in [17]) that can be obtained for the (standard) atom A. Because the partial deduction P' is covered, the atoms in the bodies of these resultants are concretisations of at least one characteristic atom in A. This means that by treating characteristic atoms (A, τ) just as a normal atoms A, but just unfolding along τ and keeping the same renaming as performed by ρ we almost get a covered and independent standard partial deduction (with renaming) as defined in [1]. The only thing that is missing are the resultants R that were pruned by imposing τ on A, plus maybe some selected negative literals N which are in theory not selectable for A because they are not ground. If we now add these resultants R and incorporate the negative literals N we will obtain a standard partial deduction with renaming as defined in [1], which is however not necessarily covered because new atoms may appear in N and the bodies of R. All we have to do is add renamed versions of the original predicate definitions and map the uncovered atoms to these new predicates by extending the renaming. We have now obtained a covered and independent partial deduction with renaming and a resulting specialised program P'' such that every derivation of P' can be mapped to a derivation of P'' (but not vice versa). We can also prove (given the conditions of the theorem concerning concretisations and coveredness) that all calls to N will be ground and succeed. Therefore soundness of the calculated answers of P' (1.⇒) and preservation of finite failure (2.⇐) follows from the standard correctness of partial deduction with renaming for P'' (see [1]). Similarly, P' can only be incomplete wrt the calculated answers (1.⇐) or finitely fail whereas the original program did not (2.⇒) if some derivation in P'' can be constructed which uses at least one of the resultants R added above. However this can only happen if some atom in G or in the leaves of the partial deductions of some $(A, \tau) \in A$ in P is not a concretisation of a characteristic atom in A, which is impossible given the conditions of the theorem. □

4 An Algorithm for Partial Deduction

We now define a possible partial deduction algorithm using concepts introduced in the previous section. As in [4, 5] we first define an abstraction operator. One can notice that, by definition, the abstraction operator preserves the characteristic trees.

Definition 15. Let A be a set of characteristic atoms. Also let, for every characteristic tree τ, A_τ be defined as $A_\tau = \{A \mid (A, \tau) \in A\}$. The operation *abstract* is defined as: $abstract(A) = \cup_\tau \{(msg(A_\tau), \tau)\}$.

In other words only one characteristic atom per characteristic tree is allowed. For example in the case that $A = \{(p(f(X)), \{((1, 1))\}), (p(b), \{((1, 1))\})\}$ we obtain $abstract(A) = \{(p(X), \{((1, 1))\})\}$.

Definition 16. Let A be an ordinary atom, U an unfolding rule and P a program. Then $chatom(A, P, U) = (A, \tau)$ where $chtree(\leftarrow A, P, U) = \tau$. We extend *chatom* to sets of atoms: $chatoms(A, P, U) = \{chatom(A, P, U) \mid A \in A\}$.

Note that A is a precise concretisation of $chatom(A, P, U)$.

The following is a formal description of an algorithm for partial deduction with characteristic atoms (more refined algorithms are possible). Please note that it is parameterised by an unfolding rule U, thus leaving the particulars of local control unspecified.

Algorithm 4.1 *Algorithm for Partial Deduction*

Input
  a program P and set of atoms A to be specialised
Output
  a specialised program P'
Initialisation
  $k := 0$ and $A_0 := chatoms(A, P, U)$
Repeat
  $A_{k+1} := abstract(A_k \cup chatoms(\{BA_P(A, \tau_A) \mid (A, \tau_A) \in A_k\}, P, U))$
Until $A_k = A_{k+1}$ (modulo variable renaming)
$P' :=$ a partial deduction of P wrt A_k and some ρ

Theorem 17. *If the number of distinct characteristic trees is finite then Algorithm 4.1 terminates and generates a partial deduction satisfying the requirements of Theorem 14 for queries G whose atoms are instances of atoms in $\mathcal{A}$.*

PROOF. Termination is a direct corollary of Proposition 20 in Appendix A. Reaching the fixpoint guarantees that all predicates in the bodies of resultants are precise concretisations of at least one characteristic atom in $\mathcal{A}_k$, i.e. we always obtain a covered partial deduction. Furthermore *abstract* always generates more general characteristic atoms (even in the sense that any precise concretisation of an atom in $\mathcal{A}_i$ is a precise concretisation of an atom in $\mathcal{A}_{i+1}$ — this follows immediately from Definitions 6 and 15). Hence, because any instance of an atom in $\mathcal{A}$ is a precise concretisation of a characteristic atom in $\mathcal{A}_0$, the conditions of Theorem 14 are satisfied. □

Example 4. We are now in a position to treat Example 2. Let $A = member(a, [a])$, $B = member(a, [a, b])$ and $\tau = \{((1, 1))\}$. For $\mathcal{A} = \{A, B\}$ the algorithm yields:

1. $\mathcal{A}_0 = \{(A, \tau), (B, \tau)\}$
2. $BA_P(A, \tau) = BA_P(B, \tau) = \emptyset$, $\mathcal{A}_1 = abstract(\mathcal{A}_0) = \{(member(a, [a|T]), \tau)\}$
3. $BA_P(member(a, [a|T]), \tau) = \emptyset$, $\mathcal{A}_2 = abstract(\mathcal{A}_1) = \mathcal{A}_1$ and we have reached the fixpoint.

A partial deduction P' wrt $\mathcal{A}_1$ and ρ with $\rho((member(a, [a|T]), \tau)) = m_1$ is:
$$m_1(X) \leftarrow$$
$\mathcal{A}_1$ is covered and all the atoms in $G = \leftarrow member(a, [a])$, $member(a, [a, b])$ are instances of an atom in $\mathcal{A}$. As predicted by Theorem 17 all atoms in G are also concretisations of characteristic atoms in $\mathcal{A}_2$ and hence Theorem 14 can be applied: we obtain the renamed goal $G' = \leftarrow m_1([])$, $m_1([b])$ and $P' \cup \{G'\}$ yields the correct result.

A system incorporating Algorithm 4.1 has been implemented. Incorporating existing unfolding rules into the system was very straightforward — something we have already hinted at earlier. The system has been used for some successful applications, like in [15] where integrity checking was pre-compiled. In addition to the examples of this paper the system is precise enough to solve all the problematic examples in [12, 13]. On some occasions a depth-bound on characteristic trees was required.

The system has also been tested for the Lam and Kusalik benchmarks (originally in[9]) by Meulemans in [21] and the results are very satisfactory, as well for code size as for execution speed. For instance the results are better than those of the SP system ([4, 5]). Further testing (and refinement) is ongoing. Table 1 is extracted from [21] and compares the Algorithm 4.1 with standard partial deduction and where termination is guaranteed by using an abstraction operation which allows only one version (i.e. one *msg*) per predicate. The *Total* row contains the normalised total speedup of all the tests (each test was given the same weight). For both approaches the same simple determinate unfolding rule with a lookahead of one level and without selecting negative literals[8] has been

---

[8] For comparison's sake with other methods which are not able to handle negation, see [21].

used. As the speedups in Table 1 show (higher figures are better), even for this simple unfolding rule the new partial deduction method pays off. We conjecture that for more sophisticated unfolding rules and for more sophisticated programs the difference will be much more dramatic.

Benchmark	Speedup with Ecological PD	Speedup with 1 *msg* per predicate
advisor	1.27	1.28
ancestor	1.01	0.99
transpose	4.37	4.37
match	0.94	0.80
contains	1.13	1.00
depth	1.56	0.97
gtrain1	1.36	0.77
gtrain2	2.01	2.01
Total	1.37	1.13

Table 1. Speedup Figures

5   Discussion and Conclusion

For the moment the technique of this paper has to impose a depth bound on characteristic trees to ensure termination. In fact the number of characteristic trees is not always bounded in a natural way. This depth bound becomes necessary for example when an accumulating parameter "influences" the unfolding, meaning that the growth of the accumulator also leads to a corresponding growth of the characteristic tree. Some examples can be found in [14]. Fortunately [14] also proposes a solution to this problem by incorporating the partial deduction technique of this paper with ideas from [20]. The basic idea is to detect growing of characteristic trees and, if necessary, generalise characteristic atoms to ensure termination. Another promising approach to solve this problem might be based pre-computing a finite and "sufficient" set of potential characteristic trees in an off-line manner.

Also note that some built-in's (like =../2, is/2) can be easily incorporated into the characteristic trees. The concretisation definition for characteristic atoms scales up and the technique will ensure correct specialisation. It should also be possible to incorporate the if-then-else into characteristic trees (and then use a specialisation technique similar to [11]).

Characteristic trees and the method proposed in this paper can probably also be useful in other areas, such as constraint logic programming or supercompilation. For further remarks see [13, 14].

The simplicity and universality of the new method comes at a (relatively small) price compared to [12, 13]. The characteristic tree τ inside a characteristic atom (A, τ) can be seen as an implicit representation of constraints on A. However in this paper these constraints are used only locally and are not propagated towards other characteristic atoms. The constraints in [12, 13] are propagated and thus used globally. Whether this has any real influence in practice remains to be seen.

In conclusion, we have presented a new framework and a new algorithm for partial deduction. The framework and the algorithm can handle *normal* logic programs and place *no* restrictions on the unfolding rule. The abstraction operator of the algorithm preserves the characteristic trees of the atoms to be specialised and ensures termination (when the number of distinct characteristic trees is bounded) while providing a fine grained control of polyvariance. All this is achieved without using constraints in the partial deduction process.

Acknowledgements

Michael Leuschel is supported by Esprit BR-project Compulog II. I would like to thank Danny De Schreye and Bern Martens for proof-reading (several versions) of this paper, for sharing their expertise and for all the encouragement and stimulating discussions. I would also like to thank Maurice Bruynooghe and John Gallagher for interesting comments and for pointing out several improvements. Finally I thank Dominique Meulemans for testing my system and anonymous referees for their helpful remarks.

References

1. K. Benkerimi and P. M. Hill. Supporting transformations for the partial evaluation of logic programs. *Journal of Logic and Computation*, 3(5):469–486, October 1993.
2. K. Benkerimi and J. W. Lloyd. A partial evaluation procedure for logic programs. In S. Debray and M. Hermenegildo, editors, *Proceedings of the North American Conference on Logic Programming*, pages 343–358. MIT Press, 1990.
3. M. Bruynooghe, D. De Schreye, and B. Martens. A general criterion for avoiding infinite unfolding during partial deduction. *New Generation Computing*, 11(1):47–79, 1992.
4. J. Gallagher. A system for specialising logic programs. Technical Report TR-91-32, University of Bristol, November 1991.
5. J. Gallagher. Tutorial on specialisation of logic programs. In *Proceedings of PEPM'93, the ACM Sigplan Symposium on Partial Evaluation and Semantics-Based Program Manipulation*, pages 88–98. ACM Press, 1993.
6. J. Gallagher and M. Bruynooghe. Some low-level transformations for logic programs. In M. Bruynooghe, editor, *Proceedings of Meta90 Workshop on Meta Programming in Logic*, pages 229–244, Leuven, Belgium, 1990.
7. J. Gallagher and M. Bruynooghe. The derivation of an algorithm for program specialisation. *New Generation Computing*, 9(3 & 4):305–333, 1991.
8. J. Komorowski. An introduction to partial deduction. In A. Pettorossi, editor, *Proceedings Meta'92*, pages 49–69. Springer-Verlag, LNCS 649, 1992.

9. J. Lam and A. Kusalik. A comparative analysis of partial deductors for pure Prolog. Technical report, Department of Computational Science, University of Saskatchewan, Canada, May 1990. Revised April 1991.

10. J.-L. Lassez, M. Maher, and K. Marriott. Unification revisited. In J. Minker, editor, *Foundations of Deductive Databases and Logic Programming*, pages 587–625. Morgan-Kaufmann, 1988.

11. M. Leuschel. Partial evaluation of the "real thing". In L. Fribourg and F. Turini, editors, Logic Program Synthesis and Transformation — Meta-Programming in Logic. *Proceedings of LOPSTR'94 and META'94*, Lecture Notes in Computer Science 883, pages 122–137, Pisa, Italy, June 1994. Springer-Verlag.

12. M. Leuschel and D. De Schreye. An almost perfect abstraction operator for partial deduction. Technical Report CW 199, Departement Computerwetenschappen, K.U. Leuven, Belgium, December 1994.

13. M. Leuschel and D. De Schreye. An almost perfect abstraction operation for partial deduction using characteristic trees. Technical Report CW 215, Departement Computerwetenschappen, K.U. Leuven, Belgium, October 1995. Submitted for Publication. Accessible via http://www.cs.kuleuven.ac.be/ lpai.

14. M. Leuschel and B. Martens. Global control for partial deduction through characteristic atoms and global trees. Technical Report CW 220, Departement Computerwetenschappen, K.U. Leuven, Belgium, December 1995. Submitted for Publication. Accessible via http://www.cs.kuleuven.ac.be/ lpai.

15. M. Leuschel and B. Martens. Partial deduction of the ground representation and its application to integrity checking. In J. Lloyd, editor, *Proceedings of ILPS'95, the International Logic Programming Symposium*, pages 495–509, Portland, USA, December 1995. MIT Press. Extended version as Technical Report CW 210, K.U. Leuven. Accessible via http://www.cs.kuleuven.ac.be/ lpai.

16. J. Lloyd. *Foundations of Logic Programming*. Springer Verlag, 1987.

17. J. W. Lloyd and J. C. Shepherdson. Partial evaluation in logic programming. *The Journal of Logic Programming*, 11:217–242, 1991.

18. B. Martens. *On the Semantics of Meta-Programming and the Control of Partial Deduction in Logic Programming*. PhD thesis, K.U. Leuven, February 1994.

19. B. Martens, D. De Schreye, and T. Horváth. Sound and complete partial deduction with unfolding based on well-founded measures. *Theoretical Computer Science*, 122(1–2):97–117, 1994.

20. B. Martens and J. Gallagher. Ensuring global termination of partial deduction while allowing flexible polyvariance. In L. Sterling, editor, *Proceedings ICLP'95*, pages 597–613, Kanagawa, Japan, June 1995. MIT Press. Extended version as Technical Report CSTR-94-16, University of Bristol.

21. D. Meulemans. Partiële deductie: Een substantiële vergelijkende studie. Master's thesis, K.U. Leuven, 1995.

22. A. Pettorossi and M. Proietti. Transformation of logic programs: Foundations and techniques. *The Journal of Logic Programming*, 19 & 20:261–320, May 1994.

23. M. Proietti and A. Pettorossi. The loop absorption and the generalization strategies for the development of logic programs and partial deduction. *The Journal of Logic Programming*, 16(1 & 2):123–162, May 1993.

24. D. Sahlin. Mixtus: An automatic partial evaluator for full Prolog. *New Generation Computing*, 12(1):7–51, 1993.

A   Termination Property of *abstract*

First we introduce the following notation: for any finite set of characteristic atoms $\mathcal{A}$ and any characteristic tree τ, let $\mathcal{A}_\tau$ be defined as $\mathcal{A}_\tau = \{A \mid (A, \tau) \in \mathcal{A}\}$. The following well-founded measure function is taken from [6] (also in the extended version of [20]):

Definition 18. Let *Term*, *Atom* denote the sets of terms and atoms, respectively. We define the function $s : Term \cup Atom \rightarrow I\!N$ counting symbols by:

- $s(t) = 1 + s(t_1) + \ldots + s(t_n)$ if $t = f(t_1, \ldots, t_n)$, $n > 0$
- $s(t) = 1$ otherwise

Let the number of distinct variables in a term or atom t be $v(t)$. We now define the function $h : Term \cup Atom \rightarrow I\!N$ by $h(t) = s(t) - v(t)$.

The well-founded measure function h has the property that $h(t) > 0$ for any non-variable t. Also if A is an atom strictly more general than B we have that $h(A) < h(B)$ (see [20]).

Definition 19. Let $\mathcal{A}$ be a set of characteristic atoms and let $T = \langle \tau_1, \ldots, \tau_n \rangle$ be a finite vector of characteristic trees. We then define the *weight vector* of $\mathcal{A}$ wrt T by $hvec_T(\mathcal{A}) = \langle w_1, \ldots, w_n \rangle$ where

- $w_i = \infty$ if $\mathcal{A}_{\tau_i} = \emptyset$
- $w_i = \sum_{A \in \mathcal{A}_{\tau_i}} h(A)$ if $\mathcal{A}_{\tau_i} \neq \emptyset$

Weight vectors are partially ordered by the usual order relation among vectors: $\langle w_1, \ldots, w_n \rangle \leq \langle v_1, \ldots, v_n \rangle$ iff $w_1 \leq v_1, \ldots, w_n \leq v_n$ and $\vec{w} < \vec{v}$ iff $\vec{w} \leq \vec{v}$ and $\vec{v} \not\leq \vec{w}$. The set of weight vectors is well founded (no infinitely decreasing sequences exist) because the weights of the atoms are well founded.

Proposition 20. *Let P be a normal program, U an unfolding rule and let $T = \langle \tau_1, \ldots, \tau_n \rangle$ be a finite vector of characteristic trees. For every finite set of characteristic atoms $\mathcal{A}$ and $\mathcal{B}$, such that the characteristic trees of their elements are in T, we have that one of the following holds:*

- *$abstract(\mathcal{A} \cup \mathcal{B}) = \mathcal{A}$ (up to variable renaming) or*
- *$hvec_T(abstract(\mathcal{A} \cup \mathcal{B})) < hvec_T(\mathcal{A})$.*

PROOF. Let $hvec_T(\mathcal{A}) = \langle w_1, \ldots, w_n \rangle$ and let $hvec_T(abstract(\mathcal{A} \cup \mathcal{B})) = \langle v_1, \ldots, v_n \rangle$. Then for every $\tau_i \in T$ we have two cases:

- $\{msg(\mathcal{A}_{\tau_i} \cup \mathcal{B}_{\tau_i})\} = \mathcal{A}_{\tau_i}$ (up to variable renaming). In this case the abstraction operation performs no modification for τ_i and $v_i = w_i$.
- $\{msg(\mathcal{A}_{\tau_i} \cup \mathcal{B}_{\tau_i})\} = \{M\} \neq \mathcal{A}_{\tau_i}$ (up to variable renaming). In this case $(M, \tau_i) \in abstract(\mathcal{A} \cup \mathcal{B})$, $v_i = h(M)$ and there are three possibilities:
  - $\mathcal{A}_{\tau_i} = \emptyset$. In this case $v_i < w_i = \infty$.
  - $\mathcal{A}_{\tau_i} = \{A\}$ for some atom A. In this case M is strictly more general than A (by definition of *msg* because $M \neq A$ up to variable renaming) and hence $v_i < w_i$.
  - $\#(\mathcal{A}_{\tau_i}) > 1$. In this case M is more general (but not necessarily strictly more general) than any atom in $\mathcal{A}_{\tau_i}$ and $v_i < w_i$ because at least one atom is removed by the abstraction.

We have that $\forall i \in \{1, \ldots, n\} : v_i \leq w_i$ and either the abstraction operation performs no modification (and $\vec{v} = \vec{w}$) or the well-founded measure $hvec_T$ strictly decreases. $\square$

Memoing Evaluation by Source-to-Source Transformation

Jens E. Wunderwald

Technische Universität München, Institut für Informatik
wunderwa@informatik.tu-muenchen.de

Abstract. This paper presents a novel implementation of memoing evaluation [SSW94] by source-to-source transformation. The transformation proceeds in two steps:

The first step consists of magic sets rewriting [BR91], a standard transformation in deductive databases, whose application to Prolog has not been considered yet.

The second transformation rewrites bottom-up rules to Prolog clauses. This new bottom-up to top-down transformation has useful applications besides memoing. It can be derived by partially evaluating a tuple-oriented semi-naive meta-interpreter for bottom-up rules, written in Prolog.

The tuple-oriented approach to bottom-up processing permits an elegant combination of negation and magic sets rewriting.

This paper also introduces a variant of supplementary magic sets tailored to the memoing application.

1 Introduction

Memoing evaluation ([War92]) terminates more often then Prolog does, it avoids recomputation of variant calls and can be used for storing data to survive a query. The basic idea of memoing is to store all calls and answers to so-called tabled predicates.

Traditionally, memoing is implemented by modification of the WAM, as in the XSB system [SSW94], or meta-interpretation using extension tables [Die87] or continuation passing [RC94]. We propose a different approach, based on a source-to-source transformation, aiming to combine the portability of the latter and the efficiency of the former approach.

Our transformation proceeds in two steps:

1. First we apply some variant of magic sets rewriting (MSR) [BR91] to the original program. MSR is a well established optimization technique, used in deductive databases for pushing selections. Application to Prolog programs has not been considered yet, because the rewritten rules are dedicated for bottom-up evaluation.

2. The second transformation rewrites bottom-up rules to Prolog clauses. This bottom-up to top-down transformation results from partial evaluation of a semi-naive tuple-oriented meta-interpreter for bottom-up rules.
   This transformation has useful applications besides memoing.

The final result of the transformation is a Prolog program, which needs some materialization technique, the dynamic database serves as the default mechanism.

The transformation is implemented by a logic program which makes use of Prolog clauses mixed with bottom-up rules.

The rest of this paper is organized as follows: The next section defines the source language for the transformations. Sections 3 and 4 describe the main transformation steps, Section 5 their semantical properties. In Section 6, we give variants of magic sets rewriting tailored for a tuple-oriented framework. Section 7 treats negation. Section 8 is about the implementation of our approach. Section 9 compares our approach to related work, Section 10 presents some benchmark results and Section 11 points to future work.

2   Scope of the Transformation

The transformation presented here processes ordinary Prolog programs. The user can indicate by compiler directives which predicates shall be tabulated.

Such directives are recommended for predicates which are called many times with variant instantiations when evaluated by SLD resolution. This includes predicates which loop because the same goal is called infinitely, e.g. when using left recursion.

A directive of the form "$\leftarrow$ table(f/a)." makes a predicate tabulated. f denotes the predicate symbol of the tabled predicate and a its mode. The mode information is a string consisting of "b"s and "f"s denoting if the corresponding argument is always called with a fully instantiated term or not[1].

MSR needs mode information, which user must provide, this is not necessary in the XSB approach.

The current implementation does not allow tabled predicates with different modes, this restriction can be overcome by renaming the predicates to special versions for every mode.

The rules defining tabled predicates should be declarative clauses: The transformation does not preserve the evaluation order of SLD resolution, therefore predicates causing side effects should be avoided in such rules.

This caveat applies specially to the cut, whose procedural semantics depends crucially on the evaluation order. However we have developed a variant of supplementary magic sets permitting usage of neck cuts.

Henceforth we will speak somewhat inexactly of *tabled rules* meaning rules defining tabled predicates, similarly we use the terms tabled atom, tabled body, etc. The same parlance will be used with bottom-up rules.

---

[1] Alternatively Prolog's "+/−"-notation may be used. "?"-arguments are subsumed by "−"-arguments, this means their bindings are not used in the magic phase. The "b/f"- notation dominates in the literature on magic sets.

3 Transformation Step 1: Magic Sets Rewriting

Notation We use uppercase letters for addressing relations resp. predicates, lowercase letters for individual atoms, literals or tuples of the corresponding relations.

"prefix_p" denotes an atom constructed from the atom p by adding prefix to the predicate symbol of p. The new predicate symbol is assumed not to occur elsewhere in the program. "prefix_P" refers to the relation prefix_p belongs to.

"Πp" denotes an atom constructed from p by using the same predicate symbol and projecting p's arguments to the positions indicated as "b" in P's mode declaration.

τ_R denotes an atom belonging to the relation R, with different free variables as arguments.

Applying MSR to tabled rules means to treat them as clauses in the language of a deductive database. For clauses which contain only tabled atoms in the body, standard MSR algorithms ([BR91]) apply directly. We use the left-to-right sideways information passing strategy inherent in Prolog rules. This means that all variable bindings obtained by evaluating the subgoals left to a goal (including the bound head variables) are used to evaluate a goal.

After MSR, a bottom-up relation magic_ΠR defines all calls to a tabled predicate R, the bottom-up relation memo_R defines the answers.

Only untabled literals in tabled rules require a little modification: they are treated as built-in predicates. Deductive databases provide built-in predicates for relations which can be defined by bottom-up rules only in an awkward or inefficient manner, e.g. list processing. The treatment of built-in predicates is not described in ([BR91]), but this is a trivial matter: they remain unchanged. This treatment means that they are evaluated by calling Prolog from the body of bottom-up rules. A preprocessor to MSR marks untabled literals in tabled bodies as built-in predicates.

As a bridge between the main Prolog program and a bottom-up rule defining a tabled predicate, we need a procedure which adds a magic tuple (magic_$\Pi \tau_R$), belonging a calls to a tabled relation R, as a bottom-up fact, evaluates all bottom-up consequences, and finally reads the bottom-up relation memo_τ_R defining this tabled predicate:

$$\tau_R \leftarrow \text{update}(\text{magic\_}\Pi \tau_R), \text{materialized}(\text{memo\_}\tau_R).$$

This rule replaces the definition of R in the original program. The exact meaning of update/1 and materialized/1 becomes clear in Section 4.

MSR results in a program with a mixture of Prolog and bottom-up rules:

1. Prolog rules defining untabled predicates remain unchanged.
2. Bridge rules connect Prolog rules and bottom-up rules.
3. Bottom-up rules define the tabled predicates of the original program. They can contain calls to Prolog predicates as built-in predicates.

Example The generalized magic sets technique rewrites the program of Fig. 1 to the program of Fig. 2. For the sake of saving space, we have omitted the rule for handling "eps" symbols. "←" discriminates bottom-up rules from Prolog rules ("←"), Helvetica-Oblique font signifies built-in predicates in tabled bodies. This example is taken from a LALR parser generator, that we have developed using tabling.

```
← table( first/bf ).

first( Terminal, Terminal ) ← terminal( Terminal ).
first( Symbol, First ) ← grammar_rule( Symbol, [Next | _] ), first( Next, First ).

grammar_rule( a, [] ). grammar_rule( a, [a, b] ). terminal( a ).
```

Fig. 1. This program defines the FIRST sets of a context free grammar. Prolog reproduces the same answer to the query "?- first(a,F)" endlessly. The loop is not immediately obvious, it lies in the data.

```
unchanged Prolog code
grammar_rule( a, [] ) . grammar_rule( a, [a, b] ) . terminal( a ) .

computing magic sets ( calls to tabled predicates )
magic_first( Next ) ← magic_first( Symbol ), grammar_rule( Symbol, [Next | _] ).

computing the tabled predicates ( answers for tabled predicates )
memo_first( Terminal, Terminal ) ← magic_first( Terminal ), terminal( Terminal ).
memo_first( Symbol, First ) ←
        magic_first( Symbol ), grammar_rule( Symbol, [Next | _] ), memo_first( Next, First ).

bridge predicates
first( A, B ) ← update( magic_first( A )), materialized( first( A, B )).
```

Fig. 2. The FIRST sets program transformed by MSR

4 Transformation Step 2: Bottom-up to Top-down Rewriting

4.1 Meta-interpreter

In order to evaluate the program resulting from MSR, we must equip Prolog with the ability to evaluate bottom-up rules. Most bottom-up systems evaluate in a set-oriented style [BR86], but there are some approaches which employ the tuple-oriented style for bottom-up evaluation ([Sch93],[Bur91]). In order to avoid the impedance mismatch of combining tuple-oriented and set-oriented evaluation, we use tuple-oriented evaluation in the bottom-up direction as well.

In order to give the reader an intuitive understanding of the ensuing transformation, we first present a meta-interpreter, written in Prolog, which evaluates bottom-up rules (Fig. 3).

```
update( Tuple ) ← not materialized( Tuple ), materialize( Tuple ), propagate( Tuple ), fail; true.
propagate( Tuple ) ← Head ← Body, occurs_in_body( Body, Tuple, Rest ), join( Rest ), update( Head )
occurs_in_body(( Tuple, Rest ), Tuple, Rest ).
occurs_in_body(( Literal, Body ), Tuple, ( Literal, Rest )) ← occurs_in_body( Body, Tuple, Rest ).
occurs_in_body( Tuple, Tuple, true ).
join(( Literal, Body )) ← holds( Literal ), join( Body ).
join( Literal ) ← holds( Literal ).
holds( BuiltInPrologLiteral ) ← !, call( BuiltInPrologLiteral ).
holds( BottomUpTuple ) ← materialized( BottomUpTuple ).
Materialization with the dynamic database
materialized( TupleOfBottomUpRelation ) ← call( TupleOfBottomUpRelation ).
materialize( TupleOfBottomUpRelation ) ← assertz( TupleOfBottomUpRelation ).
```

Fig. 3. A semi-naive, tuple-oriented bottom-up meta-interpreter

This meta-interpreter was derived from the set-oriented semi-naive evaluation algorithm [BR86] by confining the delta sets to singleton sets. Doing this, the delta sets need not to be represented explicitly, the delta information resides in the call stack of the meta-interpreter. The meta-interpreter preserves the basic property of semi-naive evaluation that a tuple is generated at most once for every possible deduction. If a tuple recursively depends on itself, i.e. there exist an infinite number of possible deductions, the cycle is detected after the first round and thus is only executed once.

Bottom-up relations must be materialized (stored), because the basic evaluation step is joining the body atoms of bottom-up relations. Materialization is implemented by a pair of predicates for reading/writing a tuple from/to a relation: materialize/1 and materialized/1. A portable prototype implementation uses the dynamic database.

This is what the meta-interpreter does: It adds a tuple to a bottom-up relation if it is new. Then all bottom-up consequences of this fact are computed. This whole process is called updating a relation. For facts which are already known, updating does nothing.

The process of computing all consequences is called propagation of a tuple. Propagation proceeds by looking for all bottom-up rules where a unifying atom occurs in the body. The tuple is joined with the other body literals of the rule which was found in the previous step. This may produce solutions for the rule's head. These head tuples are updated by recursively calling the meta-interpreter's main procedure.

Semi-naivity is accomplished by propagating a tuple immediately after its generation, only if it is new, which enforces that one newly generated tuple participates in every join.

The first subgoal of propagate/1 looks for bottom-up rules, which are assumed to be stored as "←"/2 Prolog facts.

occurs_in_body/3 tests if the bottom-up body contains a subgoal unifying with the currently propagated tuple. It returns the other body literals.

join/1 tries to prove the remaining subgoals by looking up in the current materialization for bottom-up predicates, and by calling Prolog for built-in literals. The fail in update's body enforces computation of *all* consequences.

4.2 Transformation

The meta-interpreter implementation runs fast enough for applications where efficiency is not a critical issue, such as teaching logic programming.

For real life applications, the meta-interpretation overhead must be avoided. We have applied the standard technique of compiling away the interpreter by partial deduction [Gal86]. During this process of partial evaluation, the meta-interpreter completely disappears. Instead of always partially evaluating the meta-interpreter given a concrete program, we can do the partial evaluation on an abstract program. This process leads to the bottom-up to top-down transformation, which rewrites a set of Prolog rules and bottom-up rules using the following transformation rules:

Propagation rules Each occurrence of a bottom-up atom b_k in the body of a bottom-up rule $h \leftarrow b_1, \ldots, b_{k-1}, b_k, b_{k+1}, \ldots, b_n$ produces a Prolog clause:

propagate_$b_k \leftarrow \mathcal{H}(b_1), \ldots, \mathcal{H}(b_{k-1}), \mathcal{H}(b_{k+1}), \ldots, \mathcal{H}(b_n)$, update_$h$.

$$\text{with} \quad \mathcal{H}(p) \equiv \begin{cases} p & \text{if } P \text{ is a built-in predicate} \\ \text{materialized\_}p & \text{if } P \text{ is a bottom-up predicate} \end{cases}$$

Update rules For every bottom-up relation R there is a Prolog clause:

update_$_{TR} \leftarrow$ not materialized_$_{TR}$, materialize_$_{TR}$, propagate_$_{TR}$, fail; true.

Materialization Each bottom-up relation R is maintained by a pair of materialization procedures materialize_$_{TR}$ and materialized_$_{TR}$ This offers the opportunity to select a tailored data-structure for each relation (see Section 8.1). These predicates may be inlined if their definition is very simple, which is the case for materialization with the dynamic database.

Branching rules For each bottom-up relation R the general predicates update/1, materialized/1 and materialize/1 are defined by branching to the specialized versions.

Maintenance rules Additionally, the generated Prolog program contains procedures for initializing, reading and deleting bottom-up relations.

Prolog rules The Prolog rules of the original program appear unchanged in the rewritten program.

As a final result of applying both transformation steps, we obtain a ready-to-run Prolog program.

```
propagation clauses
propagate_magic_first( Terminal ) ← terminal( Terminal ), update_memo_first( Terminal, Terminal ).
propagate_magic_first( Symbol ) ←
        grammar_rule( Symbol, [Next |_] ), memo_first( Next, First ), update_memo_first( Symbol, First )
propagate_magic_first( Symbol ) ← grammar_rule( Symbol, [Next | _] ), update_magic_first( Next ).

propagate_memo_first( Next, First ) ←
        magic_first( Symbol ), grammar_rule( Symbol, [Next | _] ), update_memo_first( Symbol, First ).

update clauses ( materialization in the dynamic database inlined )
update_magic_first( Term ) ←
        not magic_first( Term ), assertz( magic_first( Term )), propagate_magic_first( Term ), fail; true.
update_memo_first( Term, First ) ←
        not memo_first( Term ), assertz( memo_first( Term )), propagate_memo_first( Term ), fail; true.

branching clauses
update( magic_first( A )) ← update_magic_first( A )).
materialized( first( A, B )) ← memo_first( A, B ).

unchanged
first( A, B ) ← update( magic_first( A )), materialized( first( A, B )).
grammar_rule( a, [] ) . grammar_rule( a, [a, b] ) . terminal( a ) .
```

Fig. 4. The final Prolog code for computing FIRST sets

Example Fig. 4 shows result of applying the second transformation step to the program of Fig. 2.

5 Properties of the Transformations

5.1 Correctness and Completeness

Like the transformation, the correctness and completeness results for our implementation of memoing consist of two parts.

[Ram88] proves that a magically rewritten program produces the same set of answers as the original program.

In [Wun], we prove the correctness and completeness of the algorithm of Section 4 for range-restricted programs with finite Herbrand models. Range restrictedness is defined as usual, that all head variables also occur in the body, specially all facts must be ground.

The correctness proof consists of a fairly simple induction, as the basic evaluation step performs the T_P operator in a tuple-oriented fashion. Termination can be proved by showing the finiteness of the so-called materialize-and-propagate tree. An induction on the minimal length of a modus ponens proof assuming that an element of the Herbrand model is not computed shows completeness.

Note that the results about the materialize and propagate algorithm require range-restricted programs. If the original program obeys the modes given in the tabling declarations and if all tabled rules are range-restricted, magic sets rewriting produces range-restricted rules. The mode conditions demand that all arguments marked as "b" in the tabling declaration are fully instantiated at call time.

The implementation of the materialize-and-propagate algorithm presented here heavily makes use of non-declarative features of Prolog such as "!" or "fail". This may provoke some criticism, however, for implementing an *algorithm*, one needs fine control over the execution regime of the target language. Using Prolog in a procedural way is not less trust-able than using a procedural language like C++. Indeed, the Janus face of Prolog as a declarative and procedural language permits to use the same language for evaluating top-down and bottom-up rules, both written in a declarative style. The user programs on a level where the usage of non-declarative features is not visible, this minimizes the danger of errors caused by abuse of non-declarative features.

5.2 Left Recursion

Consider a left recursive ancestor program with query "anc(1,X)" and base "par(1, 2). par(2, 3). par(3, 4). par(4, 5). ...". An evaluation based upon generalized magic sets only produces one magic tuple "magic_anc(1)" which may give rise to the wrong presumption that the evaluation could miss some answers. But of course the completeness results also hold in the left recursive case. Intuitively, the magic tuple is still there when new answers for the ancestor relation arrive, therefore the computation does follow the chain of parent facts.

Much work has been devoted to rewriting programs containing left recursion because Prolog cannot handle it. However in some applications such as natural language processing, left recursion permits more natural and concise formulations. Furthermore, left recursion can yield inherently better algorithms. For the ancestor program presented above, it generates $O(1)$ magic and $O(n)$ memo tuples (n denotes the number of parent facts). A right recursive variant generates $O(n)$ magic and $O(n^2)$ memo tuples.

6 Tailored Variants of Magic Sets

6.1 Magic Sets with Binding Environments

We have developed a variant of supplementary magic sets rewriting [BR91] specially adapted to the tabling application, called magic sets with binding environments (MSBE). It also solves the well-known problem of generalized magic sets, that it recomputes the same joins. MSBE deviates from supplementary magic sets, which generate a different supplementary magic predicate for every occurrence of a tabled predicate in a body. MSBE generates only one env_magic predicate with different tags for each occurrence. The difference stems from the fact that [BR91] addresses a datalog setting, where it is impossible to gather several variables in one term argument.

MSBE maintains four bottom-up relations for each tabled predicate: In addition to the usual magic and memo relations, env_magic and env_memo relations contain additional parameters holding the binding information present at an individual body occurrence of the tabled predicate needed for evaluating the rest of the body.

The maintenance of one memo relation facilitates sharing answers for different calls to the same predicate. A new answer is joined with stored variable bindings (the env_magic predicate) to obtain specific answers for different calls. As an optimization this augmented env_memo relation needs not to be materialized, propagation suffices.

The technique of passing variable bindings in an extra parameter makes it possible to generate bottom-up rules with only one bottom-up subgoal, whereas the supplementary magic sets method generates two. This minimizes the code blow-up in the ensuing transformation which implements bottom-up evaluation.

If there are no tabled predicates between the head and a cut, MSBE treats the cut the same way as Prolog, therefore such generalized neck cuts are allowed.

If the materialization technique preserves the insertion order, i.e. tuples are retrieved in the same order they were inserted, MSBE generates answers in the same order as XSB. This makes it more intuitive to the programmer to add predicates with side effects to tabling code.

Example MSBE rewrites the Fibonacci program of Fig. 5 to the program of Fig. 6.

```
← table( fib/bf ).

fib( 0, 1 ). fib( 1, 1 ).
fib( N, Fib ) ← N > 1, N1 is N-1, fib( N1, Fib1 ), N2 is N-2, fib( N2, Fib2 ), Fib is Fib1+Fib2.
```

Fig. 5. The naive Fibonacci program

```
definitions of magic sets and memo predicates
memo_fib( 0, 1 ) ← magic_fib( 0 ).
memo_fib( 1, 1 ) ← magic_fib( 1 ).

env_magic_fib( tag_1, N1, env( N )) ← magic_fib( N ), N > 1, N1 is N - 1.
env_magic_fib( tag_2, N2, env( Fib1, N )) ← env_memo_fib( tag_1, N1, Fib1, env( N )), N2 is N - 2.

memo_fib( N, Fib ) ← env_memo_fib( tag_2, N2, Fib2, env( Fib1, N )), Fib is Fib1 + 1.

table updates
magic_fib( N ) ← env_magic_fib( _, N, _ ).

env_memo_fib( Tag, N, F, Env ) ← memo_fib( N, F ), env_magic_fib( Tag, N, Env ).
```

Fig. 6. The naive Fibonacci program rewritten with MSBE

6.2   The "Up-down" Optimization

The sliding windows optimization technique for bottom-up evaluation [NR90] permits to omit some useless evaluation steps if the evaluation can be divided into two distinct phases. The other effect of sliding windows, reduction of space consumption, is not addressed here.

The first "down" phase computes all calls to tabled relations (the magic sets), the second "up" phase only answers. This optimization is applicable if answers for tabled relations do not generate new calls to tabled predicates and if answers are used in the reverse order of corresponding calls.

Implementing this optimization in our framework is quite straight forward: The rules defining magic sets must precede the rules defining answers. Answer tuples need not to be propagated to the bodies of bottom-up rules, only magic tuples drive the computation. A little modification of bottom-up rules implements this, it just consists of marking the answer subgoals as closed for propagation. The prefix "❚" marks such closed propagation entry points.

Example Fig. 7 shows the result of applying this transformation to the naive Fibonacci program.

```
magic_fib( N1 ) ← magic_fib( N ), N > 1, N1 is N - 1.
magic_fib( N2 ) ← magic_fib( N ), N > 1, N2 is N - 2.

memo rules must follow magic rules
memo_fib( 0, 1 ) ← magic_fib( 0 ).
memo_fib( 1, 1 ) ← magic_fib( 1 ).
memo_fib( N, Fib ) ← magic_fib( N ), N > 1,
        N1 is N - 1, ❚ memo_fib( N1, Fib1 ), N2 is N - 2, ❚ memo_fib( N2, Fib2 ), Fib is Fib1 + Fib2.
```

Fig. 7. The Fibonacci program "up-down" transformed

7   Negation

The semi-naive algorithm for set-oriented bottom-up evaluation can only handle stratified negation. This gives rise to a severe problem when magic sets rewriting comes into play, as this transformation generally does not preserve stratification. The deductive database community has dedicated much work to solving this problem.

Our tuple-oriented framework can handle modularly stratified programs and does not suffer form the violation of stratification imposed by magic sets rewriting if some care is taken. This comes from the finer control over the order of generating answers facilitated by tuple-oriented evaluation. New tuples are propagated to bottom-up rules one after the other. This means that all consequences derived using an upper rule are computed *before* the consequences computable with lower rules.

This description covers negation for generalized magic sets, MSBE are treated similarly. The main idea of our implementation is to define a new relation neg_p for each tabled relation P which is called negatively. The existence of a tuple neg_p indicates that a call fact magic_p has been completely propagated. This relation is used as follows: for each negative tabled subgoal "not p" add a neg_p subgoal to the memo rule. The relation magic_P is defined as usual. Finally, the rule "neg_p ← magic_p" is added after all rules where magic_P occurs in the body.

Intuitively, a negated call is evaluated as follows: first the corresponding positive call is completely evaluated. While this is taking place, the rule containing the negated call can produce no solutions, due to absence of a neg tuple. When the positive call is finished, the corresponding neg tuple is generated and the original rule now safely performs the negated call by succeeding if no solution was found.

Example Fig. 9 shows the generalized magic sets rewritten code for the program in Fig. 8.

```
← table( win/b ).
win( X ) ← move( X, Y ), not win( Y ).
```

Fig. 8. A modularly stratified program, if move/2 is acyclic ...

```
memo_win( X ) ← magic_win( X ), move( X, Y ), neg_win( Y ), not memo_win( Y ).
The order of the following clauses matters
magic_win( Y ) ← magic_win( X ), move( X, Y ).
neg_win( Y ) ← magic_win( Y ).
```

Fig. 9. ... and its magically rewritten code

8 Implementation

8.1 Materialization

For correctly moded programs, the bottom-up rules implementing tabling are range-restricted, thus only fully instantiated terms must be materialized. Therefore a simple term comparison such as matching suffices for duplicate testing.

If one wants to lift the strict modedness, allowing partially instantiated calls or answers, the materialization technique must be able to store terms containing variables. Duplicate testing becomes harder, a variant test implements it in this case. Furthermore, new tuples may be produced which generalize older tuples. For maintaining minimal relations, the new tuple has to oust the subsumed tuple and also delete consequences of it. This introduces a non-monotonic element into the computation. For avoidance, programs should be written in a way that general tuples are produced before specializations of them. As a heuristic for accomplishing this, non-range-restricted rules should precede range-restricted rules.

For the concrete implementation of materialization, any data-structure able to store retrieve and enumerate tuples can be used. The choice of an optimal data-structure can be taken individually for each bottom-up relation. Standard Prolog only offers the dynamic database. Most Prolog implementations lack a more efficient method for maintaining a persistent update-able data-structure. As an exception, BinProlog comes with a blackboard [DBT93]. Benchmark tests indicate that sophisticated materialization techniques play a key role for reaching high performance evaluation.

For the tabling application, materialization can be slightly optimized: magic and memo tuples for one tabled relation can be stored in the same data-structure because they share the key arguments. For magic tuples, it only matters if there exists any value for a given key. The memo predicate can safely reuse the storage occupied by the dummy data from an earlier magic materialization.

8.2 The Sisyphos System

All transformations mentioned in this paper are implemented as a part of the Sisyphos system [Wun94]. The final product is a ready-to-run Prolog file. The results of both transformation steps are stored in a pretty printed form, making modification easy.

Sisyphos is implemented using Prolog and bottom-up rules. The implementation of the transformation is remarkably short (less than 60 lines of code for MSBE), but runs sufficiently fast (0.2 sec for the Fibonacci example, dominated by file i/o). Sisyphos runs on top of several Prologs[2], ports to other Prologs should be easy.

9 Related Work

Portable Approaches [RC94] and [Die87] present meta-interpreting implementations of memoing. [RC94] uses continuation passing, which is likely to cause space problems. [Die87] uses extension tables, this approach suffers form the necessity to reconstitute environments.

XSB Memoing execution of Prolog and bottom-up evaluation with MSR basically compute the same information, see Fig. 10 for an overview of corresponding concepts. This well known similarity ([War92],[Bry90]) now has led to a practical tuple-oriented implementation. Our approach eliminates the need to modify the WAM data-structures by mapping memoing evaluation to an ordinary Prolog evaluation. This makes it possible to use memoing with many Prolog systems which may have other advantages than memoing you want to benefit from.

10 Performance

All measurements were carried out on a 468 DX2 notebook with 4 MB Ram main memory and a 50 MHz CPU, running XSB (Version 1.4.1) under Linux (1.2.8). Code generated by our system is run with BinProlog (Version 4.00).

---

[2] SWI-Prolog, IF/Prolog, Eclipse and BinProlog

XSB concept	~ Magic Sets concept
call table	~ magic set
answer table	~ (modified) bottom-up rule
tabling a call	~ generating a magic tuple
tabling an answer	~ generating a bottom-up tuple
discovering a repeated call	~ duplicate testing for magic sets
non-tabled relation	~ built-in relation
waking a suspended call	≁ –
change WAM	≁ source-to-source transformation

Fig. 10. Comparison of XSB and Magic Sets

Fibonacci The naive Fibonacci program (Fig. 5) serves as a classical example of the performance improvements obtainable with tabling. A Prolog execution runs in $O(2^n)$ because every non-base call causes two recursive calls. A tabling evaluation does not execute the recursion but just reads the memoed results. It is a trivial matter to measure this basic effect of tabling.

We also investigated the effect of different materialization techniques: Using the hash table provided in BinProlog results in a one order of magnitude speed-up compared to a first argument indexing asserted database and two orders of magnitude compared to a non-indexed asserted database. The data about the influence of the rewriting algorithm indicate that MSBE performs better than generalized magic sets, except for very short rules, and "up-down" outperforms both if applicable.

In Fig. 11, we compare the runtimes obtained with XSB to two versions of our system: One with standard parameters, i.e. a rewriting and materialization technique which works for any example: generalized magic sets and the hash table allowing non-deterministic relations. The second version is generated with the up-down optimization and utilizes the fact that the Fibonacci relation is deterministic. For reference, we also included times for a linearly recursive version of Fibonacci without tabling.

Ancestor We also have measured the performance of our approach on the ancestor program, because there exist times for many deductive databases.

Concerning the recursion scheme, left recursion performs much better than right recursion, which in turn drasticly outperforms double recursion.

When comparing our system against XSB, which outperforms Coral by an order of magnitude as reported in [SSW94], we found that the structure of the base relation hardly influences the comparison. Here we present the times needed by both systems for computing all answers for the queries "anc(1,X)" (Fig. 12) and "anc(1,X),anc(2,X)" (Fig. 13) for binary-tree-shaped base relations of different sizes. "1" is the root of the tree and "2" its immediate descendant. Because XSB performs very badly for the second query, we also tried "anc(1,X),anc(2,Y),X=Y".

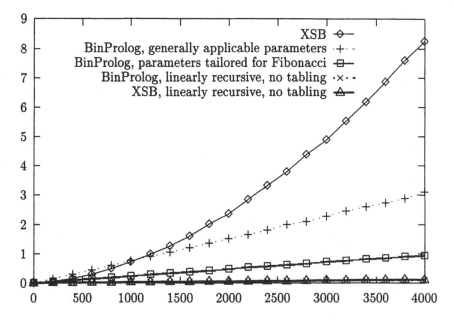

Fig. 11. Times for different evaluations of Fibonacci

11 Future Work

Some programmers may find it awkward to figure out which predicates should be tabled and with which modes this should happen. Tabling predicates not suited therefore, like append/3, results in terrible performance. Abstract interpretation solves the problem of finding modes. We are currently working on heuristics which select predicates for tabulation by criteria such as the recursion scheme and de-construction of term arguments.

Sometimes, our implementation of negation does too much work: If one counterexample for a negated call is found, this suffices to let the negated call fail, but our technique computes the full fixpoint. The kind of existential evaluation needed here needs a careful deletion of materialized relations to ensure that later positive calls to the same goal get all answers.

The main field where our system still has a prototype character is materialization techniques. What we need here is a Prolog with sophisticated hash tables, tries and other data-structures apt for tabling.

References

[BR86] F. Bancilhon and R. Ramakrishnan. An amateur's introduction to recursive query processing strategies, invited paper. In *Proceedings of SIGMOD*. 1986.

[BR91] C. Beeri and R. Ramakrishnan. On the power of magic. *The Journal of Logic Programming*, 10:255–300, January 1991.

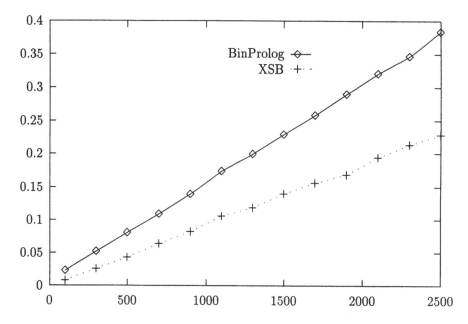

Fig. 12. Times for the left recursive Ancestor program with query anc(1,X)

[Bry90] F. Bry. Query evaluation in recursive databases: bottom-up and top-down reconciled. *Data & Knowledge Engineering*, 5:289–312, 1990.

[Bur91] W. Burgard. *Goal-Directed Forward Chaining for Logic Programs*. PhD thesis, Universität Bonn, 1991.

[DBT93] K. De Bosschere and P. Tarau. Blackboard Communication in Logic Programming. In *Proceedings of the PARCO'93 Conference*, Grenoble, France, September 1993.

[Die87] S.W. Dietrich. Extension tables: Memo relations in logic programming. In *Proceedings of the 1987 Symposium on Logic Programming*, pages 264–273, 1987.

[Gal86] J. Gallagher. Transforming logic programs by specialising interpreters. In *European Conference on Artificial Intelligence*, pages 109–122, 1986.

[NR90] J. F. Naughton and R. Ramakrishnan. How to forget the past without repeating it. In *16th International Conference on Very Large Data Bases*, 1990.

[Ram88] R. Ramakrishnan. Magic templates: A spellbinding approach to logic programs. In Robert A. Kowalski and Kenneth A. Bowen, editors, *Proceedings of the Fifth International Conference and Symposium on Logic Programming*, pages 140–159, Seatle, 1988. ALP, IEEE, The MIT Press.

[RC94] R. Ramesh and Weidong Chen. A portable method of integrating slg resolution into prolog systems. In *Logic Programming - Proceedings of the 1994 International Symposium*, pages 618–632. The MIT Press, 1994.

[Sch93] H. Schütz. *Tupelweise Bottom-up-Auswertung von Logikprorammen*. PhD thesis, Technische Universität München, 1993.

[SSW94] K. Sagonas, T. Swift, and D.S. Warren. XSB as an efficient deductive database engine. In *Proceedings of SIGMOD*. 1994.

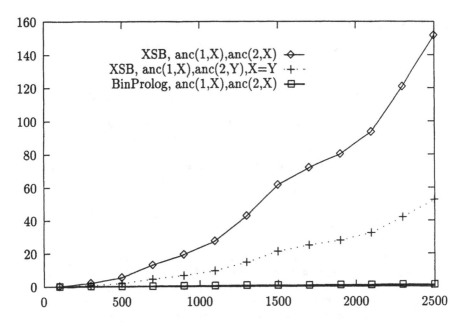

Fig. 13. Times for multi-goal queries to the left recursive Ancestor program

[War92] D. S. Warren. Memoing for logic programs with applications to abstract interpretation and partial deduction. In *Communications of ACM.* 1992.

[Wun] J. E. Wunderwald. *Adding Bottom-up Evaluation to Prolog (Preliminary Title).* PhD thesis, Technische Universität München, *to appear.*

[Wun94] J. E. Wunderwald. Logikprogrammieren mit frei wählbarer Auswertungsrichtung. In *Proceedings of the Tenth Logic Programming Workshop*, Zürich, 1994.

Transformation of Left Terminating Programs: the Reordering Problem

Annalisa Bossi[1], Nicoletta Cocco[2] and Sandro Etalle[3]

[1] Dipartimento di Matematica, Università della Calabria,
Arcavacata di Rende (Cosenza) Italy.
[2] Dipartimento di Matematica Applicata e Informatica,
Universita' di Venezia - Ca' Foscari, via Torino, 155, 30173 - Mestre-Venezia
[3] D.I.S.I - Università di Genova,
Via Dodecanneso, 35, Genova

bossi@ccusc1.unical.it, cocco@moo.dsi.unive.it, sandro@disi.unige.it

Abstract. An Unfold/Fold transformation system is a source-to-source rewriting methodology devised to improve the efficiency of a program. Any such transformation should preserve the main properties of the initial program: among them, termination. When dealing with logic programs such as PROLOG programs, one is particularly interested in preserving *left termination* i.e. termination wrt the leftmost selection rule, which is by far the most widely employed of the search rules. Unfortunately, the most popular Unfold/Fold transformation systems ([TS84, Sek91]) do not preserve the above termination property. In this paper we study the reasons why left termination may be spoiled by the application of a transformation operation and we present a transformation system based on the operations of Unfold, Fold and Switch which – if applied to a left terminating programs – yields a program which is left terminating as well.

1 Introduction

As shown by a number of applications, program transformation is a valuable methodology for the development and optimization of large programs. In this field, the unfold/fold transformation rules were first introduced by Burstall and Darlington [BD77] for transforming clear, simple functional programs into equivalent, more efficient ones. Then, such rules were adapted to logic programs both for program synthesis [CS77, Hog81], and for program specialization and optimization [Kom82].

Soon later, Tamaki and Sato [TS84] proposed an elegant framework for the transformation of logic programs based on unfold/fold rules. Their system was proven to be correct w.r.t. the least Herbrand model semantics [TS84] and the computed answer substitution semantics [KK88].

Tamaki-Sato's system became quite soon the main reference point in the literature of unfold/fold transformations of logic programs.

However, Tamaki-Sato's method cannot be applied "as it is" to most of the actual logic programs (like pure PROLOG programs) because it does not preserve left termination (here we say that a program is left terminating if all its derivations starting in a ground goal and using PROLOG's fixed "leftmost" selection rule are finite). So it can happen that a left terminating program is transformed into a non left terminating one. This is of course a situation that we need to avoid.

This problem has already been tackled in [PP91, BC94] [4], but none of these proposals includes any operation that could be employed in order to *rearrange* the atoms in the bodies of a clause. This is actually a serious limitation, in fact such an operation is often needed in order to be able to perform a subsequent fold operation. Indeed, in the majority of the examples we find in the literature, the fold operation is only possible after a rearrangement one.

In this paper we propose a new transformation system, in which we explicitly consider a *switch* operation, for which we provide specific (and needed) applicability conditions. We also provide new applicability conditions for the fold operation, and we prove that the system, when applied to a left terminating program always returns a programs which is left terminating as well.

We obtain our results by exploiting the properties of *acceptable programs*, as defined by Apt and Pedreschi in [AP90].

Section 2 contains the notation and the preliminaries on left terminating and acceptable programs. In section 3 we define the unfold/fold transformation system, and we state the main correctness results. In section 4 we will discuss and motivate the approach we have followed by showing further examples and by relating our transformation system with the ones of Tamaki and Sato [TS84] and of Seki [Sek91], as well as with other approaches to the problem of preserving termination.

The main proofs are reported in [BCE96].

2 Preliminaries

In what follows we study definite (i.e. negation-free) logic programs executed by means of the *LD-resolution* (which corresponds to the SLD resolution combined with the fixed PROLOG selection rule).

We adopt the "bold" notation (es. **B**) to indicate (ordered) sequences of objects, typically **B** indicates a sequence of atoms, $B_1, \ldots, B_n$, **t** is a sequence of terms, $t_1, \ldots, t_n$, and **x** is a sequence of variables, $x_1, \ldots, x_n$.

We work with *queries* **Q**, that is sequences of atoms, $B_1, \ldots, B_n$, instead of *goals*. Apart from this, we use the standard notation of Lloyd [Llo87] and Apt [Apt90]. In particular, given a syntactic construct E (so for example, a term, an atom or a set of equations) we denote by $Var(E)$ the set of the variables appearing in E. Given a substitution $\theta = \{x_1/t_1, \ldots, x_n/t_n\}$ we denote by $Dom(\theta)$ the set of variables $\{x_1, \ldots, x_n\}$, by $Range(\theta)$ the set of terms $\{t_1, \ldots, t_n\}$, and by $Ran(\theta)$ the set of variables appearing in $\{t_1, \ldots, t_n\}$. Finally, we define $Var(\theta) = Dom(\theta) \cup Ran(\theta)$.

Recall that a substitution θ is called *grounding* if $Ran(\theta)$ is empty, and it is called a *renaming* if it is a permutation of the variables in $Dom(\theta)$. Given a substitution θ and a set (sequence) of variables **v**, we denote by $\theta_{|\mathbf{v}}$ the substitution obtained from θ by restricting its domain to **v**.

---

[4] Another related paper is [BE94] where termination with respect to any selection rule is considered.

2.1 Left Termination and Acceptable Programs

We begin with the key definition.

Definition 1. A program P is called *left terminating* if all LD-derivations of P starting in a ground query are finite. □

Acceptable programs were introduced by Apt and Pedreschi in [AP90] in order to characterize the class of left terminating definite logic programs. Their results were successively extended to cover also general logic programs [AP93].

Given an interpretation I of a program P, and given a sequence of ground atoms $\mathbf{B} = B_1, \ldots, B_n$, we say that B_j is *reachable* (under I) if $I \models B_1, \ldots, B_{j-1}$. In fact, if I is the least model and we look at $B_1, \ldots, B_n$ as a query to be evaluated with the leftmost selection rule, the fact that $I \models B_1, \ldots, B_{j-1}$ implies that $B_1, \ldots, B_{j-1}$ will eventually be resolved by the LD-resolution process, and hence that, the (leftmost) selection rule will eventually reach (i.e. select) B_j.

Definition 2. Let $\mathbf{B} = B_1, \ldots, B_n$ be a sequence of ground atoms. Let $|\ |$ be a level mapping (i.e. a function mapping the Herbrand base into natural numbers), and I be an interpretation. Moreover, let $B_1, \ldots, B_k$ be the set of reachable atoms (under I) of $\mathbf{B}$. Then we define

$$|\mathbf{B}|_I = \sup(|B_1|, \ldots, |B_k|),$$

In other words, $|\mathbf{B}|_I$ is equal to the greatest of the level mappings of the reachable atoms of $\mathbf{B}$. □

Notice that, for any single atom B, $|B|_I = |B|$, whatever the interpretation I and the level mapping are.

Definition 3 (acceptable program). Let P be a program, $|\ |$ a level mapping for P and I a (not necessarily Herbrand) interpretation of P.

- A clause of P is *acceptable with respect to* $|\ |$ and I if I is a model of P and for every ground instance $H \leftarrow \mathbf{B}$ of it,

$$|H| > |\mathbf{B}|_I$$

In other words, for every ground instance $H \leftarrow B_1, \ldots, B_m$, and for every reachable B_i, $|H| > |B_i|$,
- P is *acceptable with respect to* $|\ |$ and I iff all its clauses are. P is called *acceptable* if it is acceptable with respect to some level mapping and interpretation of P. □

We can now fully motivate the use of acceptable programs.

Theorem 4. [AP93] A program is left terminating iff it is acceptable. □

2.2 Input positions

Modes are extensively used in the literature on Logic Programs (see for instance [AM94], usually they indicate how the arguments of a relation should be used. When dealing with termination properties mode information are particularly interesting. In fact we may relate the length of LD-derivations to some measure on input terms. This has been the basis of some approaches to proving universal termination of definite programs [Plü90, BCF94, DSF93]. In our transformation system we use just simpler information since we assume that each n-ary relation symbol p has a set of input positions $In(p) \subseteq \{1, \ldots, n\}$ associated to. For an atom A we denote by $In(A)$ the family of terms filling in the input positions of A and by $VarIn(A)$ the set of variables occurring in the input positions of A. Similar notation is used for sequences of atoms. In this paper input positions are going to be used only to broaden the range of transformations we can prove to maintain the left termination of the initial program. Throughout the paper we make the following assumption:

Assumption 1 The level mapping of an atom is uniquely determined by the terms that are found in its input positions. □

Of course this assumption imposes no syntactic restriction of the program we are going to manipulate, as we can always assume that all the positions of every relation symbol are input positions.

3 A termination preserving unfold/fold transformation system

We can now introduce the transformation system. Here we use the concept of *labelled atom*, in particular we need to label with "f" (for fold-allowing) some atoms in the bodies of the clauses of the program.

We start from the requirements on the *initial* program, which are similar to the ones proposed in [TS84]. Standardization apart is always assumed.

Definition 5 (initial program). We call a normal program P_0 an *initial program* if the following two conditions are satisfied:

(I1) P_0 is divided into two disjoint sets $P_0 = P_{new} \cup P_{old}$;
(I2) P_{new} is a non-recursive extension of P_{old}, namely all the predicates which are defined in P_{new} occur neither in P_{old} nor in the bodies of the clauses in P_{new};
(I3) all the atoms in the bodies of the clauses of P_{old} are labelled "f" and they are the only ones with such a label. □

The predicates defined in P_{new} are called *new* predicates, while those defined in P_{old} are the *old* predicates. The only difference between these conditions and the ones stated in [TS84] is the presence of **I3** which is due to the particular conditions we use for the fold operation.

The following example is inspired by the one in [Sek93].

Example 1. Let P_0 be the following program

```
c1:  path(X,[X]).
c2:  path(X,[X|Xs]) ← arc(X,Y)ᶠ, path(Y,Xs)ᶠ.

c3:  goodlist([]).
c4:  goodlist([X|Xs]) ← good(X)ᶠ, goodlist(Xs)ᶠ.

c5:  goodpath(X,Xs) ← path(X,Xs),goodlist(Xs).
```

Together with a database DB where the predicates **arc** and **good** are defined. The query **goodpath(X,Xs)** can be employed for finding a path **Xs** starting from the node **X** which contains exclusively "good" nodes. We consider the first position in all the relations as the input one. Notice that, under the assumption that the directed graph described by the relation **arc** is acyclic, the program is left terminating. Indeed, the ordering on the graph nodes induces a level mapping for the relation *arc* which can be used to prove left termination of the program. Clearly, we can choose all level mappings satisfying assumption 1.

As it is now, **goodpath** works on a "generate and test" basis: first it produces a whole path, and then it checks whether it contains only "good" nodes or not. Of course this strategy is quite naive: checking if the node is "good" or not *while* generating the path would noticeably increase the performances of the program. We can obtain such an improvement via an unfold/fold transformation. For this we split the program into $P_{old} = \{c1, \ldots, c4\} \cup DB$ and $P_{new} = \{c5\}$, thus **goodpath** is the only new predicate. This also explains the labelling used above. □

According to the usual transformation strategy, the first operation we apply is the unfold one. Unfold is the fundamental operation for program transformations and consists in applying a resolution step to the considered atom in all possible ways. Recall that the order of *the atoms in the queries and in the bodies of the clauses is relevant* since we are dealing with *LD*-resolution.

Definition 6 (unfold). Let $cl : H \leftarrow \mathbf{J}, A, \mathbf{K}.$ be a clause.
Let $\{A_1 \leftarrow \mathbf{B}_1., \ldots, A_n \leftarrow \mathbf{B}_n.\}$ be the set of clauses of P whose heads unify with A, by mgu's $\{\theta_1, \ldots, \theta_n\}$.

- *Unfolding A in cl wrt P consists of substituting cl with $\{cl'_1, \ldots, cl'_n\}$,*
  where, for each i, $cl'_i = (H \leftarrow \mathbf{J}, \mathbf{B}_i, \mathbf{K})\theta_i$. □

The unfold operation doesn't modify the labels of the atoms, no matter if the unfolded atom itself is labelled or not. Thus unfold allows to propagate the labels inside the clauses in the obvious way. This is best shown by the following example.

Example 1 (part 2) By unfolding the atom **path(X,Xs)** wrt P_0 in the body of c5, we obtain

```
c6:  goodpath(X,[X]) ← goodlist([X]).
c7:  goodpath(X,[X|Xs]) ← arc(X,Y)ᶠ,
         path(Y,Xs)ᶠ, goodlist([X|Xs]).
```

In the above clauses we can unfold **goodlist([X])** and **goodlist([X|Xs])** The resulting clauses, after a further unfolding of **goodlist([])** wrt P_0 in the clause obtained by c6, are

```
c8:   goodpath(X,[X]) ← good(X)ᶠ.
c9:   goodpath(X,[X|Xs]) ← arc(X,Y)ᶠ,
         path(Y,Xs)ᶠ, good(X)ᶠ, goodlist(Xs)ᶠ.
```

Let $P_1 = \{c1, \ldots, c4, c8, c9\} \cup DB$. □

Thanks to its correspondence to a resolution step, the unfold operation is safe wrt basically all the declarative semantics available for logic programs. It has also already been proven in [BC94] that it preserves universal termination of a query and hence also the property of being left terminating.

Now we have reached a crucial step in the transformation: in order to be able to perform the fold operation, we need to permute the atoms path(Y,Xs) and good(X). But, the rearrangement of the atoms in the body of a clause is a typical operation which does not preserve left termination. Moreover, as we'll discuss in section 4 in the context of an unfold/fold transformation system things are further complicated by the presence of the other operations. The approach we propose for guaranteeing left termination is based on the following definition.

Definition 7 (non-failing atom). Let P be a program, M_P its least Herbrand model and $cl : H \leftarrow \mathbf{J}, A, \mathbf{K}$. be a clause of P. We say that

$$A \text{ is } non\text{-}failing \text{ in } cl$$

iff for each grounding θ, such that $Dom(\theta) = Var(In(H), \mathbf{J}, In(A))$ and $M_P \models \mathbf{J}\theta$, there exists γ such that $M_P \models A\theta\gamma$. □

The reason why we call such an atom "non-failing" is the following: suppose that cl is used in the resolution process, and that the unification can bind only the variables in the input positions of H, then, if A will eventually be selected by the leftmost selection rule, the computation of the subgoal A will eventually succeed.

Note that, without restricting the domain of θ, the non-failing condition would be seldom satisfied. By restricting the set of substitutions, it becames feasible to verify it in many cases. However the condition is clearly not decidable in general.

We are now ready to introduce the switch operation.

Definition 8 (switch). Let $cl : H \leftarrow \mathbf{J}, A, B, \mathbf{K}$. be a clause of a program P. Switching A with B in cl consists of replacing cl with $cl' : H \leftarrow \mathbf{J}, B, A, \mathbf{K}$.

We say that the switch is *allowed* if the following three conditions hold:

- A is an *old* atom,
- $VarIn(B) \subseteq VarIn(H) \cup Var(\mathbf{J})$,
- A is non-failing in cl. □

Requiring that $VarIn(B) \subseteq VarIn(H) \cup Var(\mathbf{J})$ ensures that the input of B does not depend (solely) on the "output" of A, and this is a natural requirement when transforming moded programs. On the other hand, the requirement that A is non-failing in cl intuitively forbids the possibility that left termination holds, by failure of A, even if B is non-terminating; in such a case, moving B leftward would result in the introduction of a loop.

Example 1 (part 3) By permuting path(Y,Xs) with good(X) we obtain the following clause:

```
c10: goodpath(X,[X|Xs]) ← arc(X,Y)ᶠ,
         good(X)ᶠ, path(Y,Xs)ᶠ, goodlist(Xs)ᶠ.
```

Let $P_2 = \{c1, \ldots, c4, c8, c10\} \cup DB$. Notice that this operation is *allowed*, whatever the model of the program we are referring to: in fact if we take N to be the least Herbrand model of P_2 then we have that for any substitution $\theta = \{Y/t\}$ there exists a substitution γ (namely, $\gamma = \{Xs/[t]\}$) such that $N \models$ path(Y,Xs)$\theta\gamma$. So for any θ, $Dom(\theta) = \{X, Y\}$ there exists a substitution γ such that $N \models$ path(Y,Xs)$\theta\gamma$. By Herbrand's theorem, this holds for any other model M, and therefore path(Y,Xs) is non-failing (wrt any model M) in c9. □

The switch is the simplest form of reordering operation. Clearly, any permutation of the atoms in a clause body can be obtained by a finite composition of switches of adjacent atoms.

When we apply a switch operation, we *are allowed to exchange the labels of A and B* (we don't have to, though, but such an exchange may come in handy for the application of a subsequent fold operation).

Fold is the inverse of unfold when one single unfold is possible. It consists in substituting an atom A for an equivalent conjunction of literals **K** in the body of a clause c. This operation is used in all the transformation systems in order to pack back unfolded clauses and to detect implicit recursive definitions. As in Tamaki and Sato [TS84], the transformation sequence and the fold operation are defined in terms of each other.

Definition 9 (transformation sequence). A *transformation sequence* is a sequence of programs $P_0, \ldots, P_n$, $n \geq 0$, such that each program P_{i+1}, $0 \leq i < n$, is obtained from P_i by applying an unfold wrt P_i, a switch, or a fold operation to a clause of P_i. □

Definition 10 (fold). Let $P_0, \ldots, P_i$, $i \geq 0$, be a transformation sequence, cl : $H \leftarrow \mathbf{J}, \mathbf{B}, \mathbf{K}$. be a clause in P_i, and $d : D \leftarrow \mathbf{B}'$. be a clause in P_{new}. *Folding* **B** *in cl via* τ consists of replacing cl by cl' : $H \leftarrow \mathbf{J}, D\tau, \mathbf{K}$, provided that τ is a substitution such that $Dom(\tau) = Var(d)$ and such that the following conditions hold:

(F1) d is the only clause in P_{new} whose head is unifiable with $D\tau$;

(F2) If we unfold $D\tau$ in cl' wrt P_{new}, then the result of the operation is a variant of cl;

(F3) one of the atoms in **J**, or the leftmost of the atoms in **B** is labelled "f". □

Notice that the fold clearly eliminates the labels in the folded part of the body. The conditions **F1** and **F2** may appear new, but it is not difficult to prove that their combination corresponds to the combination of the conditions **F1**...**F3** of [TS84]. This is shown by the following remark 11. Therefore, apart from the fact that we take into consideration the order of the atoms in the bodies of the clauses, what distinguishes this fold definition from the one in [TS84] is condition **F3**. The comparison of our definition with the one given by Seki [Sek91] for preserving Finite

Failures is not straightforward. In fact, in [Sek91] $SLDNF-resolution$ is considered, hence, no reordering is needed. But, all the atoms in **B** have to be labelled. On the other hand, we require a much weaker condition on labelling but, since we consider $LD-resolution$, we have to take into account the order of atoms.

Remark 11. The following observations are in order:

(a) Condition **F1** can be restated as follows: "d is the only clause of P_{new} that can be used to unfold $D\tau$ in cl'".

(b) If we let $\mathbf{v} = Var(\mathbf{B'}) \setminus Var(D)$ be the set of local variables of d, then condition **F2** can also be expressed as follows:

(F2a) $\mathbf{B'}\tau = \mathbf{B}$;
(F2b) For any $x, y \in \mathbf{v}$
- $x\tau$ is a variable;
- $x\tau$ does not appear in cl';
- if $x \not\equiv y$ then $x\tau \not\equiv y\tau$;

The equivalence between **F2** and the combination of **F2a** and **F2b** follows (indirectly, though), from Theorems 6.3 and the discussion after definition 4.9 in [EG94]. These latter conditions are the "standard" ones for folding (they are present, for instance, in Seki's [Sek91, Sek93]). □

Example 1 (part 4) We can now fold path(Y,Xs), goodlist(Xs) in c10. The resulting clause is

c11: goodpath(X,[X|Xs]) ← arc(X,Y)^f, good(X)^f, goodpath(Y,Xs).

Let $P_2 = \{c1, \ldots, c4, c8, c11\} \cup DB$. Notice that because of this operation the definition of goodpath is now recursive and it checks the "goodness" of the path while generating the path itself. □

3.1 Correctness result

We can now state the main properties of the transformation system.

Theorem 12 (main). Let $P_0, \ldots, P_n$ be a transformation sequence. Suppose that P_0 is acceptable and every switch operation performed in $P_0, \ldots, P_n$ is allowed, then

- P_n is acceptable,

In particular,

- P_n is left terminating.

Proof. See [BCE96]. □

Of course, it is also of primary importance ensuring the correctness of the system from a declarative point of view. In the case of our system, the applicability conditions we propose are more restrictive than those used by Tamaki-Sato in [TS84] (which, on the other hand, do not guarantee the preservation of left termination). For this reason, all the correctness result for the declarative semantics that hold for the system of [TS84] are valid for our system as well and we have the following.

Remark 13. Let $P_0, \ldots, P_n$ be a transformation sequence.

- [TS84] The least Herbrand models of the initial and final programs coincide.
- [KK90] The computed answers substitution semantics of the initial and final programs coincide. □

Finally, since our system guarantees the preservation of left termination, and since for left termination programs the Finite Failure set coincides with the complement of the least Herbrand model, we also have the following.

Corollary 14 (preservation of finite failure). Let $P_0, \ldots, P_n$ be a transformation sequence. If P_0 is acceptable and every switch operation performed in $P_0, \ldots, P_n$ is allowed, then the finite failure set of P_n coincides with the one of P_0. □

4 Discussion and related work

Tamaki-Sato's system [TS84] was devised for definite logic program, and it is correct wrt (among others) the least Herbrand model and the computed answer substitution semantics. Later Seki proposed a new version with more restrictive applicability conditions (with the so-called *modified* fold operation) and proved that it maintains the Finite Failure set of the initial program [Sek91].

Concerning the termination issue, neither Tamaki-Sato's nor Seki's method are devised to preserve left termination of the initial program. Indeed they don't. Moreover, their definition of the (fold and unfold) operations are given *modulo reordering of the atoms in the bodies of the clauses*, which clearly does not preserve left termination. On the other hand, even the *ordered* version [5] of Tamaki-Sato's method does not preserve left termination. This is shown by the following example.

Example 2. Let P_0 be the following program

```
c1:  p  ←q, h(X).
c2:  h(s(X))  ←h(X)ᶠ.
```

Where $P_{new} = \{c_1\}$ and $P_{old} = \{c_2\}$. Notice that there is no definition for predicate q, so everything fails (finitely). Notice also that the program is left terminating. By unfolding h(X) in c1 we obtain a variant of c1, but with a different labelling :

```
c3:  p  ←q, h(Y)ᶠ.
```

Now, following the Tamaki-Sato approach, we can fold q, h(Y) in c3, using clause c1 for folding. The result is

```
c4:  p  ←p
```

---

[5] Here by *ordered version of Tamaki-Sato's method* we mean a transformation system just like Tamaki-Sato's but in which (a) no reordering is allowed in the bodies of the clauses, and (b) the definition of unfold and fold are restated (in the obvious way) so to take into consideration the order of the atoms in the bodies of the clauses. Consequently the *ordered* version of Tamaki-Sato's method has applicability conditions which are quite more restrictive that the original ones.

Now the program is clearly not left terminating any longer. ☐

This shows that for preserving left termination we need in any case a system more restrictive than the one of [TS84].

By adopting a definition of unfold and fold which takes into consideration the order of the atoms in the bodies of the clauses and by appropriately restricting the fold operation we can preserve left termination. This has been shown also in [PP91, BC94]. Unfortunately, the systems thus obtained have a serious limitation for practical applicability. Indeed, most of the examples found in the literature on unfold/fold transformations require at some point a reordering operation (this obviously applies to example 2 which is reported in the previous section); it is usually needed in order to be able to perform a subsequent fold operation.

In order to partially recover the power of the Tamaki and Sato's system while preserving termination, we introduced a switch operation. Such an operation presents subtle aspects which have to be taken into consideration. This is best shown by the following example.

Example 3. Let P_0 be the following program.

```
c1:   z  ← p, r.
c2:   p  ← qᶠ, rᶠ.
c3:   q  ← rᶠ, pᶠ.
```

Where $P_{new} = \{c1\}$ and $P_{old} = \{c2, c3\}$. Notice that r is not defined anywhere, so everything fails; notice also that this program is left terminating. By unfolding p in c1 we obtain the following clause:

```
c4:   z  ← qᶠ, rᶠ, r.
```

By further unfolding q in c4 we obtain:

```
c5:   z  ← rᶠ, pᶠ, rᶠ, r.
```

Now we permute the first two atoms, which are both labelled, obtaining:

```
c6:   z  ← pᶠ, rᶠ, rᶠ, r.
```

Notice that this switch operation *does preserve left termination*. However, if we now fold the first two atoms, using clause c1 for folding, we obtain the following:

```
c7:   z  ← z, rᶠ, r.
```

which is obviously non left terminating. ☐

In the above example we have employed the ordered version of Seki's definition of fold, i.e. the most restrictive definition of fold we could consider, surely more restrictive than the one we propose here. Nevertheless we have a situation in which the switch operation does preserve left termination in a local way while left termination will subsequently be destroyed by the application of the fold operation. This shows that the switch operation requires applicability conditions which do not just guarantee the termination properties of the actual program.

Hence, in order to preserve left termination, we have modified Tamaki-Sato's system by

- adopting a definition of unfold and fold which takes into consideration the order of the atoms in the bodies of the clauses;
- adopting a labelling rule and a restriction on folding which guarantees to preserve left termination;
- introducing the possibility to reorder atoms in the bodies by allowed switches.

Other approaches to preserving termination properties can be found in [PP91, CG94, BE94, BC94].

The work of Proietti and Pettorossi [PP91] made an important step forward in the direction of the preservation of left termination. They proposed a transformation system which is more restrictive than the ordered version of [TS84] since only unfolding the left most atom or a deterministic atom is allowed. They proved that such a system preserves the "sequence of answer substitution semantics" (a semantics for PROLOG programs, defined in [N.J84, Bau89]). This guarantees also that if the initial program is left terminating, then the resulting program is left terminating as well. They do not allow any reordering of atoms.

In [BE94] we proved that Tamaki-Sato's transformation system preserves the property of being *acyclic* [AB90]. This has to do with the preservation of termination, in fact a definite program P is *acyclic* if and only if all its derivations starting in a ground goal are finite *whichever is the selection rule employed*. Moreover, the tools used in [BE94] are quite similar to the ones used here. Unfortunately, as pointed out in [AP93], the class of acyclic programs is quite restrictive, and there are many natural programs which are left terminating but not acyclic.

The preservation of universal termination of a query with the *LD-resolution* was also studied in [BC94]. In order to capture c.a.s. and universal termination, in that paper we defined an appropriate operational semantics and splitted the equivalence condition to be satisfied into two complementary conditions: the completeness condition and the condition of being non-increasing. The validity of this second condition, which is very operational, ensures us that the transformation cannot introduce infinite derivations. We proved that, by restricting the Tamaki-Sato's original system, the whole transformation sequence is non-increasing and then it preserves also universal termination. As a consequence, acceptability of programs is also preserved by such a restricted transformation sequence. Again, however, the allowed transformations are seriously restricted by the impossibility of reordering atoms in the bodies.

More difficult is a comparison with [CG94] since they define a transformation system based only on unfold and replacement operations. The replacement operation is very powerful and it includes both fold and switch as particular cases. In [CG94]the preservation of termination is considered but the verification is "a posteriori".

References

[AB90] K. R. Apt and M. Bezem. Acyclic programs. In D. H. D. Warren and P. Szeredi, editors, *Proceedings of the Seventh International Conference on Logic Programming*, pages 617–633. The MIT Press, 1990.

[AM94] K.R. Apt and E. Marchiori.   Reasoning about Prolog programs: from modes through types to assertions.   *Formal Aspects of Computing*, 1994.

In print. Also Technical report CS-R9358, CWI, Amsterdam, The Netherlands. Available via anonymous ftp at ftp.cwi.nl, or via xmosaic at http://www.cwi.nl/cwi/publications/index.html.

[AP90]   K. R. Apt and D. Pedreschi. Studies in Pure Prolog: termination. In J. W. Lloyd, editor, *Symposium on Computational Logic*, pages 150–176. Springer-Verlag, 1990.

[AP93]   K. R. Apt and D. Pedreschi. Reasoning about termination of pure Prolog programs. *Information and Computation*, 106(1):109–157, 1993.

[Apt90] K. R. Apt. Introduction to Logic Programming. In J. van Leeuwen, editor, *Handbook of Theoretical Computer Science*, volume B: Formal Models and Semantics, pages 495–574. Elsevier, Amsterdam and The MIT Press, Cambridge, 1990.

[Bau89] M. Baudinet. *Logic Programming Semantics: Techniques and Applications*. PhD thesis, Stanford University, Stanford, California, 1989.

[BC94]   A. Bossi and N. Cocco. Preserving universal termination through unfold/fold. In G. Levi and M. Rodríguez-Artalejo, editors, *Proc. Fourth Int'l Conf. on Algebraic and Logic Programming*, volume 850 of *Lecture Notes in Computer Science*, pages 269–286. Springer-Verlag, Berlin, 1994.

[BCE96] A. Bossi, N. Cocco, and S. Etalle. Transformation of Left Terminating Programs: The Reordering Problem. Technical Report CS96-1, Dip. Matematica Applicata e Informatica, Università Ca' Foscari di Venezia, Italy", 1996.

[BCF94] A. Bossi, N. Cocco, and M. Fabris. Norms on Terms and their use in Proving Universal Termination of a Logic Program. *Theoretical Computer Science*, 124:297–328, 1994.

[BD77]   R.M. Burstall and J. Darlington. A transformation system for developing recursive programs. *Journal of the ACM*, 24(1):44–67, January 1977.

[BE94]   A. Bossi and S. Etalle. Transforming Acyclic Programs. *ACM Transactions on Programming Languages and Systems*, 16(4):1081–1096, July 1994.

[CG94]   J. Cook and J.P. Gallagher. A transformation system for definite programs based on termination analysis. In F. Turini, editor, *Proc. Fourth Workshop on Logic Program Synthesis and Transformation*. Springer-Verlag, 1994.

[CS77]   K.L. Clark and S. Sickel. Predicate logic: a calculus for deriving programs. In *Proceedings of IJCAI'77*, pages 419–120, 1977.

[DSF93] S. Decorte, D. De Schreye, and M. Fabris. Automatic Inference of Norms: a Missing Link in Automatic Termination Analysis. In D. Miller, editor, *Proc. 1993 Int'l Symposium on Logic Programming*. The MIT Press, 1993.

[EG94]   S. Etalle and M. Gabbrielli. Transformations of CLP Modules. Technical Report CS-R9515, CWI, Amsterdam, 1994.

[Hog81] C.J. Hogger. Derivation of logic programs. *Journal of the ACM*, 28(2):372–392, April 1981.

[KK88]   T. Kawamura and T. Kanamori. Preservation of Stronger Equivalence in Unfold/Fold Logic Programming Transformation. In *Proc. Int'l Conf. on Fifth Generation Computer Systems*, pages 413–422. Institute for New Generation Computer Technology, Tokyo, 1988.

[KK90]   T. Kawamura and T. Kanamori. Preservation of Stronger Equivalence in Unfold/Fold Logic Programming Transformation. *Theoretical Computer Science*, 75(1&2):139–156, 1990.

[Kom82] H. Komorowski. Partial evaluation as a means for inferencing data structures in an applicative language: A theory and implementation in the case of Prolog. In Ninth ACM Symposium on Principles of Programming Languages, Albuquerque, New Mexico, pages 255–267. ACM, 1982.

[Llo87] J. W. Lloyd. *Foundations of Logic Programming*. Springer-Verlag, Berlin, 1987. Second edition.

[N.J84] Mycroft A. N.Jones. Stepwise development of operational and denotational se-
         mantics for Prolog. In *International Symposium on Logic Programming, Atlantic
         City, NJ, (U.S.A.)*, pages 289–298, 1984.

[Plü90] L. Plümer. *Termination Proofs for Logic Programs*. Lecture Notes in Artificial
         Intelligence 446. Springer-Verlag, 1990.

[PP91]   M. Proietti and A. Pettorossi. Semantics preserving transformation rules for pro-
         log. In *ACM SIGPLAN Symposium on Partial Evaluation and Semantics-Based
         Program Manipulation (PEPM '91)*. ACM press, 1991.

[Sek91] H. Seki. Unfold/fold transformation of stratified programs. *Theoretical Computer
         Science*, 86(1):107–139, 1991.

[Sek93] H. Seki. Unfold/fold transformation of general logic programs for the Well-
         Founded semantics. *Journal of Logic Programming*, 16(1&2):5–23, 1993.

[TS84]   H. Tamaki and T. Sato. Unfold/Fold Transformations of Logic Programs. In
         Sten-Åke Tärnlund, editor, *Proc. Second Int'l Conf. on Logic Programming*, pages
         127–139, 1984.

Derivation of Concurrent Algorithms in Tempo

Steve Gregory

Department of Computer Science
University of Bristol
Bristol BS8 1TR, England

steve@cs.bris.ac.uk

Abstract

Tempo is a logic programming language that has recently been designed with the aim of allowing concurrent programs to be written in a more declarative manner than existing languages. One of the benefits of declarative programming is the potential for systematic derivation of programs — the subject of this paper. Here we present a few transformation rules that can be applied to Tempo programs, and then describe in detail the derivation of some concurrent algorithms in Tempo. An outline of the Tempo language is also included in order to make the paper self-contained.

1 Introduction

One of the major advantages of the declarative approach to programming is the ability to construct programs systematically from specifications by applying correctness-preserving transformation rules. Existing programs can be transformed to new, possibly more efficient, programs in the same way. Although it could be argued that the same technique can also be applied to "conventional" languages, it is undoubtedly far easier in a declarative context. For example, a logic program (in some executable logic programming language) can be derived from a logic specification by applying the standard rules of logic that have been established for thousands of years.

The feasibility of program transformation, along with the many other attractions of declarative programming, depends upon the target programming language being both executable and declarative. Unfortunately, most logic programming languages are only partially declarative, in that not all relevant aspects of a program's behaviour are explicit in the program. One example is termination, which, even in "pure" Prolog, is dependent on control considerations such as the order of goals and clauses: if one program P terminates, another, logically equivalent, program P' may not. The situation is made much worse by the use of non-logical primitives such as I/O, which are indispensable in "real" programs.

In this paper we address concurrent programming, a subject of increasing importance with the advent of multiprocessor architectures and computer networks. Concurrent programs comprise several processes which interact (synchronize and communicate) with each other. Programs that interact with their environment, such as the processes in a concurrent program, are often termed *reactive*. Unlike a *transformational* program, which merely terminates with a final result, a reactive program produces results incrementally throughout its execution and may not even be intended to terminate. A transformational program is considered correct if its final result is correct (partial correctness) and the program terminates. In contrast, a reactive program may be required to satisfy several properties *during its execution*.

These are usually classified into *safety* properties, those that must *always* be true, and *progress* (or *liveness*) properties, those that must *eventually* hold. Partial correctness and termination are special cases of safety and progress properties, respectively.

Concurrent logic programming languages such as Parlog (Gregory, 1987) and KL1 (Ueda and Chikayama, 1990) are declarative in the same sense as Prolog: a program explicitly describes its final result. Unfortunately, all other important (safety and progress) properties of a program are implicit and have to be preserved by proper use of control features (modes, sequencing, etc.). It follows that, if a concurrent logic program is transformed to a logically equivalent one, the only property that is guaranteed to be preserved is the final result that the program computes. This is not a very significant property in reactive programs, especially those that never terminate! Perhaps because operational semantics play such a prominent role in concurrent logic programs, there has been a trend in recent years to abandon the goal of "declarativeness" altogether. A few languages have evolved, e.g., (Foster *et al.*, 1992; McCabe and Clark, 1995), which incorporate various aspects of Parlog in an imperative framework.

In our view, it is premature to abandon the ideal of declarative concurrent programming: instead of removing the "logic" from concurrent logic programming, we should attempt to design languages that are *more* declarative than existing ones. We have moved a step in this direction with the design of Tempo (Gregory and Ramirez, 1995). Tempo is a concurrent programming language based on classical first-order logic which allows *all safety properties* to be stated declaratively, not only the program's final result.

In the next section we give a brief outline of Tempo, a full description of which can be found in (Gregory and Ramirez, 1995). Section 3 demonstrates how a specification of a classic concurrent programming problem can be transformed into various algorithms, all guaranteed to have the specified safety properties. The original contribution of this paper is the transformation method described and illustrated in Section 3, the results of which were stated without justification in (Gregory and Ramirez, 1995). The detail presented here should be sufficient to show how algorithms for other problems can be derived in Tempo.

2 Outline of Tempo

In Tempo, as in most logic programming languages, a program is a set of Horn clauses. The arguments of the head of each clause are distinct variables, so we write a *constraint definition* (a set of clauses defining a predicate) as a single clause containing a disjunction:

$$H \leftarrow Cs_1; \ \ldots; \ Cs_n.$$

(The disjunction operator ';' is less tightly binding than ',' but more tightly binding than '←'.) Each constraint definition is a complete definition of the relation being defined, so the above is equivalent to

$$H \leftrightarrow \exists V \ Cs_1 \vee \ldots \vee Cs_n$$

where V denotes the variables appearing in Cs_1, ..., Cs_n but not in H. A further syntactic restriction is that no constants or function symbols are allowed in clauses.

Precedence Constraints

The constraints in a Tempo program describe relations between *events*. Events are atomic (i.e., they have no duration), so the main attribute of an event is its *execution time*. The only primitive predicate in Tempo is the precedence constraint $X < Y$, which is read "X precedes Y" and indicates that event X occurs chronologically before event Y. Mutually unconstrained events may occur in any order, or even simultaneously. The absolute execution time of an event cannot be specified, with one exception: if $X < X$, the execution time of X must be the special value *eternity*; in this case, we call X an *eternity event*. Eternity events are *never* executed.

Figure 1 defines the '$<$' predicate more formally ((4) is a corollary of (1–3)): '$<$' is transitive and no event precedes itself except an eternity event, which is preceded by *every* event.

$$\forall X \forall Y \forall Z \ (X < Y \land Y < Z \ \rightarrow \ X < Z) \tag{1}$$
$$\forall X \forall Y \ (time(Y, eternity) \ \rightarrow \ X < Y) \tag{2}$$
$$\forall X \ (X < X \ \rightarrow \ time(X, eternity)) \tag{3}$$
$$\forall X \forall Y \ (time(Y, eternity) \land Y < X \ \rightarrow \ time(X, eternity)) \tag{4}$$

Figure 1: Properties of the '$<$' predicate

A Tempo program can describe processes (or *activities*) as partially ordered sets of atomic *events*. Events often represent transitions between successive states. For example, query (Q1) represents a *thinker* activity, which is initially in thinking state, becomes hungry (event H), starts eating (event E), and finally resumes thinking forever (event T):

```
←  thinker(H,E,T).                                          (Q1)

thinker(H,E,T) ← H < E, E < T.
```

The solution to query (Q1) is any totally ordered set of events such that H < E < T. Notice that some of these could be eternity events. Indeed, an answer substitution in which *all* events are eternity events is a valid solution to *any* Tempo query.

Operational Semantics

Although Tempo uses the familiar syntax of Horn clauses, its operational semantics is completely different from that of conventional logic programming languages such as Prolog or Parlog. Instead of merely returning an answer substitution for query variables, a Tempo interpreter actually *executes* the specified activities:

1. Instead of computing an execution time t for event E, Tempo executes an event (which we shall refer to by the variable name E) at time t. This way, events are executed in the specified order, but their execution times are implicit. For example, query (Q1) results in a sequence "*execute* H; *execute* E; *execute* T", in that order. An event that has an execution time of *eternity* is never executed; this corresponds to termination or deadlock.

2. The solution is constructed incrementally in ascending time order. That is, an event is executed as soon as its predecessors have been executed, without waiting for a complete solution. This yields useful results even if the set of events is large or infinite.

A Tempo interpreter works essentially as follows. Each event E in a query is checked to see whether it is preceded by another event, i.e., if a constraint X < E exists. If E is not preceded by any other event (it is *enabled*), it can be executed, whereupon all constraints of the form E < F are deleted and each event F (previously preceded by E) is checked in the same way to see whether it is enabled.

User-Defined Constraints

While checking whether an event E is enabled, any user-defined constraint that has E as an argument (such as `thinker(H,E,T)`) is *expanded*, i.e., replaced by its body; this is repeated until E appears only in primitive '<' constraints.

Event Trees

Many activities comprise a large or infinite set of events, for example a *philosopher*, which repeatedly cycles through the three states thinking, hungry, and eating. We cannot name each event individually in a finite specification, so instead we define relations on *trees* of events. Each event E may have one or more *offspring* events associated with it, which, for operational reasons, must be preceded by E itself. The offsprings of E are named E+1, E+2, etc., and may appear in queries and in bodies (but not heads) of constraint definitions. For example, the following recursive definition of `phil` represents a philosopher activity:

```
phil(H,E,T) ← H <* E, E <* T, T <* H+1.

X <* Z ← X < Z, X+1 <* Z+1.
```

The '+' notation can be defined formally by the following axioms:

$$p(s_1,...,s_i,X+N,t_1,...,t_j) \leftrightarrow (\exists Y\ offs(X,N,Y) \wedge X < Y \wedge p(s_1,...,s_i,Y,t_1,...,t_j))$$
$$Y = X+N \wedge Z = X+N \rightarrow Y = Z$$

where *offs(X,N,Y)* indicates that event Y is the Nth offspring of event X.

Disjunction

Disjunction is necessary to describe some problems. For example, in the mutual exclusion example that we describe below, it is necessary to ensure that one of two philosophers starts thinking before the other begins to eat. The following `mutex` constraint uses a disjunction to express this requirement:

```
mutex(E1,E2,T1,T2) ←   T1 < E2, mutex(E1+1,E2,T1+1,T2);
                       T2 < E1, mutex(E1,E2+1,T1,T2+1).
```

A Tempo program with disjunction naturally defines a search tree in which each branch admits a different ordering of events: each execution of the program must follow a single branch of this tree. Rather than attempting to perform an intelligent planning-like search for a suitable ordering, Tempo uses a special "shallow search" strategy to select a branch, which works as follows.

If a disjunctive constraint is encountered while checking whether an event E is enabled, each alternative of the constraint is checked. If E is enabled in all of the disjunction's alternatives, E is enabled by the disjunction. If E is not enabled in any alternative, E is not enabled. However, if E is enabled in some but not all of the alternatives, the disjunction is *reduced*: the alternatives that do not enable E are deleted, and E is enabled by the disjunction. This step is performed only if all other, non-disjunctive, constraints have also enabled E, and therefore E can be executed.

Concurrent Execution

A Tempo query can be solved cooperatively by a number of workers, or *processes*. A query may take the general form

$$\leftarrow \ \{Cs_1\}, \ \ldots, \ \{Cs_m\}.$$

where each Cs_i is a conjunction of constraints which is executed as a separate process. This is logically identical to the same query without the braces: it will execute the specified events in an order that satisfies the constraints in the query. The difference is purely operational: each process solves the constraints allocated to it, independently of other processes except where the processes share an event. A shared event is executed only after it has been enabled by *every* process that shares it. Shared events provide the sole mechanism for Tempo processes to communicate.

Values

The language that we have described above, and in (Gregory and Ramirez, 1995), has no explicit representation of data. However, the latest version of Tempo includes *values* (numbers, atoms, and structured terms), which can appear as arguments of constraints and can also be associated with events. This allows computation, as well as synchronization, to be expressed in Tempo. Some points mentioned above (e.g., that '<' is the only primitive) do not apply to the extended language. The extended language features will be fully described in a forthcoming paper; we shall not need to use them in the remainder of this paper.

An Example: Mutual Exclusion

The mutual exclusion problem is a classic concurrent programming example. Given a number of (philosopher) processes repeatedly executing two alternate sequences of instructions — a non-critical section (*thinking*) and a critical section (*eating*) — ensure that no more than one process executes its critical section at any time. This is a safety property. There are also various progress properties that a solution to this problem should satisfy: for example, that a philosopher that is trying to enter its critical section should eventually be able to do so.

The following Tempo query (Q2) succinctly expresses the mutual exclusion problem for two philosophers:

$$\leftarrow \ \texttt{phil(H1,E1,T1), phil(H2,E2,T2), mutex(E1,E2,T1,T2)}. \tag{Q2}$$

This is not only a straightforward "specification" of the problem, but also a Tempo program. When the program is run, the events corresponding to H1, E1, T1, etc. are executed in any order that satisfies the specification: in particular, the intervals [E1..T1], [E1+1..T1+1], ..., [E2..T2], [E2+1..T2+1], etc. do not overlap with each other. In a practical application, each event might be associated with a useful action: for example, E1 and T1 could mark the beginning and end of an operation that accesses some shared physical resource.

Because the safety properties (i.e., the order of events) are explicit in the program, they are guaranteed to be preserved by any Tempo implementation. Likewise, the order of constraints in a conjunction, and alternatives in a disjunction, is irrelevant. However, progress properties (in this example, the requirement that any process trying to enter its critical section should eventually succeed) are *not* expressed explicitly: as in most languages, these have to be preserved by reasoning about the operational behaviour of Tempo.

3 Deriving Algorithms in Tempo

The definition *Algorithm* = *Logic* + *Control* (Kowalski, 1979) applies to any logic programming language. In the case of Tempo, we argue that the *Logic* component of a program captures more aspects of behaviour than in most languages, but the *Control* component is still significant. That is, the algorithm that a Tempo program realizes depends not only on the constraints that it contains but also on the control "annotations" used. In Prolog (but not in Tempo), even changing the order of goals or clauses can result in a different algorithm, though (in both languages) more substantial changes are usually required to transform one algorithm to another.

A Tempo programmer can write concurrent algorithms by using the {} syntax outlined above. For the mutual exclusion example, query (Q2) is actually a sequential algorithm that simulates a solution. To turn it into a concurrent algorithm, the phil constraints, each representing a philosopher, need to be allocated to different processes. A simple way to do this is by annotating query (Q2) as below:

← {phil(H1,E1,T1)}, {phil(H2,E2,T2)}, {mutex(E1,E2,T1,T2)}. (Q3)

Query (Q3) represents an algorithm in which the first two (phil) processes each communicate with a third (mutex) process. When the first philosopher wants to "eat" it enables event E1. E1 can only be executed when it has also been enabled by the mutex process, effectively giving the first philosopher permission to eat. When this happens, the mutex process commits to one of the two alternatives of its disjunction: because this includes the constraint T1 < E2, the second philosopher will not be able to start eating until the first one finishes (and enables T1).

Concurrent programs are often intended to be executed in parallel, with the constituent processes possibly running on distinct physical processors. One of the most challenging aspects of concurrent programming is the wide variety of parallel architectures that exist, and the corresponding proliferation of concurrent programming paradigms and languages. For most problems, there is no universal concurrent algorithm that is well suited to all types of parallel architecture. For example, an algorithm in which processes communicate by shared variables may be efficient when run on a shared memory multiprocessor but not on a distributed machine. Also, an algorithm that involves a lot of interprocess communication may well be inefficient on a distributed architecture, where communication is expensive.

For example, query (Q3) is a perfectly correct concurrent Tempo program for mutual exclusion, but it is not necessarily efficient because:

1. The mutex process, which communicates with all phil processes, may constitute a bottleneck, especially if scaled up to a large number of philosophers.

2. The communication between a phil process and the mutex process is analogous to synchronous message passing: a shared event is executed when both processes enable it. Synchronous message passing is directly provided in some multiprocessors, but may be expensive to implement in others.

The algorithm that query (Q3) realizes is shown in an imperative style in Figure 2(a), which is reproduced from (Gregory and Ramirez, 1995). The processes named c1, c2, and s in Figure 2(a) correspond to the first, second, and third groups of constraints in (Q3), respectively.

```
% {phil(H1,E1,T1)}                  % {mutex(E1,E2,T1,T2)}           (a)
process c1:                         process s:
repeat                              repeat
    think;                              receive eat from c1 (E1)  →
    (H1)                                    receive think from c1 (T1)
    send eat to s (E1);             or  receive eat from c2 (E2)  →
    eat;                                    receive think from c2 (T2)
    send think to s (T1);          forever
forever


% {phil(H1,Eb1,T1),                 % {H1 <* E1, H2 <* E2,           (b)
   E1 <* Eb1}                           mutex(E1,E2,T1,T2)}
process c1:                         process s:
repeat                              repeat
    think;                              receive hungry from c1 (H1)  →
    send hungry to s (H1);              send eat to c1 (E1);
    receive eat from s (E1);            receive think from c1 (T1)
    eat (Eb1);                      or  receive hungry from c2 (H2)  →
    send think to s (T1);              send eat to c2 (E2);
forever                                 receive think from c2 (T2)
                                    forever


Initially: b1 := false; b2 := false;                                 (c)
% {phil(H1,E1,T1)}                  % {phil(H2,E2,T2)}
process c1:                         process c2:
repeat                              repeat
    think;                              think;
    b1 := true (H1);                    b2 := true (H2);
    repeat until not b2 (E1);           repeat until not b1 (E2);
    eat;                                eat;
    b1 := false (T1);                   b2 := false (T2);
forever                             forever
```

Figure 2: Mutual exclusion algorithms — (a) synchronous message passing;
(b) asynchronous message passing; (c) shared variables

Below we show how a Tempo program (or specification) can be transformed into another one that may be more suitable for a particular parallel architecture. Given a Tempo query $\leftarrow q$, our method is to derive a stronger query $\leftarrow q'$ (such that q' logically implies q), which will then be guaranteed to preserve all of the safety properties that $\leftarrow q$ satisfies. The objective is to obtain a Tempo program that can be executed more efficiently on the target machine than the original. Alternatively, the final Tempo program can be translated directly into a conventional language that has an efficient implementation on the target machine.

Transformation Rules

Here we outline the transformation rules that we use. These are rather standard, except for the last two, which are explained in more detail.

1. Unfolding

Given a Tempo constraint definition

$H \leftarrow Cs.$

any constraint C in a conjunction such that $C = H\theta$ can be replaced by $Cs\theta$. Because $H \leftrightarrow Cs$, the new conjunction is equivalent to the old one.

2. Folding

Given a Tempo constraint definition

$H \leftarrow Cs.$

if a conjunction contains an expression Cs' which is an instance of Cs (i.e., $Cs' = Cs\theta$), then Cs' can be replaced by $H\theta$, because $H \leftrightarrow Cs$. Again, the new conjunction is equivalent to the old one.

3. Adding redundant constraints

Any constraint that is implied by the existing constraints in a conjunction can be added to it without changing its meaning.

4. Deleting subsumed alternatives

An alternative can be removed from a disjunction if it implies at least one of the other alternatives, because $(a \vee b \leftrightarrow a)$ if $(b \rightarrow a)$. Therefore, whenever we derive a constraint definition of the form:

$p(X_1,...,X_m) \leftarrow r_1; \ r_2; \ ...; \ r_n; \ s.$

such that, for some i, $s \rightarrow r_i$, we can simplify it to:

$p(X_1,...,X_m) \leftarrow r_1; \ r_2; \ ...; \ r_n.$

5. The unfold/fold rule

Our most sophisticated transformation rule is as follows: In order to replace an expression Cs in the query by Cs', we first define two new predicates of the form:

$$p(X_1,...,X_m) \leftarrow Cs. \tag{1}$$
$$p'(X_1,...,X_m) \leftarrow Cs'. \tag{2}$$

where $X_1,...,X_m$ are all of the free variables in Cs and Cs'. We then use standard *totally correct* transformation rules (e.g., rules 1 to 4 above) to transform (1) and (2) into a pair of constraint definitions of the form (1') and (2') below:

$$p(X_1,...,X_m) \leftarrow q, \ r; \ s. \tag{1'}$$
$$p'(X_1,...,X_m) \leftarrow q', \ r'; \ s'. \tag{2'}$$

where r' and s' are identical to r and s respectively, but with every occurrence of p replaced by p'. Then, if $q' \rightarrow q$:

$$p'(X_1,...,X_m) \rightarrow p(X_1,...,X_m)$$

It is possible to prove this fact by induction on the number of constraints for predicate p appearing in r and s.[1] (Recall that the Tempo connective '$\leftarrow$' in (1, 2, 1', 2') actually denotes equivalence '$\leftrightarrow$'.)

It follows that $Cs' \rightarrow Cs$, and therefore we can replace Cs in the query by Cs', to produce a new query that logically implies the old one.

This rule is very similar to the unfold/fold method for proving the validity of replacement laws in the transformation of logic programs[2] (Boulanger and Bruynooghe, 1993; Proietti and Pettorossi, 1994). The difference is that Proietti and Pettorossi derive clauses for (1') and (2') which are *identical*, modulo predicate renaming, to prove (roughly) that $Cs' \leftrightarrow Cs$. We have a weaker requirement, that $q' \rightarrow q$, because we only need to prove that $Cs' \rightarrow Cs$.

An Algorithm for Asynchronous Message Passing

If each shared event appears on the right of a '$<$' constraint in only one process (the sender) in a Tempo query, the interprocess communication is analogous to asynchronous message passing. Because the receiver cannot delay the event's execution, it is executed as soon as the sender enables it.

Query (Q3) does not satisfy this restriction because E1 and E2 each appear on the right of '$<$' in two processes. However, we can construct a Tempo query (Q4) of the form $\leftarrow qa$, such that qa logically implies the specification s, which satisfies the restrictions corresponding to asynchronous message passing. The specification s is repeated below from (Q2):

```
← phil(H1,E1,T1), phil(H2,E2,T2), mutex(E1,E2,T1,T2).
```

First, the two phil constraints are unfolded:

```
← H1 <* E1, E1 <* T1, T1 <* H1+1,
  H2 <* E2, E2 <* T2, T2 <* H2+1, mutex(E1,E2,T1,T2).
```

Then a new event Eb1 is introduced between the two events E1 and T1; likewise, Eb2 is introduced between E2 and T2. This is done by replacing the constraint E1 <* T1 by E1 <* Eb1, Eb1 <* T1, and replacing E2 <* T2 by E2 <* Eb2, Eb2 <* T2 (we justify the validity of this replacement below). The query becomes:

```
← H1 <* E1, E1 <* Eb1, Eb1 <* T1, T1 <* H1+1,
  H2 <* E2, E2 <* Eb2, Eb2 <* T2, T2 <* H2+1,
  mutex(E1,E2,T1,T2).
```

We now add two redundant constraints to the query: H1 <* Eb1 and H2 <* Eb2 (these are subsumed by the existing constraints):

```
← H1 <* E1, E1 <* Eb1, H1 <* Eb1, Eb1 <* T1, T1 <* H1+1,
  H2 <* E2, E2 <* Eb2, H2 <* Eb2, Eb2 <* T2, T2 <* H2+1,
  mutex(E1,E2,T1,T2).
```

Folding, using the definition of the phil constraint, yields:

```
← H1 <* E1, E1 <* Eb1, phil(H1,Eb1,T1),
  H2 <* E2, E2 <* Eb2, phil(H2,Eb2,T2), mutex(E1,E2,T1,T2).
```

---

[1]   Thanks to John Gallagher for this suggestion.
[2]   Thanks again to John Gallagher for drawing my attention to this work.

Finally, this conjunction can be arranged into three groups of constraints as in the Tempo query (Q4). Event E1 now appears on the right of '<' only in the third process: it represents a "permission to eat" message sent by that process to the first philosopher. Eb1 is an event local to the first philosopher process, representing the act of "beginning to eat". Query (Q4) realizes the algorithm shown in Figure 2(b); the three groups of constraints correspond to processes c1, c2, and s, respectively.

```
←   {phil(H1,Eb1,T1), E1 <* Eb1},
    {phil(H2,Eb2,T2), E2 <* Eb2},
    {H1 <* E1, H2 <* E2, mutex(E1,E2,T1,T2)}.                    (Q4)
```

The correctness of replacing E1 <* T1 by (E1 <* Eb1, Eb1 <* T1) is justified by our unfold/fold rule. We first define a new predicate pr:

```
pr(X,Z) ← X <* Y, Y <* Z.
```

Now the two '<*' constraints are unfolded, and the right side is folded using the definition of pr, to obtain the recursive constraint definition:

```
pr(X,Z) ← X < Y, Y < Z, pr(X+1,Z+1).
```

while the '<*' constraint is defined as:

```
X <* Z ← X < Z, X+1 <* Z+1.
```

From (1) in Figure 1, we have

```
X < Y, Y < Z → X < Z
```

and so, by applying our unfold/fold rule:

```
pr(X,Z) → X <* Z
```

or, equivalently:

```
X <* Y, Y <* Z → X <* Z
```

An Algorithm for Shared Mutable Variables

Tempo can also simulate communication via shared mutable variables: variables that can be destructively modified and read by several processes. Each variable is represented by a var constraint (contained in its own process) and other processes are allowed to share events only with var processes: these shared events represent the actions of assigning a value to, and testing the current value of, the mutable variable. For example, a boolean variable, initially false, could be represented by var(AT,AF,OT,OF), where AT and AF represent assignments to true and false, respectively, and OT and OF represent observations that the variable has these respective values[3]. Assuming that the assignments to true and false strictly alternate, beginning with an assignment to true, and we only want to observe the false values, the variable can be represented by a simpler constraint varf(AT,AF,OF), defined in Tempo as follows:

```
varf(AT,AF,OF) ← OF < AT, varf(OF+1,AT,AF);
                 AF < OF, varf(OF,AT+1,AF+1).
```

---

[3] In the latest version of Tempo, a mutable variable taking an *arbitrary* value can be represented by var(A,O), where A and O are events with associated values.

The point of this transformation is that any Tempo program that fits this structure can be implemented directly by shared memory hardware: the constraint `varf(AT,AF,OF)` can be enforced by a shared mutable variable b, where the events `AT`, `AF`, and `OF` are replaced by the actions "`b:=true`", "`b:=false`", and "`wait until not b`", respectively.

An algorithm for mutual exclusion that uses shared mutable variables is shown in Figure 2(c). This is a simplified version of Peterson's (1981) algorithm with the possibility of deadlock. To render this algorithm in Tempo, we introduce a `varf` constraint for each of the shared variables `b1` and `b2`, as in query (Q5). The first two groups of constraints in (Q5) correspond to processes `c1` and `c2` in Figure 2(c).

```
←  {phil(H1,E1,T1)}, {phil(H2,E2,T2)},
   {varf(H1,T1,E2)}, {varf(H2,T2,E1)}.                    (Q5)
```

It is not at all obvious that the algorithm of Figure 2(c) satisfies the safety properties of mutual exclusion, but this is much easier to prove when the algorithm is expressed in Tempo as in query (Q5). We simply need to transform the specification

```
←  phil(H1,E1,T1), phil(H2,E2,T2), mutex(E1,E2,T1,T2).    (s)
```

into the query

```
←  phil(H1,E1,T1), phil(H2,E2,T2),
   varf(H1,T1,E2), varf(H2,T2,E1).                        (q)
```

We do this in a single step, using the unfold/fold rule: We first define two new predicates ms (equivalent to the specification) and mq (equivalent to the query):

```
ms(E1,E2,T1,T2,H1,H2) ←
    phil(H1,E1,T1), phil(H2,E2,T2), mutex(E1,E2,T1,T2).

mq(E1,E2,T1,T2,H1,H2) ←
    phil(H1,E1,T1), phil(H2,E2,T2),
    varf(H1,T1,E2), varf(H2,T2,E1).
```

and then use the unfold/fold rule to show that

```
mq(E1,E2,T1,T2,H1,H2) → ms(E1,E2,T1,T2,H1,H2)
```

The first step is to transform the definition of mq by unfolding the `varf` constraints:

```
mq(E1,E2,T1,T2,H1,H2) ←
    phil(H1,E1,T1), phil(H2,E2,T2),
    (E2 < H1, varf(H1,T1,E2+1); T1 < E2, varf(H1+1,T1+1,E2)),
    (E1 < H2, varf(H2,T2,E1+1); T2 < E1, varf(H2+1,T2+1,E1)).
```

and then distribute the conjunction:

```
mq(E1,E2,T1,T2,H1,H2) ←
    phil(H1,E1,T1), phil(H2,E2,T2),
      T1 < E2, E1 < H2, varf(H1+1,T1+1,E2), varf(H2,T2,E1+1);
    phil(H1,E1,T1), phil(H2,E2,T2),
      E2 < H1, T2 < E1, varf(H1,T1,E2+1), varf(H2+1,T2+1,E1);
    phil(H1,E1,T1), phil(H2,E2,T2),
      T1 < E2, T2 < E1, varf(H1+1,T1+1,E2), varf(H2+1,T2+1,E1);
    phil(H1,E1,T1), phil(H2,E2,T2),
      E2 < H1, E1 < H2, varf(H1,T1,E2+1), varf(H2,T2,E1+1).
```

Next, we unfold (twice) the first `phil` constraint in the first alternative of the disjunction and the second `phil` constraint in the second alternative. Changes made in this step are shown in italics:

```
mq(E1,E2,T1,T2,H1,H2) ←
    H1 < E1, H1+1 <* E1+1, E1 < T1, E1+1 <* T1+1, T1 < H1+1,
        T1+1 <* H1+1+1, phil(H2,E2,T2),
        T1 < E2, E1 < H2, varf(H1+1,T1+1,E2), varf(H2,T2,E1+1);
    phil(H1,E1,T1), H2 < E2, H2+1 <* E2+1, E2 < T2, E2+1 <* T2+1,
        T2 < H2+1, T2+1 <* H2+1+1,
        E2 < H1, T2 < E1, varf(H1,T1,E2+1), varf(H2+1,T2+1,E1);
    phil(H1,E1,T1), phil(H2,E2,T2),
        T1 < E2, T2 < E1, varf(H1+1,T1+1,E2), varf(H2+1,T2+1,E1);
    phil(H1,E1,T1), phil(H2,E2,T2),
        E2 < H1, E1 < H2, varf(H1,T1,E2+1), varf(H2,T2,E1+1).
```

Folding the first and second alternatives, using the definition of `mq`, yields:

```
mq(E1,E2,T1,T2,H1,H2) ←
    T1 < E2, E1 < H2, H1 < E1, E1 < T1, T1 < H1+1,
        mq(E1+1,E2,T1+1,T2,H1+1,H2);
    E2 < H1, T2 < E1, H2 < E2, E2 < T2, T2 < H2+1,
        mq(E1,E2+1,T1,T2+1,H1,H2+1);
    phil(H1,E1,T1), phil(H2,E2,T2),
        T1 < E2, T2 < E1, varf(H1+1,T1+1,E2), varf(H2+1,T2+1,E1);
    phil(H1,E1,T1), phil(H2,E2,T2),
        E2 < H1, E1 < H2, varf(H1,T1,E2+1), varf(H2,T2,E1+1).
```

Now we unfold the third and fourth alternatives:

```
mq(E1,E2,T1,T2,H1,H2) ←
    T1 < E2, E1 < H2, H1 < E1, E1 < T1, T1 < H1+1,
        mq(E1+1,E2,T1+1,T2,H1+1,H2);
    E2 < H1, T2 < E1, H2 < E2, E2 < T2, T2 < H2+1,
        mq(E1,E2+1,T1,T2+1,H1,H2+1);
    H1 <* E1, E1 < T1, E1+1 <* T1+1, T1 < H1+1, T1+1 <* H1+1+1,
        H2 <* E2, E2 < T2, E2+1 <* T2+1, T2 < H2+1, T2+1 <* H2+1+1,
        T1 < E2, T2 < E1, varf(H1+1,T1+1,E2), varf(H2+1,T2+1,E1);
    H1 < E1, H1+1 <* E1+1, E1 < T1, E1+1 <* T1+1, T1 <* H1+1,
        H2 < E2, H2+1 <* E2+1, E2 < T2, E2+1 <* T2+1, T2 <* H2+1,
        E2 < H1, E1 < H2, varf(H1,T1,E2+1), varf(H2,T2,E1+1).
```

and then simplify the third and fourth alternatives, using the properties of '<' given in (1) and (3) of Figure 1:

```
mq(E1,E2,T1,T2,H1,H2) ←
    T1 < E2, E1 < H2, H1 < E1, E1 < T1, T1 < H1+1,
        mq(E1+1,E2,T1+1,T2,H1+1,H2);
    E2 < H1, T2 < E1, H2 < E2, E2 < T2, T2 < H2+1,
        mq(E1,E2+1,T1,T2+1,H1,H2+1);
    time(E1,eternity), time(E2,eternity), time(T1,eternity), time(T2,eternity),
        time(H1+1,eternity), time(H2+1,eternity), H1 <* E1, H2 <* E2;
    time(E1,eternity), time(E2,eternity), time(T1,eternity), time(T2,eternity),
        time(H1,eternity), time(H2,eternity).
```

The fourth alternative, in which all variables are eternity events, is subsumed by each of the first two. It can be deleted by applying our fourth transformation rule:

```
mq(E1,E2,T1,T2,H1,H2) ←
    T1 < E2, E1 < H2, H1 < E1, E1 < T1, T1 < H1+1,
        mq(E1+1,E2,T1+1,T2,H1+1,H2);
    E2 < H1, T2 < E1, H2 < E2, E2 < T2, T2 < H2+1,
        mq(E1,E2+1,T1,T2+1,H1,H2+1);
    time(E1,eternity), time(E2,eternity), time(T1,eternity), time(T2,eternity),
        time(H1+1,eternity), time(H2+1,eternity), H1 <* E1, H2 <* E2.
```

We now define a new predicate m2, which is the same as mq except that one constraint is omitted from each of the first two alternatives:

```
m2(E1,E2,T1,T2,H1,H2) ←
    T1 < E2, H1 < E1, E1 < T1, T1 < H1+1,
        m2(E1+1,E2,T1+1,T2,H1+1,H2);
    T2 < E1, H2 < E2, E2 < T2, T2 < H2+1,
        m2(E1,E2+1,T1,T2+1,H1,H2+1);
    time(E1,eternity), time(E2,eternity), time(T1,eternity), time(T2,eternity),
        time(H1+1,eternity), time(H2+1,eternity), H1 <* E1, H2 <* E2.
```

By applying the result used in our unfold/fold transformation rule:

$$mq(E1,E2,T1,T2,H1,H2) \rightarrow m2(E1,E2,T1,T2,H1,H2)$$

In the definition of m2, the third alternative is subsumed by each of the first two, so it can be deleted by applying our fourth transformation rule:

```
m2(E1,E2,T1,T2,H1,H2) ←
    T1 < E2, H1 < E1, E1 < T1, T1 < H1+1,
        m2(E1+1,E2,T1+1,T2,H1+1,H2);
    T2 < E1, H2 < E2, E2 < T2, T2 < H2+1,
        m2(E1,E2+1,T1,T2+1,H1,H2+1).
```

We now transform the definition of ms. By unfolding all of the constraints on the right side, distributing the conjunction, and then folding using the definition of ms, we obtain the following recursive definition:

```
ms(E1,E2,T1,T2,H1,H2) ←
    T1 < E2, H1 < E1, E1 < T1, T1 < H1+1,
        ms(E1+1,E2,T1+1,T2,H1+1,H2);
    T2 < E1, H2 < E2, E2 < T2, T2 < H2+1,
        ms(E1,E2+1,T1,T2+1,H1,H2+1).
```

which is the same as the definition of m2, modulo predicate renaming, and therefore m2 and ms are equivalent.

To summarize, by transforming the definitions of ms and mq into equivalent self-recursive versions, and defining an intermediate predicate m2, we showed that

$$(q) \leftrightarrow mq(E1,E2,T1,T2,H1,H2) \rightarrow m2(E1,E2,T1,T2,H1,H2)$$
$$\leftrightarrow ms(E1,E2,T1,T2,H1,H2) \leftrightarrow (s)$$

This completes the proof that the Tempo query representing the shared variables algorithm implies the specification of the mutual exclusion problem.

4 Conclusions: Specifications vs Programs

This paper has demonstrated a way to derive concurrent algorithms within a new declarative programming language, Tempo. Here we briefly discuss the context into which Tempo fits.

Programming languages and specification languages both describe algorithms, but they are usually clearly distinguished: a programming language enables an algorithm to be executed efficiently by a real computer, while a specification language allows a human (or even a machine) to understand the algorithm and reason about it at an appropriate level of abstraction. It has been argued (Hayes and Jones, 1989) that this distinction is inevitable because the two types of language have different jobs to do and therefore have conflicting design objectives. However, history has shown that, faced with the need for two separate representations of an algorithm, programmers are likely to dispense with a formal specification and be satisfied with an informal justification of the executable program's correctness. Besides, the translation of a specification into a program remains a manual,[4] error-prone, process.

We believe that executable specification languages have an important role to play in program design. Although an executable specification may be a compromise between expressiveness and efficiency, the simplicity of a single representation of an algorithm is extremely appealing, especially for prototyping and pedagogical purposes. Tempo can be viewed as an executable specification language for concurrent systems, just as Prolog fulfils this function in its own application domain. A thorough comparison between Tempo and other concurrent languages is beyond the scope of this paper, and is the subject of ongoing research; however, we can make the following observations:

- As a programming language, Tempo has much in common with other concurrent symbolic languages such as Parlog, KL1, PCN, and April. The power of Tempo for writing real application programs is currently being tested, as features such as values are added to the language.

- As a specification language for concurrent systems, Tempo is much closer to languages based on temporal logic, e.g., Unity (Chandy and Misra, 1988) and TLA (Lamport, 1994), than process algebras (Milner, 1989). Both Unity and TLA can express the safety and progress properties of an algorithm, as well as (at an abstract level) the algorithm itself: in these languages an algorithm is correct if it logically implies the specification. This is true also in Tempo, except that a Tempo specification/algorithm can immediately be executed, and the progress properties are not explicit. An interesting aspect of TLA is that, for simplicity, it deliberately relies as far as possible on classical logic, resorting to temporal reasoning only where it is essential (mainly for progress properties). Tempo shares this aim, being based *entirely* on classical logic.

Acknowledgements

I am very grateful to John Gallagher for helpful advice on the content of this paper, and for filling in a 15-year gap in my knowledge of logic program transformation. Thanks are also due to the referees for comments on the presentation.

---

[4] If it were automated, the specification language would effectively be executable!

References

Boulanger, D. and Bruynooghe, M. 1993. Deriving unfold/fold transformations of logic programs using extended OLDT-based abstract interpretation. *Journal of Symbolic Computation 15*, pp. 495–521.

Chandy, K.M. and Misra, J. 1988. *Parallel Program Design*. Addison-Wesley.

Foster, I., Olson, R., and Tuecke, S. 1992. Productive parallel programming: The PCN approach. *Scientific Programming 1*, 1, pp. 51–66. Reprinted in *Programming Languages for Parallel Processing*, D. Skillicorn and D. Talia (Eds.), IEEE Computer Society Press, pp. 358–373, 1995.

Gregory, S. 1987. *Parallel Logic Programming in PARLOG*. Addison-Wesley.

Gregory, S. and Ramirez, R. 1995. Tempo: a declarative concurrent programming language. In *Proceedings of the 12th International Logic Programming Conference* (Tokyo, June 1995), L. Sterling (Ed.). MIT Press.

Hayes, I.J. and Jones, C.B. 1989. Specifications are not (necessarily) executable. *Software Engineering Journal 4*, 6, pp. 330–338.

Kowalski, R.A. 1979. Algorithm = Logic + Control. *Communications of the ACM 22*, 7, pp. 424–436.

Lamport, L. The temporal logic of actions. *ACM Transactions on Programming Languages and Systems 16*, 3, pp. 872–923.

McCabe, F.G. and Clark, K.L. 1995. April: Agent Process Interaction Language. In *Intelligent Agents — Lecture Notes in Artificial Intelligence 890*. Springer-Verlag.

Milner, R. 1989. *Communication and Concurrency*. Prentice Hall.

Peterson, G.L. 1981. Myths about the mutual exclusion problem. *Information Processing Letters 12*, 3, pp. 115–116.

Proietti, M. and Pettorossi, A. 1994. Synthesis of programs from unfold/fold proofs. In *Proceedings of LOPSTR93* (Louvain-la-Neuve, July 1993), Y. Deville (Ed.). Springer-Verlag.

Ueda, K. and Chikayama, T. 1990. Design of the kernel language for the Parallel Inference Machine. *Computer Journal 33*, 6, pp. 494–500.

An Argumentation-Theoretic Approach to Logic Program Transformation

Francesca Toni and Robert A. Kowalski

Department of Computing, Imperial College
180 Queen's Gate, London SW7 2BZ, UK
{ft,rak}@doc.ic.ac.uk

Abstract. We present a methodology for proving that any program transformation which preserves the least Herbrand model semantics when applied to sets of Horn clauses also preserves all semantics for normal logic programming that can be formulated in argumentation-theoretic terms [3, 4, 16]. These include stable model, partial stable model, preferred extension, stationary expansion, complete scenaria, stable theory, acceptability and well-founded semantics. We apply our methodology to prove that (some forms of) unfolding, folding and goal replacement preserve all these semantics. We also show the relationship of our methodology to that of Aravindan and Dung [1].

1 Introduction

The standard semantics for definite logic programs (i.e. the least Herbrand model semantics) is preserved by most of the program transformations studied in the literature, in particular by (some forms of) unfolding, folding and goal replacement (see [13] for a summary of these results). This paper provides a methodology for lifting these results from the definite logic program case to the normal logic program case, with respect to stable model [9], partial stable model [15], preferred extension [5], stationary expansion [14], complete scenaria [5], stable theory [10], acceptability [11] and well-founded semantics [18]. Most of the concrete cases obtained by applying our methodology [1] have been already shown elsewhere in the literature (see [1] for some of these results). Therefore, the main contribution of this paper lies in the general technique rather than in the concrete results.

All the semantics to which our methodology applies can be formulated in an argumentation framework [3, 4, 16], based upon a uniform notion of attack between sets of negative literals regarded as assumptions. We show that, to prove that any program transformation preserves all these semantics, it is sufficient to prove that there is a one-to-one correspondence between attacks before and after the transformation. This proof covers all of the semantics which can be defined in argumentation-theoretic terms, because the different semantics differ only in the way in which they build upon the same notion of attack. This technique, for proving soundness and completeness of a transformation, has already been

---

[1] with the exception that unfolding and folding preserve the acceptability semantics of [11]

used in [17] to show that abductive logic programs [16] can be transformed into normal logic programs preserving all argumentation-theoretic semantics. This general technique can be specialised to the case where the attacks before and after the transformation are exactly the same. The methodology we propose is a further specialisation of this technique, based upon the observation that all attacks are preserved if a transformation preserves the least Herbrand model semantics when it is applied to definite logic programs. The transformation must be such that it is applicable in the definite logic program case. In particular, unfolding inside negation is not allowed.

In [1], Aravindan and Dung show that (some forms of) folding and unfolding preserve the stable model, partial stable model, preferred extension, stationary expansion, complete scenaria, stable theory and well-founded semantics, due to the fact that normal logic programs before and after the application of folding and unfolding have the same semantic kernel [6] and that normal logic programs and their semantic kernels have the same semantics (for each of stable model, partial stable model, preferred extension, stationary expansion, complete scenaria, stable theory and well-founded semantics). We will show that this technique, of proving the correctness of a program transformation by proving that it preserves the semantic kernel, is equivalent to the technique of proving the correctness of a program transformation by proving that it preserves attacks. Therefore, our methodology can also be seen as a specialisation of Aravindan and Dung's. However, our methodology also generalises that of Aravindan and Dung in the sense that it applies directly to many program transformations. Whereas Aravindan and Dung consider only forlding and unfolding, ours is a general methodology for showing that, under certain conditions, any transformation that preserves the semantics of definite programs also preserves any semantics of normal logic programs that can be defined in argumentation terms.

The paper is organised as follows. First we apply the methodology to prove that the unfolding transformation, reviewed in section 2, preserves all semantics for normal logic programming which can be formulated in argumentation-theoretic terms of [3, 4, 16]. The unfolding transformation we consider is adapted from [13]. Section 3 reviews the argumentation framework and the formulation of various normal logic programming semantics in this framework. Section 4 proves that all semantics for normal logic programming formulated in the argumentation framework are preserved by unfolding. Section 5 presents the general methodology, by abstracting away from the proof in section 4. It also applies the general methodology to other transformations. Section 6 shows the relationships between our methodology and others, in particular the one in [1]. Finally, section 7 presents conclusions and discusses directions for further research.

2 Unfolding transformation

Normal logic programs are sets of clauses. A clause C is a formula of the form

$$H \leftarrow L_1, \ldots, L_n$$

where H is an atom, L_i is a literal, i.e. either an atom or the negation of an atom, for $i = 1, \ldots, n$, and all variables in $H, L_1, \ldots, L_n$ are implicitly universally quantified. H is the *head* and $L_1, \ldots, L_n$ the *body* of the clause C, referred to as *head(C)* and *body(C)* respectively. *Definite logic programs* are normal logic programs with no negative literals.

Definition 1. Let $\mathcal{P}$ be a normal logic program and let $C \in \mathcal{P}$ be a clause $H \leftarrow B_1, A, B_2$ where A is an atom and B_1, B_2 are (possibly empty) sets of literals. Suppose that

- $\{D_1, \ldots, D_m\}$, with $m > 0$, is the set of all clauses [2] in $\mathcal{P}$ such that A is unifiable with $head(D_1), \ldots, head(D_m)$ with most general unifiers $\theta_1, \ldots, \theta_m$, respectively, and
- U_j is the clause $[H \leftarrow B_1, body(D_j), B_2]\theta_j$ for $j = 1, \ldots m$.

Then, the result of *unfolding C in $\mathcal{P}$ with respect to A* is the program $(\mathcal{P}-\{C\}) \cup \{U_1, \ldots, U_m\}$.

The single unfolding step defined above can be repeated. A sequence of programs $\mathcal{P}_1, \ldots, \mathcal{P}_n$ is an *unfolding sequence* if any program $\mathcal{P}_{k+1}$, with $1 \leq k < n$, is obtained from $\mathcal{P}_k$ by applying an unfolding step.

Proving the *correctness of the unfolding transformation* (i.e. its soundness and completeness) with respect to a given normal logic programming semantics *Sem* amounts to proving that, for any unfolding sequence $\mathcal{P}_1, \ldots, \mathcal{P}_n$ and for any query [3] Q in the vocabulary of the original program $\mathcal{P}_1$: [4]

$$\mathcal{P}_1 \models_{Sem} Q \text{ if and only if } \mathcal{P}_n \models_{Sem} Q.$$

By induction, it suffices to show that, for any program $\mathcal{P}$ and for any program $\mathcal{P}'$ obtained by unfolding some clause in $\mathcal{P}$,

$$\mathcal{P} \models_{Sem} Q \text{ if and only if } \mathcal{P}' \models_{Sem} Q.$$

More generally, to prove the correctness of a sequence of transformation steps, not necessarily unfolding steps, with respect to a semantics *Sem* it suffices to prove that any such step is correct with respect to *Sem*.

In section 4, we will show correctness of the unfolding transformation with respect to all semantics *Sem* that can be formulated in the argumentation framework in terms of a single notion of *attack*.

---

[2] All variables in each of $C, D_1, \ldots, D_m$ are assumed to be standardised apart.

[3] In general, the correctness of unfolding as well as other program transformations is studied with respect to a given subset of all possible queries in the vocabulary of the original program. In this paper, for simplicity we will assume that the given subset of queries coincides with the set of all possible queries.

[4] Here and in the rest of the paper, for any program $\mathcal{P}rog$, $\mathcal{P}rog \models_{Sem} Q$ stands for "Q holds in $\mathcal{P}rog$ with respect to the semantics *Sem*".

3 An argumentation framework

The abstract argumentation framework proposed in [3, 4, 16] can be used to define many exisiting semantics for non-monotonic reasoning in general and for normal logic programming in particular.

Definition 2. An argumentation framework is a tuple $\langle T, \vdash, AB, IC \rangle$ where

- T is a *theory* in some formal language,
- $\vdash$ is a notion of *monotonic derivability* for the given language,
- AB is a set of *assumptions*, which are sentences of the language, and
- IC is a set of *denial integrity constraints with retractibles*.

Normal logic programming can be formulated as an instance of such a framework. Given a normal logic program P, the corresponding argumentation framework is $\langle T, \vdash, AB, IC \rangle$ where

- T is the set of all variable-free instances of clauses in P;
- $\vdash$ is modus ponens for the clause implication symbol $\leftarrow$;
- AB is the set of all variable-free negative literals;
- IC is the set consisting of all denials of the form $\neg[A \wedge not\ A]$, where A is a variable-free atom and *not A* is retractible.

Other non-monotonic logics, including default logic, autoepistemic logic, non-monotonic modal logic can also be understood as special cases of such a framework [3, 4, 16].

In any argumentation framework, a sentence is a non-monotonic consequence if it follows monotonically from T extended by means of an "acceptable" set of assumptions $\Delta \subseteq AB$. Various notions of "acceptability" can be defined, based upon a single notion of "attack" between sets of assumptions.

Intuitively, one set of assumptions "attacks" another if the two sets together with the theory violate an integrity constraint (i.e. the two sets together with the theory derive, via $\vdash$, the sentence which is denied by the integrity constraint), and the set which is attacked is deemed responsible for the violation. Responsibility for violation of integrity can be assigned by explicitly indicating part of the integrity constraint as *retractible* (see [12]). A set of assumptions which leads to the derivation of a retractible is deemed responsible for the violation of integrity. Thus integrity can be restored by "retracting" such an assumption. Formally:

Definition 3. Given an argumentation framework $\langle T, \vdash, AB, IC \rangle$:
a set of assumptions $\Delta' \subseteq AB$ *attacks* another set $\Delta \subseteq AB$ if and only if for some integrity constraint $\neg[L_1 \wedge \ldots \wedge L_i \wedge \ldots \wedge L_n] \in IC$ with L_i retractible,
(1) $T \cup \Delta' \vdash L_1, \ldots, L_{i-1}, L_{i+1}, \ldots, L_n$, and
(2) $T \cup \Delta \vdash L_i$.

In the simple and frequently occurring case where all retractibles in integrity constraints are assumptions and any assumption α can be derived from $T \cup \Delta$

only if $\alpha \in \Delta$, for any $\Delta \subseteq \mathcal{AB}$, then condition (2) in the definition above becomes

(2') $L_i \in \Delta$.

This simplification applies to the case of the argumentation framework corresponding to normal logic programming, where *not A* is retractible for every integrity constraint $\neg[A \wedge not\ A]$ in $\mathcal{IC}$. Therefore, the notion of attack in the argumentation framework $\langle \mathcal{T}, \vdash, \mathcal{AB}, \mathcal{IC} \rangle$ corresponding to a normal logic program $\mathcal{P}$ reduces to the following:

- a set of variable-free negative literals Δ' *attacks* another set Δ if and only if $\mathcal{T} \cup \Delta' \vdash A$, for some literal *not A* $\in \Delta$.

Various notions of "acceptability" can be defined in terms of the same, uniform notion of attack and can be applied to any non-monotonic logic defined in argumentation-theoretic terms. Here we mention some of the notions presented in [3, 4, 16]: A set of assumptions which does not *attack* itself is called

- *stable*, if and only if it *attacks* all assumptions it does not contain, where Δ *attacks* δ if and only if Δ *attacks* $\{\delta\}$;
- *admissible*, if and only if it *attacks* all sets of assumptions that *attack* it, i.e. it *defends* itself against all attacks;
- *preferred*, if and only if it is maximally admissible (with respect to set inclusion);
- *weakly stable*, if and only if for each set of assumptions that *attacks* it, the set together with the attacking set *attacks* some assumption in the attacking set which does not occur in the given set;
- *stable theory*, if and only if it is maximally weakly stable (with respect to set inclusion);
- *acceptable* [5], if and only if it is *acceptable to* the empty set of assumptions, where a set of assumptions Δ is *acceptable to* another set Δ_0 if and only if
  - $\Delta \subseteq \Delta_0$, or
  - for each set of assumptions Δ' that *attacks* $\Delta - \Delta_0$, there exists a set of assumptions Δ'' such that Δ'' *attacks* $\Delta' - (\Delta \cup \Delta_0)$ and Δ'' is *acceptable to* $\Delta \cup \Delta_0 \cup \Delta'$;
- *complete*, if and only if it is admissible and it contains all assumptions it defends, where Δ *defends* an assumption δ if and only if, for all sets of assumptions Δ', if Δ' *attacks* δ then Δ *attacks* Δ';
- *well-founded*, if and only if it is minimally complete (with respect to set inclusion).

Note that for all of these semantics, an "acceptable" set of assumptions satisfies all the denial integrity constraints, since any such set does not attack itself. Note, moreover, that the notion of integrity satisfaction is compatible with three-valued semantics for normal logic programming, since satisfaction of the integrity constraint $\neg[\underline{A} \wedge not\ A]$ does not imply that either A or *not A* must be derived.

---

[5] This notion should not be confused with the informal notion of "acceptable" set of assumptions used elsewhere in this paper.

Almost all existing semantics for normal logic programming can be expressed in argumentation-theoretic terms, as proved in [3, 4, 16]. In particular, stable models [9] correspond to stable sets of assumptions, partial stable models [15] and preferred extensions [5] correspond to preferred sets of assumptions, stable theories [10] correspond to stable theory sets of assumptions, acceptability [11] corresponds to acceptable sets of assumptions, stationary expansions [14] and complete scenaria [5] correspond to complete sets of assumptions and well-founded semantics [18] corresponds to the well-founded set of assumptions. As far as we know, these include all existing semantics except the (various versions of the) completion semantics. Moreover, the same notions of "acceptability" apply also to any other non-monotonic logic that can be defined in argumentation-theoretic terms.

In the remainder of this paper we will refer to any semantics for normal logic programming which can be expressed in argumentation-theoretic terms (see above) as "argumentation semantics".

4 Correctness of the unfolding transformation

Given a normal logic program $\mathcal{P}$ and the program $\mathcal{P}'$ obtained by unfolding some clause in $\mathcal{P}$, let $\mathcal{F}_\mathcal{P}$ and $\mathcal{F}_{\mathcal{P}'}$ be the argumentation frameworks corresponding to $\mathcal{P}$ and $\mathcal{P}'$, respectively.

In general, the Herbrand base of $\mathcal{P}$ may be larger than the Herbrand base of $\mathcal{P}'$, since the Herbrand universe of $\mathcal{P}$ may be larger than the Herbrand universe of $\mathcal{P}'$, as illustrated by the following example.

Example 1. Consider the program $\mathcal{P}$

$$p(X) \leftarrow q(a)$$
$$q(X) \leftarrow r(b)$$

and the program $\mathcal{P}'$ obtained by unfolding the first clause in $\mathcal{P}$:

$$p(X) \leftarrow r(b)$$
$$q(X) \leftarrow r(b)$$

The constant a belongs to the Herbrand universe of $\mathcal{P}$ but not to that of $\mathcal{P}'$.

As a consequence, the set of assumptions in $\mathcal{F}_\mathcal{P}$ may be larger than the set of assumptions in $\mathcal{F}_{\mathcal{P}'}$.

For simplicity, it is convenient to assume that, except for $\mathcal{P}$ and $\mathcal{P}'$, $\mathcal{F}_\mathcal{P}$ and $\mathcal{F}_{\mathcal{P}'}$ coincide, i.e. the two framework have the same monotonic derivability notion, $\vdash$, and the same sets of assumptions and integrity constraints. This assumption can be made, without loss of generality, by assuming that $\mathcal{P}$ and $\mathcal{P}'$ are formulated in the same vocabulary (Herbrand universe), which may, however, be larger than the vocabulary actually occurring in $\mathcal{P}$ and $\mathcal{P}'$ (this assumption is also adopted elsewhere, e.g. in [13]).

Theorem 4. *Given any two sets of assumptions Δ' and Δ in $\mathcal{F}_{\mathcal{P}}$ (and therefore in $\mathcal{F}_{\mathcal{P'}}$),*

Δ' *attacks* Δ *in* $\mathcal{F}_{\mathcal{P}}$ *if and only if* Δ' *attacks* Δ *in* $\mathcal{F}_{\mathcal{P'}}$.

Before proving this theorem, let us explore its consequences. Since the different argumentation semantics can all be formulated in terms of the same notion of attack and differ only in the way they use this notion (see the end of section 3), then

Theorem 5. *For any programs $\mathcal{P}rog$ and $\mathcal{P}rog'$, let $\mathcal{F}_{\mathcal{P}rog}$ and $\mathcal{F}_{\mathcal{P}rog'}$ be the corresponding argumentation frameworks. If*

(i) *there is a one-to-one onto (bijective) mapping, m, from sentences in the vocabulary of $\mathcal{P}rog$ onto sentences in the vocabulary of $\mathcal{P}rog'$, and*

(ii) *there is a one-to-one correspondence via m between attacks in $\mathcal{F}_{\mathcal{P}rog}$ and attacks in $\mathcal{F}_{\mathcal{P}rog'}$, i.e. for every sets of assumptions Δ', Δ in $\mathcal{F}_{\mathcal{P}rog}$, Δ' attacks Δ in $\mathcal{F}_{\mathcal{P}rog}$ if and only if $m(\Delta')$ attacks $m(\Delta)$ in $\mathcal{F}_{\mathcal{P}rog'}$,* [6]

then, for every argumentation semantics Sem, there is a one-to-one correspondence via m between Sem for $\mathcal{P}rog$ and Sem for $\mathcal{P}rog'$, i.e. for all queries Q in the vocabulary of $\mathcal{P}rog$,

$$\mathcal{P}rog \models_{Sem} Q \quad \text{if and only if} \quad \mathcal{P}rog' \models_{Sem} m(Q).$$

If $\mathcal{P}rog'$ is obtained by applying a transformation to $\mathcal{P}rog$, then this theorem expresses a very general technique to prove correctness of the transformation. Such a general technique is needed when the given transformation changes the vocabulary of the original program, so that to establish the correspondence between attacks, it is necessary to establish first a mapping between the vocabulary of the original program $\mathcal{P}rog$ and that of the transformed program $\mathcal{P}rog'$. This technique has been used in [17] to show that abductive logic programs [16] can be transformed correctly into normal logic programs, by mapping abducible atoms onto negative literals.

When the transformation does not change the vocabulary of the original program, as in the case of unfolding, then the mapping m can be taken to be the identity function and condition (ii) reduces to the condition that the attacks in $\mathcal{F}_{\mathcal{P}rog}$ and $\mathcal{F}_{\mathcal{P}rog'}$ are exactly the same. Therefore, theorems 4 and 5 directly imply

Corollary 6. *Let $\mathcal{P}$ be a normal logic program and $\mathcal{P}'$ be obtained by unfolding some clause in $\mathcal{P}$. Then, for every argumentation semantics Sem for normal logic programming, Sem for $\mathcal{P}$ coincides with Sem for $\mathcal{P}'$, i.e. for all queries Q in the vocabulary of $\mathcal{P}$,*

$$\mathcal{P} \models_{Sem} Q \quad \text{if and only if} \quad \mathcal{P}' \models_{Sem} Q.$$

---

[6] For every set of sentences S, $m(S) = \{m(\alpha)|\alpha \in S\}$.

Proof of theorem 4

First note that we can assume that $\mathcal{P}$ and $\mathcal{P}'$ are variable-free. If they are not, they can be replaced by all their variable-free instances over their common Herbrand universe. Then, directly from the definition of *attack*, theorem 4 is an immediate consequence of the following lemma.

Lemma 7. *For each atom A in the common Herbrand base of $\mathcal{P}$ and $\mathcal{P}'$ and for each set of assumptions Δ in $\mathcal{F}_{\mathcal{P}}$ (and therefore in $\mathcal{F}_{\mathcal{P}'}$),*
$\mathcal{P} \cup \Delta \vdash A$ *if and only if* $\mathcal{P}' \cup \Delta \vdash A$.

Lemma 7 follows from lemma 8. Here and in the rest of the paper, for any normal logic program $\mathcal{P}rog$, $\mathcal{P}rog_*$ stands for the definite logic program obtained by interpreting every negative literal, *not p*, in $\mathcal{P}rog$ syntactically as a new positive atom, p^* (see [8]). Similarly, for any set of assumptions Δ, Δ_* stands for the definite logic program obtained by interpreting every negative literal in Δ as a new positive atom.

Lemma 8. *For any normal logic program framework $(\mathcal{P}rog, \vdash, \mathcal{AB}, \mathcal{IC})$, for any set of assumptions $\Delta \subseteq \mathcal{AB}$ and for any atom A in the Herbrand base of $\mathcal{P}rog$,*
$\mathcal{P}rog \cup \Delta \vdash A$ *if and only if*
$\mathcal{P}rog_* \cup \Delta_* \vdash A$ *if and only if*
A *belongs to the least Herbrand model of* $\mathcal{P}rog_* \cup \Delta_*$.

This lemma follows directly from the fact that a ground atom A belongs to the least Herbrand model of a definite program (e.g. $\mathcal{P}rog_* \cup \Delta_*$) if and only if it is derivable from the program, as proved in [7].

Proof of lemma 7
$\mathcal{P} \cup \Delta \vdash A$
if and only if (by lemma 8)
A belongs to the least Herbrand model of $\mathcal{P}_* \cup \Delta_*$
if and only if (by the result that the unfolding transformation for definite logic programs is correct with respect to the least Herbrand model semantics [13])
A belongs to the least Herbrand model of $(\mathcal{P}')_* \cup \Delta_*$
if and only if (by lemma 8)
$\mathcal{P}' \cup \Delta \vdash A$.

This concludes the proof of theorem 4. Note that the proof of lemma 7 makes use of the property that $(\mathcal{P}')_*$ can also be obtained by applying unfolding to $\mathcal{P}_*$ (by applying the same unfolding step used to obtain $\mathcal{P}'$ from $\mathcal{P}$). In other words, the two operations $'$ and $*$ commute: $(\mathcal{P}')_* = (\mathcal{P}_*)'$.

5 General methodology

In proving the correctness of unfolding, we have used a technique which can be used more generally to prove that any transformation which preserves all attacks also preserves all argumentation semantics. Note, however, that a precondition of this technique, which holds for the unfolding transformation, is that the argumentation frameworks corresponding to the programs before and after the transformation should have the same set of assumptions, or, equivalently, that the Herbrand bases before and after the transformation coincide. We will refer to this precondition as *Property 1*.

In this section we will generalise the proof of theorem 4, to obtain a more general methodology for proving the correctness of other program transformations satisfying *Property 1* as well as other properties we will discuss next. This methodology is less powerful than the technique expressed by theorem 5 but its preconditions are easier to check. For this purpose, let us analyse the proof of theorem 4.

Theorem 4 is an immediate consequence of lemma 7, which, in turn, follows directly from two properties. The first, expressed by lemma 8, is a general property, which holds for any normal logic program in general and for the programs $\mathcal{P}$ and $\mathcal{P}'$ before and after the unfolding transformation in particular. However, the second property, that unfolding preserves the least Herbrand model semantics of definite programs, is specific (in the sense that it is not true for every transformation). We will refer to this property as *Property 2*. Its applicability depends, in turn, upon the fact that unfolding a definite program produces a definite program (*Property 3*) and the fact that unfolding commutes with the operation $*$ of interpreting negative literals as positive atoms (*Property 4*). The unfolding transformation we have considered satisfies *Property 4* because it affects only atoms (we do not allow unfolding inside negation).

No other properties, besides *Properties 1, 2, 3* and *4*, are required in the proof of the correctness of unfolding. Therefore, the same proof demonstrates the correctness, with respect to all argumentation semantics, of any transformation which satisfies *Properties 1, 2, 3* and *4*. This is the basis of our methodology, which is expressed by the following theorem.

Theorem 9. *Given any transformation Transf from normal logic programs to normal logic programs, let ' be any specific application of this transformation producing a deterministic result. Then, if for all normal logic programs $\mathcal{P}$:*

Property 1: *$\mathcal{P}'$ and $\mathcal{P}$ have the same Herbrand base;*
Properties 2 and 3: *if $\mathcal{P}$ is a definite program then*
   $-$ $\mathcal{P}'$ is a definite program (3),
   $-$ $\mathcal{P}'$ and $\mathcal{P}$ have the same least Herbrand model (2);
Property 4: *$(\mathcal{P}')_* = (\mathcal{P}_*)'$;*

then Transf is correct with respect to all argumentation semantics, Sem, i.e. for all queries Q,

$$\mathcal{P} \models_{Sem} Q \quad \text{if and only if} \quad \mathcal{P}' \models_{Sem} Q.$$

Proof: The conclusion of the theorem holds for $\mathcal{P}$ and $\mathcal{P}'$ if theorem 4 holds for $\mathcal{P}$ and $\mathcal{P}'$. Theorem 4 makes sense because *Transf* satisfies *Property 1*. Theorem 4 holds for $\mathcal{P}$ and $\mathcal{P}'$ if lemma 7 holds for $\mathcal{P}$ and $\mathcal{P}'$. But:

$$\mathcal{P} \cup \Delta \vdash A$$

if and only if (by lemma 8)

A belongs to the least Herbrand model of $\mathcal{P}_* \cup \Delta_*$.

if and only if (by *Properties 2, 3* and *4*)

A belongs to the least Herbrand model of $(\mathcal{P}')_* \cup \Delta_*$.

if and only if (by lemma 8)

$$\mathcal{P}' \cup \Delta \vdash A.$$

This concludes the proof of theorem 9.

This theorem can be used to establish the correctness of all versions of the *folding* transformation which satisfy *Property 2* (see [13]), since every version of folding satisfies the other properties. Moreover, it can be used to establish correctness of any other transformation which satisfies all four properties. Consider, for example, the following version of goal replacement, adapted from [13].

Definition 10. Given

- a normal logic program $\mathcal{P}$,
- sets of atoms G_1, G_2, possibly empty, in the vocabulary of $\mathcal{P}$,
- $C \in \mathcal{P}$, a clause $H \leftarrow B_1, G_1, B_2$, where B_1, B_2 are (possibly empty) sets of literals,

let $\{X_1, \ldots, X_n\} = vars(G_1) \cap vars(G_2)$. [7] Suppose that

- $G_1 \equiv G_2$ is an *H-valid replacement rule with respect to* $\mathcal{P}$, i.e., for all $a_1, \ldots, a_n$ in the Herbrand universe of $\mathcal{P}$,
  - $\mathcal{P}_H \models_{LHM} \exists G_1[X_1/a_1, \ldots, X_n/a_n]$ if and only if
    $\mathcal{P}_H \models_{LHM} \exists G_2[X_1/a_1, \ldots, X_n/a_n]$ [8] and
  - for all argumentation semantics $\mathcal{S}em$, for $i = 1, 2$,
    $\mathcal{P} \models_{\mathcal{S}em} \exists G_i[X_1/a_1, \ldots, X_n/a_n]$ if and only if
    $\mathcal{P}_H \models_{LHM} \exists [G_i X_1/a_1, \ldots, X_n/a_n]$,

  where $\mathcal{P}_H$ is the subset of $\mathcal{P}$ consisting of all and only Horn clauses,
- $vars(H, B_1, B_2) \cap vars(G_2) = vars(H, B_1, B_2) \cap vars(G_1) = \{X_1, \ldots, X_n\}$
- C' is the clause $H \leftarrow B_1, G_2, B_2$.

Then, the result of *H-valid replacing the goal* G_1 in $C \in \mathcal{P}$ by the goal G_2 is $(\mathcal{P} - \{C\}) \cup \{C'\}$.

This definition of H-valid goal replacement is equivalent to the definition of goal replacement in [13] except for the notion of H-valid replacement rule, which is a variation of the notion of valid replacement rule in [13].

---

[7] For any set of expressions $E_1, \ldots, E_m$, $vars(E_1, \ldots, E_m)$ stands for the set of all free variables in $E_1, \ldots, E_m$.

[8] LHM stands for least Herbrand model semantics, and, for any sentence G, $\exists G$ stands for the existential closure of G with respect to all variables occurring in G.

Let $\mathcal{P}'$ be the result of H-valid replacing the goal G_1 in $C \in \mathcal{P}$ by the goal G_2. If $G_2 \equiv G_1$ is a H-valid replacement rule with respect to $\mathcal{P}'$, then definition 10 defines a version of *reversible goal replacement*, which preserves the least Herbrand model semantics when applied to definite programs (see [13]). Moreover, it satisfies *Property 3* and it does not modify the set of predicates, by definition, i.e. it satisfies *Property 1*. Finally, since it only affects atoms in clauses, it satisfies *Property 4*. As a consequence, by theorem 9, this form of reversible goal replacement preserves all argumentation semantics.

6 Comparisons

The general methodology (theorem 9) is a special case of the general technique of proving the correctness of a transformation by proving that attacks are preserved by the transformation. This general technique, in turn, is a special case of the even more general technique (theorem 5) for proving correctness of a program transformation by proving that there is a one-to-one correspondence between attacks before and after the transformations. Theorem 5 generalises the method used in [17] to show that abductive logic programs [16] can be transformed correctly into normal logic programs.

In the remainder of this section we compare our methodology with the technique used by Aravindan and Dung in [1] to prove that (some forms of) unfolding and folding are correct with respect to a number of semantics for normal logic programming. We will see that their technique is equivalent to the method, used in section 4 (for unfolding), of proving that the attack relations before and after the transformation are identical.

The method in [1] uses the notion of semantic kernel, given by the following definition which is adapted from [6].

Definition 11. Given a normal logic program $\mathcal{P}rog$, let $\mathcal{S}_{\mathcal{P}rog}$ be the operator on sets of variable-free clauses of the form
$$H \leftarrow \Delta \quad \text{with } \Delta \text{ a (possibly empty) set of negative literals}$$
defined as follows:
$\mathcal{S}_{\mathcal{P}rog}(I) = \{ H \leftarrow \Delta', B_1, \ldots, B_m \mid \Delta' \text{ is possibly empty, } m \geq 0,$
$\qquad H \leftarrow \Delta', H_1, \ldots, H_m \text{ is a variable-free instance of a clause in } \mathcal{P}rog,$
$\qquad H_i \leftarrow B_i \in I, \text{ for } i = 1, \ldots, m \}.$
Then, the *semantic kernel* of $\mathcal{P}rog$, $SK(\mathcal{P}rog)$ in short, is the least fix point of $\mathcal{S}_{\mathcal{P}rog}$, i.e. (since $\mathcal{S}_{\mathcal{P}rog}$ is continuous) $SK(\mathcal{P}rog) = \bigcup_{i \geq 1} \mathcal{S}^i_{\mathcal{P}rog}(\emptyset)$.

Note that, in the construction of $SK(\mathcal{P}rog)$, one application of the operator $\mathcal{S}_{\mathcal{P}rog}$ amounts to performing a step of monotonic reasoning, leaving the non-monotonic part (the negative literals) untouched.

In [1], it is proved that unfolding and folding preserve the semantic kernel of programs, i.e. for any logic program $\mathcal{P}$ and for any logic program $\mathcal{P}'$ obtained by applying folding or unfolding to $\mathcal{P}$, $SK(\mathcal{P}) = SK(\mathcal{P}')$. As a consequence, unfolding and folding preserve all semantics Sem for normal logic programming for which it can be shown that, for any logic program $\mathcal{P}rog$ and query $\mathcal{Q}$, $\mathcal{P}rog$

$\models_{Sem} Q$ if and only if $SK(Prog) \models_{Sem} Q$. These semantics include all the argumentation semantics for normal logic programming we have considered in this paper.

Theorems 13 and 14 below imply that, for the purpose of proving the correctness of a transformation with respect to any argumentation semantics for normal logic programming, the two techniques of showing that the transformation preserves the semantic kernel and of showing that it preserves all attacks are equivalent. These theorems are stated in terms of the following definition which is adapted from [2]:

Definition 12. For any normal program $Prog$ and sets of assumptions Δ', Δ in the argumentation framework corresponding to $Prog$
Δ' is a *locally minimal attack against* Δ if and only if
there exists a subset $Prog'$ of the set of all variable-free instances of clauses in $Prog$ such that

- $Prog' \cup \Delta' \vdash A$ for some $not\ A \in \Delta$, and
- there exists no $\Delta'' \subset \Delta'$ such that $Prog' \cup \Delta'' \vdash A$.

Intuitively, a locally minimal attack is a minimal attack with respect to some subset of the program. A locally minimal attack can be thought of as the set of negative literals that occur in clauses directly involved in the derivation of the complement A of an assumption $not\ A$ in the attacked set. Since programs can have redundant clauses, including clauses which are subsumed by other clauses, the set of all negative literals in a derivation is not guaranteed to be minimal in an absolute sense.

Locally minimal attacks are important because they subsume all other attacks, as expressed by the following

Theorem 13. *For any normal logic program $Prog$ and sets of assumptions Δ', Δ in the argumentation framework corresponding to $Prog$,*
Δ' attacks Δ if and only if
there exists $\Delta'' \subseteq \Delta'$ such that Δ'' is a locally minimal attack against Δ.

This theorem follows directly from the monotonicity of $\vdash$. (See [16] for the full proof.) An important consequence of this theorem is that a transformation preserves all argumentation semantics if and only if it preserves all locally minimal attacks. In fact, via theorem 13, all notions of "acceptable" set of assumptions in section 3 can be reformulated in terms of locally minimal attacks and $\subseteq$. For example, a set of assumptions Δ is *stable* if and only if none of its subsets is a locally minimal attack against Δ and some subset of Δ is a locally minimal attack against every assumption Δ does not contain.

The following theorem establishes the equivalence between semantic kernels and locally minimal attacks.

Theorem 14. *Given a normal logic program $Prog$, let $\langle Prog, \vdash, AB, IC \rangle$ be the corresponding argumentation framework. Then, for every set of assumptions Δ in $\langle Prog, \vdash, AB, IC \rangle$ and atom H in the vocabulary of $Prog$:*

$(H \leftarrow \Delta) \in SK(\mathcal{P}rog)$ *if and only if*
Δ *is a locally minimal attack against* $\{not\, H\}$.

The proof of this theorem can be found in the appendix.

7   Conclusions and future work

We have presented a methodology for proving that some program transformations, e.g. unfolding, folding and (a form of) goal replacement, preserve many semantics for normal logic programming, namely all argumentation semantics for normal logic programming (these include all known semantics except the completion semantics). This methodology is a special case of the more general technique, introduced in [17], of showing that there is a one-to-one correspondence between attacks before and after a transformation.

We are investigating the application of the proposed methodology to show the correctness of other program transformations. Clause elimination and introduction do not satisfy *Property 1* of theorem 9. Therefore, the methodology cannot be applied to these transformations. Note, however, that these transformations do not preserve all argumentation semantics. For example, given the normal logic program $\mathcal{P}$

$$p \leftarrow not\, q$$

the program $\mathcal{P}'$ obtained by introducing the extra clause

$$r \leftarrow not\, r$$

is not equivalent to $\mathcal{P}$ under the stable model semantics. In fact, $\mathcal{P}$ has a single stable model $\{p\}$ while $\mathcal{P}'$ has no stable model. Whether some restricted forms of clause elimination and introduction might preserve all argumentation semantics (including the stable model semantics), and whether our methodology can be generalised to prove this are open issues that require further investigation.

Finally, another interesting topic for future research is the generalisation of our methodology to prove the correctness of transformations for other non-monotonic logics including default, autoepistemic and non-monotonic modal logic, which can be formalised in the argumentation framework of section 3.

Acknowledgements

This research was supported by the Fujitsu Research Laboratories. The authors are grateful to Alberto Pettorossi, Maurizio Proietti and each other for helpful discussions, and to the anonymous referees for helpful suggestions.

References

1. C. Aravindan, P.M. Dung, On the correctness of unfold/fold transformation of normal and extended logic programs. *Journal of Logic Programming* 24(3):201–217 (1995)
2. C. Aravindan, P.M. Dung. Belief dynamics, abduction and databases. *Proc. 4th European Workshop on Logic in AI* (1994)
3. A. Bondarenko, F. Toni, R. A. Kowalski, An assumption-based framework for non-monotonic reasoning. *LPNMR'93* (A. Nerode and L. Pereira eds.) MIT Press, 171–189
4. A. Bondarenko, P. M. Dung, R. A. Kowalski, F. Toni, An abstract, argumentation-theoretic framework for default reasoning. Technical Report (1995)
5. P.M. Dung, Negation as hypothesis: an abductive foundation for logic programming. *ICLP'91* (K. Furukawa ed.) MIT Press, 3–17
6. P.M. Dung, K. Kanchanasut, A fixpoint approach to declarative semantics of logic programs. *NACLP'89* 1:604–625
7. M.H. van Emden, R.A. Kowalski, The semantics of predicate logic as a programming language. *ACM* 23(4):733–742 (1976)
8. K. Eshghi, R.A. Kowalski, Abduction compared with negation as failure. *ICLP'89* (G. Levi and M. Martelli eds.) MIT Press, 234–255
9. M. Gelfond, V. Lifschitz, The stable model semantics for logic programs. *ICLP'88* (K. Bowen and R.A. Kowalski eds.) MIT Press, 1070–1080
10. A.C. Kakas, P. Mancarella, Stable theories for logic programs. *ILPS'91* (V. Saraswat and K. Ueda eds.) MIT Press, 85–100
11. A.C. Kakas, P. Mancarella, P.M. Dung, The Acceptability Semantics for Logic Programs. *ICLP'94* (P. Van Hentenryck ed.) MIT Press, 504–519
12. R.A. Kowalski, F. Sadri, Knowledge representation without integrity constraints. Imperial College Technical Report (1988)
13. A. Pettorossi, M. Proietti, Transformation of logic programs. *Journal of Logic Programming* 19/20:261–320 (1994)
14. T.C. Przymusinski, Semantics of disjunctive logic programs and deductive databases. *DOOD'91* (C. Delobel, M. Kifer, and Y. Masunaga eds.) 85–107
15. D. Saccà, C. Zaniolo, Stable models and non determinism for logic programs with negation. *ACM Symposium on Principles of Database Systems*, ACM Press, 205–217 (1990)
16. F. Toni, Abductive logic programming, PhD Thesis, Imperial College (1995)
17. F. Toni, R.A. Kowalski. Reduction of abductive logic programs to normal logic programs. *ICLP'95* (L. Sterling ed.) MIT Press, 367–381
18. A. Van Gelder, K.A. Ross, J.S. Schlipf, The well-founded semantics for general logic programs. *Journal of the ACM*, 38(3):620–650 (1991)

Appendix

Proof of theorem 14. As in the proof of theorem 4, we will assume (without loss of generality) that $Prog$ is variable-free.

First, we define the notion of *minimal derivability*. For any normal program $Prog$, set of assumptions Δ in the argumentation framework corresponding to $Prog$ and atom A in the vocabulary of $Prog$,

$Prog \cup \Delta \vdash_{min} A$ ($Prog \cup \Delta$ *minimally derives* A)
if and only if there exists $Prog' \subseteq Prog$ such that
$Prog' \cup \Delta \vdash A$ and there exists no $\Delta' \subset \Delta$ such that $Prog' \cup \Delta' \vdash A$.
By definition, Δ is a locally minimal attack (with respect to $Prog$) against Δ'
if and only if $Prog \cup \Delta \vdash_{min} A$ for some *not* $A \in \Delta'$. Therefore, theorem 14
directly follows from the following lemma:

Lemma 15. *Given a normal logic program* $Prog$,
$\quad H \leftarrow \Delta \in SK(Prog)$ *if and only if* $Prog \cup \Delta \vdash_{min} H$.

In the proof of this lemma $\vdash^i$ will indicate derivability by applying the modus
ponens inference rule i times and $\vdash^i_{min}$ will indicate $\vdash_{min}$ as defined above but
with $\vdash$ replaced for by $\vdash^i$.

Proof of lemma 15
$H \leftarrow \Delta \in SK(Prog)$ if and only if $H \leftarrow \Delta \in \mathcal{S}^j_{Prog}(\emptyset)$, for some $j \geq 1$. By
induction on j, we prove that, for all $j \geq 1$,
$\quad H \leftarrow \Delta \in \mathcal{S}^j_{Prog}(\emptyset)$ if and only if $Prog \cup \Delta \vdash^j_{min} H$,
which directly proves the lemma.

- If $j = 1$ then $H \leftarrow \Delta \in \mathcal{S}^j_{Prog}(\emptyset)$ if and only if $H \leftarrow \Delta \in Prog$ if and
only if $\{H \leftarrow \Delta\} \cup \Delta \vdash^1 H$ if and only if $Prog \cup \Delta \vdash^1_{min} H$.

- If $j > 1$ then let us assume the inductive hypothesis that, for each $1 \leq k < j$,
$H' \leftarrow \Delta' \in \mathcal{S}^k_{Prog}(\emptyset)$ if and only if $Prog \cup \Delta' \vdash^k_{min} H'$.
Then, $H \leftarrow \Delta \in \mathcal{S}^j_{Prog}(\emptyset)$
  if and only if (by definition)
$H \leftarrow \Delta', H_1, \ldots, H_m \in Prog$, with $m \geq 0$, and for all $i = 1, \ldots, m$ there
exists some k_i with $1 \leq k_i \leq j - 1$ such that $H_i \leftarrow B_i \in \mathcal{S}^{k_i}_{Prog}(\emptyset)$, and $\Delta = \Delta' \cup B_1 \cup \ldots \cup B_m$
  if and only if (by inductive hypothesis)
$H \leftarrow \Delta', H_1, \ldots, H_m \in Prog$, with $m \geq 0$, and for all $i = 1, \ldots, m$ there exists
some k_i with $1 \leq k_i \leq j - 1$ such that $Prog \cup B_i \vdash^{k_i}_{min} H_i$, i.e. there exists $Prog_i$
$\subseteq Prog$ such that $Prog_i \cup B_i \vdash^{k_i} H_i$ and B_i is minimal with respect to $Prog_i$
  if and only if
$\bigcup_{1 \leq i \leq m} Prog_i \cup \{H \leftarrow \Delta', H_1, \ldots, H_m\} \cup \Delta \vdash^{k+1} H$, with k the maximum of
the k_i and B_i is minimal with respect to $Prog_i$
  if and only if (since at least one of the k_i is necessarily $j - 1$),
$\bigcup_{1 \leq i \leq m} Prog_i \cup \{H \leftarrow \Delta', H_1, \ldots, H_m\} \cup \Delta \vdash^j H$ and B_i is minimal with
respect to $Prog_i$
  if and only if (due to the minimality of the B_i with respect to $Prog_i$)
$Prog \cup \Delta \vdash^j_{min} H$. This concludes the proof.

Complexity of Horn Programs

Erik Aarts*

[1] Research Institute for Language and Speech, Trans 10, 3512 JK Utrecht, The Netherlands
[2] Dept. of Mathematics and Computer Science, Plantage Muidergracht 24, 1018 TV
Amsterdam, The Netherlands

Abstract. This paper gives a method to estimate the space and time complexity
of Horn programs executed under the OLDT search strategy (also called Earley
Deduction or memoing).

1 Introduction

This article is about the complexity of Horn programs, whose syntax is the same as
the syntax of pure Prolog programs. The resolution strategy we use is different from
Prolog, but the declarative semantics of programs is the same. In the sequel we will
use the word "Prolog" also for Horn programs with OLDT resolution. The worst case
time complexity of programs written in an imperative language (like Pascal or C) can
be estimated by straightforward means. These programs are deterministic so we can
follow the execution step by step. The number of steps is counted by estimating the
cost of smaller procedures, e.g. multiplying the number of times that a "while" loop
is executed with the number of steps needed in the loop. A disadvantage is that the
code of larger programs gets incomprehensible very soon. This is solved by presenting
pseudo-code. However, in pseudo-code the reader has to guess the details. In fields like
computational linguistics and artificial intelligence we often see algorithms explained
by "real" Prolog code. This can be done because real Prolog code is easier to read
than, e.g., C or Pascal code. An algorithm presented this way, has no open-ended
details. For Prolog programs, however, the complexity analysis is not so easy. The main
problem is that Prolog programs are intended to be non-deterministic. Computers are
deterministic machines, however. Therefore any Prolog interpreter has to deal with the
non-determinism in some deterministic way. Standard interpreters perform a depth-first
search through the search space with backtracking. Backtracking is what makes the
analysis of Prolog programs so hard. The only attempt to estimate the runtime of Prolog
programs in the context of standard interpreters is from Lin (1993). This method is
discussed in the next section.

This article does not solve the problem of estimating the runtime for standard
interpreters. However, we can estimate the time complexity easier than in Lin (1993)
if we use an interpreter called the *Earley interpreter*. The Earley interpreter does not

---
* The author was sponsored by project NF 102/62-356 ('Structural and Semantic Parallels in
Natural Languages and Programming Languages'), funded by the Netherlands Organization for
the Advancement of Research (NWO). He can be reached via E-mail: aarts@fwi.uva.nl.
His home page is http://www.fwi.uva.nl/~aarts/.

backtrack, but it keeps an administration of what goals have been tried and what the result was. It differs in two ways from the standard interpreter:

- Improved proof search. Prolog programs have a very clear meaning from a logical point of view. Standard interpreters do not behave properly however. They do not always find a proof although there exists one, because they end up in an infinite loop. One can "program around" this but then we leave the path of declarative programming. The Earley interpreter does what it should do. It can only get in a loop if terms can grow arbitrarily long. The method presented in this chapter is meant to be used for problems with a finite search space, i.e., decidable problems.
- Longer runtime. Because the interpreter has to do a lot of bookkeeping the runtime will be longer in general. This is the major disadvantage of the method presented here: in order to estimate the runtime we use an interpreter that increases the runtime. Lin (1993) does not have this disadvantage. There are two arguments in favor of our method. First, there are cases in which the bookkeeping can speed up algorithms as well. It can even speed up an exponential time algorithm to a polynomial time algorithm. Second, the overhead is small. The overhead is linear in the *size of the terms* during execution of the Prolog program. When the size of the terms does not grow exponentially but remains polynomial, we stay in the same complexity class (for classes that are insensitive for the degree of the polynomial, like $\mathcal{P}$). The method presented in this article is suited especially to prove that some problem is in $\mathcal{P}$.

The main reason to switch from the standard interpreter to the Earley interpreter is the possibility to prove runtime bounds for Earley interpreters in a pretty straightforward way. We will describe a simple method to deduce the runtime of an algorithm from two sources: the number of possible instantiations of the variables in the program and the length of the instantiations. If a Prolog programmer knows how the variables in his program behave, he can deduce the runtime in a simple manner.

The main idea behind our approach is the following. The Earley interpreter stores all attempts to prove something (i.e. it stores all "procedure" calls). Furthermore it stores all solutions (and all partial solutions). Because of this we are sure that every procedure is executed only once for every call. When the procedure is called a second time the answer can be looked up and, in general, this costs less time than recomputing it. This is called *memoization* or *tabulation* or *tabling*. The search strategy is called Earley Deduction (or OLDT resolution). The Earley Deduction proof procedure is due to Warren (1975). It was first published in Pereira and Warren (1983). A good introduction is Pereira and Shieber (1987, pp. 196-210). Similar ideas can be found in Warren (1992), Tamaki and Sato (1986) (OLDT resolution) and Vieille (1989) (SLD-AL resolution) and van Noord (1993).

The fact that all problems are solved only once makes it much easier to estimate the time complexity: we only have to count the number of procedure calls multiplied with the amount of time spent in the procedure for each call.

The structure of this article will be as follows. First we describe what other research has been done on this topic. Then we describe a non-deterministic Prolog interpreter that does exactly what should be done according to the declarative meaning. Then we show two methods to make the interpreters deterministic. The first one leads to the standard interpreter. The second method leads to the Earley interpreter.

When it is clear how the Earley interpreter works we start our complexity analysis. The result of the counting will be a complexity formula in which one has to fill in the length and the number of all possible instantiations for the variables. We will sketch some ideas about further research. Finally we will say something about existing implementations of Prolog interpreters which are able to follow the search strategy we describe here.

2   Other Research

The complexity of Prolog programs has remained largely unexplored up till now. The PhD thesis of Lin (Lin 1993) and the article Debray and Lin (n.d.) are the only treatments of the problem of complexity of Prolog programs. Lin (1993) explains what research has been done further and why this other research does not cover the problem of complexity of logic programs. In this section we will explain the ideas behind the approach of Lin and Debray and compare it to our approach.

Lin (1993) starts from the work that has been done on functional programming. Functional programs are deterministic, contrary to logic programs. The functional programming approach has been extended in order to deal with non-determinism. The second starting point is that the analysis is done (semi-)automatically. A system called CASLOG (Complexity Analysis System for LOGic) has been implemented. This system takes as input an annotated Prolog program and produces formulas which are estimates for the time and space complexity.

The formulas are computed by looking at *size differences*. In imperative programming languages iteration is implemented with *while statements*. Examination of the *guard* of the while statement tells how many times the loop is executed. In functional and logic programming, iteration is implemented by *recursion*. The depth of a recursion can not be estimated as easily as the number of iterations in a while statement. The depth of a recursion can be estimated by looking at the size differences of the terms in the procedure call. Suppose we call a procedure with a list of length n. Within this procedure, there is a recursive call with a list of length $n - 1$. Then we can conclude that the depth of the recursion is n. This description is only a clue for the method that CASLOG uses. We refer to Lin (1993) for more details.

Our approach differs from Lin's as follows. Basically, our method is by hand and Lin's is automatically. The method of Lin is fairly complex. When the system computes some estimate it is hard to see *why* the estimate is correct. In our approach it is clear how the estimates are obtained (because the analysis is done by hand). A second difference is that Lin's approach does not always work well. Take for example a program that computes the transitive closure of a graph. The difference in the procedure calls is not in the size of the arguments, the arguments are just vertices. The advantage of doing the analysis by hand is that we can apply the method to problems where the size difference is not important. The third difference is that Lin assumes the standard proof search (depth-first with backtracking) whereas we start from OLDT-resolution (or Earley Deduction). The standard proof search is much more common, OLDT resolution is hardly used in practice as yet. For experienced Prolog programmers, the main drawback of OLDT resolution is that it is slower than standard search in general. The advantage is that it has a better semantics, i.e., there is no gap between procedural and declarative semantics.

3 Prolog interpreters

We restrict ourselves to *pure* Prolog in this article. We assume that the standard Prolog terminology is known. The declarative meaning of a program can be defined as follows.

Definition 1. A query ? - $Q_1, Q_2, \ldots, Q_n$ is *true* iff there is a substitution σ_1 such that the atoms $\sigma_1(Q_1)$ and ... and $\sigma_1(Q_n)$ are true.
An atom G is *true* if and only if there is a clause C : - $B_1, B_2, \ldots, B_n$ in the program ($B_1, \ldots, B_n$ can be empty, then C is a fact) and a substitution σ_2 such that $\sigma_2(C)$ is identical to G and the atoms $\sigma_2(B_1)$ and ... and $\sigma_2(B_n)$ are true.

Often there are infinitely many substitutions that make a query true. Then we are interested in the most general substitutions. A substitution σ_1 is more general than a substitution σ_2 if there is a substitution σ_3, not the identity, such that $\sigma_2 = \sigma_3 \circ \sigma_1$, where $\circ$ is the function composition operator. A substitution σ is a solution for a query if the substitution makes the query true and there is no more general substitution that makes the query true. But even then a query can have infinitely many solutions. If there is no solution the query is false. We define the *most general unifier* (mgu) and the *most general common instance* (mgci) as usual and assume that $Var(mgci(A, B)) \cap Var(A) = \emptyset$ and $Var(mgci(A, B)) \cap Var(B) = \emptyset$ for all A, B (every most general unifier contains fresh variables).

When we have the declarative meaning as defined in Definition 1 in mind, a non-deterministic interpreter can be given that follows the declarative meaning precisely. The interpreter answers yes if there is a proof (but not vice versa). The non-deterministic interpreter is in Figure 1.

The only non-determinism in this interpreter is the guessing of a clause. In standard interpreters this non-determinism is eliminated by performing a depth-first search. This strategy often leads to problems. Consider the following program. It computes the reflexive transitive closure of a graph.

```
path(X,Z) :-
          path(X,Y),
          edge(Y,Z).
path(X,X).

edge(a,b).
edge(b,c).
edge(c,a).
edge(c,d).
```

Prove goal:

Given a goal G, guess a clause C :- $B_1, B_2, \ldots, B_n$ in the program and compute $mgci(G, C)$. Suppose $mgci(G, C) = f(C) = g(G)$. Prove the list of goals $f(B_1), f(B_2), \ldots f(B_n)$. The result is the substitution h. If $n = 0$ (C is a fact), then h is the identity. The result of proving goal G is the substitution $h \circ g$.

Prove list of goals:

Given a list of goals $Q_1, \ldots, Q_n$, prove goal Q_1. The result will be a substitution σ_1 such that $\sigma_1(Q_1)$ is derivable. Then prove the list of goals $\sigma_1(Q_2), \ldots, \sigma_1(Q_n)$. The result of proving $\sigma_1(Q_2), \ldots, \sigma_1(Q_n)$ is a substitution $\sigma_n \circ \ldots \circ \sigma_2$. The result of proving $Q_1, \ldots, Q_n$ is $\sigma_n \circ \ldots \circ \sigma_2 \circ \sigma_1$. Th result of proving the empty list is the identity function.

Fig. 1. Non-deterministic interpreter

Suppose we have a query ?- path(a,d). A depth-first searching Prolog interpreter will try to prove the following goals: path(a,d), path(a,Var1), path(a,Var2), path(a,Var3), path(a,Var4), etc. The interpreter will never get out of this loop.

Earley interpreters are defined as follows. The basic datastructure we use is called the *item*. Items have the same form as clauses: they are pairs of heads and bodies. The head of the item is the head of some clause after some substitution. The body of the item is a (possibly empty) remainder of the same clause after the same substitution. Items are used to store partial results when proving a query. This is done as follows. Consider the interpreter in Figure 1. We have to prove some goal, and therefore we take an arbitrary clause from the program. After computing the $mgci$ of the goal and the head of the clause, we obtain the item $\langle f(C), [f(B_1), f(B_2), \ldots, f(B_n)] \rangle$. Now we try to prove $f(B_1)$. This gives us the substitution σ_1 and the new item $\langle \sigma_1(f(C)), [\sigma_1(f(B_2)), \ldots, \sigma_1(f(B_n))] \rangle$. We prove $\sigma_1(f(B_2))$, find σ_2, and obtain $\langle \sigma_2(\sigma_1(f(C))), [\sigma_2(\sigma_1(f(B_3))), \ldots, \sigma_2(\sigma_1(f(B_n)))] \rangle$. In every step the body becomes shorter. Finally, the body is empty. The final item $\langle \sigma_n(\ldots(\sigma_1(f(C))), [] \rangle$ is a solution for the goal we tried to prove.

The data structure the Earley interpreter uses has been described now. The control structure is as follows. We keep an *agenda* of items that wait to be processed and a *table* of items that have been processed. When we process an item from the agenda we first look whether it occurs in the table. If it does, we can simply discard it because it has been processed earlier. If it does not occur in the table there are two possibilities:

- the body is empty. That means that the item is a solution. We combine the solution with the items in the table that are waiting for that solution. This gives us new items which are placed on the agenda again. This operation is called completion.
- The body is not empty. Two operations are executed:

- prediction. The first element of the body is unified with the head of clauses in the program. New items are put on the agenda again.
- completion. The first element of the body is combined with solutions in the table.

We will implement two interpreters: one that generates all solutions and one that stops after it has found the first solution. If we want to generate all solutions, then we stop when the agenda is empty. When we want only one solution, we can stop when the first solution appears in the table.

The algorithms sketched above can be implemented in Prolog as follows. The main predicate for the one-solution interpreter is prove_one. It is called with the goal we want to prove as argument. For the all-solutions interpreter the main predicate is prove_all. This predicate is called with the goal and with a variable that will be instantiated to the list of all solutions. We can change between depth-first and breadth-first behaviour simply by swapping two arguments in some append predicate.

The program clauses are of the form Goal ::- Body in order to separate them from the clauses of the meta-interpreter.

Observe that the meta-interpreter is almost deterministic (with the *if-then-else* constructor we could make it deterministic). The interpreter in Figure 1 (with some extensions for the impure parts of the meta-interpreter) defines the procedural semantics of the meta-interpreter in a deterministic way.

```
% Earley interpreter.
% needs: findall, member, append, numbervars.

?- op(1150,xfx,::-).

prove_all(Goal,Solutions) :-
        findall(item(Goal,Goals),(Goal ::- Goals),Agenda),
        extend_items_all(Agenda,[],Table),
        findall(Goal,member(item(Goal,[]),Table),Solutions).

extend_items_all([],Table,Table).
extend_items_all([Item|Agenda1],Table1,Table2) :-
        memberv(Item,Table1),
        extend_items_all(Agenda1,Table1,Table2).
extend_items_all([Item|Agenda1],Table1,Table3) :-
        \+ memberv(Item,Table1),
        Table2 = [Item|Table1],
        new_items(Item,Table1,Items),
        append(Items,Agenda1,Agenda2),   % depth-first
%       append(Agenda1,Items,Agenda2),   % breadth-first
        extend_items_all(Agenda2,Table2,Table3).
```

```
prove_one(Goal,YN) :-
        findall(item(Goal,Goals),(Goal ::- Goals),Agenda),
        extend_items_one(Agenda,[],Goal,YN).

extend_items_one(_,Table,Goal,yes) :-
        member(item(Goal,[]),Table).
extend_items_one([],Table,Goal,no) :-
        \+ member(item(Goal,[]),Table).
extend_items_one([Item|Agenda1],Table,Goal,YN) :-
        \+ member(item(Goal,[]),Table),
        memberv(Item,Table),
        extend_items_one(Agenda1,Table,Goal,YN).
extend_items_one([Item|Agenda1],Table1,Goal,YN) :-
        \+ member(item(Goal,[]),Table1),
        \+ memberv(Item,Table1),
        Table2 = [Item|Table1],
        new_items(Item,Table1,Items),
        append(Agenda1,Items,Agenda2),   % breadth-first
        extend_items_one(Agenda2,Table2,Goal,YN).
```

```
new_items(item(Goal1,[]),Table,Items) :-
        findall(item(Goal2,Goals),
                member(item(Goal2,[Goal1|Goals]),Table),
                Items).
new_items(item(Goal1,[Goal2|Goals1]),Table,Items) :-
        findall(item(Goal2,Goals2),
                (Goal2 ::- Goals2),
                Items1),
        findall(item(Goal1,Goals1),
                member(item(Goal2,[]),Table),
                Items2),
        append(Items1,Items2,Items).

memberv(Item,Table) :-
        member(Item2,Table),
        variant(Item,Item2).

variant(X,Y) :-
        \+ (\+ (numbervars(X,0,_),numbervars(Y,0,_),X == Y)).
```

The definition of the predicates append, member, \+ (not), findall and numbervars follows the standard conventions. append is a predicate for the concatenation of two lists. member is a predicate for membership of a list. When the atom findall(X,condition(X),Solutions) has been proved, Solutions

- $\{X \mid condition(X)\}$. numbervars replaces all variables in a term by special constants. This operation makes two terms identical when they are alphabetic variants. A sample programs is (facts are rules with an empty body):

```
path(X,Z) ::-
        [path(X,Y),
         edge(Y,Z)].
path(X,X) ::- [].

edge(a,b) ::- [].
edge(b,c) ::- [].
edge(c,a) ::- [].
edge(c,d) ::- [].
```

The predicates just given are repeated here with a little comment.

prove_all The main goal is used to predict items. These items are put in the agenda. The interpreter is started with extend_items_all. When extend_items_all is finished we search in the table for all solutions.

extend_items_all If the agenda is empty we are finished. If an item from the agenda is in the table, it can be discarded. If an item is not in the table as yet, it is added and new items are generated. These new items are put in front or behind the agenda, corresponding with depth-first and breadth-first behaviour respectively.

new_items If the item is a solution, it is combined with items in the table that wait for that solution (completion). In the second clause the item is not a solution, some atoms in the body are to be proved. We predict new items and try to combine the given item with solutions. If the next goal in the body has been processed earlier, we will predict items that are already in the table.

memberv, variant Here we check whether there is an alphabetic variant in the table. Observe that two items never share any variables. *Variables are only shared within an item.*

The one-solution interpreter only differs from the all-solutions interpreter in the fact that the first stops when the first solution is found, whereas the latter goes on untill the agenda is empty.

The one-solution interpreter has two advantages over the standard Prolog interpreter with a depth first strategy. The first is that for these simple programs the declarative meaning and the procedural meaning coincide: if the interpreter answers "yes" to a query then the query is indeed derivable from the facts. On the other hand, if an atom is derivable then the interpreter will answer "yes". Standard interpreters get in an infinite loop in our example program PATH. The second advantage is that "a problem is never solved twice". The reuse of results of subcomputations in Prolog interpreters is called *memoing* or *tabling*. The technique is also known in general as *dynamic programming*.

Memoing can save us a lot of time. For some programs (like naive Fibonacci) the expected runtime decreases from exponential time to polynomial time.

4 Space Complexity

Because it is much easier to reason about space complexity than about time complexity of the interpreter we gave in the previous section we start with a space complexity analysis. This analysis is also a good stepping stone towards the time complexity analysis in the next section. We will define two ways to look at decidability problems in Prolog theorem proving. The first is:

PROLOG THEOREM PROVING
INSTANCE: A query Q and a program P.
QUESTION: Is there a substitution f such that $f(Q)$ follows from P?

This problem is undecidable in general. E.g., in (Shapiro 1984) it is described how a Prolog program can simulate a Turing Machine. The problem is semi-decidable: if the answer is yes we can give an algorithm that finds a proof in finitely many steps. An algorithm with this property is the one-solution interpreter. This interpreter searches its proofs under a breadth-first regime and is therefore guaranteed to stop if there exists a proof.

In this article we will define classes of programs as follows. We define predicates to be *fixed* or *free*. All programs in a class must have identical clauses for the fixed predicates, but differ in the clauses for the free predicates. In this article all free predicates are defined with ground facts only. When there are no free predicates, the class contains only one program. The set of clauses for the fixed predicates in some class is called the *core program*.

PROLOG THEOREM PROVING FOR CORE PROGRAM P
INSTANCE: A query Q and a set of clauses R.
QUESTION: Is there a substitution f such that $f(Q)$ follows from $P \cup R$?

P defines the fixed predicates, and R the free predicates. We define PROLOG THEOREM PROVING FOR PROGRAM P as a special case of PROLOG THEOREM PROVING FOR A CORE PROGRAM P, namely, when $R = \emptyset$. In the rest of this paper we will only consider programs for which these problems are decidable. The path program, that we presented earlier, consists of two predicates: path and edge. We can see the path predicate as fixed and the edge predicate as free. This enables us to define upperbounds for various graphs and not just for one graph (because we can vary the edges).

The space complexity of PROLOG THEOREM PROVING FOR CORE PROGRAM P is the size of the table when the computation of the one-solution interpreter has finished.

This is not quite true because there can be many duplicates in the agenda. We have to modify the interpreter a bit. We have to make sure that items neither occur in the agenda nor in the table before we put them in the agenda. Then we know that the size of the agenda plus the size of the table is smaller than the size of the final table at any point in the computation. In order to save space we do not show the implementation here.

Because we can not predict when the first solution is found by the one-solution interpreter, we will assume the worst scenario, where the computation ends because the agenda is empty. In fact we estimate the complexity of the one-solution interpreter and the all-solutions interpreters simultaneously.

In order to estimate the size of the final table we have to count

- the number of items in the table, and
- the length of the items.

We will index our clauses from now on. The function $l(i)$ denotes the number of atoms in the body of clause i. For every clause $C_i : - B_{i1}, B_{i2}, \ldots, B_{in}$ (i is the index, n replaces $l(i)$ for some i sometimes), the items in the table are of the following form:

$$\langle f(C_i), [f(B_{i1}), f(B_{i2}), \ldots, f(B_{in})] \rangle.$$
$$\langle \sigma_1(f(C_i)), [\sigma_1(f(B_{i2})), \ldots, \sigma_1(f(B_{in}))] \rangle.$$
$$\langle \sigma_2(\sigma_1(f(C_i))), [\sigma_2(\sigma_1(f(B_{i3}))), \ldots, \sigma_2(\sigma_1(f(B_{in})))] \rangle.$$
$$\vdots$$
$$\langle \sigma_n(\ldots(\sigma_1(f(C_i))), [\,] \rangle$$

If we want to know the number of items we have to estimate the number of possible substitutions $f, \sigma_1 \circ f, \sigma_2 \circ \sigma_1 \circ f, \ldots, \sigma_n \circ \ldots \circ f$, for every clause i in the program. In general the number of substitutions is infinite but we count here the number of substitutions with a given query and program under the proof procedure specified in the one-solution and all-solutions provers. Substitutions that are alphabetic variants are not allowed, we count just the number of "alphabetically different" substitutions. We introduce a notation for the number of possible substitutions for a set of variables. The functions $\#_i(Var(X), j)$ (where $Var(X)$ is a set of variables) return the number of possible substitutions of the variables in $Var(X)$ after proving $Bi1$ through Bij, i.e. the number of possible $\sigma_j \circ \ldots \circ \sigma_1 \circ f$. The positions in the body and the various B_{ij} are related as follows:

$$\overset{0}{\bullet} \; B_{i1} \; \overset{1}{\bullet} \; \ldots \ldots \; B_{ij} \; \overset{j}{\bullet} \; B_{i(j+1)} \; \overset{j+1}{\bullet} \; \ldots \ldots \; B_{i(l(i))} \; \overset{l(i)}{\bullet}$$

We first have to see which variables occur in the substitutions (i.e., for which variables the substitution is not the identity mapping). We will call these variables the *relevant variables*. Suppose we want to count the items of the following form:

$$\langle \sigma_j(\ldots \sigma_1(f(C_i))), [\sigma_j(\ldots \sigma_1(f(B_{i(j+1)}))), \ldots, \sigma_j(\ldots \sigma_1(f(B_{in})))] \rangle.$$

Then the following variables are *not* relevant:

- Variables that occur in $B_{i1}, \ldots, B_{ij}$, but neither in $B_{i(j+1)}, \ldots, B_{in}$ nor in C_i. These variables are not relevant, simply because they do not occur in the item.
- Variables that occur in $B_{i(j+1)}, \ldots, B_{in}$, but neither in $B_{i1}, \ldots, B_{ij}$ nor in C_i. These variables are not relevant, because they are uninstantiated.

The other variables are relevant. These can be divided in two groups:

- The variables in C_i. These are called the *head variables* $HV(i)$. $HV(i) = Var(C_i)$
- Variables that occur both in $B_{i1}, \ldots, B_{ij}$ and in $B_{i(j+1)}, \ldots, B_{in}$ but not in C_i. These variables are called the *relevant body variables* $RV(i,j)$. $RV(i,j) = (Var(B_{i1}) \cup \ldots \cup Var(B_{ij})) \cap (Var(B_{i(j+1)}) \cup \ldots \cup Var(B_{in}))$.

The number of items in the final table is:

$$\sum_{i=1}^{k} \sum_{j=0}^{l(i)} \#_i(HV(i) \cup RV(i,j), j)$$

We will apply this formula in the example program PATH.

```
path(X,Z) ::-
        [path(X,Y),
         edge(Y,Z)].
path(W,W) ::- [].

edge(a,b) ::- [].
edge(b,c) ::- [].
edge(c,a) ::- [].
edge(c,d) ::- [].
```

The number of items is:
$\#(\{X, Z\} \cup \emptyset, 0) + \#(\{X, Z\} \cup \{Y\}, 1) + \#(\{X, Z\} \cup \emptyset, 2) +$
$\#(\{W\} \cup \emptyset, 0) +$
$\#(\emptyset \cup \emptyset, 0) +$
$\#(\emptyset \cup \emptyset, 0) +$
$\#(\emptyset \cup \emptyset, 0) +$
$\#(\emptyset \cup \emptyset, 0)$

We know that the variables in this programs can only be substituted by a vertex in the graph (a, b, c or d). We denote the number of vertices in the graph as $|V|$ and the number of edges as $|E|$, and fill in the formula:

$$|V|^2 + |V|^3 + |V|^2 + |V| + 1 + \ldots + 1$$

We sum $|E|$ times 1. Because $|E| \leq |V|^2$, the formula equals $\mathcal{O}(|V|^3)$.

The space complexity does not depend on the number of items only, but also on the length of the items. We introduce the function $\#\#_i$ that does not count the number of substitutions, but the number of *symbols needed to write down* all substitutions. The number of instantiations and the length of the instantiations behave different if they are estimated for a set of variables. Suppose we have two variables, $A1$ and $A2$. The number of possible substitutions for $A1$ is n_1. The number of possible substitutions for $A2$ is n_2. The average length of the substitutions for $A1$ and $A2$ is l_1 and l_2 respectively. Then the number of possible substitutions for $\#_i(\{A, B\})$ is $n_1 \times n_2$. The average length of all substitutions is $l_1 + l_2$, and $\#\#_i(\{A, B\})$ is $(n_1 \times n_2) \times (l_1 + l_2)$. We have to *multiply* the possibilities and *add* the lengths. Because variables are often dependent it will in general not be the case that $\#_i(\{X, Y\}) = \#_i(X) \times \#_i(Y)$. If a variable occurs twice in a $\#\#_i(\ldots)$ formula we can leave one out. We are interested in estimates only, therefore we define that $\#_i(X, j) = \mathcal{O}(\#_i(X, j))$ and $\#\#_i(X, j) = \mathcal{O}(\#\#_i(X, j))$.

We assume that the length of clauses in the program is bounded by a constant. The space complexity of PROLOG THEOREM PROVING FOR CORE PROGRAM P is now:

$$\sum_{i=1}^{k} \sum_{j=0}^{l(i)} \#\#_i(HV(i) \cup RV(i, j), j)$$

In the example, we assume that the number of symbols needed to write down a vertex is bounded by a constant. In that case, the space complexity of the problem is $\mathcal{O}(|V|^3)$.

5 Time Complexity

In the previous section we saw how the space complexity of a problem can be estimated. In this section we will consider the time complexity. Observe that the Earley interpreter is deterministic. Therefore it can be converted to a program in an imperative language in a straightforward way. We will assume that this has been done. We will describe the time complexity of PROLOG THEOREM PROVING FOR CORE PROGRAM P in terms of this imperative interpreter. We count the number of steps of the all-solutions interpreter because we can not predict when the first solution of a problem has been found. Therefore we assume that the algorithm terminates when the agenda is empty.

We know that all items in the table and the agenda are different. Therefore the procedure extend_items_all will be executed as many times as there are items in the final table: $\sum_{i=1}^{k} \sum_{j=0}^{l(i)} \#_i(HV(i) \cup RV(i, j), j)$. Within this procedure, we have to execute the procedure new_items. Within the procedure new_items we perform *prediction* and *completion*. We can divide the table in two parts. First, we have items of the form item(Goal1, [Goal2|Goals]). The number of items of this form is $\sum_{i=1}^{k} \sum_{j=0}^{l(i)-1} \#_i(HV(i) \cup RV(i, j), j)$. Secondly, we have items of the form item(Goal, []). There are $\sum_{i=1}^{k} \#_i(HV(i), l(i))$ such items in the final table (observe that $RV(i, l(i)) = \emptyset$). If we sum all completion steps, we see that every item of the form item(Goal1, [Goal2|Goals]) is compared exactly once with every item of the form item(Goal, []) to check whether the second is a solution for the first. Therefore the total number of completion steps is

$$\sum_{i=1}^{k} \sum_{j=0}^{l(i)-1} \#_i(HV(i) \cup RV(i, j), j) \times \sum_{i=1}^{k} \#_i(HV(i), l(i))$$

In a completion step, we have to unify two atoms. The time needed is the sum of the length of the two atoms. If the length of the atoms in the program, is bounded by a constant, then the total time needed for all completion steps is (## is the sum of the length of all possible substitutions):

$$(\sum_{i=1}^{k} \sum_{j=0}^{l(i)-1} \#\#_i(HV(i) \cup RV(i,j),j) \times \sum_{i=1}^{k} \#_i(HV(i),l(i))) \; +$$

$$(\sum_{i=1}^{k} \sum_{j=0}^{l(i)-1} \#_i(HV(i) \cup RV(i,j),j) \times \sum_{i=1}^{k} \#\#_i(HV(i),l(i)))$$

The number of prediction steps is estimated as follows. We do a prediction step once for every item of the form item(Goal1, [Goal2|Goals]), thus $\sum_{i=1}^{k} \sum_{j=0}^{l(i)-1} \#_i(HV(i) \cup RV(i,j),j)$ times. We have to compare Goal2 with every clause in the program. Say the number of clauses for free predicates in the program is $|R|$. Then we have to execute $\sum_{i=1}^{k} \sum_{j=0}^{l(i)-1} \#_i(HV(i) \cup RV(i,j),j) \times |R|$ unifications. Under the assumption that the length of the clauses of R is bounded by a constant, the total time needed in the prediction steps amounts to $\sum_{i=1}^{k} \sum_{j=0}^{l(i)-1} \#\#_i(HV(i) \cup RV(i,j),j) \times |R|$.

Without proof we state that putting items in the agenda and the table is less complex than the other operations. The total time needed for all operations together is:

$\sum_{i=1}^{k} \sum_{j=0}^{l(i)-1} \#\#_i(HV(i) \cup RV(i,j),j) \times \sum_{i=1}^{k} \#_i(HV(i),l(i)) \; +$

$\sum_{i=1}^{k} \sum_{j=0}^{l(i)-1} \#_i(HV(i) \cup RV(i,j),j) \times \sum_{i=1}^{k} \#\#_i(HV(i),l(i)) \; +$

$\sum_{i=1}^{k} \sum_{j=0}^{l(i)-1} \#\#_i(HV(i) \cup RV(i,j),j) \times |R| \; + \sum_{i=1}^{k} \sum_{j=0}^{l(i)} \#\#_i(HV(i) \cup RV(i,j),j)$

This can be simplified to:

$(\sum_{i=1}^{k} \sum_{j=0}^{l(i)-1} \#\#_i(HV(i) \cup RV(i,j),j) \times (\sum_{i=1}^{k} \#_i(HV(i),l(i)) + |R|)) \; +$

$(\sum_{i=1}^{k} \sum_{j=0}^{l(i)-1} \#_i(HV(i) \cup RV(i,j),j) \times \sum_{i=1}^{k} \#\#_i(HV(i),l(i)))$

We can use this formula to estimate the time complexity of the sample program PATH in the previous section: $\sum_{i=1}^{k} \sum_{j=0}^{l(i)-1} \#\#_i(HV(i) \cup RV(i,j),j) =$

$\sum_{i=1}^{k} \sum_{j=0}^{l(i)-1} \#_i(HV(i) \cup RV(i,j),j) = \mathcal{O}(|V|^3)$

$\sum_{i=1}^{k} \#\#_i(HV(i),l(i)) = \sum_{i=1}^{k} \#_i(HV(i),l(i)) = \mathcal{O}(|V|^2 + |E|)$

$|R| = |E|$.

The time complexity is $\mathcal{O}(|V|^3 \times (|V|^2 + |E|)) = \mathcal{O}(|V|^5)$, because $|E| \leq |V|^2$.

The upper bound on the time complexity is high, merely because we use a very simple interpreter. It is possible to write an interpreter that is much more efficient. This has been done in Aarts (1995). It is e.g. possible to eliminate the unification in the completer step. This can be done as follows. Every item with a non-empty body is associated with two keys. The first key tells how the clause was "called". When we have proved the rest of the body, this key can be used to find all items that are waiting for this solution. The second key tells what items can be a solution for the first atom in the body. The keys are computed in the prediction step. With this usage of keys we can immediately see whether a given solution "fits" a waiting item. A disadvantage is that the number of items grows a little bit: we not only store the substitutions for the head variables after some part of the body has been proven, but we also store the substitutions when nothing has been proved yet (the "call").

In Aarts (1995) it is shown how we obtain a simple formula for the time complexity, if we restrict ourselves to *well-moded* and *nicely-moded* programs (Apt and Pellegrini 1994). We obtain a bound of $|E|$ for the time complexity of the path program with this improved method.

6 Further research

As said in the introduction, the approach taken in this article is modest. We have proven an upper bound for the time complexity of Prolog programs in a pretty straightforward way. The bad thing is that the bound is often higher than one would desire. In order to get the right semantics we have to do the so-called *occur check* in every unification. Arguing against the occur check, Pereira (1993, p. 547) states:

> "it was felt that the cost of a procedure call in a reasonable programming language should not depend on the sizes of the actual parameters"

In the previous we saw that the complexity *does* depend on the size of the parameters. There are two sources for this. First we perform the occur check. Secondly, we make copies of the parameters when we store them in the tables and we have to compare parameters all the time. This comparison is often not necessary. E.g. if we have a DCG there will be many copies of tails of the input sentence. Instead of copying this list we would like to copy pointers to positions in this list. If we want to compare two terms in this case, we only have to see whether two pointers point to the same address. And we do not have to compare the two lists. In a practical system we could do the following. We first look whether two pointers point to the same address. If they do, then we are sure they are identical and we don't have to compare or copy anything. If they point to different addresses we have to compare them. It is still possible that they are the same.

```
firstpart([a,b]).        firstpart([a]).
secondpart([c]).         secondpart([b,c]).
pred1 :-
        firstpart(X),
        secondpart(Y),
        append(X,Y,Z),
        pred2(Z).
```

We have to compute twice whether pred2 ([a,b,c]), but the two terms [a,b,c] will be represented internally in a different way. Theoretically the "trick" does not help us much, but in practice it can be an improvement. In practice the size of the parameters will often be eliminated.

7 Existing implementations of Earley interpreters

Currently there are (at least) three implementations of the Earley interpreter. The first is a very experimental implementation by the author. This implementation can be found at `"http://www.fwi.uva.nl/~aarts/prolog.html"`.

The interpreter has been written in Prolog and runs under Quintus, Sicstus and SWI Prolog. A nice feature is high-level tracing, where we can inspect proof trees after the execution of the program. The high-level tracer stimulates a declarative programming style. The second implementation is SLG. This is also a meta-interpreter in Prolog. It supports the third truth value for non-stratified programs. It has been developed by W. Chen and D.S. Warren. The third implementation is XSB. XSB has been developed at the University of New York at Stony Brook by D.S. Warren et al. This interpreter allows both Earley and standard deduction. The idea is that one can use the standard interpreter for simple, deterministic, predicates where tabling is a useless overhead. Complex non-deterministic predicates can be tabled. XSB has been written in C and is a fast Prolog interpreter. The home page of the XSB Group (where XSB and SLG can be found) is: `"http://www.cs.sunysb.edu/~sbprolog/"`.

References

Aarts, Erik: 1995, *Investigations in Logic, Language and Computation*, PhD thesis, Research Institute for Language and Speech, University of Utrecht.

Apt, K. R. and Pellegrini, A.: 1994, On the occur-check free Prolog programs, *ACM Toplas* **16**(3), 687–726.

Debray, Saumya K. and Lin, Nai-Wei: n.d., Cost Analysis of Logic Programs, Available as ftp://cs.arizona.edu/people/debray/papers/cost_analysis.ps.

Lin, Nai-Wei: 1993, *Automatic Complexity Analysis of Logic Programs*, PhD thesis, Department of Computer Science, University of Arizona. Available as ftp://cs.arizona.edu/caslog/naiwei93.tar.Z.

van Noord, Gertjan: 1993, *Reversibility in Natural Language Processing*, PhD thesis, Utrecht University.

Pereira, F. and Warren, D.H.: 1983, Parsing as deduction, *Proceedings of the 21st Ann. Meeting of the ACL*, MIT, Cambridge, Mass., pp. 137–144.

Pereira, Fernando: 1993, Review of "The Logic of Typed Feature Structures" (Bob Carpenter), *Computational Linguistics* **19**(3), 544–552.

Pereira, Fernando C.N. and Shieber, Stuart M.: 1987, *Prolog and Natural Language Analysis*, Vol. 10 of *CSLI Lecture Notes*, Stanford.

Shapiro, Ehud Y.: 1984, Alternation and the Computational Complexity of Logic Programs, *Journal of Logic Programming* **1**, 19–33.

Tamaki, H. and Sato, T.: 1986, OLDT resolution with tabulation, *Proc. of 3rd Int. Conf. on Logic Programming*, Springer-Verlag, Berlin, pp. 84–98.

Vieille, L.: 1989, Recursive query processing: the power of logic, *Theoretical Computer Science* **69**, 1–53.

Warren, David H.D.: 1975, Earley deduction, unpublished note.

Warren, David S.: 1992, Memoing for Logic Programs, *Communications of the ACM* **35**(3), 94–111.

Studying the Cost of Logic Languages in an Abstract Interpretation Framework for Granularity Analysis

M.M. Gallardo, J.M. Troya

Dpto. de Lenguajes y Ciencias de la Computación
Universidad de Málaga
(gallardo,troya)@tecmal.ctima.uma.es

Abstract

The execution of a concurrent logic program on a distributed system is very dependent on the program granularity and the communication costs. We present a framework based on the abstract interpretation technique to obtain information about these program characteristics and show how its execution time can be improved using the analysis.

The method proposed is realized partially in compile time and partially during execution in order to minimize the runtime overhead. The static part mainly consists of a mode analysis and a type analysis. Using this latter analysis we develop one algorithm to obtain the size relationships between the terms in the heads of the program clauses. This information is essential for building the functions which give the process cost and the communication cost.

We also show how to use the static analysis to transform a concurrent logic program into a distributed program. During transformed program execution, a process will be moved to a remote node only if the relation between the computational and communication costs given by the analysis will improve its execution.

1 Introduction

The expressiveness of logic programming languages allows us to solve many problems in a very elegant way. But it is necessary to realize efficient implementations in order to use them in real applications. One possibility is to carry this out on parallel machines, exploiting the intrinsic parallelism of these languages. However, efficient implementations on these machines must limit parallelism in order to fit the fine granularity of logic programs to the characteristics of parallel architecture. This is why logic program granularity is one the most important fields of study in which to achieve efficient parallelism.

In general, the execution of a program on a parallel system depends strongly on the partitioning, allocation and scheduling of processes among processors [14]. The granularity of a program represents the average size of its processes. The analysis can be applied to sequential languages to infer optimum partitioning of the program into processors or to concurrent languages with intrinsically very fine granularity for joining processes, ensuring that the granularity of the parallel program is coarse enough for a given system without losing too much parallelism.

The granularity analysis is especially important in declarative languages which have architecture independent characteristics. Also, the performance of distributed systems is very dependent on communication costs and therefore a granularity analysis must look for a good communication/computation relation. The granularity has been studied in several contexts. [10,11] present two different frameworks to improve the execution of concurrent logic programs, by ordering the clause body atoms in order to avoid suspensions in a grain, and by analyzing the relation between the grain cost and the communication cost. [16,19] consider the problem of including the granularity information in the programs by using compile time analyses. They approximate the cost of every program clause even if the clause is recursive. However, the communication cost is not taken into account in these works. In [6] authors present a compile time granularity analysis of logic languages by estimating the complexity of every program predicate. They extract upper bounds to this complexity, and use this value to decide when the sequential execution of a task will improve the execution. So they discuss the problem of "sequentializing" parallel programs instead of parallelizing sequential programs. The method used to obtain the size relations gives good information only if the program considered uses lists. However, our framework can be used to obtain this information even if the program uses more general structures because we abstract the atom structure. Also, as we have separated the processes of analyzing the type of program atoms and the size relations, further improvements of this latter analysis can provide more accurate results. On the other hand, in [6] the cost communication is not considered. Finally, [8] is the first version where we present our framework to analyze the concurrent logic program granularity.

Static and dynamic analysis can be carried out to obtain information about this size. A runtime granularity analysis provides very exact information about the grain size but it has a large execution overhead. On the other hand, compile time granularity analyses have no overheads, but they can only generate approximate information. Another possibility is to consider a hybrid method which infers all possible information during compilation, completing it with runtime parameters only known during execution.

Following the ideas of [5,16], we have developed a framework to analyze the granularity of concurrent logic programs which deduces both computational and communication costs. In this framework it is essential to know the size relations between the terms which appear in the clause heads. Here, we present a static analysis based on a type analysis which provides this information. Many type analyses have been developed in the literature, for example [3,12]. In these analyses very approximate type information is obtained. Our type analysis gives less approximate information because it only keeps the term structure and the variable name explicit, but, on the other hand, it provides the type information efficiently. Anyway, this information is enough to analyze the term cost and therefore it is sufficient for our purposes.

The type analysis uses the abstract interpretation technique, so it is well structured and is accomplished completely in compile time. The principal contribution of the method is its simplicity. Moreover, it can be applied to a program although the direction of its data is unknown, and in addition different programming styles do not affect the obtained results.

The method proposed for analyzing the granularity of a program consists in associating each program clause (considering all its possible data directions) with two functions: one providing the computational cost of the clause and the other one giving the communication cost produced if the atoms in the body clause are moved to remote processors.

The usual method, used in [16,19] to obtain the computational cost of a program predicate constituted by two or more clauses consists in calculating the arithmetic mean of each clause cost. The results may be very "approximate" if the clauses have very different behaviors. To partially solve this, we present a way of modifying the framework in order to obtain more accurate information when programs with these characteristics are analyzed.

The information given by the analysis can be used to transform a concurrent logic program into a distributed program. The transformation consists of adding a set of atoms to the body of every transformed program clause. During execution, these atoms calculate the process and communication cost using the data size, and decide if distributing some body atoms improves the execution.

The paper is structured as follows: section 2 gives an overview of the method proposed for analyzing the granularity. Section 3 defines the abstract interpretation and shows how it is used to deduce the size relation between the clause head terms. Section 4 shows how to infer the computational cost of a clause from the previous information and explains how the abstract interpretation can be used to obtain more accurate results concerning the computational cost of a predicate. Section 5 presents an application of the analysis and finally the conclusions and the future work are given in the section 6.

In the following, knowledge about concurrent logic languages, which were classified in [15], and abstract interpretation is assumed. This technique was first used in [4] in the context of imperative languages. However, in the last decade, many works have been developed on declarative languages [2,13,18]. The method has been developed on the concurrent logic language KL1 [9,17], but many of the results could be adapted to other logic languages.

2 Overview of the method

The granularity of concurrent logic programs is very fine, so the analysis must provide enough information to decide when the performance improves if the processes are distributed. The method combines different analyses that are fundamentally carried out in compilation, but they are also completed during execution with runtime parameters which make the approach more precise. This situation is formally established in the following definitions:

Definition 2.1: A static analysis of granularity consists of the 3-uple (G^c, F_T^c, F_C^c) where: $G^c=(V^c, E^c)$ is a directed and labeled graph representing the program structure; $F_T^c:V^c \rightarrow N \rightarrow [0,1]$ gives the relative size of every atom represented in the graph by the vertices; and $F_C^c : E^c \rightarrow N \rightarrow R^1$ gives the size of the communication overhead between the atoms connected by the arcs of the graph.

The graph G^c is really a set of directed and labeled graphs related to the program clauses. There is a graph in G^c for each data direction that a program clause may have during different program executions. This graph is obtained as the fixed point of an abstract immediate consequence operator. The abstract domain models each program term with the atoms which consume or produce it. An atom produces a term if it writes on some variable(s) in the term. Similarly, an atom consumes a term if it reads some variable(s) in the term.

The development of this analysis is not the subject of this paper, so we shall only present an example to illustrate how it works. Consider the following KL1 program used to reverse a list:

C1:	nrev([ ],Y):-	C3:	append([ ],L,L1):-
	Y = [ ].		L1 = L.
C2:	nrev([X|Xs],Y):-	C4:	append([X|Xs],L,[Y|Zs]):-
	nrev(Xs,Ys),		Y = X,
	append(Ys,[X],Y).		append(Xs,L,Zs).

Figure 1

Abstract interpretation will produce the graph (related to the clause C_2) in Figure 2 in which the program data direction is perfectly established. The atom head (*nrev1*) sends the variables X and Xs to the body atoms (*append* and *nrev2*). In the body, *nrev2* sends Ys to *append* and finally, the variable Y flows from the atom *append* to head atom *nrev1*.

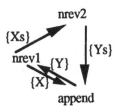

Figure 2

Given a clause atom p (p also being the name of the atom in the graph), the compile time cost function $F_T^c(p)$ represents the cost of executing p in relation to the rest of the atoms in the clause. Finally, if p_1 and p_2 are two atoms in a clause that share a variable, the compile time communication function $F_C^c((p_1,p_2))$ gives the communication cost (that is, the number of write/read operations) that is carried out if these two atoms are distributed to two different system processors.

Section 3 presents the abstract interpretation, based on a type analysis used to build these two functions.

During execution, the 3-uple (G^e, F_T^e, F_C^e) is built using the compile time granularity analysis (G^c, F_T^c, F_C^c) and the data size. The graph $G^e=(V^e, E^e)$ is a

---

[1]N and R denote the sets of natural and real numbers.

dynamic graph which is expanded at each execution step. It represents the program state at each moment during execution, that is, V^e is formed by the set of processes[2] in execution. Two processes are in E^e if they actually share data. Again, a more detailed explanation about how this graph is formally defined is not the purpose of this paper.

The runtime computational cost function F_T^e and the runtime communication cost function F_C^e provides information about the program at each point during its execution. So, if *Proc* is the set of active processes, these functions are calculated as follows:

$$F_T^e : Proc \rightarrow N \qquad\qquad F_T^e(p) = F_T^c(v)(k)$$

$$F_C^e : Proc \; x \; Proc \rightarrow N \qquad\qquad F_C^e((p_1,p_2)) = k'F_C^c(a)(label(p_1,p_2))$$

v being the vertex which abstracts the process p in the graph G^c, and a the arc which abstracts the communication between the processes p_1 and p_2. The value k' is a constant that depends on the architecture of the system, that is, on the distance of the nodes to which the processes p_1 and p_2 will be sent, if we decide to distribute them. k represents the data size of p, and $label(p_1,p_2)$ is the size of the data that flows from p_1 to p_2. We name them in this way as they constitute the label of the arc (p_1,p_2) in the graph G^e. In fact, $F_C^e((p_2,p_1))$ must be also evaluated to calculate the total communication cost.

During the execution of a program, the set of processes in execution will be represented by the dynamic graph G^e. If a goal atom is selected to be reduced by using a clause, the compile time cost function F_T^e and the communication cost function F_C^e may be inspected. The inputs of these functions are the size of the parameters of F_T^c and F_C^c, which are known during execution. So, with the information provided by F_T^e and F_C^e, the decision to move one atom in the body of a clause to a different processor can be made.

3 Obtaining size relations

In the previous section, we have presented a framework for analyzing the granularity of concurrent logic programs. Two analyses are mainly developed in this framework: a mode analysis and a type analysis. In this section we present this latter one in more detail. The type analysis is used here to deduce the size relations between some arguments of the clause heads. This information is now employed to obtain the computational and communication cost functions, as is explained below.

Let us consider a generic KL1 clause $C \equiv h\text{:-}\, g|b_1,...,b_m$. The execution cost of C can be defined as $T(n) = a + T_{b1}(s_1(n)) + ... + T_{bm}(s_m(n))$, where:

1. - a represents the cost of head unification plus guard evaluation[3].

2. - n is the size of the iteration parameter of the clause. This concept was introduced in [19].

---

[2]We call program atoms processes during execution.
[3]All guards are flat.

3. - $s_i(n)$ is the size of the iteration parameter[4] of the atom b_i calculated in terms of n.

The abstract interpretation presented here generates enough information to calculate the functions s_i. For example, let us consider the program in the Figure 1. Assuming that the first parameter of the predicates *append* and *nrev* is their iteration parameter, we can define the execution cost of C_2 as $T_{nrev}(n) = a + T_{append}(s_1(n)) + T_{nrev}(s_2(n))$. s_1 and s_2 are built using the size relations. In this way, if after analyzing the program in the Figure 1 we obtain that the size of the first and second arguments[5] of *nrev/2* are equal, that is, $<nrev/2, t_1 = t_2>$, then we can deduce that $s_1(n) = n - 1$. To obtain $s_2(n) = n - 1$, it is not necessary to use the size relations.

Also, the abstraction will provide these size relations even though they are not referred to whole head clause arguments. For example, given the KL1 programs: $p(X,Y) :- Y = X$, and $p(f(X,Y)) :- Y = X$, both act in a similar way when they are called with the goals $:- p(a,Y)$ and $:- p(f(a,Y))$, respectively. Our approach will infer that, in these two programs, the size of the variable Y is equal to the size of a, that is, the costs of these predicates are equivalent by using our abstraction. Next, the abstract interpretation used to deduce the size relations is given.

3.1 Abstract interpretation

We use a bottom-up abstract interpretation to deduce the size relations. This section presents the abstract domain considered along with the abstract immediate consequence operator. The abstract atoms provided by the application of this operator are used to obtain the size relation of a predicate in the following way. Firstly, an algorithm which provides the size relations of an abstract atom is presented. Next, we apply this algorithm to the abstract atoms obtained in the iterations of the abstract operator and, finally, with this information we show how to deduce the size relation of a predicate.

The abstract interpretation proposed infers the structure of the terms to which variables are bound. Also, the abstraction keeps visible the name of the term variables.

Definition 3.1: Given a KL1 program P, the abstract domain defined to represent the type information is: $D = \{1\} \cup Var \cup (\underset{n \geq 0}{\cup} D^n)$ where $D^n = \underset{\leftarrow \ n \ \rightarrow}{D \times \cdots \times D}$, the symbol 1 represents any program constant, Var is a denumerable set of symbols, and the Cartesian product models the term structure.

Definition 3.2: If $Term_P$ denotes the set of terms that can be built using the functor symbols, constants and variables of a KL1 program P, then the abstraction function $\alpha: Term_P \rightarrow D$ is defined as follows. Given $t \in Term_P$ then

a) if $arity(t) = 0$ then

    a1) $\alpha(t) = t$ if $t \in Var$ a2) $\alpha(t) = 1$ if t is a program constant

b) if $arity(t) = n$ then

    b1) $\alpha(t) = (\alpha(t_1),..., \alpha(t_n))$ t_i being the n arguments of t.

---

[4]We are assuming that each program predicate has an iteration parameter.
[5]t_i represent the size of the ith argument of the associated program predicate.

So, under this abstraction, the terms $f(X,b)$ and $g(X,a)$ are equivalent, that is, $\alpha(f(X,b)) = \alpha(g(X,a)) = (X,1)$.

In this context an abstract substitution is a map $\mu : Var \to D$ with finite support. The application of an abstract substitution to an abstract term, the composition of abstract substitutions and the most general abstract unifier of a set of abstract terms can be defined in the usual way.

Many abstract interpretations are top-down as they approximate the operational semantics of the language. However, it is also possible to use a bottom-up abstract interpretation [1] which has the advantage of being independent of the initial goal. Here, we adopt this last strategy and define the abstract immediate consequence operator as follows:

Definition 3.3: Given a KL1 program P, the immediate consequence operator $T : 2^D \to 2^D$ related to the abstraction $<D, \alpha, Term_P>$ is defined as:

$$T(I) = \{h\tau / C \equiv h <\text{-}G{:}b_1,...,b_n \in Clause_P \text{ and } b_i* \in I \text{ and}$$

$$\tau = amgu((b_1\alpha,...,b_n\alpha),(b_1*\rho,...,b_n*\rho)) \}$$

where $Clause_P$ is the set of program clauses, $amgu$ is the most general abstract substitution that makes its arguments equal, and the substitution ρ changes the variables of the abstract atoms b_i* for fresh variables.

In general, when an abstract interpretation is defined, the abstract domain is a finite or noetherian lattice, so the immediate consequence operator finds its fixed point in finite time. However, this cannot be assured with the previous definition, (supposing that the "more instantiated than" order has been defined on D), since we can find terms with any depth in D. The definition of D can be modified by only taking into account the abstract term structure up to a certain depth given by the code program. This would produce a noetherian and non-finite domain. However, the discussion about the building of this domain would exceed the size of this paper and so we will assume that it can be achieved. In any case, in this work, the termination of the algorithm proposed is provided by a different line of reasoning that will be discussed later.

The behaviour of T is illustrated in the following example. Again, let us consider the program in Figure 1:

- $T(\emptyset) = \{nrev(1,1), append(1,L,L)\}$

- $T^2(\emptyset) = T(\emptyset) \cup \{nrev((X1,1),(X1,1)), append((X1,1),L,(X1,L))\}$

- $T^3(\emptyset) = T^2(\emptyset) \cup ......$

Next, an algorithm is presented for obtaining the size relations between the abstract terms of an abstract atom. The notion of *path* is used in this algorithm. Given an abstract atom a with arity n, a *path* in a is defined as a non empty sequence of integers $c_1c_2...c_m$ such that $c_1 \leq n$, and $c_2...c_m$ is a path in the term placed in the argument c_1 of a. Given a path $\alpha = c_1c_2...c_m$ in an abstract atom a, the abstract term placed at the end of the path is denoted by $end\_path(a,\alpha)$. Moreover, $Var\_path(a)$ is used to represent those paths that end in a variable term.

For example, $end\_path(((X,Y),Z),1\ 1) = X$, and $Var\_path(((X,Y),Z)) = \{1\ 1, 1\ 2, 2\}$

Here, the size relation of a program predicate p/n is an expression that combines different subterms and which is verified by all the atoms (with predicate symbol p and arity n) in the success set of the program considered. This relation will be equivalently called *fixpoint size relation* in the rest of the paper.

Algorithm: Given an abstract atom a, and a family of paths Δ in a that represents the input and output terms of the atom, the following algorithm finds the size relations between the abstract terms placed at the end of these paths.

a) First the set $Eq(a) = \{t_{\alpha_1} = t_{\alpha_2} : \alpha_1, \alpha_2 \in Var\_path(p),\ end\_path(p, \alpha_1) = end\_path(p, \alpha_2)\}$ is built. For example:

$$Eq(append((X1,1),L,(X1,L))) = \{t_{11} = t_{31}, t_2 = t_{32}\}$$

b) Let Δ be the set $\{\alpha_1, ..., \alpha_k\}$. To continue the example, we will suppose that $\Delta = \{1,2,3\}$

b1) For each $i = 1, ..., k$, we introduce in the initially empty set E the expression $t_{\alpha_i} = t_{\alpha_{i1}} + t_{\alpha_{i2}} + \cdots + t_{\alpha_{im}} + cte$, where $\{\alpha_{i1}, ..., \alpha_{im}\}$ are the paths that can be found by a depth-first traversal in the subterm $end\_path(a, \alpha_i)$, and cte represents the cost of the constants.

In the previous example, $E = \{t_1 = 2 + t_{11}, t_3 = 1 + t_{31} + t_{32}\}$

Here, we assume that the cost of each functor and constant is 1.

b2) The following steps are repeated for each expression $t_{\alpha_i} = t_{\alpha_{i1}} + t_{\alpha_{i2}} + \cdots + t_{\alpha_{im}} + cte$ in E.

b21) If t_{α_j} exists in $t_{\alpha_i} = t_{\alpha_{i1}} + t_{\alpha_{i2}} + \cdots + t_{\alpha_{im}} + cte$, such that $t_{\alpha_j} = t_{\beta_j}$ belongs to $Eq(a)$, t_{α_j} is substituted by t_{β_j} and the expression $t_{\alpha_i} = t_{\beta_1} + t_{\beta_2} + \cdots + t_{\beta_m} + cte$ is obtained, otherwise the expression is not modified.

In the example, taking the first expression from E, $t_1 = 2 + t_{31}$ is obtained.

b22) For each expression $t_{\alpha_i} = t_{\beta_1} + t_{\beta_2} + \cdots + t_{\beta_m} + cte$ (*) obtained in b21) the following process is realized:

1.- If each $\beta_i \in \{\alpha_1, ..., \alpha_k\}$, the expression is already a size relation.

2.- If $\beta_i \notin \{\alpha_1, ..., \alpha_k\}$ exists, we look at the set E for an equation in which t_{β_i} appears. If this equation exists, we use it to substitute t_{β_i} in (*), and the iteration starts again from point b2).

We carry out this process until point 1 can be chosen. If this is not possible because we have used all expressions in $Eq(a)$ and E, then the equation is discarded.

To finish our example: $t_1 = 2 + t_3 - 1 - t_{32} \overset{b21)}{=} 1 + t_3 - t_2$, that is, the size relation obtained is $t_3 = t_1 + t_2 - 1$

The value - 1 appears in the size relation because the list obtained by appending two lists has only one empty list at its end.

Theorem: Given an abstract atom a , and $\Delta = \{\alpha_1,..., \alpha_n\}$ a family of paths in a, the previous algorithm can find any size relation that exists between the terms placed at the end of these paths.

The proof is based on the fact that the algorithm obtains the size relations by only substituting some values in the expresions in E with the expresions in $Eq(a)$. It is sufficient to prove that from the size relation, by carrying out the same substitutions but in opposite way, the expression $0 = 0$ can be obtained. Thus, the algorithm can find this size relation by realizing the same process in the reverse way.

3.2 Deduction of the predicate size relations

In the previous section we have presented the way to obtain the size relation of an abstract atom. However, we need to know the size relations of every program predicate. To achieve this, we carry out the following. First, we apply the previous algorithm to each abstract atom in the set produced in every iteration of T, and secondly, we analyze the size relations obtained to decide whether we have yet generated all program predicate size relations and so we can stop the iteration, or we have to carry on looking for new relations. This is described below in detail.

We assume that the mode analysis explained in section 1 provides the information about the input and output paths of a predicate. In this analysis, a program clause can have different modes, depending on the data directions in the environment. However, the algorithm does not use the direction of a path explicitly, therefore even if the direction of a path is modified, the algorithm will not be affected.

We now show how the size relations are obtained using the previous example. The set SR_i represents the size relations provided by the corresponding iteration.

- $T(\varnothing) = \{nrev(1,1), append(1,L,L)\}$

$\qquad SR_1 = \{ <nrev/2,\{[t_1 = 1, t_2 = 1]\}>, <append/3,\{[t_1 = 1, t_2 = t_3]\}> \}$

- $T^2(\varnothing) = T(\varnothing) \cup \{nrev((X1,1),(X1,1)), append((X1,1),L,(X1,L))\}$

$\qquad SR_2 = \{ <nrev/2,\{[t_1 = 1, t_2 = 1],[t_1 = t_2]\}>,$

$\qquad\qquad\qquad <append/3,\{[t_1 = 1, t_2 = t_3], [t_3 = t_1 + t_2 - 1]\}> \}$

- $T^3((\varnothing) = T^2(\varnothing) \cup ....$

$\qquad SR_3 = \{ <nrev/2,\{[t_1 = 1, t_2 = 1],[t_1 = t_2]\}>,$

$\qquad\qquad\qquad <append/3,\{[t_1 = 1, t_2 = t_3], [t_3 = t_1 + t_2 - 1]\}> \}$

....

Figure 3

In this example, two interrelated problems are shown. First, we have not yet defined how to relate the size relations of a predicate obtained in different iterations; and secondly it is not clear when the process of extracting size relations must stop. We now discuss these two points.

In the following, P represents a KL1 program, p/n a program predicate with arity n, and Δ the set of paths having the same meaning as in the algorithm. sr and sr_i ($i \in N$) represent size relations related to p/n and $SR_i = \{<p/n,Sr>: p/n \in P\}$ contains the size relations obtained by applying the algorithm to the set $T^i(\varnothing)$, where $Sr = \{sr_1,...,sr_k\}$.

To relate the size relations obtained in different iterations of T, we define the following partial order over the set of size relations of a program predicate. If sr_1 and sr_2 are two size relations then $sr_1 \leq sr_2$ iff $sol(sr_1) \subseteq sol(sr_2)$, where $sol(sr)$ is the set of solutions of sr. As a predicate can have different clauses defining its behaviour, Sr may be formed by a disjunction of different size relations. Therefore, if the partial order is extended to a set of size relations, the way of constructing the sequence $\{T^n(\varnothing) : n \geq 0 \}$ implies that the relations obtained in successive iterations of T always verify this partial order. The following Proposition shows how the size relation of a predicate can be found, supposing that it exists.

Proposition 1: If the fixpoint size relation fsr of a predicate exists, then $fsr = max\{sr : sr \in Sr_i \ i \geq 0 \}$and $SR_i = \{...,<p/n,Sr_i>,...\}$.

Proof: Every atom with the functor symbol p/n in the success set of P verifies the size relation of fsr, therefore $sr \leq fsr$ for all $sr \in Sr_i$. If the size relation $max\{sr : sr \in Sr_i \ i \geq 0 \}$ exists then the smallest size relation that verifies this expression is the maximum size relation.

The Proposition 2 shows how the search of a predicate size relation can be simplified.

Proposition 2: Given $Sr = \{sr_1,...,sr_k\}$, if the size relation $sr = max(sr_1,...,sr_k)$ exists, where $max(sr_1,...,sr_n)$ is the maximum size relation with respect to the partial order defined, and $sr \in Sr$, then we can substitute the set $\{sr_1,...,sr_k\}$ by $\{sr\}$ in the set Sr.

This Proposition is obtained from the previous one, and means that if there is a size relation in the set Sr that is greater than the rest of the size relations, we can simplify Sr by eliminating the small relations. Therefore, in the example as $sol(\{t_1 = 1, t_2 = t_3\}) \subseteq sol(\{t_3 = t_1 + t_2 - 1\})$ and $sol(\{t_1 = 1, t_2 = 1\}) \subseteq sol(\{t_1 = t_2\})$, we can redefine SR_2 and SR_3 as follows: $SR_2 = \{<nrev/2,\{[t_1 = t_2]\}>, <append/3,\{[t_3 = t_1 + t_2 - 1]\}>\}$

To determine the predicates without size relations we introduce the notion of dimension. The intuition behind this concept is that if $\Delta = \{\alpha 1,..., \alpha n\}$ then the maximum set of points that verify a size relation is defined by a set of expressions such as $t_{\alpha 1} = f(t_{\alpha i1},...,t_{\alpha in})$. Therefore, the number expressions obtained in different iterations of T is bounded. At most an expression like this can be obtained.

The *dimension* of the size relation $t_{\alpha 1} = f(t_{\alpha 2},...,t_{\alpha n})$ is $n - 1$. Considering this, the following Proposition is verified.

Proposition 3: Given sr_1, $sr_2 \in Sr$, and $SR_i = \{<p/n,Sr>: p/n \in P\}$, if $sol(sr_2) \not\subseteq sol(sr_1)$ and sr_1 has the maximum dimension, then the predicate p/n has no fixpoint size relation.

Proof: It is not possible to build a size relation whose set of solutions strictly contains these two sets of solutions as sr_1 has the maximum dimension.

As a consequence, if $sol(sr_1) \cap sol(sr_2) = \varnothing$ then the fixpoint does not exist as occurs in the following example:

$p(X,Y):- Y = X.$ $\qquad\qquad$ $p(X,[X1|Y]):- X1 = X, p(X,Y).$

As has been shown before the size relations obtained by applying the algorithm, Δ being $\{1,2\}$, are:

- $T(\emptyset) = \{p(X,X)\}$
- $T^2(\emptyset) = \{p(X,X),\ p(X,(X,X))\}$

$SR_1 = \{<p/2,\{t_1 = t_2\}>\}$

$SR_2 = \{<p/2,\{[t_1 = t_2],\ [t_2 = 1 + 2*t_1]\}>\}$

The maximum dimension of the fixpoint size relation of $p/2$ is 1, and so are the dimensions of $t_1 = t_2$ and $t_2 = 1 + 2*t_1$; thus by applying Proposition 3 to SR_2 it can be deduced that the predicate $p/2$ has no fixpoint size relation. as obviously $sol(t_1 = t_2) \cap sol(t_2 = 1 + 2*t_1) = \emptyset$.

3.3 Termination

Proposition 1 gives the fixpoint size relation when it exists, and Proposition 3 presents a situation where the fixpoint size relation of a predicate does not exist. However, the second problem mentioned above is not solved. That is, it is necessary to establish when the iteration of T must stop, or equivalently when the maximum has been found, if it exists. This aspect is studied in this section.

To deduce the termination of T we use the mode analysis. This analysis associates each program clause with a set of graphs. Each graph relates the clause variables with the set of their producers and consumers. This information is useful for deducing the size relations.

Definition 3.4: Given $C \equiv p :\text{-} g \mid b_1,...,b_m$ and sr a size relation of p/n, then sr is a fixpoint size relation of C using $sr_1,...,sr_m$ if sr can be inductively deduced from C, $sr_1,...,sr_m$ and the mode analysis. The following example clarifies this definition.

Let us suppose that the mode information given by the mode analysis of the program clause $p(X,Y) :\text{-} q(X,Z),r(Z,Y)$ is as follows: X is provided by the environment, Z is produced by q and consumed by r, and Y is produced by r and consumed by the environment. If $sr_1 = [t_1 = t_2]$ and $sr_2 = [t_1 = t_2]$ are the size relations of q and r respectively, and $sr = [t_1 = t_2]$ is the size relation to be deduced, we can build the following sequence using the mode analysis: $t_2 = t_Y \underset{sr_2}{=} t_Z \underset{sr_1}{=} t_X = t_1$

The following definition explains how to obtain the fixpoint size relation of a predicate: this relation must be a fixpoint size relation of every program clause that defines this predicate.

Definition 3.5: Let us suppose that $C \equiv p :\text{-} g \mid b_1,...,b_m$ is a program clause. If the fixpoint size relation fsr_i of b_i has been found (for all $i = 1,...,m$), a size relation of p/n is a fixpoint size relation of C if we can deduce sr from C, by using $fsr_1,...,fsr_m$ and the mode analysis as has been defined before. With this new concept, the following Proposition is asserted:

Proposition 4: The fixpoint size relation of a predicate is a size relation sr that is a fixpoint size relation for all the clauses that define the program predicate.

Applying this to the example shown in the Figure 3, the fixpoint size relation of *append* and *nrev* are $t_3 = t_1 + t_2 - 1$ and $t_1 = t_2$, respectively.

To summarize, Proposition 4 shows that in order to find the fixpoint size relation of a predicate, we have to iterate until finding a size relation that is a fixpoint size relation of all predicate clauses. Proposition 2 explains how to simplify the size relations obtained in every iteration of T. The process of finding the fixpoint size relations of a predicate is finite due to the fact that the dimension of this size relation is bounded. Proposition 3 gives the termination of this process when the fixpoint size relation of a predicate does not exist.

4 Communication and computational costs

To obtain the cost function of a predicate, we need to know which is the iteration parameter. In our work, this will be the input parameter whose size changes in every iteration of the immediate consequence operator T. This is established by calculating the difference (in absolute value) between the sizes of the parameters for each predicate in the first iteration of the operator, and the rest of the iterations. Given this definition, several arguments could be iteration parameters. In this case, only one of them will be chosen. The program predicates in Figure 1 only have an input argument, and so this is the iteration parameter.

Now we can calculate the computational and communication cost of the program in Figure 1.

$$T_{append}(n) = 1 + T_{append}(n - 1) \qquad\qquad T_{append}(0) = 1$$

If this recurrence equation is solved then $T_{append}(n) = n + 1$ is obtained, where n represents the size of the iteration parameter of the predicate *append*.

$$T_{nrev}(n) = 1 + T_{append}(n - 1) + T_{nrev}(n - 1) \qquad T_{nrev}(0) = 1$$

After resolving the recurrence equation, $T_{nrev}(n) = \dfrac{n^2 + 3n + 2}{2}$ is obtained, where n represents the size of the iteration parameter of *nrev*.

Finally, with this information, it is possible to carry out the compile time granularity analysis in the way explained in section 1. We assume that the mode analysis presented in Figure 2 has been previously carried out.

$$F_T{}^{\mathcal{C}}(nrev1)\,(n) = 1 \qquad\qquad F_T{}^{\mathcal{C}}(append)\,(n) = \frac{2n}{n^2 + 3n + 2}$$

$$F_T{}^{\mathcal{C}}(nrev2)\,(n) = \frac{n^2 + 3n + 2}{(n-1)^2 + 3(n-1) + 2}$$

The communication cost is calculated by using the size of the variables shared by the processes which are explicit in the mode analysis:

$$F_C{}^{\mathcal{C}}(nrev1,nrev2)(n) = n - 1 \qquad\qquad F_C{}^{\mathcal{C}}(nrev1,append)(n) = 1$$

$$F_C{}^{\mathcal{C}}(nrev2,append)(n) = n - 1 \qquad\qquad F_C{}^{\mathcal{C}}(append,nrev1)(n) = n$$

4.1. A possible improvement of the cost analysis

In general, the predicates of a program consists of several clauses. This means that some measurements must be carried out to obtain the total cost of the predicates. One possibility is to consider the average sum of the costs of each predicate clause. However, the measure obtained in this way can be very imprecise if the clauses display very different behaviours.

Let us suppose, for example, that a predicate is formed by two clauses, one of them with linear cost, and the other one with exponential cost. Obviously, a very imprecise measure is obtained if we only consider the average of both costs when the first clause is committed to continue an execution.

Sometimes the programmer places particular constants in the arguments of the predicate clauses to direct the execution of a program. In this case, the above mentioned problem can be more efficiently solved because the value of these constants can be used to identify the selected clause during execution. Let us consider the following example:

> list_processing(reverse,L,RL):-   list_processing(empty_list,L,EL):-
>   nrev(L,RL).   empty_list(L,EL).
> list_processing(sort,L,SL):-   empty_list([],X):- X = true
>   qsort(L,SL).   empty_list([_|_],X):- X = false.
> list_processing(reverse,L,RL):-
>   nrev(L,RL).

The execution cost of the predicate *list_processing* depends strongly on the constant placed in the first argument. If the constant *reverse* is provided to *list_processing*, the execution cost is the one obtained previously. However, if the constant *empty_list* arrives, the execution cost is constant.

The abstract interpretation defined in section 3 can be modified to integrate this new information. This can be simply done by keeping visible those constants having the meaning previously mentioned. So, the new abstract domain would be: $D = \{1\} \cup Var \cup Const \cup (\bigcup_{n \geq 0} D^n)$ and the abstraction function is defined in order to make two abstract terms equivalent only if the special constants are placed exactly in the same term positions. This work is developed in [7].

Given this new domain, we associate a family of computational cost functions to each predicate (instead of associating one function only). Each function will correspond to a predicate clause. During execution, depending on the value of the constant, a clause will be chosen and the associated computational cost function will indicate the cost of this reduction with more precision.

5 Application of the analysis

We now show how to transform a concurrent logic program into a distributed program using the analysis developed here. The idea consists in implementing a static and a dynamic scheduler using the information given by the static granularity analysis.

The static scheduler will analyze every program clause and will annotate the body atoms which could be moved to remote processors during the program execution because its computation cost is high. Also, the body of the clauses will be augmented with a new atom called the dynamic scheduler. There will be a different dynamic scheduler in every clause. The role of this atom is to evaluate the computational and communication cost functions of the clause body atoms using the data size known in runtime. With this information the dynamic scheduler will decide if the annotated atoms have to be moved to remote processors, taking into account a constant dependent on the system. To illustrate the transformation we utilize the quicksort program:

$qsort([],L):- L = [].$
$qsort([X|Xs],Y):-$
  $split(Xs,X,L,G),$
  $qsort(L,SL), qsort(G,SG),$
  $append(SL,[X|SG],Y).$

$qsort([],L):- L = [].$
$qsort([X|Xs],Y):-$
  $split(Xs,X,L,G),$
  $qsort(L,SL) @ node(V_1),$
  $qsort(G,SG) @ node(V_2),$
  $append(SL,[X|SG],Y),$
  $qsort\_scheduler(V_1,V_2,U,DataSize).$

$qsort\_scheduler(V_1,V_2,U,DataSize):-$

  $--$ *V_1 will be bound to a remote node if the relation between the*
  $--$ *communication and computational costs and the system dependent*
  $--$ *constant U implies that the distribution of qsort(L,SL) will*
  $--$ *improve the execution.*

We assume that the *split* and *append* code is not modified by the transformation. The static scheduler will deduce the relation between the clause cost and the costs of the body atoms. As the two body atoms *qsort* have the same cost function, the scheduler will annotate these two atoms indicating that any of them may be distributed during the execution. The new body atom scheduler will distribute one atom *qsort* if the relation between the computational and communication cost, calculated taking into account the data size *DataSize*, does not exceed the system dependent constant U. The distribution simply consists in binding the variables V_1 and V_2 to the processor where the corresponding atoms must be executed.

6 Conclusions and future work

This paper presents a general framework for analyzing the granularity of concurrent logic languages. The method mainly contains two analyses: a mode analysis and a type analysis. This latter analysis is used to obtain the size relations between the atom terms. We develop the algorithm which provides this.

We are implementing an environment which includes this approach to obtain information about the grain size in concurrent logic languages like KL1. It has been shown that the use of abstract interpretation is of high interest due to the possibility of combining different analyses with a common technique to generate non-trivial information. Finally, we are studying the set of programs that can be definitely analyzed with our method. The improvement that appears in Section 4.1 may increase the utility of the approach.

References

[1] Barbuti R., R. Giacobazzi, G. Levi. *A General Framework for Semantics-Based Bottom-up Abstract Interpretation of Logic Programs*. ACM Transactions on Programming Languages and Systems vol 15, nº 1, January 1993. Pages 133-181

[2] Bruynooghe M. *A Practical Framework for the Abstract Interpretation of Logic Programs*. Journal of Logic Programming 10(2):91-124 (Feb. 1991)

[3] Cortesi, A., Le Charlier, B., Van Hentenryck, P. 1994. *Combinations of abstract domains for logic programming*. In proceedings of the 21st ACM Symposium on Principles of Programming Languages.

[4] Cousot P., R. Cousot. *Abstract interpretation: A Unified Lattice Model for Static Analysis of Programs by Construction or Approximation of Fixpoints*. Proc. 4th Ann. ACM Symp. Principles of Programming Languages, Los Angeles, California (1977) 238-252.

[5] Debray S.K., N-W Lin. *Cost Analysis of Logic Programs*. ACM Transactions on Programming Languages and Systems Vol 15 N° 5. November 1993. Pages 826-875

[6] Debray S.K., N-W Lin, M. Hermenegildo. *Task Granularity Analysis in Logic Programs*. In Proc. of the 1990 ACM Conf. on Programming Language Design and Implementation, pg. 174-188. ACM Press, June 1990.

[7] Gallardo M., J. M. Troya. *Parlog Programs Non-termination Analysis*. Eighth Conference on Logic Programming. Guizzeria, Italy.(1993)

[8] Gallardo M., J. M. Troya. *Granularity Analysis of Concurrent Logic Languages based on Abstract Interpretation*. In Proceedings of the Joint Conference GulpProde94.

[9] Ichiyoshi, N., Mitazaki T., Taki K., *A distributed implementation of Flat GHC on the Multi-PSI*. Logic programming: Proc. of the 4th Int. Conf., MIT Press, 1987.

[10] King A., P. Soper. *Schedule Analysis of Concurrent Logic Programs*. Proceedings of the Joint International Conference and Symposium on Logic Programming. Apt Editor 1992.

[11] King A., P. Soper. *Granularity Analysis of Concurrent Logic Programs*. In the fifth International Symposium on Computer and Information Sciences, Nevsehir, Cappadocia, Turkey.

[12] King, A. 1994. *Depth-k sharing and freeness*. In Proceedings of the 11th International Conference on Logic Progrmming. MIT Press, Cambridge, Mass., 553-568.

[13] Mellish C. S. *Abstract Interpretation of Prolog Programs*. Third International Conference on Logic Programming, n. 225 Lecture Notes in Computer Science. Imperial College, Springer-Verlg, July 1986.

[14] Sarkar V. *Partitioning and Scheduling Parallel Programs for Multiprocessors*. MIT Press, Cambridge MA, 1989.

[16] Tick E. *Compile-time Granularity Analyisis for Parallel Logic Programming*. Proceeding of the International Conference on fifth generation computer system.

[17] Ueda K., *Guarded Horn Clauses*. Ph. D. Thesis, Graduate School, University of Tolyo, 1986.

[18] Warren R., M. Hermenegildo, S. Debray. *On the Practicality of Global Flow Analysis of Logic Programs*. Fifth International Conference and Symposium on Logic Programming. MIT Press, August 1988.

[19] Zhong X., E. Tick, S. Durvuru, A. Hansen, A.V.S. Sastry, R. Dudararajan, *Towards and Efficient Compile-Time Analysis Algorithm*. Proceedings of the International Conference on fifth Generation Computer Systems, 1992. Ed ICOT.

Towards Automatic Control
for CLP(χ) Programs

Fred Mesnard

Iremia, Université de la Réunion
15, avenue René Cassin - BP 7151 - 97 715 Saint-Denis Messag. Cedex 9
France
fred@univ-reunion.fr

Abstract. We discuss issues of control for constraint logic programs. The problem we try to solve is to find, from the text of a program, a computation rule which ensures finiteness of the computation tree. In a single framework, we address two related areas, namely the generation of control annotations and the local level of control for partial deduction.

1 Introduction

We discuss issues of control for constraint logic programs [9], [3], [10]. It is well known that for the same goal, one computation rule can give rise to a finite computation tree and another one to an infinite computation tree. So the problem we try to solve is how to find, from the text of a program, a computation rule which ensures finiteness of the computation tree. In a single framework, we address two related areas, namely the generation of control annotations and the local level of control for partial deduction (see [13] for a discussion of local versus global level of control).

The paper is organized as follows: Sect. 2 justifies the switch to $\mathcal{Q}^+$. In Sect. 3, we briefly discuss the derivation of interargument relations. Then we focus on the inference of control information in Sect. 4. Section 5 presents a class of computation rules, which can lifted to the original computation domain (Sect. 6). At last, we summarize our approach, compare it with related work and conclude by sketching possible extensions of the proposed method in Sect. 7.

2 From CLP(χ) to CLP($\mathcal{Q}^+$)

The first step in the approach we propose is to switch from χ to $\mathcal{Q}^+$ by using an approximation A which consists in an algebraic morphism associated to a syntactic transformation. (By $\mathcal{Q}^+$, we mean the structure $\langle \mathbb{Q}^+; \{0, 1, +\}; \{=, \geq\}\rangle$ where $\mathbb{Q}^+$ denotes the set of non-negative rational numbers). The approximation A captures a notion of size for the elements of χ. We now define more precisely what we call an approximation.

Let $\chi = \langle D_\chi; F_\chi; \{=_\chi\} \cup C_\chi \rangle$ where D_χ is the domain of χ, F_χ is a set of functions and C_χ a set of relations, be a solution-compact structure without any limit element [10]. Let $\psi = \langle D_\psi; F_\psi; \{=_\psi\} \cup C_\psi \rangle$ be another solution-compact structure.

Definition 1. An *approximation* A consists in a pair of functions $\langle A_{sx}, A_{sm} \rangle$ where:

1. A_{sx} is a mapping from $F_\chi \cup \{=_\chi\} \cup C_\chi$ to $F_\psi \cup \{=_\psi\} \cup C_\psi$ such that:
   (a) for every function or relation symbol s, $arity(s) = arity(A_{sx}(s))$;
   (b) $A_{sx}(F_\chi) \subseteq F_\psi$;
   (c) $A_{sx}(=_\chi) = =_\psi$;
   (d) $A_{sx}(C_\chi) \subseteq C_\psi$.
2. A_{sm} is a mapping from D_χ to D_ψ such that for every $\widetilde{e_\chi} \in \widetilde{D_\chi}$:
   (a) for every function f_χ, $A_{sm}(f_\chi(\widetilde{e_\chi})) =_\psi A_{sx}(f_\chi)(A_{sm}(\widetilde{e_\chi}))$;
   (b) for every relation c_χ, if $\models_\chi c_\chi(\widetilde{e_\chi})$ then $\models_\psi A_{sx}(c_\chi)(A_{sm}(\widetilde{e_\chi}))$.

Example 1. Let $List(\chi) = \langle D_\chi^*; \{<>\} \cup \bigcup_{e \in D_\chi} \{< e >\} \cup \{\cdot\}; \{=_{List(\chi)}\} \rangle$ where the constant $<>$ denotes the empty list, the constants $< e >$ denote the lists $< e >$ and $\cdot$ is the concatenation of lists. We define the approximation A from $List(\chi)$ to Q^+:

$$A_{sx}(<>) = 0, \ A_{sx}(< e >) = 1, \ A_{sx}(\cdot) = + \ and \ A_{sm}(< e_1, \ldots, e_n >) = n.$$

One verifies that $A = \langle A_{sx}, A_{sm} \rangle$ satisfies the definition 1.

Let V be a denumerable set of variables and P be a finite set of predicate symbols. The set of *terms, constraints, atoms, programs, goals* are defined as usual. If we extend A_{sx} on $V \cup P$ with $A_{sx}(x) = x$ (resp. $A_{sx}(p) = p$) for every variable x (resp. for every predicate symbol p), then A may be naturally extended on terms, constraints, atoms, programs and goals.

Example 2. Consider the CLP(List(χ)) program P:

$$p(< x_1, x_2, x_3, x_4, x_5 >, < x_5, x_4, x_3, x_2, x_1 >, <>) \leftarrow \diamond$$
$$p(< x_1, x_2 > .x, y. < y_1 > .y, < y_1 > .z) \leftarrow \diamond p(y, x.x. < x_1, y_1, x_2 >, z)$$

Here is its approximation $A(P)$ in CLP(Q^+):

$$p(5, 5, 0) \leftarrow \diamond$$
$$p(x + 2, 2y + 1, z + 1) \leftarrow \diamond p(y, 2x + 3, z)$$

For a more rigorous treatment and some properties of approximations (e.g. $A(M_P) \subseteq M_{A(P)}$), we refer the reader to [14]. The original idea of such mappings was already present in [21] and developed in [2].

Let us go back to our main subject. The following result gives a first justification for switching to Q^+: termination in Q^+ implies termination in $List(\chi)$.

Theorem 2. *Let A be an approximation from CLP(χ) to CLP(ψ), P a CLP(χ) program and $A(P)$ its approximation, G a goal and $A(G)$ its approximation, R_2 a computation rule for CLP(ψ). If the $(A(P), R_2)$-computation tree for $A(G)$ is finite, then the $(P, R_2 \circ A)$-computation tree for G is finite.*

Note that in Theorem 2, $R_2 \circ A$ means that we first abstract the goal, then choose a literal, denoted by its rank in the goal (cf definition 8) using R_2. So $R_2 \circ A$ is indeed a computation rule for $CLP(\chi)$. Moreover, because of condition 2(b) of definition 1, a branch of the $(P, R_2 \circ A)$-computation tree for G may lead to a failure node, though its corresponding branch in $CLP(\psi)$ may be longer and lead to a success node. A proof of Theorem 2 is given in [14].

A second justification for choosing Q^+ instead of $\mathcal{N} = \langle \text{IN}; \{0, 1, +\}; \{=, \geq\}\rangle$ lies in the fact that many problems are much easier to solve in Q^+ than in $\mathcal{N}$. We believe that the achieved efficiency largely outweighs the loss in accuracy.

3 Inference of Interargument Relations

For termination analysis, it is essential to have information about the relationship between between the sizes of the arguments of a predicate (see for instance the examples 5 and 6 of Sect. 4). In the logic programming framework, the research devoted to the derivation of interargument relations (IR) begun with [20] and is nicely summarized in [5]. We just mention some of the main results obtained so far.

In [22], the authors show how one may compute by abstract interpretation IR's of the form: $\forall(x_1, \ldots, x_n) \, p(x_1, \ldots, x_n) \rightarrow \bigwedge_{1 \leq j \leq m} \left[\sum_{1 \leq i \leq n} c_i^j x_i = k^j\right]$.

In [6], the class of "3-recursive" $CLP(\mathcal{Z})$ logic procedures is defined as follows:

$$p(\tilde{x}) \leftarrow \xi(\tilde{x}) \diamond$$
$$p(\tilde{x} + \tilde{a}) \leftarrow \Phi_1(\tilde{x}) \diamond p(\tilde{x})$$
$$p(\tilde{x} + \tilde{b}) \leftarrow \Phi_2(\tilde{x}) \diamond p(\tilde{x})$$
$$p(\tilde{x} + \tilde{c}) \leftarrow \Phi_3(\tilde{x}) \diamond p(\tilde{x})$$

where $\tilde{a}$, $\tilde{b}$ and $\tilde{c}$ are vectors of integers, $\xi(\tilde{x}), \Phi_1(\tilde{x}), \Phi_2(\tilde{x})$ and $\Phi_3(\tilde{x})$ are finite linear arithmetic constraints. Such a procedure p can be *exactly* characterized by a finite disjunction of arithmetic constraints. The authors have enumerated all the 512 cases, and for each case, they have computed the characterization. As a consequence, the computational cost of the inference of the meaning of a 3-recursive procedure is almost constant.

In [18], for the class of "linear recursive logic programs satisfying the translativeness property", a technique is presented which enables the derivation of IR's in the form of polyhedral convex sets.

At last, we require that the inferred IR's are added as constraints to the original program P, which leads to a specialized version P_{spec} of P. Note that as the IR's are logical consequences of the least model of P, we preserve the meaning of P (i.e. $M_P = M_{P_{spec}}$).

4 Inference of Control Information

A basic idea for termination relies on associating to every recursive predicate a measure which decreases at each recursive call. For sake of simplicity, we disallow mutually recursive procedures, i.e. we assume that the transitive closure of the dependency graph D_P (see the definition 11 in the appendix) of the program P is antisymmetric.

Definition 3. A *measure* $\mu = (\mu_1, \ldots, \mu_n)$ where the $\mu'_i s \in \mathbb{Q}^+$ is a mapping from $(\mathbb{Q}^+)^n$ to $\mathbb{Q}^+$ such that: $\forall (a_1, \ldots, a_n) \in (\mathbb{Q}^+)^n \quad \mu(a_1, \ldots, a_n) = \sum_{i=1}^{n} \mu_i a_i$.

For a recursive predicate p of P, we are interested in measures which effectively decreases in the least model M_P of P, i.e. we need a link with the semantics of p.

Definition 4. A measure μ_p associated to a recursive predicate p is *valid* if for each clause $p(\tilde{t}) \leftarrow c \diamond \tilde{B}$ defining p in P, for each solution θ of c such that $\tilde{B}\theta \in M_P$, for each atom $p(\tilde{s})$ appearing in $\tilde{B}$, we have: $\mu_p(\tilde{t}\theta) \geq \mu_p(\tilde{s}\theta) + 1$.

Example 3. $\mu_p^1 = (2, 1, 0)$ *and* $\mu_p^2 = (0, 0, 1)$ *are valid measures for the approximated version of the program defined in example 2 because:* $\forall(x, y, z) \in (\mathbb{Q}^+)^3, 2x + 4 + 2y + 1 \geq 2y + 2x + 3 + 1$ *and* $\forall z \in \mathbb{Q}^+, z + 1 \geq z + 1$.

However, we have to weaken definition 4, in order to automate the computation of measures.

Definition 5. A measure μ_p associated to a recursive predicate p is *t-valid* (t for textually) if for each clause $p(\tilde{t}) \leftarrow c \diamond \tilde{B}$ defining p in P, for each solution θ of c, for each atom $p(\tilde{s})$ appearing in $\tilde{B}$, we have: $\mu_p(\tilde{t}\theta) \geq \mu_p(\tilde{s}\theta) + 1$.

Example 4. *In example 3, we have in fact shown that* μ_p^1 *and* μ_p^2 *are t-valid measures for p, but :*

Proposition 6. *If* μ_p *is t-valid for p, then* μ_p *is valid for p.*

Of course, the converse is false.

Example 5. The measure $\mu_q = (1)$ *is valid q:*

$$q(1) \leftarrow \diamond$$
$$q(2x) \leftarrow \diamond q(x)$$

because $q(x) \in M_q$ *implies* $x \geq 1$ *but* μ_q *is not t-valid. The non-recursive clauses are indirectly useful to termination analysis: they enable the derivation of inter-argument relations which should be added to the program before computing valid measures. In our example, it gives:*

$$q(1) \leftarrow \diamond$$
$$q(2x) \leftarrow x \geq 1 \diamond q(x)$$

Now $\mu_q = (1)$ *is t-valid.*

Automatic discovery of t-valid measures is a consequence of a result of [19]:

Theorem 7. *There exists a complete polynomial procedure for deciding the existence of a t-valid measure for any logic procedure defined using a single predicate symbol.*

This procedure, based on the duality theorem of linear programming (see [19]), can be adapted to compute the coefficients of μ [14]. For a more general logic procedure p where $r_1, \ldots, r_n$ appears in the definition of p, we abstract the meaning of each r_i by a constraint supposed to be the "most precise rational superset" of the meaning of r_i, and then we apply Theorem 7.

Example 6. Consider the following program P:

$$p(0) \leftarrow \diamond$$
$$p(x) \leftarrow \diamond r(x, y), p(y)$$
$$r(x + u, 0) \leftarrow 3 \geq u \geq 1 \diamond$$
$$r(x + 1, y + 1) \leftarrow \diamond r(x, y)$$

Let us assume that we are interested in finding a valid measure for p and that we have inferred : $\forall x \in \mathbb{Q}^+ [p(x) \Rightarrow x \geq 0]$ and $\forall (x, y) \in (\mathbb{Q}^+)^2 [r(x, y) \Rightarrow x \geq y + 1]$. We first specialize P into P_{spec}:

$$p(0) \leftarrow \diamond$$
$$p(x) \leftarrow x \geq y + 1 \diamond r(x, y), p(y)$$
$$r(x + u, 0) \leftarrow 3 \geq u \geq 1 \diamond$$
$$r(x + 1, y + 1) \leftarrow x \geq y + 1 \diamond r(x, y)$$

Then we forget r, which gives P' :

$$p'(0) \leftarrow \diamond$$
$$p'(x) \leftarrow x \geq y + 1 \diamond p'(y)$$

Roughly speaking, the least model of P' is generally a superset of the least model of P_{spec}. Then we compute (Theorem 7) $\mu_{p'} = (1)$, which is t-valid for P' and t-valid for P_{spec}.

We conclude that on the one hand, the notion of validity refers directly to the semantics of the program. On the other hand, the notion of t-validity refers to the text of the program but remains computable.

5 An Extended Resolution for CLP($\mathcal{Q}^+$)

The operational semantics we intend is an extension of the standard top-down execution of CLP. The computation tree can be incomplete by having any goal as a leaf and the computation rule uses and updates a history of the computation. Let us be more precise.

Let c (resp. t) be a constraint (resp. a term) of CLP($\mathcal{Q}^+$). *Min(c;t)* denotes the least (rational) value of t in c. *Bounded(c;t)* is true iff the set of values for t in c is bounded by a (rational) number. Let P be a program which defines a set π of predicate symbols. Let Rec be the subset of π denoting the recursive procedures of P. Let V be a countable set of variables. Let At be the set of atoms defined using π, $\{0,1,+\}$ and V. A *supervised atom* is a pair $\langle p(\bar{t}), m \rangle$ where $p(\bar{t}) \in At$ and $m \in \mathbb{Q}^+$. The set of all supervised atoms is denoted by $SupAt$ and its powerset by 2^{SupAt}. Finally, let $Hist \in 2^{SupAt}$ and RES be the set of all resolvents.

Definition 8. An *extended computation rule* (ecr) $R : RES \times 2^{SupAt} \to \mathbb{N} \times 2^{SupAt}$ verifies:

1. $R(\leftarrow c \diamond, Hist) = \langle 0, Hist \rangle$
2. $R(\leftarrow c \diamond A_1, \ldots, A_{n+1}, Hist) = \langle i, Hist' \rangle$ with $0 \leq i \leq n + 1$.

Definition 9. Given a goal G and an extended computation rule R, the *extended computation tree* $\tau_{G,R}$ is the smallest tree such that:

1. $\langle G, \phi \rangle$ is the root of $\tau_{G,R}$,
2. if $\langle G', Hist' \rangle$ is a node such that $R(G', Hist') = \langle 0, Hist' \rangle$ then $\langle G', Hist' \rangle$ is a leaf,
3. if $\langle G', H' \rangle$ is a node where $G' = \leftarrow c \diamond A_1, \ldots, A_i, \ldots, A_{n+1}$ and $R(G', H') = \langle i, H'' \rangle$ with $i \geq 1$ then the node has a child $\langle \leftarrow c \diamond A_1, \ldots, \tilde{B}, \ldots, A_{n+1}, H'' \rangle$ for each clause of P: $Head \leftarrow c' \diamond \tilde{B}$ such that $c, c', A_i = Head$ is satisfiable. Moreover, each atom of $\tilde{B}$ with the same predicate symbol as A_i is marked as **checked**.

We are now in position to define the class $\mathcal{R}$ of ecr's we are interested in, parameterized by a function $SelectAtom : RES \times 2^{SupAt} \to \mathbb{N}$ which has to satisfy the postcondition $0 \leq SelectAtom(\leftarrow c \diamond A_1, \ldots, A_k) \leq k$ (see Fig. 1).

So $ExtendedComputationRule$ provides a shell which uses and computes histories. The idea is that it divides G into non-recursive and recursive atoms, which in turn is divided into checked, bounded and unbounded atoms. If an unbounded atom is selected, then it adds the atom and its current minimum value for its measure to the history. In any case, it checks that unfolding the selected atom is allowed wrt the updated history. Note that once a function $SelectAtom$ has been chosen, which may embody various heuristics criteria, we hold a particular ecr which satisfies the definition 8. Moreover, any ecr of $\mathcal{R}$ ensures termination.

Theorem 10. *Let P be a $CLP(\mathcal{Q}^+)$ program such that its dependency graph is antisymmetric. Assume that a valid measure is associated with each recursive predicate. Let R be an extended computation rule $\in \mathcal{R}$. Then for any goal G, the extended computation tree $\tau_{G,R}$ is finite.*

The proof is given in the appendix. We propose two particular ecr's which illustrate the range of $\mathcal{R}$.

If $SelectAtom$ chooses the leftmost atom $\in NR \cup C \cup B$, then we don't need to compute and check the history before we allow this choice (see the proof

$ExtendedComputationRule(G, H) =$
let $\ i = SelectAtom(G, H)$
in $\ \ $ if $i = 0$ then $\langle 0, H \rangle$
$\quad$ else
$\qquad$ let $\ G = \leftarrow c \diamond p_1(\tilde{t}_1), \ldots, p_{k+1}(\tilde{t}_{k+1})$
$\qquad\qquad NR = \{j \mid 1 \leq j \leq k+1, p_j \notin Rec\}$
$\qquad\qquad R = \{j \mid 1 \leq j \leq k+1, p_j \in Rec\}$
$\qquad\qquad C = \{j \mid j \in R, p_j(\tilde{t}_j) \text{ is marked as checked }\}$
$\qquad\qquad B = \{j \mid j \in R \setminus C, Bounded(c; \mu_{p_j}(\tilde{t}_j))\}$
$\qquad\qquad U = \{j \mid j \in R \setminus (B \cup C)\}$
$$\left\{ \begin{array}{l} p_i(\tilde{h}_1) \leftarrow c_1 \diamond \ldots \\ \phantom{p_i(\tilde{h}_1)} \vdots \qquad\qquad\qquad \text{the n clauses of } P \text{ defining } p_i \\ p_i(\tilde{h}_n) \leftarrow c_n \diamond \ldots \end{array} \right.$$
$\qquad\qquad H' = $ if $i \in U$ then $H \cup \{\langle p_i(\tilde{t}_i), Min(c, \mu_{p_i}(\tilde{t}_i)) \rangle\}$
$\qquad\qquad\qquad$ else H
$\qquad\qquad stop = \exists j, 1 \leq j \leq n, \exists \langle q(\tilde{s}), m \rangle \in H',$
$\qquad\qquad\qquad\qquad m < Min(c, c_j, \tilde{t}_i = \tilde{h}_j; \mu_q(\tilde{s}))$
$\quad$ in
$\qquad\qquad$ if $stop$ then $\langle 0, H \rangle$
$\qquad\qquad$ else $\langle i, H' \rangle$

Fig. 1. The function $ExtendedComputationRule$.

of Theorem 10). As a consequence, *such an extended computation rule can be directly wired in a CLP system with a delay primitive.* A complete example is presented in Sect. 6.

On the other end of the scale, we may unfold as much as possible by selecting an atom $\in NR \cup C \cup B$ such that *stop* remains false. We postpone as far as we can the selection of atoms $\in U$ because it implies an increase of the history which potentially refrains the unfolding.

To conclude, it seems reasonable to mix the approaches in a *two-level top-down execution* as follows. Given a goal, we prove it using directly the CLP system with a delay primitive. If there are remaining frozen goals, and if the user agrees, we may unfold them using a meta-interpreter with a smarter ecr as explained above. We call R_{ext} such an ecr.

6   Back to CLP(χ)

We now present a complete example which sketches how one might come back to the original domain of computation. Consider the CLP($\mathbb{Q}, List(\mathbb{Q})$) program:

$sort(<>, <>) \leftarrow \diamond$

$$sort(< x > .y, z) \leftarrow \diamond sort(y, t), insert(t, x, z)$$

$$insert(<>, x, < x >) \leftarrow \diamond$$
$$insert(< x > .y, w, < w, x > .y) \leftarrow w \leq x \diamond$$
$$insert(< x > .y, w, < x > .z) \leftarrow w > x \diamond insert(y, w, z)$$

First, we approximate it in CLP($\mathcal{Q}^+$):

$$sort(0, 0) \leftarrow \diamond$$
$$sort(y + 1, z) \leftarrow \diamond sort(y, t), insert(t, -, z)$$

$$insert(0, -, 1) \leftarrow \diamond$$
$$insert(y + 1, -, y + 2) \leftarrow \diamond$$
$$insert(y + 1, -, z + 1) \leftarrow \diamond insert(y, -, z)$$

Second, inference of interargument relations may conclude that:

$$\forall(y, z) \in (\mathbb{Q}^+)^2 \, insert(y, -, z) \Rightarrow z = y + 1$$
$$\forall(x, y) \in (\mathbb{Q}^+)^2 \, sort(x, y) \Rightarrow x = y$$

We add the information to the program:

$$sort(0, 0) \leftarrow \diamond$$
$$sort(y + 1, z) \leftarrow z = t + 1, y = t \diamond sort(y, t), insert(t, -, z)$$

$$insert(0, -, 1) \leftarrow \diamond$$
$$insert(y + 1, -, y + 2) \leftarrow \diamond$$
$$insert(y + 1, -, z + 1) \leftarrow z = y + 1 \diamond insert(y, -, z)$$

Third, we compute the valid measures for $sort$ and $insert$:

$$\mu^1_{insert}(x, -, z) = (1, 0, 0) \text{ and } \mu^2_{insert}(x, -, z) = (0, 0, 1)$$
$$\mu^1_{sort}(x, y) = (1, 0) \text{ and } \mu^2_{sort}(x, y) = (0, 1)$$

Note that it is useless at this point to try to infer new interargument relations. Fourth, we lift to the original program either by relating lists to their length, e.g. $\mu^1_{insert}(x, -, z) = l$ where $x :: l$ and using R_{ext} (see the end of Sect. 5) or by compiling the valid measures we found (such a compilation can be easily automated):

$$sort(x, y) \leftarrow x :: l, y :: l \diamond freeze(l, sort'(x, y))$$
$$sort'(<>, <>) \leftarrow \diamond$$
$$sort'(< x > .y, z) \leftarrow y :: l, t :: l, z :: l + 1 \diamond sort'(y, t), insert(t, x, z)$$

$$insert(x, y, z) \leftarrow x :: l, z :: l + 1 \diamond freeze(l, ins'(x, y, z))$$
$$ins'(<>, x, < x >) \leftarrow \diamond$$
$$ins'(< x > .y, w, < w, x > .y) \leftarrow w \leq x \diamond$$
$$ins'(< x > .y, w, < x > .z) \leftarrow y :: l, z :: l + 1, w > x \diamond ins'(y, w, z)$$

The proof of any query about $sort$ and $insert$ on a CLP system with the $freeze$ primitive will stop. For instance:

$$> 1 < x < y \diamond sort(n, n), insert(l, x + 1, m),$$
$$insert(m, 4y, n), sort(l, < 2y, 3x + 1 >);$$
$$\{1 < x < y, 2y \leq 3x + 1, n =< x + 1, 2y, 3x + 1, 4y >,$$
$$l =< 2y, 3x + 1 >, m =< x + 1, 2y, 3x + 1 >\}$$
$$>$$

7 Discussion

Let us first summarize our approach for the control of a CLP(χ) program P.

1. We abstract P to $A(P)$ in CLP(Q^+).
2. We compute interargument relations and add them to $A(P)$
3. We compute the valid measures for $A(P)$.
4. We lift to CLP(χ) either by compiling the measures in order to prove the queries directly with the underlying CLP system or we explicitly run a meta-interpreter based on the extended resolution of Sect. 5.

Before we discuss related work, we point out that our approach can be extended by allowing multiple valid measures for a procedure and mutual recursion.

Termination. Of course we owe a lot to the works on compile-time termination analysis of logic programs. This research begun with [20], [16] and [21]. Once again, we refer the reader to the survey of D. De Schreye and S. Decorte [5]. But we believe that there is no essential difference between termination and local control for partial deduction. Moreover, as most constraint logic programming systems supply a delay primitive, termination analysis should not rely so much on the left-to-right computation rule. We briefly come back to this point at the end of this section.

Automatic control generation. In [15], Naish presents a technique for deriving wait-declarations from the text of the program. However, termination is not guaranteed. Later he notices that non-linearity (when a variable appears more than once in a goal) may lead to non-termination of annotated programs (also true for [11]). Consider the program:

$$append(<>, y, y) \leftarrow \diamond$$
$$append(< x_1 > .x, y, < x_1 > .z) \leftarrow \diamond append(x, y, z)$$

where a call to $append(x, y, z)$ is delayed until $nonvar(x)$ or $nonvar(z)$. It is for instance the DELAY control declaration given for $append$ in the module for lists processing of the Gödel programming language [8]. The proof of the goal $G :\leftarrow \diamond append(< x_1 > .x, y, x)$ does not terminate.

Using our technique, we compute the interargument relation for the approximated version of append: $append(x, y, z) \Rightarrow z = x+y$ and the two valid measures: $\mu^1_{append} = (1, 0, 0)$ and $\mu^2_{append} = (0, 0, 1)$. Then we compile this knowledge to obtain:

$$append(x, y, z) \leftarrow x :: l_x, y :: l_y, z :: l_z, l_z = l_x + l_y \diamond$$
$$freeze(l_x, once(v, append'(x, y, z))),$$
$$freeze(l_z, once(v, append'(x, y, z)))$$
$$append'(<>, y, y) \leftarrow \diamond$$
$$append'(< x_1 > .x, y, < x_1 > .z) \leftarrow \diamond append'(x, y, z)$$

$$once(v, G) \leftarrow \diamond free(v), !, eq(v, cst), G$$
$$once(v, G) \leftarrow \diamond$$

Now the proof of the goal $\leftarrow \diamond append(< x_1 > .x, y, x)$ fails because the constraint $< x_1 > .x :: 1 + l_x, y :: l_y, x :: l_x, l_x = 1 + l_x + l_y$ is unsatisfiable.

Local control in partial deduction. Ensuring finite unfolding is one of the problems of partial deduction. Various ad hoc solutions, e.g. imposing an arbitrary depth bound to the derivations, have been proposed, which obviously do not really address the problem. Our technique is firmly based on the criterion established in [1]. The first difference is that we directly move to the CLP(Q^+). It allows a smooth integration of interargument relations, and makes the implementation easier and more efficient. The major improvement is that we rely on the concept of valid measures, related to the semantics of the program, to control the unfolding. We illustrate this point. Consider the program given in example 2.
The unfolding of the goal $G: \leftarrow \diamond p(7, 9, z)$ gives:

$$G_1 : \langle \leftarrow \diamond p(7, 9, z); \phi \rangle$$
$$G_2 : \langle \leftarrow z = z_1 + 1 \diamond p(4, 13, z_1); \phi \rangle$$
$$G_3 : \langle \leftarrow z = z_2 + 2 \diamond p(6, 7, z_2); \phi \rangle$$
$$G_4 : \langle \leftarrow z = z_3 + 3 \diamond p(3, 11, z_3); \phi \rangle$$
$$G_5 : \langle \leftarrow z = z_4 + 4 \diamond p(5, 5, z_4); \phi \rangle$$
$$G_6 : \langle \leftarrow z = 4 \diamond; \phi \rangle$$

because the valid measure $\mu_p^1(x, y, z) = 2x + y$ is bounded for G. As the first argument increases from G_2 to G_3, the second argument and the sum of the two arguments increase from G_1 to G_2, and the minimum value of the third argument remains 0, the partial deduction process as described in [1] stops at G_3.
The unfolding of the goal $G' :\leftarrow \diamond p(x + 7, y + 9, z)$ under μ_p^1 gives :

$$G_1 : \langle \leftarrow \diamond p(x + 7, y + 9, z); \phi \rangle$$
$$G_2 : \langle \leftarrow z = z_1 + 1 \diamond p(y/2 + 4, 2x + 13, z_1); \{\langle p(x + 7, y + 9, z_1 + 1), 23 \rangle\} \rangle$$
$$G_3 : \langle \leftarrow z = z_2 + 2 \diamond p(x + 6, y + 7, z_2); \{\langle p(x + 7, y + 9, z_2 + 2), 23 \rangle\} \rangle$$
$$G_4 : \langle \leftarrow z = z_3 + 3 \diamond p(y/2 + 3, 2x + 11, z_3); \{\langle p(x + 7, y + 9, z_3 + 3), 23 \rangle\} \rangle$$
$$G_5 : \langle \leftarrow z = z_4 + 4 \diamond p(x + 5, y + 5, z_4); \{\langle p(x + 7, y + 9, z_4 + 4), 23 \rangle\} \rangle$$
$$G_6 : \langle \leftarrow x = 0, y = 0, z = 4 \diamond; \{\langle p(x + 7, y + 9, 4), 23 \rangle\} \rangle$$

or

$$G_7 : \langle \leftarrow z = z_5 + 5 \diamond p(y/2 + 2, 2x + 9, z_5); \{\langle p(x + 7, y + 9, z_5 + 5), 23 \rangle\} \rangle$$
$$G_8 : \langle \leftarrow z = z_6 + 6 \diamond p(x + 4, y + 3, z_6); \{\langle p(x + 7, y + 9, z_6 + 6), 23 \rangle\} \rangle$$

Once again, the unfolding process described in [1] stops at G_3. In our case, the derivation is stopped at G_8 because otherwise, the history would be violated. From this extended computation tree, we may extract the property: $\forall(x, y, z) \in (\mathbb{Q}^+)^3 p(x+7, y+9, z) \Leftrightarrow (x = y = 0 \wedge z = 4) \vee (p(x+4, y+3, z) \wedge z \geq 6)$ true in the least $\mathcal{Q}^+$-model of the program. Or, if we only keep the deterministic part of the extended computation tree: $\forall(x, y, z) \in (\mathbb{Q}^+)^3 p(x + 7, y + 9, z) \Leftrightarrow p(x + 5, y + 5, z) \wedge z \geq 4$.

To conclude, we believe that the following points deserve further work. It seems feasible to adapt the approach we propose in this paper to other termination criteria [12]. Deterministic goals should be taken into account in order to reduce the size of the computation tree [7], [17]. The switch from χ to $\mathcal{Q}^+$ could be automated [4]. At last, it would nice if we could compute the "maximal" class of goals such that there is no remaining frozen goal in the computation tree. As in [14], a starting point could be to add a second layer of abstraction using CLP($\mathcal{BOOL}$).

Never-ending stories never end ...

Acknowledgments

I would like to thank the referees and the participants of LOPSTR'95 — and especially Alberto Pettorossi — for their helpful comments.

References

1. M. BRUYNOOGHE, D. DE SCHREYE, and B. MARTENS. A general criterion for avoiding infinite unfolding during partial deduction. *New Generation Computing*, 11(1):47–79, 1992.
2. P. CODOGNET and G. FILÉ. Computations, abstractions and contraints in logic programming. *Proc. of ICCL'92*, 1992.
3. A. COLMERAUER. An introduction to Prolog III. *CACM*, 33 (7):70–90, July 1990.
4. S. DECORTE, F. STEFAAN, and D. DE SCHREYE. Automatic inference of norms : a missing link in automation termination analysis. In *Logic Programming - Proceedings of 1993 International Symposium*, pages 420–436, 1993.
5. D. DE SCHREYE and S. DECORTE. Termination of logic programs: the never-ending story. *Journal of Logic Programming*, pages 1–199, 1993.
6. L. FRIBOURG and M. VELOSO PEIXOTO. Bottom-up evaluation of datalog programs with arithmetic constraints: The case of 3 recursive rules. Technical report, L.I.E.N.S, France, 1994.
7. R. GIACOBAZZI and L. RICCI. Detecting determinate computations by bottom-up abstract interpretation. Technical report, Università di Pisa, 1992.
8. P. HILL and J. LLOYD. *The Gödel Programming Language.* MIT Press, 1994.
9. J. JAFFAR and J.L. LASSEZ. Constraint logic programming. Technical Report 74, Monach University, Australia, 1986.
10. J. JAFFAR and M.J. MAHER. Constraint logic programming: a survey. *J. Logic Programming*, pages 503–581, 1994.

11. S. LÜETTRINGHAUS-KAPPEL. Control generation for logic programs. *Proc. of 10th ICLP*, pages 478–495, 1993.
12. B. MARTENS and D. DE SCHREYE. Automatic finite unfolding using well-founded measures. *Journal of Logic programming*, To appear.
13. B. MARTENS and J. GALLAGHER. Ensuring global termination of partial deduction while allowing flexible polyvariance. *Proc. of ICLP'95*, 1995.
14. F. MESNARD. *Etude de la terminaison des programmes logiques avec contraintes, au moyen d'approximations*. PhD thesis, Université Paris VI, 1993.
15. L. NAISH. Negation and control in prolog. In *LNCS 238*. Springer-Verlag, 1985.
16. L. PLÜMER. *Termination proofs fo logic programs*. Springer-Verlag, 1989.
17. B. SAGLAM and J.P. GALLAGHER. Approximating constraint logic programs using polymorphic types and regular descriptions. Technical report, University of Bristol, Dpt of Computer Science, 1995.
18. K. SOHN. Constraints among argument sizes in logic programs. *Proc. of PODS'94*, pages 68–74, 1994.
19. K. SOHN and A. VAN GELDER. Termination detection in logic programs using argument sizes. *Proc. of PODS'91*, pages 216–226, 1991.
20. J.D. ULLMAN and A. VAN GELDER. Efficient tests for top-down termination of logical rules. *Journal of the ACM*, 35(2):345–373, 1988.
21. K. VERSCHAETSE and D. DE SCHREYE. Deriving termination proofs for logic programs, using abstract procedures. *Proc. of the 8th ICLP*, pages 301–315, 1991.
22. K. VERSCHAETSE and D. DE SCHREYE. Derivation of linear size relations by abstract interpretation. In *LNCS 631*, pages 296–310. Springer Verlag, 1992.

A Proof of Theorem 10

Let us give a precise meaning of the dependency graph of a program.

Definition 11. Given a program P with π_P as its set of predicate symbols, we define its dependency graph D_P as the subset of $\pi_P \times \pi_P$ such that $(p, q) \in D_P$ iff there is a clause $p(\tilde{s}) \leftarrow \dots, \diamond \dots, q(\tilde{u}), \dots$ in P. Let D_P^+ be the transitive closure of D_P.

Let P be a (specialized) $\mathrm{CLP}(\mathcal{Q}^+)$ program. We assume that D_P is antisymmetric and that a valid measure μ_p is associated to each recursive predicate symbol p (i.e. such that $(p, p) \in D_P$). Let $ConstAt_P$ be the set of constraint atoms built from the vocabulary defined in P, i.e. $ConstAt_P = \{c \diamond p(\tilde{t}) | c \text{ is a } \mathcal{Q}^+ - constraint,\ p(\tilde{t})\ a\ \pi_P - atom\}$. We have the following propositions:

Definition 12. A constraint atom $c \diamond p(\tilde{t})$ is bounded by $m \in \mathbb{Q}^+$ if m is the greatest lower bound of the set $\{\mu_p(\tilde{t}\theta) | \theta \text{ is a solution of } c\}$.

Proposition 13. *Suppose $c \diamond p(\tilde{t})$ is bounded by m. Let $p(\tilde{s}) \leftarrow c' \diamond \dots, p(\tilde{u}), \dots$ be a clause of P defining p. If $c, c', \tilde{t} = \tilde{s}$ is solvable, then $c, c', \tilde{t} = \tilde{s}' \diamond p(\tilde{u})$ is bounded by m' and $m \geq m' + 1$.*

Definition 14. On $ConstAt_P$ we define a relation $>_P$:
$c \diamond p(\tilde{t}) >_P c' \diamond q(\tilde{s})$ if
$$\begin{cases} p \neq q, (p,q) \in D_P^+ \\ or \\ p = q, c \diamond p(\tilde{t}) \text{ bounded } m_1, c' \diamond p(\tilde{s}) \text{ bounded by } m_2, m_1 \geq m_2 + 1 \end{cases}$$

Proposition 15. $\langle ConstAt_P, >_P \rangle$ *is a partially ordered well-founded set.*

From now on, we stick to the concepts and definitions of [1] to prove the main result of the paper.

Theorem 10 *Let R be an extended computation rule. Then for any goal G, the extended computation tree $\tau_{G,R}$ is finite.*

Proof. Let $p_1, \ldots, p_N$ be the N recursive predicate symbols of P. We construct a *hierarchical prefounding* (see the definition in [1]) for $\tau_{G,R}$ as follows:

$$R_0 = \{A_i | \langle G, H \rangle \equiv \langle \leftarrow c \diamond A_1, \ldots, A_{n+1}, H \rangle \in \tau_{G,R},$$
$$R(G, H) = \langle i, H' \rangle, i \geq 1, A_i = p(\tilde{t}), [(p,p) \notin D_p \text{ or } Bounded(c, p(\tilde{t}))]\}$$

and for $1 \leq k \leq N$:

$$R_k = \{A_i | \langle G, H \rangle \equiv \langle \leftarrow c \diamond A_1, \ldots, A_{n+1}, H \rangle \in \tau_{G,R},$$
$$R(G, H) = \langle i, H' \rangle, i \geq 1, A_i = p_k(\tilde{t}), [(p_k, p_k) \in D_p \text{ and } \neg Bounded(c, p_k(\tilde{t}))]\}$$

Note that:

1. We have a finite partition $R_0, \ldots, R_N$ of the set of selected goals in $\tau_{G,R}$. The classes $(C_0, C_1, C_2, \ldots)$ of resolvents from $\tau_{G,R}$ are defined as in the first part of the corresponding definition in [1].
2. Propositions 13 and 15 show that C_0 contains no infinite sequence of direct successors.
3. Let $\langle W_1, >_1 \rangle = \ldots \langle W_N, >_N \rangle = \langle \mathbb{Q}^+, \geq +1 \rangle$, which is a well-founded set. Let $\langle G, H \rangle \equiv \langle \leftarrow c \diamond A_1, \ldots, A_{n+1}, H \in \tau_{G,R}$ be an element of C_i such that $R(G, H) = \langle j, H' \rangle, i \geq 1, A_j = p_k(\tilde{t})$. We define $f_i : C_i \rightarrow \mathbb{Q}^+$ as $f_i(G, H) = Min(c; \mu_k(\tilde{t}))$.
4. For any element $\in C_m \cap C_n$ we have $f_m = f_n$.

To finish the proof, it remains to show that each f_i is monotonic. Let $\langle G; H \rangle$ the first element appearing in $\tau_{G,R}$ such that $\langle G; H \rangle \in C_i$. Let $G =\leftarrow c \diamond \tilde{C}, p(\tilde{s}), \tilde{D}$ where R chooses to unfold $p(\tilde{s})$. Let $p(\tilde{t}) \leftarrow c' \diamond \tilde{B}, p(\tilde{u}), \tilde{E}$ be a clause of P defining p. Then the node has as direct descendant: $\langle \leftarrow c, c', \tilde{s} = \tilde{t} \diamond \tilde{C}, \tilde{B}, p(\tilde{u}), \tilde{E}, \tilde{D}; H \cup \{\langle p(\tilde{s}), Min(c, \mu_p(\tilde{s})) \rangle\} \rangle$. Assume that $\langle G''; H'' \rangle$ is the first descendant $\in C_i$ of $\langle G; H \rangle$. In general, we have $\langle G''; H'' \rangle = \langle \leftarrow c, c', \tilde{s} = \tilde{t}, c'' \diamond \tilde{A}, p(\tilde{u}), \tilde{F}; H \cup \{\langle p(\tilde{s}), Min(c, \mu_p(\tilde{s})) \rangle\} \cup H''' \rangle$.

Let us show $f_i(G, H) \geq f_i(G'', H'') + 1$. On the one hand, we have:

$$Min(c; \mu_p(\tilde{s})) = Min(c, c', \tilde{s} = \tilde{t}; \mu_p(\tilde{s}))$$

$$= Min(c, c', \tilde{s} = \tilde{t}, c''; \mu_p(\tilde{s}))$$
$$= Min(c, c', \tilde{s} = \tilde{t}, c''; \mu_p(\tilde{t}))$$

because the unfolding from $\langle G; H \rangle$ to $\langle G'; H' \rangle$ then to $\langle G''; H'' \rangle$ are allowed. On the other hand, recall that μ_p is a valid measure for p. Hence:

$$Min(c, c', \tilde{s} = \tilde{t}, c''; \mu_p(\tilde{t})) \geq 1 + Min(c, c', \tilde{s} = \tilde{t}, c''; \mu_p(\tilde{u}))$$

So we obtain:

$$Min(c; \mu_p(\tilde{s})) \geq 1 + Min(c, c', \tilde{s} = \tilde{t}, c''; \mu_p(\tilde{u}))$$

i.e.

$$f_i(G, H) \geq f_i(G'', H'') + 1$$

We conclude the proof by noting that in general, for the descendants $\in C_i$ of $\langle G; H \rangle$ we have, with $n \geq 1$:

$$Min(c; \mu_p(\tilde{s})) \geq 1 + n + Min(c, c', \tilde{s} = \tilde{t}, c'', c'''; \mu_p(\tilde{v}))$$

$\square$

Ideal Refinement of Datalog Programs

Giovanni Semeraro, Floriana Esposito and Donato Malerba

Dipartimento di Informatica - Università degli Studi di Bari
Via E. Orabona 4 - 70126 Bari, Italy
{semeraro, esposito, malerbad}@vm.csata.it

Abstract. In model inference, refinement operators are exploited to change in an automated way incorrect clauses of a logic program. In this paper, we present two refinement operators for Datalog programs and state that both of them meet the properties of *local finiteness, properness,* and *completeness (ideality)*. Such operators are based on the quasi-ordering induced upon a set of clauses by the generalization model of *θ-subsumption under object identity*. These operators have been implemented in a system for theory revision that proved effective in the area of electronic document classification.

1 Introduction

In a logical framework for the inductive inference of theories from facts, a fundamental problem is the definition of *locally finite, proper,* and *complete (ideal)* refinement operators. Indeed, when the aim is to identify in the limit [11] a finite axiomatization of a theory - a *model* - expressed in a logical language, it becomes relevant to develop incremental operators that allow for the refinement of theories which turn out to be *too weak* or *too strong*.

Shapiro [31] presented a framework for the inductive inference of logic theories. He developed an incremental inductive inference algorithm, the Model Inference System (MIS), that can identify in the limit any model in a family of complexity classes of first order theories. Despite of its scientific importance, this system proved very inefficient on real-world tasks and was able to infer only simple logic programs from a small number of examples.

The *ideality* of the refinement operators plays a key role when the efficiency and the effectiveness of the learning systems is an unnegligible requirement [34].

Theoretical studies in Inductive Logic Programming (ILP) have shown that, when full Horn clause logic is chosen as representation language and either *θ-subsumption* or *implication* is adopted as generalization model, there exist no ideal refinement operators [34, 35]. Research efforts in the area of ILP have been directed to improve the efficiency of the learning systems by restricting full first order Horn clause logic by means of suitable language biases, such as linkedness [15], *ij*-determinacy [21], Datalog (i.e., function-free) clauses [23, 27], rule models [17], antecedent description grammars [3], clause sets [1] and literal templates [33]. However, these language biases are not sufficient to solve the problem of defining ideal refinement operators. Indeed, as Niblett says [22], *"it is an open question as to which restrictions on full first order logic are compatible with complete non-redundant refinement operators."*

In this paper, we define two ideal refinement operators for the space of Datalog clauses. These definitions rely on a weaker ordering than θ-subsumption, namely θ_{oi}-subsumption.

In Section 2, we briefly recall the definition of the generalization model based on θ_{oi}-subsumption and give the basic definitions concerning the refinement operators. The non-existence of ideal refinement operators for Datalog clauses under θ-subsumption is investigated in Section 3. Novel refinement operators for Datalog clauses ordered by θ_{OI}-subsumption are defined in Section 4. Moreover, we point out that such operators are ideal. Section 5 presents an application of these operators to the real-world task of electronic document classification.

2 Preliminaries and Definitions

We assume the reader to be familiar with the notions of *substitution, literal, fact, Horn clause* and *definite clause* [19]. A clause $C = l_1 \vee l_2 \vee \ldots \vee l_n$, is considered as the set of its literals, that is, $C = \{ l_1, l_2, \ldots, l_n \}$. $|C|$ denotes the number of literals in C - the *length* of C - while $size(C)$ denotes the number of symbol occurrences in C (excluding punctuation) minus the number of distinct variables occurring in C. Furthermore, we will denote with $vars(C)$, $consts(C)$, and $terms(C)$ the set of the variables, of the constants and of the terms occurring in C, respectively. Henceforth, any two clauses will be always assumed to be variable disjoint. This does not limit the expressiveness of the adopted language since any two non-variable disjoint clauses always can be standardized apart.

Henceforth, by clause we mean *Datalog* clause. Datalog is a language for deductive databases. Here, we refer to [16] for what concerns the basic notions about deductive databases. The vocabulary of a Datalog program P is composed of *intensional database symbols*, denoted with *IDB*'s, and *extensional database symbols*, denoted with *EDB*'s. P is made up of a set of Datalog clauses of the form

$$Q(x_1, x_2, \ldots, x_n) :- \varphi \qquad\qquad n \geq 0$$

where:

- the head $Q(x_1, x_2, \ldots, x_n)$ consists of an IDB Q of arity n, $n \geq 0$, and of a list of n arguments
- the body φ is a set of literals, which can be equality atoms and relational atoms. Both these kinds of atoms must be positive in Datalog. Negations of such atoms are allowed in *Datalog*. If the only negations are inequalities in the bodies, we have a sublanguage of *Datalog*, called *Datalog*.

Let us denote with **L** a language that consists of all the possible Datalog clauses built from a finite number of predicates. We distinguish two subsets of **L**, namely $\mathbf{L_o}$ and $\mathbf{L_h}$, which are the language of observations and the language of hypotheses, respectively. Shortly, the model inference problem can be stated as follows. Given two sets of ground facts E^+ (positive examples) and E^- (negative examples), expressed in the language of observations $\mathbf{L_o}$, and a background knowledge B in the language **L** (in our setting, B is bound to be a set of ground atoms), the model inference problem consists in finding a logic program P (theory) such that $P \cup B \vdash E^+$ (*completeness*) and $P \cup B \not\vdash E^-$ (*consistency*).

In the literature of machine learning, it is possible to find many examples of algorithms that solve model inference problems. They can be roughly subdivided into *batch* and *incremental*, according to the fact that training examples - $E^+ \cup E^-$ - are completely available at learning time or not, respectively. For instance, MIS is an incremental algorithm based on the Popperian methodology of conjectures and refutations [26]. The importance of this algorithm is not limited to the area of machine learning, but extends to algorithmic debugging of logic programs.

MIS is able to infer a logic theory from a sequence of examples by modifying incrementally a conjecture (a logic program) whenever a contradiction occurs between the conjectured theory and the given examples, that is to say, whenever the current theory is either not complete (*too weak*) or not consistent (*too strong*). Part of MIS is the contradiction backtracing algorithm, that allows the system to trace back any contradiction to the false clause that caused it, as well as to construct a counterexample that shows the falsity of that clause. Specifically, MIS starts from a strong conjecture and deletes any over-general (too strong) clause. When the conjecture becomes too weak, specializations of deleted clauses can be added until a complete and consistent conjecture is found.

Computing the specializations of a previously removed clause is the task of a downward refinement operator, which performs a general-to-specific search through the space of the Horn clauses rooted into the deleted clause (*specialization hierarchy*). However, a specialization hierarchy is an infinite search space, since the possible downward refinements of any clause are infinite. Refinement operators take advantage of the structure given to the specialization hierarchy by the definition of a quasi-ordering upon it, in order to control the search and avoid the combinatorial explosion. The most frequently adopted quasi-orderings are those induced by the notions of logical implication and θ-subsumption [24]. Nevertheless, the search remains computationally expensive. Indeed, the algorithm in MIS is exponential.

Recently, Ling [18] has developed a system, called SIM, with the aim at overcoming the overall inefficiency of MIS. SIM performs a specific-to-general search, which strongly relies on positive examples to compute the generalizations of clauses that turn out to be too weak. An upward refinement operator takes care of this task.

Here, we recall the notion of object identity, given in [29] for function-free and constant-free clauses. This notion is the basis for the definition of both an equational theory for Datalog clauses and a quasi-ordering upon them.

Definition 1 (Object Identity) *Within a clause, terms denoted with different symbols must be distinct.*

In Datalog, the adoption of the object identity assumption can be viewed as a method for building an equational theory into the ordering as well as into the inference rules of the calculus (resolution, factorization and paramodulation) [25].

Such equational theory is very simple, since it consists of just one further axiom schema, in addition to the canonical set of equality axioms (reflexivity, symmetry, transitivity, and subsitutivity of both the function and the predicate letters) [2]:

$$\forall C \in \mathbf{L}, \ \forall t, s \in terms(C),$$
$$\neg t = s \Rightarrow \neg t = s \in body(C) \qquad \text{(OI)}$$

The (OI) axiom can be viewed as an extension of Reiter's *unique-names* assumption [28] to non-ground terms. Henceforth, we will use $t \neq s$ as an abbreviation for $\neg t = s$. Note that the substitutivity axiom for function letters is useless in Datalog, since no function symbols occur in a Datalog clause.

Under object identity assumption, the Datalog clause $C = P(x) :- Q(x, x), Q(y, a)$ is an abbreviation for the following Datalog* clause

$$C_{oi} = P(x) :- Q(x, x), Q(y, a) \ \| \ [x \neq y], [x \neq a], [y \neq a]$$

where P, Q denote predicate letters, x, y variables, a is a constant and the inequations attached to the clause can be seen as constraints on its terms. These constraints are generated in a systematic way by the (OI) axiom. In addition, they can be dealt with in the same way as the other literals in the clause. Therefore, under object identity, any Datalog clause C generates a new Datalog* clause C_{oi} consisting of two components, called $core(C_{oi})$ and $constraints(C_{oi})$, where $core(C_{oi}) = C$ and $constraints(C_{oi})$ is the set of the inequalities generated by the (OI) axiom.

We can formally introduce the ordering relation defined by the notion of θ-subsumption under object identity -θ_{oi}-*subsumption* - upon the set of Datalog clauses.

Definition 2 (θ_{oi}-subsumption ordering) Let C, D be two Datalog clauses. We say that D θ-*subsumes* C *under object identity* (D θ_{oi}-*subsumes* C) if and only if (iff) there exists a substitution σ such that (s.t.) $D_{oi}.\sigma \subseteq C_{oi}$.
In such a case, we say that D is *more general than or equal to* C (D *is an upward refinement of* C and C *is a downward refinement of* D) *under object identity* and we write $C \leq_{oi} D$.
We write $C <_{oi} D$ when $C \leq_{oi} D$ and $not(D \leq_{oi} C)$ and we say that D *is more general than* C (D *is a proper upward refinement of* C) or C *is more specific than* D (C *is a proper downward refinement of* D) or D *properly* θ_{oi}-*subsumes* C. We write $C \sim_{oi} D$, and we say that C and D are *equivalent clauses under object identity*, when $C \leq_{oi} D$ and $D \leq_{oi} C$.

Henceforth, we will denote with $\leq_{\theta}$ the θ-subsumption ordering, with $\leq_{oi}$ the θ_{oi}-subsumption ordering and with $\leq$ indifferently either θ-subsumption or implication ordering. •
We write $C < D$ when $C \leq D$ and $not(D \leq C)$. We write $C \sim D$ when $C \leq D$ and $D \leq C$.

θ_{oi}-subsumption is a strictly weaker order relation than θ-subsumption. Indeed, the following result holds.

Proposition 1. *Let* C, D *be two Datalog clauses,* $C \leq_{oi} D \Rightarrow C \leq_{\theta} D$.
Proof. From Definition 2, $C \leq_{oi} D$ means that there exists a substitution σ s.t. $D_{oi}.\sigma \subseteq C_{oi}$. Thus, $core(D_{oi}).\sigma \subseteq core(C_{oi})$. But, $core(D_{oi}) = D$ and $core(C_{oi}) = C$, therefore it holds also $D.\sigma \subseteq C$.   q.e.d.

Example. Let C and D be the following clauses:

$$C = P(x) :\text{-} Q(x, x) \qquad D = P(x) :\text{-} Q(x, y), Q(y, x)$$
and $\quad C_{oi} = P(x) :\text{-} Q(x, x) \qquad D_{oi} = P(x) :\text{-} Q(x, y), Q(y, x) \ \| \ [x \neq y]$

the corresponding clauses under object identity.
It holds that $C \leq_{\theta} D$, since $D.\sigma \subseteq C$, where $\sigma = \{y/x\}$. Conversely, it holds that $not(C \leq_{oi} D)$, since the substitution $\sigma = \{y/x\}$ violates the constraint $[x \neq y]$ in $constraints(D_{oi})$ and it is easy to see that no substitution θ s.t. $D_{oi}.\theta \subseteq C_{oi}$ can exist.   □

The following result provides a practical characterization of the notion of θ_{oi}-subsumption.

Proposition 2. *Let* C, D *be two Datalog clauses,*
$C \leq_{oi} D \quad \Leftrightarrow \quad \forall \sigma$ such that $D_{oi}.\sigma \subseteq C_{oi}$:
σ is injective and $\sigma : vars(D) \rightarrow vars(C) \cup (consts(C) - consts(D))$
A proof of Proposition 2 can be found in [9].

Definition 3 (Downward Refinement) Given a quasi-ordered set $(L_h, \leq)$:
1) a *downward refinement operator* ρ is a mapping from L_h to 2^{L_h}, $\rho : L_h \rightarrow 2^{L_h}$ s.t.
   for every C in L_h, $\rho(C)$ is a subset of the set $\{ D \in L_h \mid D \leq C \}$
2) let ρ be a downward refinement operator and C a clause in L_h, then
   $\rho^0(C) = \{C\}$ $\rho^n(C) = \{ D \mid \exists E \in \rho^{n-1}(C)$ and $D \in \rho(E) \}$
   $\rho^*(C) = \bigcup_{n \geq 0} \rho^n(C) = \rho^0(C) \cup \rho^1(C) \cup ... \cup \rho^n(C) \cup ...$
   are the sets of *zero-step downward refinements*, *n-step downward refinements* and *downward refinements* of C, respectively.
3) ρ is *locally finite* iff $\forall C \in L_h$: $\rho(C)$ is finite and computable
   ρ is *proper* iff $\forall C \in L_h$: $\rho(C) \subseteq \{ D \in L_h \mid D < C \}$

ρ is *complete* iff $\forall C, D \in \mathbf{L_h}$, if $D < C$ then $\exists E$ s.t. $E \in \rho^*(C)$ and $E \sim D$

ρ is *ideal* iff it is locally finite, proper and complete.

4) let $C, D_1, D_2, D_3, \ldots,$ be clauses in $\mathbf{L_h}$,

if $C < \ldots < D_{n+1} < D_n < \ldots < D_3 < D_2 < D_1$ and there is no $A \in \mathbf{L_h}$ s.t. $\forall n \geq 1 : C < A \leq D_n$, then $(D_n)_{n\geq1}$ is an *unlimited infinite strictly descending chain* of C.

Definition 4 (Upward Refinement) Given a quasi-ordered set $(\mathbf{L_h}, \leq)$:

1') an *upward refinement operator* δ is a mapping from $\mathbf{L_h}$ to $2^{\mathbf{L_h}}$, $\delta : \mathbf{L_h} \to 2^{\mathbf{L_h}}$ s.t. for every C in $\mathbf{L_h}$, $\delta(C)$ is a subset of the set $\{ D \in \mathbf{L_h} \mid D \geq C \}$

2') let δ be an upward refinement operator and C a clause in $\mathbf{L_h}$, then

$\delta^0(C) = \{C\}$ $\qquad\qquad \delta^n(C) = \{ D \mid \exists E \in \delta^{n-1}(C) \text{ and } D \in \delta(E) \}$

$\delta^*(C) = \bigcup_{n\geq0} \delta^n(C) = \delta^0(C) \cup \delta^1(C) \cup \ldots \cup \delta^n(C) \cup \ldots$

are the sets of *zero-step upward refinements*, *n-step upward refinements* and *upward refinements* of C, respectively.

3') δ is *locally finite* iff $\forall C \in \mathbf{L_h} : \delta(C)$ is finite and computable

δ is *proper* iff $\forall C \in \mathbf{L_h} : \delta(C) \subseteq \{ D \in \mathbf{L_h} \mid C < D \}$

δ is *complete* iff $\forall C, D \in \mathbf{L_h}$, if $C < D$ then $\exists E$ s.t. $E \in \delta^*(C)$ and $E \sim D$

δ is *ideal* iff it is locally finite, proper and complete.

4') let $C, D_1, D_2, D_3, \ldots,$ be clauses in $\mathbf{L_h}$,

if $D_1 < D_2 < D_3 < \ldots < D_n < D_{n+1} < \ldots < C$ and there is no $A \in \mathbf{L_h}$ s.t. $\forall n \geq 1 : D_n \leq A < C$, then $(D_n)_{n\geq1}$ is an *unlimited infinite strictly ascending chain* of C.

3 Non-existence of Ideal Refinement Operators for Datalog Clauses

In [34], several refinement operators are reviewed and compared. None of them meets the property to be ideal. In fact, it is possible to prove that, even in the space of Datalog clauses ordered by $\leq$, there exist no ideal refinement operators, neither downward nor upward ones. This result is a straightforward consequence of similar results due to van der Laag and Nienhuys-Cheng [34] for unrestricted search spaces under θ-subsumption (p. 256) and implication (p. 258). Here, we recall only the former result.

*"**Theorem 4.3.** Let L be a first-order language that contains at least one predicate or function symbol of arity ≥ 2 and let C be the set of all clauses in L, then an ideal downward or upward refinement operator for $<C, \geq>$ does not exist."*

The non-existence of ideal downward refinement operators follows directly from the existence of unlimited infinite strictly ascending chains of a clause C in an unrestricted search space. Dually, the non-existence of ideal upward refinement operators follows from the existence of unlimited infinite strictly descending chains of a clause C.

Indeed, if we consider the sequence of clauses, reported in [34, p. 256] (x_i and y_j denote variables)

$C = q :- P(x_1, x_2), P(x_2, x_1)$

$E_n = q :- P(x_1, x_2), P(x_2, x_1), P(y_1, y_2), P(y_2, y_3), \ldots, P(y_{n-1}, y_n), P(y_n, y_1) \qquad n \geq 3$

an example of unlimited infinite strictly ascending chain of C is $(E_{3n})_{n\geq1}$.

Such a chain is composed of Datalog clauses. Moreover, since all the clauses in the chain are not self-resolving, this chain does exist under θ-subsumption as well as under logical implication. As to the difference between θ-subsumption and implication, for our purposes it is enough to say that the incompleteness of θ-subsumption wrt implication concerns exclusively the tautological and the self-resolving clauses, that is, if C is tautological or D is self-resolving then $C \models D$ is not equivalent to $D \leq_\theta C$ [12].

Most systems that learn Horn clauses from examples adopt the language bias of linkedness in order to restrict the search space and to avoid generating quite insignificant clauses. A formal definition of linkedness can be found in [15, 29]. The unlimited infinite chain $(E_{3n})_{n \geq 1}$ consists of clauses that are not linked, therefore it could be guessed that, if the learning system adopts such a language bias, it is possible to define an ideal downward refinement operator. Unfortunately, even in the space of linked Datalog clauses there exists an unlimited strictly ascending chain of infinite length of a clause C, denoted with $(D_{3n})_{n \geq 1}$, where

$C = Q(z) :- P(z, x_1, x_2), P(z, x_2, x_1)$

$D_n = Q(z) :- P(z, x_1, x_2), P(z, x_2, x_1), P(z, y_1, y_2), P(z, y_2, y_3), \ldots, P(z, y_{n-1}, y_n), P(z, y_n, y_1)$

As to the upward refinement operators, the following example of an unlimited infinite strictly descending chain of a clause C is given in [34, page 255]:

$G_n = q :- \{ P(x_i, x_j) \mid 1 \leq i, j \leq n, i \neq j \}$ $\qquad\qquad n \geq 2$

$C = q :- P(x_1, x_1)$

Similarly to the downward case, it is possible to change properly the chain $(G_n)_{n \geq 2}$ in order to obtain the following unlimited infinite strictly descending chain of a clause C, that consists of linked Datalog clauses:

$F_n = Q(z) :- \{ P(z, x_i, x_j) \mid 1 \leq i, j \leq n, i \neq j \}$ $\qquad\qquad n \geq 2$

$C = Q(z) :- P(z, x_1, x_1)$

Graphical descriptions of the chains $(D_{3n})_{n \geq 1}$ and $(F_n)_{n \geq 2}$ are given in Figure 1, inspired by similar figures in [35].

In the literature, the research efforts made in order to solve the problem of defining ideal refinement operators have tended towards the introduction of further constraints in the definition of refinement. For instance, Shapiro [32] restricts the definition of refinement by introducing the concept of size of a clause C. Indeed, his definition states that *"A clause D is a refinement of a clause C if $C \vdash D$ and size(C) < size(D)."*

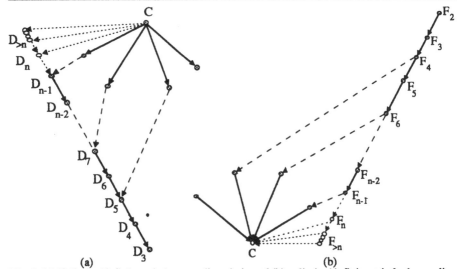

(a)　　　　　　　　　　　　　　(b)

Fig. 1. (a) Unlimited infinite strictly ascending chain and (b) unlimited infinite strictly descending chain of a clause C in the space of linked Datalog clauses ordered by θ-subsumption.

Interestingly, the same problem can be found in the area of automated deduction. Loveland [20, page 200] gives a definition of θ-subsumption which is slightly different from the classical one, as reported in [2, 21, 24] (the difference is underlined). Indeed, according to Loveland, "*a clause C θ-subsumes D iff there exists a substitution θ such that $C.\theta \subseteq D$ and C has no more literals than D*." In this case, the restriction is brought to the level of the definition of θ-subsumption and concerns the number of literals in a clause. Lemma 4.1.1 in [20, page 208] states that "*every sequence of clauses in which each clause properly θ-subsumes its predecessor is of finite length*." The constraint on the number of literals is a necessary condition for the validity of that lemma. In fact, both chains $(E_{3n})_{n\geq 1}$ and $(D_{3n})_{n\geq 1}$ cease to exist, since the number of literals in the upper clauses $(E_{3(n+1)}$ and $D_{3(n+1)})$ exceeds the number of literals in the lower ones $(E_{3n}$ and D_{3n}, respectively). Furthermore, it is well known in the area of automated theorem proving that if the definition of θ-subsumption is not tightened by the constraint on the number of literals, then each factor of a clause is removed because it is θ-subsumed by the clause itself [4, page 228]. The damaging effect is that the simplification rule of factorization, which is a major step in improving the efficiency of a deduction system, is no longer applied. On the other hand, if we do not restrict to reduced clauses, Loveland's definition of θ-subsumption contradicts the notion of logical equivalence of clauses, as stated by the definition of the relation $\sim$. Indeed, if we adopt Loveland's definition, the two clauses $P(x)$:- $Q(x, y)$ and $P(x)$:- $Q(x, y), Q(x, z)$ are no longer equivalent because of their different lengths.

4 Ideal Refinement Operators for Datalog Programs

Before giving the formal definition of the operators for refining Datalog programs and stating that both of them meet the property to be ideal, we need to enunciate (and prove) the result that in the space of Datalog clauses ordered by θ_{OI}-subsumption there exist no unlimited infinite strictly ascending/descending chains of some clause C. To this purpose, we give preliminarily the following proposition.

Proposition 3. *Let C and D be Datalog clauses,*
$$C \sim_{OI} D \text{ iff } C \text{ and } D \text{ are alphabetic variants.}$$
A proof of Proposition 3 is given in [9].

Proposition 3 has several implications that can be relevant. First, the problem of removing redundancy from a clause, also known as the problem of establishing whether a clause is reduced and, if not, finding an algorithm for reducing it, is cast to the problem of establishing if two clauses are alphabetic variants, when θ-subsumption (or implication) is replaced by θ_{OI}-subsumption. The problem of reducing a clause requires a test for θ-subsumption, which is NP-complete [10]. Proposition 3 abates the computational complexity of the clause reduction problem under θ_{OI}-subsumption to $O(n^2)$, where n is the number of literals in the clause. In other words, removing redundancy from a clause, which is a major problem in several areas of computer science [13], can be coped with in an efficient way for clauses constrained by the OI-equational theory.

In logic-based machine learning, top-down systems perform a general-to-specific search to learn the body of a clause whose head contains (a proper variabilization of) the predicate to be learned. Specifically, the search is performed in the specialization hierarchy rooted in $P(x_1, x_2, ..., x_n)$:- , where P is the predicate to be learned, and proceeds by selecting literals to be added to the body of an inconsistent clause, one literal at a time. One of the problems that affect some of these systems is that there is no formal warranty that the learning process terminates, as pointed out in [29], and this is due to the fact that these systems do not perform a θ-subsumption equivalence test for efficiency reasons. In [29], it is proved the following result.

"Proposition 11. *Let C and D be two definite Horn clauses:*

$$C \text{ reduced, } C \subset D \text{ and } vars(C) = vars(D) \Rightarrow [C]_{\sim} \neq [D]_{\sim}"$$

where $[\varphi]_{\sim}$ denotes the class of clauses that are equivalent to φ under θ-subsumption.

This result allows the learning system to avoid performing the θ-subsumption equivalence test in the case the added literal does not introduce *new* variables, i.e. variables *local* to the literal itself. Unfortunately, this condition is not met in the general case, thus the θ-subsumption equivalence test is still needed. Furthermore, Proposition 11 requires the clause *C* to be reduced. Adding a literal to a clause does not always produce a reduced clause, even if the added literal does not introduce any new variable. The following example illustrates this last case.

Example[1]. Let *C* be the reduced clause:

$$C = H(x) :- P(x, y), Q(y), P(x, z), R(z)$$

Adding the literal $l_1 = \neg R(y)$ to (the body of) *C* yields the clause *D*,

$$D = H(x) :- P(x, y), Q(y), P(x, z), R(z), R(y)$$

which is a proper downward refinement of *C*, in accordance with Proposition 11, but it is no longer reduced. Thus, adding to *D* a further literal l_2 which does not introduce new variables does not guarantee the resulting clause *E* were a proper downward refinement of *D*, because the first condition of Proposition 11 - "*C reduced*" - is no longer satisfied. Indeed, if $l_2 = \neg Q(z)$ then we have:

$$E = H(x) :- P(x, y), Q(y), P(x, z), R(z), R(y), Q(z)$$

which is logically equivalent to *D*, even though the literal l_2 has no new variable. □

Coming back to the problem of defining ideal refinement operators, the most relevant consequence of Proposition 3 is the absence in the space $(L_h, \leq_{oi})$ of unlimited infinite strictly ascending/descending chains of a clause *C*, as stated by the following result.

Proposition 4. *Given the space $(L_h, \leq_{oi})$ and a clause C in L_h,*
(a)   there exist no (unlimited) infinite strictly ascending chains of C,
(b)   there exist no unlimited infinite strictly descending chains of C.
A proof of Proposition 4 can be found in [9].

Now, we can formally define two refinement operators for Datalog clauses ordered by θ_{oi}-subsumption.

Definition 5 (Downward Refinement : the operator $\rho_{oi}(C)$)
Let *C* be a Datalog clause. Then, $D \in \rho_{oi}(C)$ when exactly one of the following holds:
(i) $D = C.\theta$, where $\theta = \{ x/a \}$, $a \notin consts(C)$, $x \in vars(C)$, that is, θ is a substitution, *a* is a constant not occurring in *C* and *x* is a variable that occurs in *C*.
(ii) $D = C \cup \{\neg l\}$, where *l* is an atom such that $\neg l \notin C$.

Definition 6 (Upward Refinement : the operator $\delta_{oi}(C)$)
Let *C* be a Datalog clause. Then, $D \in \delta_{oi}(C)$ when exactly one of the following holds:
(i) $D = C.\gamma$, where $\gamma = \{ a/x \}$, $a \in consts(C)$, $x \notin vars(C)$, that is, γ is an antisubstitution (or inductive substitution), *a* is a constant occurring in *C* and *x* is a variable that does not occur in *C*.

---

1. Thanks to J. U. Kietz for suggesting this example.

(ii) $D = C - \{\neg l\}$, where l is an atom such that $\neg l \in C$.

Proposition 5.

ρ_{ol} *is an ideal downward refinement operator for Datalog clauses ordered by θ_{ol}-subsumption.*

δ_{ol} *is an ideal upward refinement operator for Datalog clauses ordered by θ_{ol}-subsumption.*

Proof.

ρ_{OI}

(local finiteness)

(i) ρ_{ol} is locally finite because, given a clause C, both $vars(C)$ and the number of constants in L_h is finite. This last condition is motivated by the fact that the set of constants occurring in the target clause, which must be a downward refinement of C, is a subset of the constants in $B \cup E^+ \cup E^-$ *(domain closure assumption)*. Indeed, it is useless to consider constants that are not either in the background knowledge or in at least one of the training examples.

(ii) ρ_{ol} is locally finite because it adds only one literal at a time. Furthermore, we supposed that both the number of predicates and the number of constants in L_h is finite. Finally, observe that the renamings of a clause (which could be generated by choosing different variable names) are equivalent under θ_{ol}-subsumption.

(properness)

Trivial in case (i).

In case (ii), let us denote with D any element of $\rho_{ol}(C)$.

$D \leq_{ol} C$ because $C \subset D$, thus C θ_{ol}-subsumes D through the empty substitution. Moreover, the condition $\neg l \notin C$ implies that C and D have different lengths, thus they are not alphabetic variants. Then, from Proposition 3 it follows that $not(D \sim_{ol} C)$.

(completeness)

We must prove that $\forall C, D \in L_h$, if $D <_{ol} C$ then $\exists F$ s.t. $F \in \rho^*_{ol}(C)$ and $F \sim_{ol} D$.

Let C and D be two clauses in L_h such that $D <_{ol} C$. This implies that there exists an injection σ such that $C.\sigma \subseteq D$. Moreover, it holds $consts(C) \subseteq consts(D)$.

Let E be the clause obtained by replacing each constant in D (if any) but not in C (i.e. in $consts(D) - consts(C)$) with a new variable.

Let $consts(D) - consts(C)$ be the set $\{a_1, a_2, ..., a_n\}$, and $\{x_1, x_2, ..., x_n\}$, $n \geq 0$, be the set of the corresponding new variables. Thus, we have defined an *antisubstitution*

$$\eta: \{a_1, a_2, ..., a_n\} \rightarrow \{x_1, x_2, ..., x_n\} \text{ s.t. } \eta(a_i) = x_i, i = 1, 2, ..., n.$$

By construction, $D \in \rho^n_{ol}(E)$. In fact, D is obtained by applying n times the point (i) of Definition 5. We must prove that $E \in \rho^*_{ol}(C)$.

Let us observe that the constants in E, if any, are also constants in C. If we consider the previous injection σ such that $C.\sigma \subseteq D$, then we can define the following substitution

$$\mu: vars(C) \rightarrow vars(E) \cup consts(E)$$

$$\mu(x) = \begin{cases} \sigma(x) & \text{if } \sigma(x) \notin \{a_1, a_2, ..., a_n\} \\ \eta(\sigma(x)) & \text{otherwise} \end{cases}$$

It results that $C.\mu \subseteq E$ and μ is an injection because σ and η are both injections, and the range of η and $vars(D)$ are disjoint sets.

Finally, it is possible to obtain E starting from C by applying the point (ii) of Definition 5 t times, where $t = |D| - |C|$. Specifically, the literals to be added to C are taken one at a time from the *residual* of E from C wrt μ, denoted with $Res_\mu(E, C)$ and defined as the set $E - C.\mu$. In formulae, $E = C \cup Res_\mu(E, C)$.

This completes the proof since we have found E s.t. $D \in \rho^*_{ol}(E)$ and $E \in \rho^*_{ol}(C)$. Moreover, we have an upper bound to the number of downward refinement steps required to produce D from C, since we have shown that $D \in \rho^{n+t}_{ol}(C)$.

δ_{ol}

(local finiteness)

(i) and (ii). Preliminarily, let us denote with $PGEN_{ol}(C)$ the set $\{ [D]_{\sim_{ol}} \in \mathbf{L}_h \mid C <_{ol} D \}$ of the proper upward refinements under θ_{ol}-subsumption of a clause C in $\mathbf{L}_h$ up to renamings ($[D]_{\sim_{ol}}$ denotes the class of clauses in $\mathbf{L}_h$ that are equivalent to D under θ_{ol}-subsumption). δ_{ol} is locally finite because, given a clause C, $\delta_{ol}(C) \subseteq PGEN_{ol}(C)$ and $PGEN_{ol}(C)$ is a finite set from Proposition 4.

(properness)

Trivial in case (i).

In case (ii), let us denote with D any element of $\delta_{ol}(C)$.

$D \subset C$ is equivalent to $core(D_{ol}) \subset core(C_{ol})$. In addition, $D \subset C$ implies that $constraints(C_{ol}) \subseteq constraints(D_{ol})$. Therefore, D θ_{ol}-subsumes C through the empty substitution. Moreover, the condition $\neg l \in C$ implies that C and D have different lengths, thus they are not alphabetic variants. Then, from Proposition 3 it follows that $not(D \sim_{ol} C)$.

(completeness)

We must prove that $\forall C, D \in \mathbf{L}_h$, if $C <_{ol} D$ then $\exists F$ s.t. $F \in \delta^*_{ol}(C)$ and $F \sim_{ol} D$.

Let C and D be two clauses in $\mathbf{L}_h$ such that $C <_{ol} D$. This implies that there exists an injective substitution σ such that $D.\sigma \subseteq C$. Moreover, it holds $consts(D) \subseteq consts(C)$.

Let E be the clause obtained by replacing each constant in C (if any) but not in D (i.e. in $consts(C) - consts(D)$) with a new variable.

Let $consts(C) - consts(D)$ be the set $\{a_1, a_2, ..., a_n\}$, and $\{x_1, x_2, ..., x_n\}, n \geq 0$, be the set of the corresponding new variables. Thus, we have defined an *antisubstitution*

$$\eta: \{a_1, a_2, ..., a_n\} \to \{x_1, x_2, ..., x_n\} \text{ s.t. } \eta(a_i) = x_i, i = 1, 2, ..., n.$$

It is worth noting that η coincides with $\sigma^{-1}.\lambda$, where λ is a variable renaming from $vars(D)$ to $\{x_1, x_2, ..., x_n\}$. By construction, $E \in \delta^n_{ol}(C)$. In fact, E is obtained by applying n times the point (i) of Definition 6.

We must prove that $D \in \delta^*_{ol}(E)$. This is the case when $t = |D| - |C| > 0$ (if $t = 0$ then $E \sim_{ol} D$). In such a case, we can easily refine E by applying the point (ii) of Definition 6 t times, so that we can write: $D \in \delta^t_{ol}(E)$.

This completes the proof since we have found E s.t. $D \in \delta^*_{ol}(E)$ and $E \in \delta^*_{ol}(C)$. Moreover, we have an upper bound to the number of upward refinement steps required to produce D from C, since we have shown that $D \in \delta^{n+t}_{ol}(C)$. q.e.d.

A nice property of the operators ρ_{ol} and δ_{ol} is that, if a clause C properly θ_{ol}-subsumes a clause D then $size(D) > size(C)$. Indeed, point (i) of Definition 5 increases the size of a clause by 1, while point (ii) increases the size of the clause at least by 1 - when all the arguments of the atom l are new variables - and at most by $n + 1$, where n is the arity of the predicate in l - when l does not introduce new variables. Dually, point (i) of Definition 6 decreases the size of a clause by 1, while point (ii) decreases the size of the clause at least by 1 - when all the arguments of the dropped atom l are new variables - and at most by $n + 1$ - when all the arguments of l are *old* variables.

Another observation is that the notions of generality (*subsumption*) and refinement unify for spaces of Datalog clauses ordered by θ_{OI}-subsumption, while Shapiro (and Niblett) needs a definition of refinement that does not coincide with that of the quasi-ordering of the clauses (based on logical implication).

Furthermore, if C properly θ_{OI}-subsumes D, then D (C) is in the set of the k-step downward (upward) refinements of C (D), with $k \le size(D) - size(C)$. In formulae,

$$D \in \rho^k_{OI}(C), \qquad C \in \delta^k_{OI}(D), \qquad k \le size(D) - size(C)$$

Practically speaking, this means that the chain of refinements from C to D is guaranteed not to exceed length k. Thus, it is possible to establish syntactically and statically (that is, just by looking at the clauses and computing their sizes) an upper bound to the computational effort required to refine an incorrect clause, if we already have some kind of background information about the structure of the clauses (the *template*) in the Datalog program to be learned, or if we are able to compute the highest complexity of each clause in some way (for instance, from the set $B \cup E^+ \cup E^-$, through the process of *pattern reconstruction* described in [7]).

Example. Consider the following two clauses (we omit writing the inequations attached to each clause).

$$C = P(x) :\text{-} Q(x, y) \qquad D = P(x) :\text{-} Q(x, y), Q(a, b)$$

It holds: $size(C) = 5 - 2 = 3$, $size(D) = 8 - 2 = 6$.

Figure 2 shows a portion of the space of the Datalog clauses ordered by θ_{OI}-subsumption. Specifically, it is the specialization hierarchy rooted in C.

D can be obtained by C in $size(D) - size(C) = 3$ downward refinement steps, that is, $D \in \rho^3_{OI}(C)$, through the following sequence of application of the operator ρ_{OI} (the path in bold-face in Figure 2).

$C' = P(x) :\text{-} Q(x, y), Q(u, v)$	$C' \in \rho_{OI}(C)$	(point (ii) of Def. 5)
$C'' = P(x) :\text{-} Q(x, y), Q(a, v)$	$C'' \in \rho_{OI}(C')$	(point (i))
$D = P(x) :\text{-} Q(x, y), Q(a, b)$	$D \in \rho_{OI}(C'')$	(point (i))

In addition, D can be obtained from C in one step by just applying the point (ii) of Definition 5, with $l = Q(a, b)$ (the dashed edge in Figure 2).

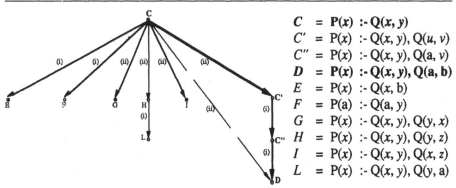

$$
\begin{aligned}
C &= P(x) :\text{-} Q(x, y) \\
C' &= P(x) :\text{-} Q(x, y), Q(u, v) \\
C'' &= P(x) :\text{-} Q(x, y), Q(a, v) \\
D &= P(x) :\text{-} Q(x, y), Q(a, b) \\
E &= P(x) :\text{-} Q(x, b) \\
F &= P(a) :\text{-} Q(a, y) \\
G &= P(x) :\text{-} Q(x, y), Q(y, x) \\
H &= P(x) :\text{-} Q(x, y), Q(y, z) \\
I &= P(x) :\text{-} Q(x, y), Q(x, z) \\
L &= P(x) :\text{-} Q(x, y), Q(y, a)
\end{aligned}
$$

Fig. 2. A portion of the specialization hierarchy rooted in the clause $C = P(x) :\text{-} Q(x, y)$. Each node denotes a proper downward refinement of C. An edge from φ to ψ denotes the fact that $\psi \in \rho_{OI}(\varphi)$. Edges are labelled by either (i) or (ii), according to the corresponding point of Definition 5 that has been applied.

Dually, C can be obtained from D in at most three upward refinement steps, when a specific-to-general search is performed through the generalization hierarchy rooted in D. Figure 3 shows this search space. The path (D, C'', C', C) in bold-face in Figure 3 mirrors the sequence of application of the operator δ_{ol}.

$C'' = P(x) :\text{-} Q(x, y), Q(a, v)$	$C'' \in \delta_{ol}(D)$	(point (i) of Def. 6)
$C' = P(x) :\text{-} Q(x, y), Q(u, v)$	$C' \in \delta_{ol}(C'')$	(point (i))
$C = P(x) :\text{-} Q(x, y)$	$C \in \delta_{ol}(C')$	(point (ii))

and $C \in \delta^3_{ol}(D)$. Again, alternatively C can be obtained from D in one step by applying the point (ii) of Definition 6, with $l = Q(a, b)$, that is, it holds $C \in \delta_{ol}(D)$. This case is shown by the dashed edge in Figure 3.

5 Application to Document Classification

The refinement operators ρ_{ol} and δ_{ol} have been implemented in a new version of INCR/H [5], an incremental system for revising logic theories expressed as linked constant-free Datalog programs. The restriction of the search space to linked constant-free clauses allows INCR/H to optimize the search for one of the *most general (specific) downward (upward) refinements* of an over-general (over-specific) clause under θ_{ol}-subsumption.

For practical purposes, given an incorrect program, the only relevant refinements are those able to restore the properties of consistency and completeness of the program. Therefore, we restricted the scope of the operators ρ_{ol} and δ_{ol} by pruning the search space of all those clauses that either are inconsistent with the negative examples or do not preserve the completeness of the whole Datalog program. Details about the pruning strategies adopted by the downward refinement operator can be found in [8].

Several experiments have been designed to verify on an empirical basis whether such operators were efficient and effective when they are exploited to cope with a real-world task of program refinement. All the experiments have been carried out in the area of *electronic document classification*, which aims at identifying the membership class of a document [6]. In fact, wherever paper documents are handled, a primary demand is that of grouping documents into classes, according to criteria that usually differ from an

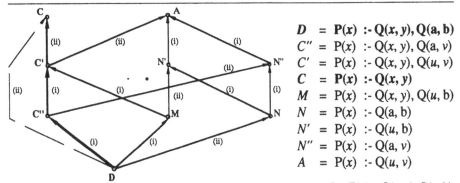

$$
\begin{aligned}
D &= P(x) :\text{-} Q(x, y), Q(a, b) \\
C'' &= P(x) :\text{-} Q(x, y), Q(a, v) \\
C' &= P(x) :\text{-} Q(x, y), Q(u, v) \\
C &= P(x) :\text{-} Q(x, y) \\
M &= P(x) :\text{-} Q(x, y), Q(u, b) \\
N &= P(x) :\text{-} Q(a, b) \\
N' &= P(x) :\text{-} Q(u, b) \\
N'' &= P(x) :\text{-} Q(a, v) \\
A &= P(x) :\text{-} Q(u, v)
\end{aligned}
$$

Fig. 3. A portion of the generalization hierarchy rooted in the clause $D = P(x) :\text{-} Q(x, y), Q(a, b)$. Each node denotes a proper upward refinement of D. An edge from φ to ψ denotes the fact that $\psi \in \delta_{ol}(\varphi)$. Edges are labelled by either (i) or (ii), according to the corresponding point of Definition 6 that has been applied.

environment to another, such as the common subject or the kind of processing the documents must undergo. In most cases, documents belonging to the same class have a set of relevant and invariant layout characteristics, called *page layout signature*, which allows the document to be recognized. The page layout of a document is reconstructed by a process of layout analysis and is translated into a linked clause. An example of the page layout of a document and the corresponding description as a Datalog ground clause is given by Figure 4.

Logic-based document classification relies on a set of simple Datalog programs in order to identify the membership class of the document. In our setting, each class of documents is associated with a set of range-restricted linked constant-free Datalog clauses with the same head. These clauses are learned from a training set of positive and negative instances of the class. Instances are Datalog descriptions of real documents in a computer-revisable form. For our experiments, we considered a database of 171 single-page documents (faxes, forms and letters), belonging to five document classes from specific firms (*AEG, Olivetti, SIFI, SIMS* and *SOGEA*) and to a further set of nine heterogeneous documents (*Reject*). Each document is a positive example for the class it belongs to and, at the same time, is a negative example for all the other classes. The only exceptions are represented by the nine documents in *Reject*, which are exploited as negative examples for all five classes to be learned. For each class, the two refinement operators have been tested separately. The experiments have been replicated ten times for both the refinement operators, by randomly splitting the database of 171 documents into two subsets, namely a *learning* set and a *test* set. In turn, the learning set has been subdivided into *training* set and *tuning* set. The learning set has been exploited in two distinct ways, according to the mode - batch or incremental - adopted to learn the Datalog programs. For the batch mode, this set has been entirely given to INDUBI/H [6], an empirical learning system, as its input. For the incremental mode, only the training set has been used by INDUBI/H in order to produce the first version of the Datalog programs, while the tuning set has been exploited to correct incrementally omission and commission errors made by

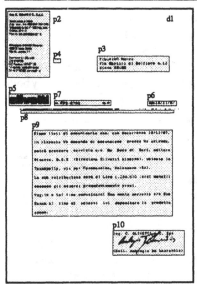

Olivetti(d1) :-
part_of(d1,p2), part_of(d1,p3), part_of(d1,p4), part_of(d1,p5),
part_of(d1,p6), part_of(d1,p7), part_of(d1,p8), part_of(d1,p9),
part_of(d1,p10),
width-medium(p2), width-medium-large(p3), width-smallest(p4),
width-medium(p5), width-medium-small(p6), width-medium-large(p7),
width-very-very-large(p8), width-very-very-large(p9),
width-medium-large(p10),
height-medium-large(p2), height-small(p3), height-smallest(p4),
height-very-small(p5), height-very-very-small(p6),
height-very-very-small(p7), height-smallest(p8), height-large(p9),
height-medium-small(p10),
type-text(p2), type-text(p3), type-text(p4), type-picture(p5), type-text(p6),
type-text(p7), type-text(p8), type-text(p9), type-mixture(p10),
position-top-left(p2), position-top(p3), position-top-left(p4),
position-top-left(p5), position-top-right(p6), position-top(p7),
position-center(p8), position-center(p9), position-bottom-right(p10),
on_top(p5,p8), on_top(p6,p8), on_top(p7,p8), on_top(p9,p10),
to_right(p2,p4), to_right(p5,p7),
aligned-both-columns(p2,p5), aligned-only-lower-row(p5,p7),
aligned-only-left-col(p4,p7), aligned-both-rows(p7,p6),
aligned-only-right-col(p8,p9), aligned-only-upper-row(p4,p3)

Fig. 4. Page layout of an Olivetti letter and its Datalog description.

the programs, if any, through the operators ρ_{ol} and δ_{ol}. The tuning set is made up of only positive (negative) examples in every replication concerning the upward (downward) refinement operator. As a consequence, only omission (commission) errors may occur when testing the upward (downward) operator. Lastly, the test set has been exploited to evaluate the predictive accuracy of the Datalog programs on unclassified documents.

Table 1 shows the results concerning the upward refinement operator. This table compares the programs learned in batch mode with those learned incrementally along two dimensions, namely their predictive accuracy on the test set ($P.A.$) and the computational time taken by the learning system to produce the programs ($Time$). Specifically, the *batch time* is relative to the training set for the batch mode, while the *incremental time* is computed as the sum of the computational time concerning the training set for the incremental mode plus the time concerning the tuning set. Values concerning $P.A.$ are percentages, while those concerning $Time$ are expressed in seconds. All the reported figures refer to the averages on the ten replications.

Table 2 illustrates the results of two statistical methods exploited to evaluate the significance of the observed differences as to $P.A.$ and $Time$ for each class, namely the paired t test (parametric) and the Wilcoxon test (nonparametric). Both the tests have been performed as two-sided tests at a 0.01 level of significance.

Each entry in the table contains the t value and the corresponding significance value for the t test, the W value and the corresponding critical value for the Wilcoxon test.

It is well-known that the t test requires that the population data be normally distributed, when used with small sample sizes (less than 30). Conversely, the Wilcoxon test does not make any assumption on the distribution of the population data. In our setting, the sample size is 10, i.e. the number of replications, thus the t test might seem to be unsuitable. However, we performed preventively the Cucconi's normality test [14] in order to establish whether the population data are normally distributed. Such a test allows us to state that the population is normally distributed at a 0.01 level of significance.

Table 1 shows that the batch-learned programs outperform the incrementally-learned ones for all the classes, with the exception of *SIFI*, as regards the predictive accuracy (shaded boxes). However, Table 2 states that, on the ground of the results obtained by both

Upward Refinement		batch	incr.
AEG	P.A. %	99.1	98.3
	Time (secs)	318.6	148.0
Olivetti	P.A. %	96.6	96.3
	Time (secs)	298.8	222.0
SIFI	P.A. %	98.5	99.0
	Time (secs)	183.4	141.8
SIMS	P.A. %	98.6	98.5
	Time (secs)	367.3	259.2
SOGEA	P.A. %	98.9	98.8
	Time (secs)	132.4	103.4

Table 1. Comparison of the average predictive accuracies on the test set ($P.A.$) and the average computational times ($Time$) for the upward refinement operator.

Upward Refinement	t test				Wilcoxon test			
	batch vs. incremental				batch vs. incremental			
	P.A.		Time		P.A.		Time	
	t value	sign. value	t value	sign. value	W value	crit. value	W value	crit. value
AEG	1.309	.2229	7.751	.0001		3		45
Olivetti	.194	.8506	2.502	.0334	-1	32	43	45
SIFI	-.889	.3974	6.405	.0001	-8	10		45
SIMS	.096	.9238	3.718	.0046	1	10		45
SOGEA	.142	.8905	3.893	.0057	1	21		45

Table 2. Results of the paired two-sided t test and of the Wilcoxon test for the upward refinement operator.

tests, there is no statistically significant difference between the two programs (the probability of error in rejecting the hypothesis that the two average values are equal is greater than 0.01), with the exception of the class AEG for the Wilcoxon test (shaded box). On the contrary, there is a statistically significant improvement when learning the program in incremental mode wrt learning it in batch mode, as regards the computational time, for all the classes, with the exception of Olivetti for the Wilcoxon test (shaded boxes).

The results concerning the downward refinement operator are reported in Table 3. Again, the comparison between the Datalog programs learned in batch mode with those learned incrementally has been focused on the values of the predictive accuracies on the test set (P.A.) and of the computational times (Time) for each class, averaged on the ten replications.

An analysis of Table 3 leads us to observe that the incremental approach determines an increase in the predictive accuracy of all the programs with the exception of the class SIMS (shaded boxes). Moreover, the incremental method outperforms the batch one for all the classes as to the computational times, as expected.

By pairwise comparing the average predictive accuracies and computational times obtained by the two methods by means of both the paired two-sided t test and the two-sided Wilcoxon test (Table 4), we can conclude that neither the increases nor the decreases of the predictive accuracies are statistically significant, with the exceptions of the results concerning the class SIFI (shaded boxes) for both tests. Indeed, in such a case, the probability of error in rejecting the hypothesis that the two average values are equal is less than the level of significance 0.01 for both tests. Conversely, the differences in the computational times are always statistically significant (shaded boxes).

The overall analysis of the experimental results shows that the differences of the predictive accuracies between the batch method and the incremental one are not statistically significant in most cases (9 out of 10 for the t test, and 8 out of 10 for the Wilcoxon test) and in one case (out of two) in which they are significant, the use of the refinement operators ρ_{ol} and δ_{ol} allows INCR/H to generate Datalog programs which outperform those learned by INDUBI/H. In addition, by comparing the percentage values of the predictive accuracies, the incremental approach behaves

Downward Refinement		batch	incr.
AEG	P.A. %	97.8	99.8
	Time (secs)	508.4	200.5
Olivetti	P.A. %	97.7	98.1
	Time (secs)	490.9	334.1
SIFI	P.A. %	98.7	99.7
	Time (secs)	194.4	138.3
SIMS	P.A. %	98.4	97.4
	Time (secs)	446.8	252.4
SOGEA	P.A. %	98.0	98.6
	Time (secs)	194.3	54.6

Table 3. Comparison of the average predictive accuracies on the test set (P.A.) and the average computational times (Time) for the downward refinement operator.

Downward Refinement	t test				Wilcoxon test			
	batch vs. incremental				batch vs. incremental			
	P.A.		Time		P.A.		Time	
	t value	sign. value	t value	sign. value	W value	crit. value	W value	crit. value
AEG	-2.212	.0543	9.413	.0001	-30	39	55	45
Olivetti	-.440	.6704	6.721	.0001	-2	21	55	45
SIFI	-3.354	.0085	12.902	.0001	-28	28	55	45
SIMS	1.103	.2987	14.078	.0001	12	28	55	45
SOGEA	-.745	.4754	16.522	.0001	-6	15	55	45

Table 4. Results of the paired two-sided t test and of the Wilcoxon test for the downward refinement operator.

better than the batch one in 5 cases out of 10. As to the computational times, the decrease occurs in all the cases and, in addition, it is nearly always statistically significant.

6 Conclusions and Future Work

This paper has presented two operators for refining Datalog clauses ordered by θ_{oi}-subsumption. The weakening of the generalization model from θ-subsumption to θ_{oi}-subsumption allows the refinement operators to satisfy the properties of local finiteness, properness, and completeness, which are deemed fundamental to get effective revisions of incorrect programs.

These operators have been embodied in an incremental learning system for theory revision. Extensive experimentation in the area of electronic document processing has shown that the operators are able to refine effectively and efficiently Datalog programs for document classification. Indeed, when used to classify new documents, the revised programs have a predictive accuracy statistically comparable or better than that of programs learned *from scratch*, that is, in batch mode rather than starting from incorrect programs and refining them incrementally. Nevertheless, as expected, the overall efficiency of the learning process results largely increased when the operators ρ_{oi} and δ_{oi} are used, since the computational time almost halves - it decreases from an average of more than 52 minutes (3153.3 seconds) to less than 31 minutes (1854.3 seconds). These promising results lead us to integrate the operators into PLRS [30], the learning module of IBIsys, a software environment for office automation distributed by Olivetti.

Future work will extend the scope of the refinement operators along three dimensions - Datalog⁻ programs, introduction of functions in the language, and ambivalent clauses.

Acknowledgment

We thank Prof. Shan-Hwei Nienhuys-Cheng, Dr. Patrick van der Laag, and the anonymous referees who made insightful comments on several drafts of this paper.

References

1. Bergadano, F., and Gunetti, D., Learning Clauses by Tracing Derivations, *Proceedings of the Fourth International Workshop on Inductive Logic Programming, ILP-94*, S. Wrobel (Ed.), GMD-Studien Nr.237, 11-29, 1994.
2. Chang, C.-L. and Lee, R. C.-T*., *Symbolic Logic and Mechanical Theorem Proving*, Academic Press, 1973.
3. Cohen, W. W., Rapid Prototyping of ILP Systems Using Explicit Bias, *Proceedings of the IJCAI-93 Workshop on Inductive Logic Programming*, F. Bergadano, L. De Raedt, S. Matwin, S. Muggleton (Eds.), 24-35, 1993.
4. Eisinger, N., and Ohlbach, H. J., Deduction Systems Based on Resolution, in *Handbook of Logic in Artificial Intelligence and Logic Programming, Volume 1, Logical Foundations*, D. M. Gabbay, C. J. Hogger and J. A. Robinson (Eds.), Oxford Science Publications, 183-271, 1993.
5. Esposito, F., Malerba, D., and Semeraro, G., INCR/H: A System for Revising Logical Theories, *Proceedings of the MLnet Workshop on Theory Revision and Restructuring in Machine Learning*, ECML-94, Arbeitspapiere der GMD N.842, S. Wrobel (Ed.), 13-15, 1994.
6. - , Multistrategy Learning for Document Recognition, *Applied Artificial Intelligence: An International Journal*, 8:33-84, 1994.
7. Esposito, F., Malerba, D., Semeraro, G., Brunk, C., and Pazzani, M., Traps and Pitfalls when Learning Logical Definitions from Relations, in *Methodologies for Intelligent Systems - Proceedings of the 8th International Symposium, ISMIS '94*, Lecture Notes in Artificial Intelligence 869, Z. W. Ras and M. Zemankova (Eds.), Springer-Verlag, 376-385, 1994.
8. Esposito, F., Fanizzi, N., Malerba, D., and Semeraro, G., Downward Refinement of Hierarchical Datalog

Theories, *Proceedings of the Joint Conference on Declarative Programming, GULP-PRODE'95*, M. Alpuente and M. I. Sessa (Eds.), 148-159, 1995.

9. - , *Locally Finite, Proper and Complete Operators for Refining Datalog Programs*, LACAM Technical Report No. 95-014, Dipartimento di Informatica, Università di Bari, June 1995.

10. Garey, M. R., and Johnson, D. S., *Computers and Intractability: A Guide to the Theory of NP-Completeness*, Freeman, New York, 1979.

11. Gold, E. M., Language identification in the limit, *Information and Control*, 10:447-474, 1967.

12. Gottlob, G., Subsumption and Implication, *Information Processing Letters*, 24:109-111, 1987.

13. Gottlob, G., and Fermüller, C. G., Removing redundancy from a clause, *Artificial Intelligence*, 61:263-289, 1993.

14. Grigoletto, F., *Notes in statistics, Part II* (in italian), CLEUP, Padova, 1975.

15. Helft, N., Inductive Generalization: A Logical Framework, in *Progress in Machine Learning - Proceedings of EWSL 87: 2nd European Working Session on Learning*, I. Bratko & N. Lavrac (Eds.), Sigma Press, Wilmslow, 149-157, 1987.

16. Kanellakis, P. C., Elements of Relational Database Theory, in *Handbook of Theoretical Computer Science, Volume B, Formal Models and Semantics*, J. Van Leeuwen (Ed.), Elsevier Science Publ., 1073-1156, 1990.

17. Kietz, J. U., and Wrobel, S., Controlling the Complexity of Learning in Logic through Syntactic and Task-Oriented Models, in *Inductive Logic Programming*, S. Muggleton (Ed.), Academic Press, 335-359, 1992.

18. Ling, X., Inductive Learning from Good Examples, *Proceedings of the 12th International Joint Conference on Artificial Intelligence*, J. Mylopoulos and R. Reiter (Eds.), Sydney, Australia, 751-756, 1991.

19. Lloyd, J. W., *Foundations of Logic Programming*, Second Edition, Springer-Verlag, New York, 1987.

20. Loveland, D. W., *Automated Theorem Proving: A Logical Basis*, North-Holland, Amsterdam, 1978.

21. Muggleton, S., and Feng, C., Efficient Induction of Logic Programs, in *Inductive Logic Programming*, S. Muggleton (Ed.), 281-298, Academic Press, 1992.

22. Niblett, T., A note on refinement operators, in *Machine Learning: ECML-93 - Proceedings of the European Conference on Machine Learning*, Lecture Notes in Artificial Intelligence 667, P. B. Brazdil (Ed.), Springer-Verlag, 329-335, 1993.

23. Pazzani, M. , and Kibler, D., The utility of knowledge in inductive learning, *Machine Learning*, 9:57-94, 1992.

24. Plotkin, G. D., A Note on Inductive Generalization, in *Machine Intelligence 5*, B. Meltzer and D. Michie (Eds.), Edinburgh University Press, 153 - 163, 1970.

25. - , Building-in Equational Theories, in *Machine Intelligence 7*, B. Meltzer and D. Michie (Eds.), Edinburgh University Press, 73-90, 1972.

26. Popper, K. R., *Conjectures and refutations: The Growth of Scientific Knowledge*, Harper Torch Books, New York, 1968.

27. Quinlan, J. R., Learning Logical Implications from Relations, *Machine Learning*, 5:239-266, 1990.

28. Reiter, R., Equality and domain closure in first order databases, *Journal of ACM*, 27:235-249, 1980.

29. Semeraro, G., Esposito, F., Malerba, D., Brunk, C., and Pazzani, M., Avoiding Non-Termination when Learning Logic Programs: A Case Study with FOIL and FOCL, in *Logic Program Synthesis and Transformation - Meta-Programming in Logic*, Lecture Notes in Computer Science 883, L. Fribourg and F. Turini (Eds.), Springer-Verlag, 183-198, 1994.

30. Semeraro, G., Esposito, F., and Malerba, D., Learning Contextual Rules for Document Understanding, *Proceedings of the 10th Conference on Artificial Intelligence for Applications (CAIA'94)*, IEEE Computer Society Press, Los Alamitos, CA, 108-115, 1994.

31. Shapiro, E. Y., An Algorithm that Infers Theories from Facts, *Proceedings of the 7th International Joint Conference on Artificial Intelligence*, Vancouver, Canada, 446-451, 1981.

32. - , *Inductive Inference of Theories from Facts*, Technical Report 192, Department of Computer Science, Yale University, New Haven, Connecticut, 1981.

33. Tausend, B., Representing Biases for Inductive Logic Programming, in *Machine Learning: ECML-94 - Proceedings of the European Conference on Machine Learning*, Lecture Notes in Artificial Intelligence 784, F. Bergadano and L. De Raedt (Eds.), Springer-Verlag, 427-430, 1994.

34. van der Laag, P. R. J., and Nienhuys-Cheng, S.-H., A Note on Ideal Refinement Operators in Inductive Logic Programming, *Proceedings of the Fourth International Workshop on Inductive Logic Programming, ILP-94*, S. Wrobel (Ed.) , GMD-Studien Nr.237, 247-260, 1994.

35. - , Existence and Nonexistence of Complete Refinement Operators, in *Machine Learning: ECML-94 - Proceedings of the European Conference on Machine Learning*, Lecture Notes in Artificial Intelligence 784, F. Bergadano and L. De Raedt (Eds.), Springer-Verlag, 307-322, 1994.

Guiding Program Development Systems by a Connection Based Proof Strategy

Christoph Kreitz   Jens Otten   Stephan Schmitt

Fachgebiet Intellektik, Fachbereich Informatik
Technische Hochschule Darmstadt
Alexanderstr. 10, 64283 Darmstadt, Germany
{kreitz,jeotten,steph}@intellektik.informatik.th-darmstadt.de

Abstract. We present an automated proof method for constructive logic based on Wallen's matrix characterization for intuitionistic validity. The proof search strategy extends Bibel's connection method for classical predicate logic. It generates a matrix proof which will then be transformed into a proof within a standard sequent calculus. Thus we can use an efficient proof method to guide the development of constructive proofs in interactive proof/program development systems.

1 Introduction

According to the *proofs-as-programs* paradigm of program synthesis the development of verifiably correct software is strongly related to proving theorems about the satisfiability of a given specification. If such a theorem is proven in a constructive manner then the proof construction implicitly contains an algorithm which is guaranteed to solve the specified problem. In contrast to 'deductive' synthesis for which classical proof methods are sufficient, however, synthesis techniques based on this paradigm have rely on *constructive* logics for their adequacy. Therefore computer systems which support the development of constructive proofs and the extraction of programs from proofs are very important for program synthesis.

Such systems (e.g. NuPRL [6], Oyster [5], Isabelle [14], LEGO [15]) are usually designed as *interactive* proof editors supported by a *tactic* mechanism for programming proofs on the meta-level. Most of them are based on a very expressive constructive theory. To allow a proper interaction between the system and its users this theory is usually formulated as natural deduction or sequent calculus and includes a calculus for predicate logic similar to Gentzen's [8] calculi for intuitionistic logic. It has been demonstrated that these systems can be used quite successfully, if properly guided, but the degree of automatic support is very weak. A user often has to deal with subproblems which appear trivial to him since they depend solely on predicate logic. A formal proof, however, turns out to be rather tedious since existing tactics dealing with predicate logic are far from being complete.

On the other hand, theorem provers like Setheo [9], Otter [20], or KoMeT [2] have demonstrated that formal reasoning in *classical predicate logic* can be automated sufficiently well. It would therefore be desirable to integrate techniques from automated theorem proving into already existing program synthesis tools. This would not only liberate the users of a proof development system from having to solve problems from first order logic by hand but would also make it possible to generate simple (non-recursive) algorithms fully automatically.

Two problems have to be solved for this purpose. Firstly, since a *constructive proof* contains much more information than a classical one many of the well known classical normal forms and equivalences are not valid constructively. Despite of the success in the classical case there is not yet an efficient proof procedure for constructive logics and therefore the existing classical proof methods need to be extended. Secondly, we have to take into account that efficient *proof search* must be based on some internal characterization of validity which avoids the usual redundancies contained in natural deduction and sequent proofs while for the sake of comprehensibility (and for an extraction of programs in the usual fashion) the proof *representation* must be based on the formal calculus underlying the program development system. This makes it necessary to convert the internal representation of proofs into a more natural one.

We have developed a complete proof procedure for constructive first-order logic and a technique for integrating it into a program development system based on a sequent calculus. As a starting point we have used a proof procedure called the *connection method* [3, 4] which has successfully been realized in theorem provers for classical predicate logic like Setheo [9] and KoMeT [2]. It is based on a characterization for the classical validity of logical formulae which recently has been extended by Wallen [19] into a matrix characterization of *intuitionistic* validity. We have considerably extended the connection method according to this characterization and developed a method for converting matrix proofs into sequent proofs. The combined procedure, whose structure is depicted in figure 1, is currently being implemented as a proof tactic of the NuPRL proof development system [6] and will thus support the efficient construction of proofs and verified routine programs within a rich constructive theory. It proceeds in three steps.

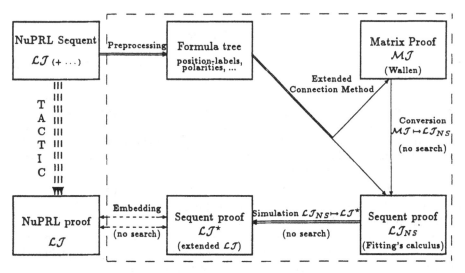

Fig. 1. Structure of the combined proof procedure

1. In a preprocessing step a NuPRL sequent will be converted into a formula tree augmented by information (such as polarities, position labels and type-labels) which will be helpful for guiding the proof search.

2. In the second step we use our extended connection method to search for a proof according to Wallen's matrix characterization. While originally we were interested only in constructing a matrix proof which should be translated into a sequent proof afterwards our investigations have shown that it is helpful to exploit the close relation between a matrix proof and a proof in Fitting's [7] sequent calculus $\mathcal{LJ}_{NS}$[1] and to consider the structure of the corresponding sequent proof already *during* the proof search and design our proof procedure as a hybrid method combining the connection method with the sequent calculus. The result of our proof search procedure will be a matrix proof which can already be considered as the skeleton of an $\mathcal{LJ}_{NS}$-proof.

3. In the final step the information gained during proof search will be used to construct a standard sequent proof which is valid in NuPRL. Since our proof search already yields the structure of a sequent proof in $\mathcal{LJ}_{NS}$ we are liberated from having to convert a matrix proof ($\mathcal{MJ}$) into an $\mathcal{LJ}_{NS}$-proof. Nevertheless the proof still needs to be converted since Fitting's *non-standard* sequent calculus $\mathcal{LJ}_{NS}$ is more complex than the standard Gentzen-like calculus $\mathcal{LJ}$ used in program development systems. For reasons which we shall discuss in section 4 our proof transformation will proceed in two smaller steps which do not involve any additional search.

In the rest of this paper we shall describe the essential components of our procedure. After explaining how to construct the augmented formula tree in section 2 we shall elaborate the extended connection method in section 3. In section 4 we shall then discuss the procedure for constructing a standard sequent proof acceptable for the NuPRL System. We conclude with a few remarks on implementation issues and future investigations.

2 Constructing the Augmented Formula Tree

In the first step of our procedure a given sequent has to be converted into a formula tree which then can be investigated by the proof search method. Except for dealing with a few peculiarities of NuPRL[2] this is can be done by a standard procedure which collects the assumptions (antecedent) of a sequent on the left hand side of an implication whose right hand side is the sequent's conclusion (succedent) and adds universal quantifiers for all the free variables. Constructing a tree representation of the resulting formula again uses a standard technique. As an example, figure 2 presents the formula tree of the formula

$$F \equiv (S \wedge (\neg(T \Rightarrow R) \Rightarrow P)) \Rightarrow (\neg((P \Rightarrow Q) \wedge (T \Rightarrow R)) \Rightarrow (S \wedge \neg\neg P))$$

which we shall later use as a running example for our proof procedure.

In this tree each node represents a sub-term of the given formula and is marked by its major logical connective. In addition to that it is associated with a polarity, a position label, and a type label. These informations are necessary for guiding the proof search and can be computed while constructing the formula tree.

---

[1] When developing his matrix characterization for intuitionistic validity Wallen [19] has used Fitting's formulation of the sequent calculus as theoretical framework to prove his characterization theorems.

[2] Some of the assumptions declare the type of certain variables or the wellformedness of certain expressions and may simply be ignored.

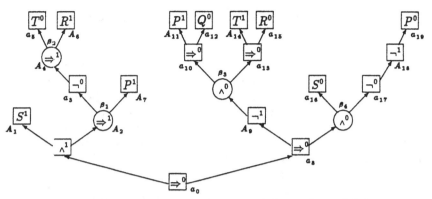

Fig. 2. Formula tree with polarities, positions, and type labels

- The *polarity* (0 or 1) of a node indicates whether the corresponding sub-formula would occur negated (1) in a normal form of the given formula or not (0). The polarity of the root is 0 and the polarity of other nodes is determined recursively by the polarity and the connective of their parents. In figure 2 the polarity of each node occurs on top of its connective.

  Pairs of atomic formulae with the same predicate symbol but different polarities (so-called *connections*) correspond to the axioms in a sequent proof and are a key notion in the matrix characterization of validity.

- While polarities are important for both classical and intuitionistic proof methods the *position labels* (*positions*) are necessary only for constructive reasoning. They encode the fact that in intuitionistic sequent calculi the order of rule applications cannot be permuted as easily as in classical logic. Special nodes ($\Rightarrow^0$, $\forall^0$, $\neg^0$, and atoms with polarity 0) correspond to rules which – when being used in a top-down fashion in order to *reduce* the node – will delete formulae from the actual sequent. In a proof these rules have to be applied as late as possible.

  By analyzing the sequence of positions on the paths from the root to two connected atomic formulae (the *prefixes* of the formulae) one can determine whether the two atoms can form an axiom which closes some subproof and in which order the corresponding rules need to be applied in order to construct this subproof. Technically this is done by assigning constants (position labels with small letters) to the special nodes and variables to the others. By trying to unify the prefixes of two connected atoms one may then check whether both atoms can be reached by a sequence of rule applications at the same time. In figure 2 we have assigned positions to nodes containing a negation, implication, universal quantifier, or an atom. All other nodes are not significant for building prefixes.

- *Type labels*[3] express a property of sequent rules which is important mostly during proof search. Nodes of type β (i.e. $\wedge^0$, $\vee^1$, and $\Rightarrow^1$) are particularly important since the corresponding rules would cause a proof to branch into two independent subproofs. In order to complete the proof each of these subproofs (encoded by a *path*) must be closed with an axiom (i.e. a connection). Thus investigating β-branches not yet closed will help identifying those connections which will contribute to a progress in the remaining proof search. In figure 2 we have marked β-nodes by circles and labels $\beta_1, \ldots \beta_4$. Nodes of other types remain unmarked.

---

[3] The assignment of types to nodes follows the laws of the tableaux calculus [1].

3 The Connection Method for Constructive Logics

After constructing the augmented formula tree a proof search will focus on 'connections' between atomic formulae which can be shown to be 'complementary'. According to the characterization of validity all 'paths' through the formula tree must contain such a connection. In our procedure the set of all paths (within a subproof under consideration) which are not yet investigated will be encoded by the 'active path'. This will help to guide the search efficiently. Before describing our procedure in detail we shall briefly explain the notions of connections, paths, and complementarity and resume Wallen's matrix characterization for intuitionistic validity.

3.1 A Matrix Characterization for Intuitionistic Validity

In propositional classical logic a formula F is valid if there is a spanning set of connections for F. A *connection* is a pair of atomic formulae with the same predicate symbol but different *polarities* such as P^1 and P^0. A set of connections *spans* a formula F if every *path* through F^4 contains at least one connection. This characterization also applies to predicate logic if the connected formulae can be shown to be *complementary*, i.e. if all the terms contained in connected formulae can be made identical by some (*first-order*/quantifier) substitution σ_Q.

In *sequent calculi* like Gentzen's $\mathcal{LK}$ and $\mathcal{LJ}$ [8] or Fitting's calculi [7] the difference between classical and intuitionistic reasoning is expressed by certain restrictions on the intuitionistic rules. If rules are applied in a top down fashion these restrictions cause formulae to be deleted from a sequent. Applying a rule (i.e. *reducing* a sub-formula) too early may delete a formula which later will be necessary to complete the proof. Because of this *non-permutability* of rules in intuitionistic sequent calculi the order of rule applications must be arranged appropriately. In Wallen's matrix characterization this requirement is expressed by an *intuitionistic* substitution σ_J which makes the prefixes of connected atoms identical. A *prefix* of a node A consists of the sequence of position labels on the path from the root to A and encodes the sequence of rules which have to be applied in order to isolate the sub-formula described by A. The prefix of the atom R^0 in figure 2, for instance, is $a_0 a_8 A_9 a_{13} a_{15}$.

Both the first-order and the intuitionistic substitution can be computed by unification algorithms (see section 3.3) and put restrictions on the order of rule-applications (see [19] or [11]). $\sigma_J(B) = b_1...b_n$ for instance, means that all the special positions $b_1...b_n$ *must* have been reduced *before* position B and after its predecessor. Otherwise certain sub-formulae which are necessary assumptions for applying the sequent rule corresponding to B would not be available. Similarly $\sigma_Q(x) = t$ requires all the Eigenvariables of t to be introduced by some rule before the quantifier corresponding to x can be reduced. Together with the ordering of the formula tree the *combined substitution* $\sigma := (\sigma_Q, \sigma_J)$ determines the ordering $\lhd$ in which a given formula F has to be reduced by the rules of the sequent calculus. This ordering must be acyclic since otherwise no proof for F can be given. If $\lhd$ is acyclic then σ is called *admissible*.

---

[4] A *path* through F is a subset of the atoms of F which corresponds to a horizontal path through the (nested) *matrix representation* of F. See [19, p. 215] for a complete definition.

During the proof search it may become necessary to create multiple instances of the same sub-formula. The number of copies generated to complete the proof is called *multiplicity* μ. Again, a multiplicity may be due to a quantifier or specific to intuitionistic reasoning. Altogether, the following theorem has been proven in [19].

Theorem 1 Matrix characterization of intuitionistic validity.
A formula F is intuitionistically valid if and only if there is
  – *a multiplicity μ,*
  – *an admissible combined substitution $\sigma := (\sigma_Q, \sigma_J)$,*
  – *a set of connections which are complementary under σ*
such that every path through the formula F contains a connection from this set.

3.2   Connection Based Proof Search

In Bibel's classical connection method [3, 4] the search for a matrix proof of a given formula proceeds by considering connections between atomic formulae whose sub-terms can be unified. The selection of appropriate connections is guided by the *active path* and the set of *open goals*. Developing a procedure which constructs intuitionistic proofs on the basis of theorem 1 means extending the key concepts for guiding the search procedure accordingly. This allows a formulation of our procedure which is similar to the one of the classical connection method operating on logical formulae in non-normal form.

Our investigations have shown that during the proof search one should not only consider paths and connections but also the branching structure of the corresponding (partial) sequent proof. This structure provides valuable informations about the reduction ordering $\lhd$ to be constructed and helps selecting appropriate connections guiding the search process. Furthermore, it allows to consider *local* substitutions (see [11, section 5]) instead of global ones, i.e. substitutions which can be applied independently within sub-proofs of a sequent proof. Such a local view reduces the number of copies of sub-formulae which have to be generated to find a (global) sub-stitution and keeps the search space and the proof size smaller. Since it also simplifies the conversion of the 'abstract proof' into a humanly comprehensible sequent proof we have designed our proof search procedure as a hybrid method which generates a matrix proof and the structure of the corresponding sequent proof simultaneously.

We shall now describe our search strategy by developing a proof for the formula

$$F \equiv (S \wedge (\neg(T \Rightarrow R) \Rightarrow P)) \Rightarrow (\neg((P \Rightarrow Q) \wedge (T \Rightarrow R)) \Rightarrow (S \wedge \neg\neg P))$$

whose formula tree has already been presented in figure 2. To simplify our illustration we shall from now on display only a skeleton of this tree in which only positions with type label β, branches rooted at such a β-position (i.e. a,b,...,h – also called β-branches), and atomic formulae are marked.

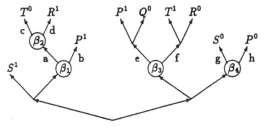

Our search procedure will consider connections between atomic formulae whose sub-terms and prefixes can be unified and build the skeleton of a sequent proof whose nodes and branches are labeled similarly to the formula tree. The search is guided by the *active β-path* and the set of *open subgoals* in the partial sequent proof. These notions extend the original concepts mentioned above and are roughly defined as follows (see [13] for precise definitions).

Definition 2.

1. The *β-prefix* of an atom A is the set of all (labels of) β-branches that dominate A in the formula tree.
2. The *active β-path* $\mathcal{P}_\beta$ for a branch u in the sequent proof is the set of labels of branches on the path between u and the root of the proof tree.
3. The *active path* $\mathcal{P}$ for a branch u of the proof tree is the set of atoms whose *β-prefix* is a subset of $\mathcal{P}_\beta(u)$.[5]
4. The set of *open subgoals* $\mathcal{C}_\beta$ is the set of open branches in the sequent proof structure (i.e. branches which are not closed by an axiom).

To prove F we begin by selecting an arbitrary atomic formula, say P^1, in branch 'e' of the formula tree and connect it with the atom P^0 in the 'h'-branch. This means that in a sequent proof we have to reduce two β-positions, namely β_3 and β_4. Unifying the prefixes of P^1 and P^0 (see section 3.3) of the two atoms leads to the substitution $\sigma_J \equiv \{A_9 \backslash a_{17}B, \ A_{18} \backslash Ba_{10}C, \ A_{11} \backslash Ca_{19}\}$ where B and C are new variables. Within an intuitionistic sequent proof the node marked by a_{17} must therefore be reduced before A_9, a_{10} before A_{18}, and a_{19} before A_{11}. Furthermore β_4 must be reduced before a_{17} and A_9 before β_3 according to the ordering of the formula tree in figure 2. Thus σ_J induces the reduction ordering $\beta_4 \lhd \beta_3$ and we have to split into the branches 'g' and 'h' (corresponding to β_4) before we split the 'h'-branch into 'e' and 'f' (corresponding to β_3). This closes the 'e'-branch in the sequent proof as shown in figure 3.

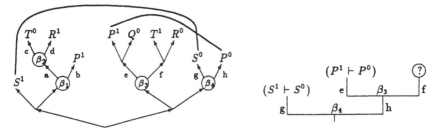

Fig. 3. The first and second proof step

In the next step we choose the 'g'-branch from the set $\mathcal{C}_\beta = \{g, \ f\}$ of open subgoals. The active β-path $\mathcal{P}_\beta = \{g\}$ for 'g' induces an active path $\mathcal{P} = \{S^1, S^0\}$. The only atom S^0 in the 'g'-branch of the formula tree can therefore be connected to S^1 in the active path without further reductions of β-nodes. The unification of the prefixes of S^1 and S^0 consists of a simple matching which extends σ_J by $\{A_1 \backslash a_8 a_{16}\}$. This closes branch 'g' in the sequent proof.

---

[5] $\mathcal{P}$ is thus the set of atoms (in the *formula tree*) which can be reached from the root or any position corresponding to a element of $\mathcal{P}_\beta(u)$ without passing through a β-position.

The only open branch is now the 'f'-branch ($C_\beta = \{f\}$). In the formula tree this branch contains the two atoms R^0 and T^1. We select R^0 and connect it with R^1 in branch 'd' of the formula tree. In the active path $\mathcal{P} = \{S^1, P^0, R^0, T^1\}$ for 'f' ($\mathcal{P}_\beta = \{h,f\}$) this atom is not yet included. Thus we have to reduce β_1 which splits the proof into 'a' and 'b' and β_2 which splits the 'a'-branch into 'c' and 'd'. The unification of the prefixes of R^0 and R^1 extends σ_J by $\{A_2\backslash a_8 a_{17}D, B\backslash Da_3E, A_4\backslash Ea_{13}a_{15}, A_6\backslash\epsilon\}$. Together with the tree ordering ($\beta_4 < a_{17}$, $\beta_1 = A_2 < a_3$, $A_9 < \beta_3 < a_{13}$, $A_4 = \beta_2$) it induces the reduction ordering $\beta_4 \lhd \beta_1 \lhd \beta_3 \lhd \beta_2$. Therefore we have to insert the β-split into 'a' and 'b' *between* the reduction of β_4 and β_3 (leaving the rest of the partial sequent proof unchanged), split into the branches 'c' and 'd' *after* reducing β_3, and close the 'd'-branch by the axiom $R^1 \vdash R^0$. The result is shown in figure 4.

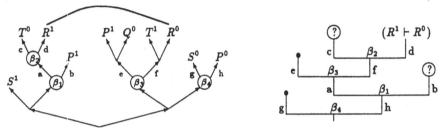

Fig. 4. The third proof step

After the third step the two branches 'b' and 'c' remain open ($C_\beta = \{b, c\}$). The active β-paths for 'b' ($\mathcal{P}_\beta = \{h, b\}$) and for 'c' ($\mathcal{P}_\beta = \{h,a,f,c\}$) induce active paths $\mathcal{P} = \{S^1, P^0, P^1\}$ and $\mathcal{P} = \{S^1, P^0, T^1, R^0, T^0\}$ respectively. To close these branches we connect P^1 in the 'b'-branch of the formula tree to P^0 in the active path for 'b' and T^0 in the 'c'-branch to T^1 in the active path for 'c'. Again the unification of the prefixes consists of a simple matching. It extends σ_J by $\{A_7\backslash a_3 E a_{10} C a_{19}, A_{14}\backslash a_{15}a_5\}$ which shows that now every branch in the sequent proof can be closed.

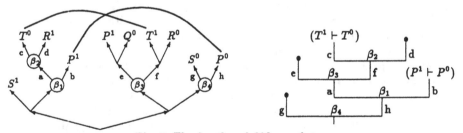

Fig. 5. The fourth and fifth proof step

This concludes the intuitionistic proof for F. All the paths through F contain a connection which is complementary under σ_J. Furthermore, a complete sequent proof can easily be constructed from the proof skeleton obtained in the process since the order in which all the other nodes have to be reduced is determined by the reduction ordering induced by σ_J and the ordering of the formula tree for F. The resulting sequent proof is presented in figure 6.

A full description of the complete proof search strategy for first-order intuitionistic logic which we just have illustrated is rather complex and shall therefore not be presented in this paper. Details can be found in [13].

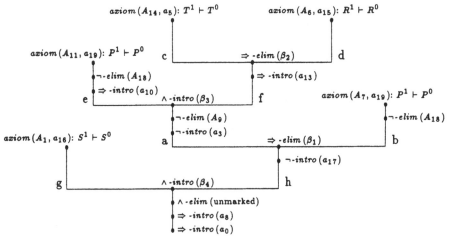

Fig. 6. Complete representation of the resulting sequent proof

3.3 Prefix-Unification

The efficiency of the proof search procedure described above strongly depends on the efficiency of the unification algorithms computing both the first-order and intuitionistic substitutions. While the first-order substitution σ_Q can be computed by well-known efficient unification algorithms we had to develop a specialized string-unification procedure for computing the intuitionistic substitution σ_J.

In general string-unification is very complicated and no efficient algorithm could be given so far. Fortunately, however, we do not have to unify arbitrary strings but only strings corresponding to the prefixes of two connected atoms. This enables us to put certain restrictions on the pairs of strings which have to be unified.

1. Since the prefix of a node is the sequences of position labels on the path from the root to the node we know that a position label (i.e. either a variable or a constant character) occurs at most once in the prefix string. Thus we only have to consider *strings without duplicates*.

2. Secondly prefixes correspond to branches in a formula tree. Therefore in two prefixes *equal position labels* can occur *only at the beginning*. Once the two prefixes diverge the remaining substrings are completely disjoint.

These two restrictions will cause prefix-unification to be much simpler than general string unification. We may simply skip common substrings at the beginning of the two prefixes and know that the remaining substrings will not have any variables in common. Prefix-unification can be realized as an extension of bidirectional matching where variables of one string will be matched against substrings of the other and, if necessary, vice versa.

Using bidirectional matching we can already compute a unifier for the prefixes of P^0 ($a_0a_8a_{17}A_{18}a_{19}$) and P^1 ($a_0a_8A_9a_{10}A_{11}$) in the first step of our proof search. A_9 can be instantiated by a_{17}, A_{18} by a_{10}, and A_{11} by a_{19}. In most cases, however, unification will be more complex. The prefix $a_0A_2A_7$ of the atom P^1 in the 'b'-branch, for instance, contains two adjoint variables. There are several possibilities for unifying it with the prefix of P^0: the variable A_2 may be instantiated with either ϵ, a_8, a_8a_{17}, $a_8a_{17}A_{18}$, or $a_8a_{17}A_{18}a_{19}$ and A_7 will receive values correspondingly. Thus in general there will be more than one unifier for each pair of prefix-strings.

Furthermore we have to consider the fact that during proof search our unification procedure will be called several times and may yield different strings to be assigned to a given variable. The variable A_9, for instance will receive a value both by unifying the prefixes of P^0 and P^1 in the first step and by unifying the prefixes of R^0 and R^1 in the third. Therefore we should make sure that the strings assigned to a variable by our unification procedure are not already too specific since otherwise we will run into contradictions. The prefixes of P^0 and P^1 could also be unified by $\sigma_J = \{A_{18}\backslash a_3 a_{10}, A_9 \backslash a_{17}, A_{11} \backslash a_{19}\}$ which is much more compatible with the unifier required for the prefixes of R^0 and R^1. The unification algorithm should therefore create only the *most general unifiers* of two prefixes and thus leave room for specializations in the following steps of our proof search. A most general unifier (short *mgu*) takes into account that the strings assigned to variables within the two prefixes may overlap. In the case of P^0 and P^1 it would have to express that the end of (the string assigned to) A_9 may overlap with the beginning of A_{18} and that the end of A_{18} may overlap with the beginning of A_{11}. The only fixed information is that A_9 must begin with a_{17}, A_{11} must end with a_{19}, and A_{18} must contain a_{10}. All these informations can be encoded by introducing two new variables B and C and setting the most general unifier to $\{A_{18} \backslash Ba_{10}C, A_9 \backslash a_{17}B, A_{11} \backslash Ca_{19}\}$.

Taking the above considerations into account our prefix-unification algorithm tries to compute the most general descriptions of all the possibilities for overlapping two prefix strings. We shall now describe this algorithm by an example unification of the prefixes $a_0 A_2 a_3 A_4 A_6$ of R^1 and $a_0 a_8 A_9 a_{13} a_{15}$ of R^0 (which is the same as $a_0 a_8 a_{17} B a_{13} a_{15}$ because of the earlier assignment $\{A_9 \backslash a_{17} B\}$).

Our procedure starts by writing down the string $a_0 A_2 a_3 A_4 A_6$ in a way such that constants will receive a small slot (one character) and variables will receive slots of variable size (it suffices to reserve a slot of the size of the second string). In the rows below we write down the second string such that (except for the common substring a_0) each constant occurs in the range of a variable while the range of variables (e.g. B) may be stretched arbitrarily to make this possible. In the first row we begin by stretching the variables as little as possible. Below we will then systematically enumerate all the possibilities for extending the range of one or more variables. The most general unifier can then easily be computed: the assignment of constants is obvious and new variables will have to be generated if two variables overlap. For unifying the prefixes if R^1 and R^0 the most general unifiers are constructed according to the following diagram.

a_0	A_2	a_3	A_4	A_6	σ_J
a_0	a_8 a_{17} —— B ——	a_{13} a_{15}	ϵ		$\{A_2 \backslash a_8 a_{17} D,\ B \backslash Da_3 E,\ A_4 \backslash Ea_{13}a_{15},\ A_6 \backslash \epsilon\}$
a_0	a_8 a_{17} —— B —————	a_{13} a_{15}			$\{A_2 \backslash a_8 a_{17} D,\ B \backslash Da_3 E,\ A_4 \backslash Ea_{13},\ A_6 \backslash a_{15}\}$
a_0	a_8 a_{17} —— B ————————	a_{13} a_{15}			$\{A_2 \backslash a_8 a_{17} D,\ B \backslash Da_3 A_4 F,\ A_6 \backslash Fa_{13}a_{15}\}$

The simple procedure illustrated above does in fact compute all the most general unifiers for two prefix-strings in a way which is considerably more efficient than the one presented in [10]. Among other advantages it generates unifiers step by step instead of computing them all at once.[6] Since it will seldomly be the case that we will

---

[6] There may be up to $\frac{1}{2}\frac{(2n)!}{(n!)^2} \in \mathcal{O}(\frac{2^{2n}}{\sqrt{n}})$ mgu's where n is the depth of the formula tree.

have to check all possible unifiers during a proof search[7] it leads to a very efficient proof search procedure. A complete description of the unification algorithm and its properties can be found in [12, 13].

4 Conversion into Standard Sequent Proofs

While the connection method is very efficient for *finding* proofs according to the matrix characterization of validity its results cannot directly be used for the construction of programs from the proof. Therefore it is necessary to convert matrix proofs back into sequent proofs which are closer to 'natural' mathematical reasoning. This is comparably easy for classical propositional logic but becomes rather difficult for predicate or intuitionistic logic (see e.g. [16, section 3]) since the reduction ordering $\lhd$ induced by σ_Q and σ_J has to be taken into account.

Fortunately, our proof search procedure described in the previous section already constructs a sequent proof in Fitting's [7] *non-standard* sequent calculus $\mathcal{LJ}_{NS}$. In contrast to standard sequent calculi like Gentzen's $\mathcal{LJ}$ [8] which are used in program development systems it allows the occurrence of more than one formula in the succedent of a sequent. Thus for integrating our procedure into an program development system we only have to convert this $\mathcal{LJ}_{NS}$-proof into a proof within a *standard* sequent calculus.

To understand the differences between these calculi consider the rules shown on the left half of figure 7 where Γ and Δ are *sets* of formulae. When using the two calculi in an analytic manner (i.e. reading the rules from the conclusion to the premises) the different treatment of succedents results in different non-permutabilities of the rules in a sequent proof. The $\neg$-*elim* rule in $\mathcal{LJ}$, for instance, would cause a deletion of the actual succedent formula C and a standard proof could not be finished if C is still relevant. The application of the corresponding $\mathcal{LJ}_{NS}$-rule, however, does not cause any problems. On the other hand the $\neg$-*intro* rule could stop $\mathcal{LJ}_{NS}$-proofs because relevant succedent formulae Δ which are not involved in the reduction itself would be deleted. The corresponding rule in the standard calculus is not dangerous in this sense and does not cause any non-permutabilities in the $\mathcal{LJ}$-proofs.

$\mathcal{LJ}$:

$$\frac{\Gamma, \neg A \vdash A}{\Gamma, \neg A \vdash C} \ \neg\text{-}elim$$

$$\frac{\Gamma, A \vdash}{\Gamma \vdash \neg A} \ \neg\text{-}intro$$

$\mathcal{LJ}_{NS}$:

$$\frac{\Gamma, \neg A \vdash A, \Delta}{\Gamma, \neg A \vdash \Delta} \ \neg\text{-}elim$$

$$\frac{\Gamma, A \vdash}{\Gamma \vdash \neg A, \Delta} \ \neg\text{-}intro$$

$\mathcal{LJ}^\star$:

$$\frac{\Gamma, \neg A \vdash A \vee \Delta_S}{\Gamma, \neg A \vdash \Delta_S} \ \neg(\vee)\text{-}elim$$

$$\frac{\dfrac{\Gamma, A \vdash}{\Gamma \vdash \neg A} \ \neg\text{-}intro}{\Gamma \vdash \neg A \vee \Delta_S} \ \vee\text{-}intro \ 1$$

Fig. 7. Example rules of $\mathcal{LJ}$ and $\mathcal{LJ}_{NS}$ and the simulation of $\mathcal{LJ}_{NS}$-rules in $\mathcal{LJ}^\star$.

In [17, chapter 2] we have shown that because of the strong differences between the rules of the calculi $\mathcal{LJ}_{NS}$ and $\mathcal{LJ}$ it is not possible to transform every $\mathcal{LJ}_{NS}$-proof into a corresponding $\mathcal{LJ}$-proof without changing the structural information contained in the proof. Thus a transformation of $\mathcal{LJ}_{NS}$-proofs into standard sequent proofs would require an additional search process. To solve this problem we have

---

[7] This will only be necessary if unification fails in some later step of the proof search.

extended Gentzen's calculus $\mathcal{LJ}$ into an extended standard sequent calculus $\mathcal{LJ}^\star$ which is compatible with $\mathcal{LJ}_{NS}$. This calculus essentially simulates a set of formulae in the succedent by a disjunction of these formulae and thus uses only sequents containing at most one succedent formula. On the other hand it is a simple extension of $\mathcal{LJ}$ since it requires only a few rules in addition to those of the calculus $\mathcal{LJ}$. For example the $\mathcal{LJ}_{NS}$-rule $\neg\neg$-$elim$ (figure 7) will be simulated by such a new rule $\neg(\vee)$-$elim$ in the calculus $\mathcal{LJ}^\star$ (where Δ_S is the disjunction of the elements contained in Δ). The simulation of the $\neg$-$intro$ rule of $\mathcal{LJ}_{NS}$ does not require new rules since it can be expressed by existing $\mathcal{LJ}$-rules as shown in figure 7. All additionally rules which are required to extend $\mathcal{LJ}$ are summarized in figure 8. The only structural rule $\vee$-$change$ A_i ensures that it is sufficient to reduce only the leftmost formula of the succedent disjunction Δ_S. For detailed presentation of the development of these rules and its correctness we refer again to [17].

$$\frac{\Gamma \vdash A_i \vee (\Delta_S \setminus\!\setminus A_i)}{\Gamma \vdash \Delta_S} \; \vee\text{-}change \; A_i$$

$$\frac{\Gamma, \neg A \vdash A \vee (\Delta_S)}{\Gamma, \neg A \vdash \Delta_S} \; \neg(\vee)\text{-}elim \qquad \frac{\Gamma, A \Rightarrow B \vdash A \vee (\Delta_S) \quad \Gamma, B \vdash \Delta_S}{\Gamma, A \Rightarrow B \vdash \Delta_S} \; \Rightarrow(\vee)\text{-}elim$$

$$\frac{\Gamma \vdash A \vee (\Delta_S) \quad \Gamma \vdash B \vee (\Delta_S)}{\Gamma \vdash (A \wedge B) \vee (\Delta_S)} \; \wedge(\vee)\text{-}intro \qquad \frac{\Gamma \vdash A \vee (B \vee (\Delta_S))}{\Gamma \vdash (A \vee B) \vee (\Delta_S)} \; \vee(\vee)\text{-}intro$$

$$\frac{\Gamma \vdash A[x/t] \vee \exists x.A}{\Gamma \vdash \exists x.A} \; \exists(\vee)^\star\text{-}intro \; t \qquad \frac{\Gamma \vdash A[x/t] \vee ((\exists x.A) \vee (\Delta_S))}{\Gamma \vdash (\exists x.A) \vee (\Delta_S)} \; \exists(\vee)\text{-}intro \; t$$

Fig. 8. The additionally required rules of $\mathcal{LJ}^\star$

Using the complete rule set of $\mathcal{LJ}^\star$ and the rule mapping procedure guiding the application of these rules (depending on the actual succedent of the $\mathcal{LJ}_{NS}$-proof) the non–permutabilities of each non–standard proof could be simulated exactly in an $\mathcal{LJ}^\star$-proof. Figure 9 shows an informal presentation of the transformation procedure. Its input is an $\mathcal{LJ}_{NS}$-proof of a given formula which is represented as a list of $\mathcal{LJ}_{NS}$ rules.[8] From the output of the procedure we obtain a corresponding $\mathcal{LJ}^\star$-proof, i.e. a list of $\mathcal{LJ}^\star$ rules. The *proof structure* (by which we mean the multi-set of axiom formulae) will not be violated by such a transformation.

Consider, for instance, the following application of the $\Rightarrow$-$elim$ rule in $\mathcal{LJ}_{NS}$:

$$\frac{\forall x.A(x) \vee B(x) \vdash \exists y.A(y), \, \exists x.B(x) \qquad \forall x.A(x) \vee B(x), \, \exists z.\neg A(z) \vdash \exists x.B(x)}{\forall x.A(x) \vee B(x), \, \exists y.A(y) \Rightarrow \exists z.\neg A(z) \vdash \exists x.B(x)}$$

In the left subgoal two succedent formulae were generated. We have shown in [16] that these two succedent formulae cannot be simulated within an $\mathcal{LJ}$-proof. Consequently we will have fundamental differences in the resulting proof structures. In contrast to this, our transformation procedure transforms any complete $\mathcal{LJ}_{NS}$-proof of the above sequent into an $\mathcal{LJ}^\star$-proof while preserving the structure of the $\mathcal{LJ}_{NS}$-proof (i.e. using the same instances of the axiom formulae). Figure 10 gives an example of such a proof generated by our procedure.

---

[8] After branching into two independent subproofs the proof of "left" subgoal precedes the proof of the "right" one in this list. So we can avoid a more complicated list structure for representing the branching structure of the $\mathcal{LJ}_{NS}$-proof.

function transform ($\mathcal{LJ}_{NS}$-list, $\mathcal{LJ}^*$-list)
  let r the head of $\mathcal{LJ}_{NS}$-list **and** t the tail of $\mathcal{LJ}_{NS}$-list
  let r' the corresponding $\mathcal{LJ}$-rule
  if for the actual succedent [9] $|\Delta| = \emptyset$ **then**
    append $[r']$ to $\mathcal{LJ}^*$-list
  else
    if for the actual succedent $|\Delta| = 1$ **then** append
$$l = \begin{cases} [op(\vee)\text{-}elim], & \text{if } r = op\text{-}elim,\ op \in \{\Rightarrow, \neg\} \\ [\exists(\vee)^*\text{-}intro], & \text{if } r = \exists\text{-}intro \\ [\varepsilon^{10}], & \text{if } r = \vee\text{-}intro \\ [r'], & \text{otherwise} \end{cases}$$
      to $\mathcal{LJ}^*$-list
    else
      if for the actual succedent $|\Delta| > 1$ **then** append
$$l = \begin{cases} [op(\vee)\text{-}elim], & \text{if } r = op\text{-}elim,\ op \in \{\Rightarrow, \neg\} \\ [\vee\text{-}change^{11}, op(\vee)\text{-}intro], & \text{if } r = op\text{-}intro,\ op \in \{\exists, \vee, \wedge\} \\ [\vee\text{-}change, \vee\text{-}intro1, r'], & \text{if } r \in \{\Rightarrow\text{-}intro, \neg\text{-}intro, \forall\text{-}intro, axiom\} \\ [r'], & \text{otherwise} \end{cases}$$
        to $\mathcal{LJ}^*$-list
  fi fi fi
  if $t \neq [\ ]$ **then** call transform (t, $\mathcal{LJ}^*$-list) **else** return $\mathcal{LJ}^*$-list **fi**

call transform ($\mathcal{LJ}_{NS}$-list, nil)

Fig. 9. The transformation procedure $\mathcal{LJ}_{NS} \longmapsto \mathcal{LJ}^*$.

The concept of proof structure, the calculus $\mathcal{LJ}^*$, and the transformation of $\mathcal{LJ}_{NS}$–proofs into $\mathcal{LJ}^*$–proofs have been investigated in detail in [17, chapter 2]. Altogether we have proven the following properties.

Theorem 3.

1. *The calculus $\mathcal{LJ}^*$ is a standard calculus which is sound and complete.*
2. *Each $\mathcal{LJ}_{NS}$–proof can be represented in $\mathcal{LJ}^*$ in a structure-preserving way.*
3. *Each rule of $\mathcal{LJ}^*$ can be simulated by applying a fixed set of $\mathcal{LJ}$–rules (including the cut).*

Using the proof of theorem 3 we have embedded the calculus $\mathcal{LJ}^*$ into the Nu-PRL proof development system [6] by simulating its rules via proof tactics guiding the application of $\mathcal{LJ}$-rules. Furthermore we have implemented a procedure transforming $\mathcal{LJ}_{NS}$-proofs into $\mathcal{LJ}^*$-proofs which is comparably simple (in contrast to the one presented in [18]) and keeps the size of the resulting proof small. As a consequence we can transform matrix proofs into standard sequent proofs *without any additional search* and integrate our proof search method into larger environments for reasoning about programming and many other kinds of applied mathematics.

---

[9] ε denotes the *empty* rule which does not affect the actual sequent in the $\mathcal{LJ}^*$-proof.

[10] The application of the $\vee$-*change* rule additionally requires the formula which has to be changed to the leftmost succedent position. This formula is uniquely determined by the actual $\mathcal{LJ}_{NS}$-rule r and has been omitted here for simplicity.

[11] By this we mean the actual succedent Δ in the $\mathcal{LJ}_{NS}$-proof wrt. to the rule r.

$$
\cfrac{
  \cfrac{
    \cfrac{
      \cfrac{A(a) \vdash A(a)}{A(a) \vdash A(a) \lor (\exists y.A(y) \lor \exists x.B(x))} \; \text{V-intro 1}
    }{A(a) \vdash \exists y.A(y) \lor \exists x.B(x)} \; \exists(\text{V})\text{-intro } a \qquad \boxed{\text{Subgoal 1}}
  }{
    \cfrac{A(a) \lor B(a) \vdash \exists y.A(y) \lor \exists x.B(x)}{\forall x.A(x) \lor B(x) \vdash \exists y.A(y) \lor \exists x.B(x)} \; \text{V-elim } a \qquad \boxed{\text{Subgoal 2}}
  } \; \text{V-elim}
}{
  \forall x.A(x) \lor B(x), \exists y.A(y) \Rightarrow \exists z.\neg A(z) \vdash \exists x.B(x)
} \; \Rightarrow(\text{V})\text{-elim}
$$

$\boxed{\text{Subgoal 1:}}$

$$
\cfrac{
  \cfrac{
    \cfrac{B(a) \vdash B(a)}{B(a) \vdash B(a) \lor (\exists x.B(x) \lor \exists y.A(y))} \; \text{V-intro 1}
  }{B(a) \vdash \exists x.B(x) \lor \exists y.A(y)} \; \exists(\text{V})\text{-intro } a
}{
  B(a) \vdash \exists y.A(y) \lor \exists x.B(x)
} \; \text{V-change } \exists x.B(x)
$$

$\boxed{\text{Subgoal 2:}}$

$$
\cfrac{
  \cfrac{
    \cfrac{
      \cfrac{A(a) \vdash A(a)}{A(a) \vdash A(a) \lor \exists x.B(x)} \text{V-intro 1} \qquad
      \cfrac{\cfrac{\cfrac{B(a) \vdash B(a)}{B(a) \vdash B(a) \lor (\exists x.B(x) \lor A(a))}\text{V-intro 1}}{B(a) \vdash \exists x.B(x) \lor A(a)}\exists(\text{V})\text{-intro } a}{B(a) \vdash A(a) \lor \exists x.B(x)}\text{V-change } \exists x.B(x)
    }{A(a) \lor B(a) \vdash A(a) \lor \exists x.B(x)} \text{V-elim}
  }{\forall x.A(x) \lor B(x) \vdash A(a) \lor \exists x.B(x)} \text{V-elim } a
}{
  \cfrac{\forall x.A(x) \lor B(x), \neg A(a) \vdash \exists x.B(x)}{\forall x.A(x) \lor B(x), \exists z.\neg A(z) \vdash \exists x.B(x)} \exists\text{-elim } a
} \; \neg(\text{V})\text{-elim}
$$

Fig. 10. The resulting $\mathcal{LJ}^*$-proof [12]

5 Conclusion

We have developed an automated proof procedure for intuitionistic logic and a technique for integrating it into proof/program development systems based on the sequent calculus. For this purpose we have extended Bibel's connection method for classical predicate logic [3, 4] into a procedure operating on formulae in non-normal form which is complete for first-order intuitionistic logic and developed an efficient algorithm for the unification of prefix-strings. Furthermore we have designed an extended standard sequent calculus which makes it possible to convert the abstract proof into a proof acceptable for the program development system without any additional search. Our method is currently being realized as a tactic for solving subproblems from first-order logic which arise during a program derivation.

Our work demonstrates that it is possible to make techniques from automated theorem proving directly applicable to program synthesis. By an emphasis on connections and open branches in the proof structure the search space is drastically reduced in comparison with methods based on natural deduction or sequent calculi while a very compact proof representation avoids the notational redundancies contained in them. Since we also construct the skeleton of a sequent proof already during the proof search the transformation of the resulting 'abstract proof' into a humanly comprehensible sequent proof turns out to be comparably easy. Thus our proof-technology combines the strengths of well-known proof search methods (i.e. completeness and efficiency) with those of interactive, tactics supported proof development systems (i.e. safety, flexibility, and expressivity of the underlying theory) and thus extends the deductive power of these systems in a safe and efficient way.

---

[12] For better overview we omit the *axiom* rules

Although we have based our implementation on the NuPRL proof development system [6] our methodology can also be used to guide other systems based on natural deduction or sequent calculi. Due to the similarity of intuitionistic logic and modal logics it could also be extended to automate reasoning in these logics. Very likely the same proof-technology will be, at least in principle, usable for some subset of linear logic and calculi which describe formal methods in software engineering (although a matrix-characterization for validity still has to be developed). Besides exploring these possibilities our future work will focus on techniques for improving the efficiency of the proof search like the preprocessing steps used in Setheo [9] and KoMeT [2] and the use of typing information during unification. Furthermore we shall investigate how inductive proof methods can be integrated into program synthesis systems by the same technology. All these steps will help a user of a program development system to focus on the key ideas in program design while being freed from having to deal with all the formal details that ensure correctness.

References

1. E. W. BETH. *The foundations of mathematics*. North–Holland, 1959.
2. W. BIBEL, S. BRÜNING, U. EGLY, T. RATH. Komet. In *Proceedings of the 12th CADE*, LNAI 814, pp. 783–787. Springer Verlag, 1994.
3. W. BIBEL. On matrices with connections. *Jour. of the ACM*, 28, p. 633–645, 1981.
4. W. BIBEL. *Automated Theorem Proving*. Vieweg Verlag, 1987.
5. A. BUNDY, F. VAN HARMELEN, C. HORN, A. SMAILL. The Oyster-Clam system. In *Proceedings of the 10th CADE*, LNCS 449, pp. 647–648. Springer Verlag, 1990.
6. R. L. CONSTABLE ET. AL. *Implementing Mathematics with the NuPRL proof development system*. Prentice Hall, 1986.
7. M. C. FITTING. *Intuitionistic logic, model theory and forcing*. North–Holland, 1969.
8. G. GENTZEN. Untersuchungen über das logische Schließen. *Mathematische Zeitschrift*, 39:176–210, 405–431, 1935.
9. R. LETZ, J. SCHUMANN, S. BAYERL, W. BIBEL. SETHEO: A high-performance theorem prover. *Journal of Automated Reasoning*, 8:183–212, 1992.
10. H. J. OHLBACH. A resolution calculus for modal logics. Ph.D. Thesis (SEKI Report SR-88-08), Universität Kaiserslautern, 1988.
11. J. OTTEN, C. KREITZ. A connection based proof method for intuitionistic logic. In *Proceedings of the 4th Workshop on Theorem Proving with Analytic Tableaux and Related Methods*, LNAI 918, pp. 122–137, Springer Verlag, 1995.
12. J. OTTEN, C. KREITZ. T-String-Unification: Unifying Prefixes in Non-Classical Proof Methods. Report AIDA-95-09, FG Intellektik, TH Darmstadt, 1995.
13. J. OTTEN. Ein konnektionenorientiertes Beweisverfahren für intuitionistische Logik. Master's thesis, TH Darmstadt, 1995.
14. L. PAULSON. Isabelle: The next 700 theorem provers. In Piergiorgio Odifreddi, editor, *Logic and Computer Science*, pp. 361–386. Academic Press, 1990.
15. R. POLLACK. *The theory of LEGO - a proof checker for the extendend calculus of constructions*. PhD thesis, University of Edinburgh, 1994.
16. S. SCHMITT, C. KREITZ. On transforming intuitionistic matrix proofs into standard-sequent proofs. In *Proceedings of the 4th Workshop on Theorem Proving with Analytic Tableaux and Related Methods*, LNAI 918, pp. 106–121, Springer, 1995.
17. S. SCHMITT. Ein erweiterter intuitionistischer Sequenzenkalkül und dessen Anwendung im intuitionistischen Konnektionsbeweisen. Master's thesis, TH Darmstadt, 1994.
18. G. TAKEUTI. *Proof Theory*. North–Holland, 1975.
19. L. WALLEN. *Automated deduction in nonclassical logic*. MIT Press, 1990.
20. L. WOS ET. AL. Automated reasoning contributes to mathematics and logic. In *Proceedings of the 10th CADE*, LNCS 449, p. 485–499. Springer Verlag 1990.

Towards an Object-Oriented Methodology for Deductive Synthesis of Logic Programs*

Kung-Kiu Lau[1] and Mario Ornaghi[2]

[1] Fachgebiet Intellektik, Fachbereich Informatik
Technische Hochschule Darmstadt
Alexanderstr. 10, D-64283 Darmstadt, Germany
lau@intellektik.informatik.th-darmstadt.de (or kung-kiu@cs.man.ac.uk)
[2] Dipartimento di Scienze dell'Informazione
Universita' degli studi di Milano, Via Comelico 39/41, Milano, Italy
ornaghi@hermes.mc.dsi.unimi.it

Abstract. Quality software must be reusable, extensible, and reliable. Object-oriented programming purports to achieve these attributes by the use of classes and inheritance (informally). In this paper, we show how our existing approach to deductive synthesis of logic programs can serve as the basis for an object-oriented methodology for formal program development that achieves reusability, extensibility and correctness (formally).

1 Introduction

Object-oriented programming is very much seen as the standard bearer of the software industry nowadays, because it purports to achieve the key attributes of any quality software: *reusability*, *extensibility*, and *reliability* (see e.g. [12, 13]). Object-oriented programming achieves reusability and extensibility by using a *class* as the basic modular unit, and a mechanism called *inheritance* to define new classes from existing ones. Reliability results from the ability to monitor *assertions* and *invariants* contained in classes. However, at present, there is no single standard (formal) characterisation of object-oriented programming (see [7]), so we shall adopt the common view of object-oriented programming, as expressed in e.g. [13, 16] (based on imperative programming).

In an object-oriented system, the basic modular unit is a *class*, which describes an implementation of an abstract data type (ADT), including a set of procedures, called *methods*, that implement operations on the ADT. A class can be composed with other classes to define new classes, through *inheritance*, to form larger, composite classes. If a class C_2 inherits class C_1, then C_1 is a *superclass* of C_2; or conversely, C_2 is a *subclass* of C_1. At execution time, instances of a class are created dynamically. Such instances are called *objects*. An object contains actual *data* (of the type of its ADT). Its methods, when invoked by *messages* sent by other objects, are used to manipulate its data. An object therefore has an internal state. Thus a class is a (compile-time) template for generating a family of (run-time) objects with the same data type and methods.

---

* The first author is on leave from the Department of Computer Science, University of Manchester, UK, and is supported by the European Union HCM project on Logic Program Synthesis and Transformation, contract no. 93/414.

Code reuse arises through inheritance as well as through *dynamic binding*. Inheritance allows code reuse, since the code for the methods in a class is generated only once, and 'inherited' by all the objects of any subclass. If a method has different implementations in different subclasses, then dynamic binding allows any common code for different implementations of the method to be placed in the superclass, and be reused with different subclasses.

However, apart from monitoring assertions and invariants at run-time, current object-oriented programming technology does not support formal program development, i.e. the development of object-oriented programs that are guaranteed to be (formally) correct (wrt their specifications). In this paper, we outline (the beginnings of) such an approach for logic programs, based on our existing approach to deductive synthesis of logic programs. In order to avoid confusion, we shall use *classes* and *objects* only in the sense of conventional object-oriented programming, as described above, and we will not employ these terms when describing elements or features of our approach. However, we will of course relate our approach to object-oriented programming.

Our starting point is a well-defined and well-understood (global) context, that we call a *framework*. A framework is a theory that embodies our knowledge of the problem domain in question. Within this theory, we define semantically notions similar to classes and inheritance in object-oriented programming, and thus characterise modularity and reusability at a semantic level, rather than at code level.

More importantly, *correctness*, both of programs and of their composition, can be defined in a framework. Moreover, the framework itself can be used to state precise conditions under which program composition and reuse preserve correctness. Thus our approach not only offers modularity and reusability, but it also has the additional property of formal correctness, not just of modules and module composition, but also of reuse. This we believe is an advancement over the current object-oriented technology, and in this paper we will discuss how we can use our approach as a basis for an object-oriented methodology for logic program synthesis.

The paper is organised as follows. In Section 2 we give a brief overview of our existing approach. In particular, we describe frameworks (corresponding to ADT's), and steadfast logic programs (corresponding to methods). Then, in Section 3, we discuss how our existing approach can be the basis of a fully object-oriented program synthesis methodology.

2 An Overview of Our Existing Approach

In our existing approach to logic program synthesis a specification S is given in the context of a (first-order) theory $\mathcal{F}$, which we call a *specification framework* (or just *framework* for short). The purpose of a framework is to provide a well-defined context for program specifications, and for reasoning about program synthesis.

Synthesis is *deductive*, i.e. it iteratively derives (using some synthesis method)[3] from a specification S of a relation r a sequence of programs $P_0 \subseteq \cdots \subseteq P_n$, such that P_n, when the synthesis process halts, is *totally correct* wrt S.

A detailed description of our approach, including criteria for correctness and for determining when to halt the synthesis process (with a totally correct program), can be found in [9]. Here we give a brief overview of its key elements that are relevant to this paper.

2.1 Specification Frameworks

A framework is a first-order theory that embodies all the relevant knowledge of the problem domain of interest. Such a theory could be regarded as an axiomatisation of a collection of ADTs. However, it has more than the usual ADTs, since it can also contain *any* relevant axioms for reasoning about ADTs (e.g. induction axioms), as well as other axioms for reasoning about the domain (e.g. stating that in a library each book has a title, a list of authors, and so on).

We endow frameworks with *isoinitial semantics* [1, 8, 14]. It is closely related to initial semantics used in algebraic ADTs [17]. In initial semantics the *intended models* are initial models, whereas in isoinitial semantics they are isoinitial models. We choose isoinitial semantics because the existence of an isoinitial model corresponds to the existence of steadfast programs.

A framework may be *closed*, i.e. completely defined, or it may be *open*, i.e. it may contain *parameters*. A closed framework has only one intended model (unique up to isomorphism), whereas an open framework has a class of intended models.

Example 1. The following *closed* framework formalises Peano Arithmetic, denoted by $\mathcal{PA}$,

> **Framework $\mathcal{PA}$;**
> SORTS: *Nat*;
> FUNCTIONS: 0 $: \rightarrow Nat$;
> s $: Nat \rightarrow Nat$;
> $+, \cdot : (Nat, Nat) \rightarrow Nat$;
> AXIOMS: $\forall x(\neg 0 = s(x)) \wedge \forall x, y(s(x) = s(y) \rightarrow x = y)$;
> $\forall(H(0) \wedge \forall i(H(i) \rightarrow H(s(i))) \rightarrow \forall x H(x))$;
> $\forall x(x + 0 = x)$;
> $\forall x, y(x + s(y) = s(x + y))$;
> $\forall x(x \cdot 0 = 0)$;
> $\forall x, y(x \cdot s(y) = x + x \cdot y)$

The intended model of $\mathcal{PA}$ (under isoinitial semantics) is the standard structure of natural numbers.

---

[3] Synthesis methods are not relevant to this paper. A survey can be found in [6].

155

Example 2. The following *open* framework formalises a theory of lists, with list element type and ordering as *parameters*:[4]

> **Framework** $\mathcal{LIST}(Elem, \lhd)$;
>
> IMPORT: $\mathcal{PA}$;
>
> SORTS: $Nat, Elem, List$;
>
> FUNCTIONS: $nil : \to List$;
> $\quad\quad\quad . : (Elem, List) \to List$;
> $\quad\quad\quad nocc : (Elem, List) \to Nat$;
>
> RELATIONS: $elemi : (List, Nat, Elem)$;
>
> D-AXIOMS: $\neg nil = a.B \land (a_1.B_1 = a_2.B_2 \to a_1 = a_2 \land B_1 = B_2)$;
> $\quad\quad (H(nil) \land \forall a, J\,(H(J) \to H(a.J))) \to \forall L\,H(L)$;
> $\quad\quad nocc(x, nil) = 0$;
> $\quad\quad a = b \to nocc(a, b.L) = nocc(a, L) + 1$;
> $\quad\quad \neg a = b \to nocc(a, b.L) = nocc(a, L)$;
> $\quad\quad elemi(L, 0, a) \leftrightarrow \exists B : List(L = a.B)$;
> $\quad\quad elemi(L, s(i), a) \leftrightarrow \exists b, B\,(L = b.B \land elemi(B, i, a))$;
>
> P-AXIOMS: $x \lhd y \land y \lhd x \leftrightarrow x = y$;
> $\quad\quad x \lhd y \land y \lhd z \to x \lhd z$

The intended models of $\mathcal{LIST}(Elem, \lhd)$ are the usual list structures with a partial ordering $\lhd$ on the (parametric) element type.

Natural numbers, the function $nocc(x, L)$ (number of occurrences of x in L), and the relation $elemi(L, i, a)$ (a occurs in L at position i) have been introduced to get an *expressive* specification framework, as we will see later.

Frameworks can be built incrementally through the operations of *framework composition* and *framework extension*. The *composition operation* behaves properly, if the frameworks involved are *adequate*.

Definition 1. A closed framework C is *adequate* iff it has an isoinitial model $\mathcal{I}$.

It turns out that, for every ground literal $L, \mathcal{I} \models L$ iff $C \vdash L$. Thus, in an adequate closed framework C, the axioms completely define the intended meaning of the symbols of its signature.

We shall denote an open framework by $\mathcal{F}(\Pi) = \mathcal{D} \cup \mathcal{P}(\Pi)$, where Π are the parameters, $\mathcal{D}$ the d-axioms, and $\mathcal{P}(\Pi)$ the p-axioms. The latter state properties that are assumed to be verified by the parameters, and may contain *only* parameters. In Example 2 we assume (as the p-axioms state) that $\lhd$ is a partial ordering. The d-axioms characterise the other symbols, that we will call *defined symbols* of the framework.

---

[4] In the axioms, external universal quantifiers have been omitted, variables of sort *Elem* are in lower-case, and variables of sort *List* are in upper-case.

Definition 2. An open framework $\mathcal{F}(\Pi)$ is *adequate* iff, for every adequate closed framework C that satisfies the proof obligation $C \vdash \mathcal{P}(\Pi)$,[5] $\mathcal{F}(\Pi) \cup C$ is an adequate closed framework. We call $\mathcal{F}(\Pi) \cup C$ a *closed instance* of $\mathcal{F}(\Pi)$.

Adequacy of $\mathcal{F}(\Pi) = \mathcal{D} \cup \mathcal{P}(\Pi)$ means that, whenever we have the information on the parameters Π (given by C), we get a closed framework, i.e. that the axioms of $\mathcal{D}$ completely define the meaning of the defined symbols (in terms of the meaning of the parameters).

An *extension operation* introduces a new defined symbol r through a set D_r of axioms, that we call a *definition* of r. Since adequacy is essential for framework composition, we allow only definitions that preserve adequacy, and we also call such definitions *adequate*.

Definition 3. Let C be a closed framework with isoinitial model $\mathcal{I}$. A definition D_r of a relation r is *adequate* in C iff $C \cup D_r$ is an adequate closed framework, and it has an intended model $\mathcal{I}_r$ that is an expansion[6] of $\mathcal{I}$ (by r).

Let $\mathcal{F}(\Pi)$ be an open framework. A definition D_r is *adequate* in $\mathcal{F}(\Pi)$ iff it is adequate in every closed instance $\mathcal{F}(\Pi) \cup C$ of $\mathcal{F}(\Pi)$.

We consider *recursive definitions* and *explicit definitions*. A recursive definition of a function or a relation is adequate if it satisfies suitable sufficient conditions. Essentially, we require that it is like a primitive recursive definition, like the axioms introducing $+$ and $\cdot$ in $\mathcal{PA}$.

An explicit definition of a relation r has the form $\forall x(r(x) \leftrightarrow R(x))$, where R is a formula of the old language, that we call the *defining formula*. If $R(x)$ is *quantifier-free* or contains only *bounded quantifiers*, then the definition is adequate. Otherwise, a sufficient condition for adequacy is the derivability of a steadfast program for computing the defined relation. For example, in $\mathcal{LIST}(Elem, \lhd)$ we can explicitly define length as follows:

$$len(L, n) \leftrightarrow \forall i(i < n \leftrightarrow \exists a(elemi(L, i, a)))$$
$$\forall L, n\, (n = l(L) \leftrightarrow len(L, n))$$

In $len(L, n)$ the length n of a list L is defined as its first empty position. The derivability of a program for computing len proves adequacy. Moreover, since we can prove $\forall L \exists! n\, len(L, n)$, we can explicitly define the function l.

Similarly, we can introduce the most useful relations and functions on lists, like $L|M$ (the *concatenation* function), $x \in L$ (x is a member of list L), $perm(L, M)$ (L is a *permutation* of M), $ord(L)$ (L is *ordered*), and so on. We say that $\mathcal{LIST}(Elem, \lhd)$ is *expressive*.

2.2 Steadfast Logic Programs

The standard notion of *correctness* in logic program synthesis is defined for *closed* programs only. It can be stated in terms of specification frameworks as

---

[5] Here, for the sake of simplicity, we assume that the intersection of the signatures of C and $\mathcal{F}(\Pi)$ coincides with Π.

[6] See e.g. [5].

follows: in a closed framework C, a program P for computing r, specified by (the adequate definition) $\forall(r(x) \leftrightarrow R(x))$, is correct wrt the specification iff P's minimum Herbrand model is isomorphic to the intended model of C (restricted to the signature of P).

Steadfastness extends this to *open* programs. An open program, denoted by $P : \delta \Leftarrow \pi$, contains the definitions of a set δ of relation symbols in terms of a set π of parameters; to be more precise, the *defined relations* δ occur in the heads of the clauses of P, whilst the *parameters* π occur only in the bodies. Open programs can arise in both *closed* and *open* frameworks.

In a closed framework C, steadfastness can be defined as follows:

Definition 4. $P : \delta_1 \Leftarrow \pi_1$ is *steadfast* in C iff, for every correct (closed) program $\{Q : \delta_2 \Leftarrow\}$ for computing δ_2, with $\delta_2 \supseteq \pi_1$ and $\delta_2 \cap \delta_1 = \emptyset$, $\{P \cup Q : \delta_1 \cup \delta_2 \Leftarrow\}$ is a correct program for computing $\delta_1 \cup \delta_2$.

Thus programs that are steadfast within a closed framework behave like correct units that can be composed in a correct way.

Example 3. In $\mathcal{PA}$ we can specify the relations $\forall(prod(x, y, z) \leftrightarrow z = x \cdot y)$ and $\forall(sum(x, y, z) \leftrightarrow z = x+y)$. Since the defining formulas are quantifier-free, these definitions are adequate. We can derive the open program

Framework:- $\mathcal{PA}$
Program:- prod : $prod \Leftarrow sum$
$prod(x, 0, 0) \leftarrow$ $prod(x, s(y), z) \leftarrow prod(x \cdot y, w), sum(w, x, z)$

The program prod is *open*, since it does not contain clauses for computing the parameter *sum*. Therefore, it cannot be used for computing. However it is *steadfast* in $\mathcal{PA}$. This means that, for every (closed) program sum for computing *sum*, if sum is correct (in $\mathcal{PA}$), then {prod $\cup$ sum} is a (closed) correct program for computing *prod*.

In an open framework $\mathcal{F}(\Pi)$, the meaning of the defined symbols is characterised in terms of the parameters Π. Since the latter are supplied by a closed framework, steadfastness can be defined as follows:[7]

Definition 5. Let $\mathcal{F}(\Pi)$ be an open framework, and $P : \delta \Leftarrow \pi$ be an open program. P is *steadfast* in $\mathcal{F}(\Pi)$ iff it is steadfast in every closed instance $\mathcal{F}(\Pi) \cup C$.

This means that $P : \delta \Leftarrow \pi$ is (closed and) correct wrt to its specification whenever $\mathcal{F}(\Pi)$ becomes closed, and correct closed programs for computing π are supplied. The parameters of π that belong to Π will be called *framework-parameters*, to distinguish them from those that do not belong to Π, which we will call

---

[7] A more abstract, model-theoretic characterisation, can be found in [10].

program-parameters. The programs for computing framework-parameters can be supplied only after the instantiation $\mathcal{F}(\Pi) \cup \mathcal{C}$ by a closed framework $\mathcal{C}$, while those for the program-parameters can be supplied either before or after such an instantiation. Note that, in a closed framework, an open program has only program-parameters. These parameters may be completely specified, e.g. *sum* in the program prod in Example 3, or partially defined, as we will see in the next example.

Example 4. In $\mathcal{LIST}(Elem, \lhd)$ sorting can be defined in the usual way, by the adequate explicit definition:

$$sort(x, y) \leftrightarrow perm(x, y) \wedge ord(y) \tag{1}$$

From (1) we can synthesise the following open program for *sort*:

$$
\begin{array}{|l|}
\hline
\qquad\qquad \textbf{Framework:- } \mathcal{LIST}(Elem, \lhd) \\
\hline
\hline
\qquad \textbf{Program:- } \text{merge sort} : sort \Leftarrow merge, split \\
\hline
\quad sort(nil, nil) \leftarrow \\
sort(x.nil, x.nil) \leftarrow \\
\quad sort(x.y.A, W) \leftarrow split(x.y.A, I, J) \wedge sort(I, U) \wedge sort(J, V) \wedge \\
\qquad\qquad\qquad merge(U, V, W) \\
\hline
 \\
\hline
\end{array}
\tag{2}
$$

The program-parameters *split* and *merge* can be specified by the *partial definition*:

$$
\begin{aligned}
&split_{max}(x, i, j) \leftrightarrow (perm(x, i|j) \wedge i \prec x \wedge j \prec x) \\
&\forall x, y, a \exists i, j\, split(x.y.a, i, j) \wedge \forall x, i, j\, (split(x, i, j) \rightarrow split_{max}(x, i, j)) \\
&ord(x) \wedge ord(y) \rightarrow (merge(x, y, z) \leftrightarrow ord(z) \wedge perm(x|y, z)).
\end{aligned}
\tag{3}
$$

where $\prec$ is the well founded relation $x \prec y \leftrightarrow l(x) \leq 1 \vee l(x) < l(y)$. (3) allows many possible interpretations. It reflects a design decision to split the input list, then sort the sublists and merge the sorted sublists. Even if the meaning of the program-parameters *split* and *merge* is left open, we can prove that the program (2) is steadfast (in $\mathcal{LIST}(Elem, \lhd)$) wrt the specification (1), that is, it is correct in every closed instance of $\mathcal{LIST}(Elem, \lhd)$, i.e. for any element type *Elem* and any (partial) ordering relation $\lhd$, whenever *merge* and *split* compute relations that satisfy the partial definitions (3). Thus it can be composed with different programs for *merge* and *split* to yield different sorting algorithms based on merging, e.g. insertion sort (as we will see in Section 3.2).

Intuitively, steadfastness can be seen as a kind of 'two-dimensional' parametric correctness, viz. with respect to both program-parameters and framework-parameters.

3 Towards an Object-Oriented Methodology

Using frameworks and steadfastness, we can synthesise correct programs in an object-oriented manner. In this section, we shall discuss the elements of such a methodology.

3.1 Classes and Inheritance

In object-oriented programming, a class is an implementation of an ADT, with methods that implement operations on the ADT. A framework contains axioms that formalise an ADT (or more generally a problem domain), and adequate definitions which serve as program specifications. Thus a framework can be considered to be a class, in which adequate definitions are declarative specifications of methods. Moreover, like classes, we can construct a hierarchy of frameworks with an inheritance mechanism. In this section, we explain how to construct frameworks by *framework extension* and *framework composition*, and how inheritance works between super- and sub-frameworks.

In a *framework extension*, new axioms and, possibly, new symbols are added, either to strengthen properties of the parameters, or to axiomatise new defined symbols, or to make stronger assumptions.

An *extension* $\mathcal{G}(\Delta)$ of a framework $\mathcal{F}(\Pi)$ (where Δ is a possibly empty list of new parameters) will be of the following form:

Framework $\mathcal{G}(\Delta)$;

IMPORT: $\mathcal{F}(\Pi)$;

SORTS: ...

FUNCTIONS: ...

RELATIONS: ...

D-AXIOMS: ...

P-AXIOMS: ...

THEOREMS: ...

where the new symbols of $\mathcal{G}$ (namely, the signature introduced after the import statement) must not occur in $\mathcal{F}(\Pi)$.

When adding new axioms, we must ensure that adequacy is preserved, i.e. that the extension is *adequate*. Once adequacy has been established, the new framework $\mathcal{G}(\Delta)$ inherits all the axioms, theorems, definitions and steadfast programs that have been developed in $\mathcal{F}(\Pi)$.

Since, in general, it may be not easy to establish adequacy, extensions by arbitrary axioms are rarely used.[8] As we said in Section 2.1, we use *recursive definitions* and *explicit definitions*.

Recursive definitions are used to build the core of a framework, that is to introduce a *few* basic operations and relations, needed to get an *expressive* initial framework. Let us consider for example Presbürger Arithmetic, i.e. $\mathcal{PA}$ without $\cdot$.

---

[8] We shall discuss this at the end of the section.

It is a complete theory. However, its completeness is not a symptom of deductive power, but of lack of expressiveness. We cannot explicitly define $\cdot$, for example, and therefore we have to add it by a recursive definition.

Once we have $\cdot$, we get the expressive framework $\mathcal{PA}$, where all the computable functions and relations can be explicitly defined. Adequate explicit definitions are our main tool to introduce new defined relations and functions, that can be used as specifications of new programs or simply as useful abbreviations. In $\mathcal{LIST}(Elem, \lhd)$, we have seen the example of *perm*, *ord*, used to define *sort*, and of *sort* itself, used to derive a family of sorting algorithms.

We also allow extension by new parameters. In this case, if the (possible) new p-axioms are consistent, then adequacy is (trivially) preserved.

In a *framework composition*, two frameworks are put together. For example, let us assume that we have a closed framework C containing the (closed) sort $Elem_C$ and an ordering relation $\lhd_C$. It can be composed with the open framework $\mathcal{LIST}(Elem, \lhd)$, and we obtain a closed framework. Moreover, if C contains a program for deciding $\lhd_C$, we can compose it with the open sorting program already contained in $\mathcal{LIST}$, and we get a closed sorting program.

We recall that an open framework is of the form $\mathcal{F}(\Pi) = \mathcal{D} \cup \mathcal{P}(\Pi))$, where Π are the parameters, $\mathcal{D}$ the d-axioms, and $\mathcal{P}(\Pi)$ the p-axioms. The operation of composition is defined as follows.

Definition 6. Let $\mathcal{F}_1(\Pi_1) = \mathcal{D}_1 \cup \mathcal{P}_1(\Pi_1)$ and $\mathcal{F}_2(\Pi_2) = \mathcal{D}_2 \cup \mathcal{P}(\Pi_2)$ be two open frameworks. Let us assume that:

(a) the intersection of the signatures of $\mathcal{F}_1$ and $\mathcal{F}_2$ is contained in Π_1;
(b) the proof-obligation $\mathcal{F}_2(\Pi_2) \vdash \mathcal{P}_1(\Pi_1)$ holds.

Then the composition operation $\mathcal{F}_1[\mathcal{F}_2]$ is defined and yields the framework $\mathcal{G}(\Delta)$ such that Δ contains Π_2 and the (possible) symbols of Π_1 that are not defined by $\mathcal{F}_2$, the signature is the union of the signatures of $\mathcal{F}_1$ and $\mathcal{F}_2$, and the axioms are the union of those of $\mathcal{F}_1$ and $\mathcal{F}_2$.

If (a) and (b) are not satisfied, then $\mathcal{F}_1[\mathcal{F}_2]$ is not defined. The obligation (a) is rather restrictive; it can be avoided by using signature morphisms. We do not have the space to present them here. They have been introduced in the algebraic approach (see e.g. [17]) and can be used in our approach, essentially in the same way.

Now, let $\mathcal{F}(\Pi) = \mathcal{D} \cup \mathcal{P}(\Pi)$ be an adequate open framework and C be an adequate closed framework that defines all the parameters Π. Then $\mathcal{G} = \mathcal{F}[C]$ is a closed instance of $\mathcal{F}$. Since $\mathcal{F}$ and C are adequate, $\mathcal{G}$ is an adequate closed framework.

Moreover we can easily see that $\mathcal{F}_1[\mathcal{F}_2[C]] = (\mathcal{F}_1[\mathcal{F}_2])[C]$. Therefore we have:

Theorem 7. *If $\mathcal{F}_1$ and $\mathcal{F}_2$ are adequate, and $\mathcal{F}_1[\mathcal{F}_2]$ is defined, then $\mathcal{F}_1[\mathcal{F}_2]$ yields an adequate framework.*

This theorem shows the operation $\mathcal{F}_1[\mathcal{F}_2]$ preserves the adequacy property. It is obvious that all the theorems that have been proved (separately) in $\mathcal{F}_1$

and $\mathcal{F}_2$ are inherited. Moreover, it can be shown that composition preserves the steadfastness of the programs that have been derived (separately) in $\mathcal{F}_1$ and $\mathcal{F}_2$. Thus adequate definitions and steadfast programs are also inherited.

The operations of framework extension and framework composition can be combined for building frameworks in an object-oriented manner. In object-oriented terminology, a framework is a class, and its steadfast programs are the methods of the class. An adequate extension $\mathcal{G}(\Delta)$ of $\mathcal{F}(\Pi)$ is a *subclass* of $\mathcal{F}(\Pi)$. Subclasses inherit from their parent classes. For example, the framework $\mathcal{LIST}(Elem, \lhd)$ has been built up as an extension of $\mathcal{PA}$. It inherits $\mathcal{PA}$ (by importing it), and introduces the new parameters $Elem$, $\lhd$ and the new defined symbols nil, :, $nocc$, $elemi$.

As another example, we can define the purely parametric class of partial orderings $\mathcal{PO}(Elem, \lhd)$, with signature containing only the two parameters $Elem$ and $\lhd$: $(Elem, Elem)$, and the axioms that state that $\lhd$ is a partial ordering. Then we can build the subclass $\mathcal{TO}(Elem, \lhd)$ by adding the axiom $\forall x, y : Elem(x \lhd y \lor y \lhd x)$, that states that the ordering $\lhd$ is also total.

Framework composition works like *class composition*, and the associated inheritance is a kind of *multiple inheritance*: $\mathcal{F}_1[\mathcal{F}_2]$ inherits from both $\mathcal{F}_1$ and $\mathcal{F}_2$. For example, let $\mathcal{LIST}(Elem)$ be the framework for lists without $\lhd$, then $\mathcal{LIST}(Elem, \lhd)$ can be generated by the composition:

$$\mathcal{LIST}(Elem, \lhd) = \mathcal{LIST}(Elem)[\mathcal{PO}(Elem, \lhd)].$$

It inherits from both $\mathcal{LIST}(Elem)$ and $\mathcal{PO}(Elem, \lhd)$.

An interesting fact is that subclass inheritance and composition inheritance are orthogonal: if $\mathcal{G}_1$ is an (adequate) extension of $\mathcal{F}_1$, and $\mathcal{G}_2$ is an (adequate) extension of $\mathcal{F}_2$, then, if $\mathcal{G}_1[\mathcal{G}_2]$ is defined, it is an adequate extension of $\mathcal{F}_1[\mathcal{F}_2]$. For example, since we know that $\mathcal{TO}(Elem, \lhd)$ is an extension of $\mathcal{PO}(Elem, \lhd)$, we automatically know that $\mathcal{LIST}(Elem)[\mathcal{TO}(Elem, \lhd)]$ is an extension of $\mathcal{LIST}(Elem)[\mathcal{PO}(Elem, \lhd)]$ (from which it therefore inherits). This allows propagation of extensions to various frameworks.

The above discussion shows how reusability is supported by the inheritance property of the framework operations we have considered. Now we briefly comment on reliability. There are three kinds of correctness problems:

- Informal correctness wrt the intuitive definition of a data type or an informal problem domain.
- Formal correctness of framework extensions and compositions.
- Formal correctness of program composition.

Formal correctness of framework extension and composition is guaranteed by the adequacy of the operations, as we have already discussed. Formal correctness of program composition will be (further) addressed in Section 3.3. Here, we briefly comment on informal correctness. Since this cannot be treated formally, we should build a possibly small, intuitively correct formalisation, that we call a *top-level* framework. When we are convinced that the top-level framework meets our informal idea of the problem domain, and we have a sufficiently expressive and adequate framework, then we extend it by adequate definitions. Adequate definitions are safe and completely modular. Indeed each definition is completely independent of the others, since it is eliminable and gives rise to a conservative extension. This means that, even if we discover that it does not meet our intuitive specification, we can modify it (and the related steadfast programs) without affecting any other part of the framework. This cannot be done, in general, with other kinds of definitions, since they may be non-eliminable (they increase the expressive power and cannot be eliminated, if they have been used elsewhere), or even non-conservative (they allow us to prove new theorems, that may have been used in other parts of the framework).

3.2 Synthesising Methods

Having shown how to construct classes (frameworks), we now show how in a given class, we can synthesise methods (steadfast programs), in an object-oriented style, i.e. in a hierarchical, modular manner.

Example 5. In the framework $\mathcal{LIST}(Elem, \lhd)$, from the specification (1) of sorting in Example 4 (in Section 2.2), we can derive different steadfast programs Ps, and from these programs we can in turn derive different (steadfast) programs to compute the parameters of Ps. Thus we can synthesise a hierarchy of (steadfast) sorting programs in a modular way. Let us see some examples.

As we saw in Example 4, from (1) we can synthesise the steadfast program (2) for merge sort. By using different specialisations of *split* to obtain different implementations, we can get different sorting programs. For instance, let us consider the adequate explicit definition

$$split1(x, i, j) \leftrightarrow \exists a, A(x = a.A \wedge i = [a] \wedge j = A \wedge split_{max}(a.A, [a], A))$$

Now *split1* satisfies (3). Therefore it can replace *split* in (2), and we can derive the following (open) steadfast program, where *split1* disappears and the second clause of (2) is subsumed by the second one of (4):

$$
\begin{array}{|l|}
\hline
\quad\text{Framework:- } \mathcal{LIST}(Elem, \lhd) \\
\hline
\text{Program:- insertion sort : } sort \Leftarrow merge \\
sort(nil, nil). \\
sort(x.A, W) \leftarrow sort(A, V) \wedge merge([x], V, W) \\
\hline
\end{array}
\qquad (4)
$$

Now we can rewrite the method *merge* to obtain insertion sort. Alternatively, from (1), we can synthesise the following steadfast program for partition sort:

$$
\boxed{
\begin{array}{c}
\textbf{Framework:-}\ \mathcal{LIST}(Elem, \lhd) \\[4pt]
\hline \\[-6pt]
\boxed{
\begin{array}{l}
\textbf{Program:-}\ \text{partition sort}\ :\ sort \Leftarrow P, concat \\[2pt]
\hline \\[-6pt]
sort(nil, nil). \\
sort(x.nil, x.nil) \leftarrow \\
\quad sort(a.A, Z) \leftarrow P(a.A, I, J, K) \wedge sort(I, I') \wedge sort(J, J') \wedge \\
\qquad\quad sort(K, K') \wedge concat(I', J', V) \wedge concat(V, K', Z)
\end{array}
}
\end{array}
}
\tag{5}
$$

where P is a *partition* relation partially defined by:

$$
P_{max}(X, I, J, K) \leftrightarrow perm(X, I|J|K) \wedge less(I, J) \wedge less(J, K) \wedge
$$
$$
I \prec X \wedge J \prec X \wedge K \prec X,
$$
$$
\forall x, X\ \exists I, J, K(P(x.X, I, J, K) \wedge \forall X, I, J, K(P(X, I, J, K) \rightarrow P_{max}(X, I, J, K))
$$

where $less(A, B) \leftrightarrow \forall a, b\, (a \in A \wedge b \in B \rightarrow a \lhd b)$ and the well-founded relation $\prec$ is defined by $A \prec B \leftrightarrow l(A) \leq 1 \vee l(A) < l(B)$.

From (5) we can derive a family of programs by specialising P in different ways. For instance, by the (adequate) specialisation $P_1(X, I, J, K) \leftrightarrow \exists a, A(X = a.A \wedge J = [a] \wedge P_{max}(a.A, I, [a], K))$ we can get the following program for quick sort:

$$
\boxed{
\begin{array}{c}
\textbf{Framework:-}\ \mathcal{LIST}(Elem, \lhd) \\[4pt]
\hline \\[-6pt]
\boxed{
\begin{array}{l}
\textbf{Program:-}\ \text{quick sort}\ :\ sort \Leftarrow part1, concat \\[2pt]
\hline \\[-6pt]
sort(nil, nil) \leftarrow \\
sort(a.A, Z) \leftarrow P_1(a.A, I, [a], K) \wedge sort(I, I') \wedge sort(K, K') \wedge \\
\qquad concat(I', [a], V) \wedge concat(V, K', Z)
\end{array}
}
\end{array}
}
$$

Now $P_1(a.A, I, [a], K)$ can be rewritten by the usual partition relation for quick sort, defined by $part1(A, I, a, K) \leftrightarrow P_1(a.A, I, [a], K)$. Finally, we can derive a steadfast program for computing such a relation.

These sorting programs are steadfast. Each open steadfast program can be used as a correct schema for program composition, over different instances of the parameters (both program- and framework-parameters). Thus our family of steadfast programs can be reused for generating code for different sorting algorithms in different problem domains. In object-oriented programming terms, they provide a basis for constructing libraries of 'correct' classes for sorting.

3.3 Reusability of Methods

A distinguishing feature of the methods (steadfast programs) in our classes (frameworks) is their *reusability* wrt both program-parameters and framework-parameters, as demonstrated by the example in the previous section. However, in general, such reusability is not always as straightforward as the example suggests. In this section, we take a closer look at this issue.

A steadfast program is a unit $P : \delta \Leftarrow \pi$, and it is defined in the context of a framework $\mathcal{F}(\Pi)$. We require that the symbols of δ have been introduced by adequate (explicit) definitions. If a parameter q of π is a framework-parameter (i.e. q belongs to Π), then the axioms for q are the parameter axioms of the framework. Otherwise q is a program-parameter, and is a new symbol introduced in (an extension to) the framework either by an adequate definition or by a partial definition, as we have seen in Section 2.2.

The composition of two programs $P_1 : \delta_1 \Leftarrow \pi_1$ and $P_2 : \delta_2 \Leftarrow \pi_2$, denoted by $P_1 + P_2$, is defined if $\delta_1 \cap \pi_2 = \emptyset$. We have:

$$P_1 + P_2 : \delta_1 \cup \delta_2 \Leftarrow (\pi_1 - \delta_2) \cup \pi_2$$

Here the framework has an important role, since every symbol used in a program must be defined by the framework. We have two cases. In the first case, the meaning of a symbol q is *completely* characterised by an explicit definition, and we can use q in many different programs, without any further constraint. In the second case, a program-parameter q (of a program P) has been introduced by a partial definition (i.e. set of axioms) D_q. In this case q *cannot* be used as a parameter in other programs, and we have to synthesise programs for q using a synthesis method that also works correctly for partial definitions.[9]

If a set of symbols δ has been introduced in $\mathcal{F}(\Pi)$ by adequate or partial definitions, then a program $P : \delta \Leftarrow \pi$ can be derived directly in $\mathcal{F}(\Pi)$. Another program $Q : \delta \Leftarrow \pi$ could be derived later, in a subclass of $\mathcal{F}(\Pi)$ obtained by framework extension or composition. Both P and Q can be used in the subclass. More generally, in a given class we may have many programs with the behaviour $\delta \Leftarrow \pi$, and we can use any one of them. Correctness follows from the fact that the meaning of the defined symbol has been stated by the framework *once and for all*, and the programs are steadfast with respect to this meaning.

Example 6. Let $\mathcal{F}(Elem, \lhd, \ldots)$ be a framework that inherits $\mathcal{LIST}(Elem, \lhd)$ and uses the merge sort program to perform some other computation. Now, let $\mathcal{F}[C]$ be a closed instance, where the elements have been instantiated by binary numbers. Then we can restart from the adequate explicit definition of *sort* and derive a new sort program, e.g. a distribution sort program. Since we have derived it starting from the same definition of sort, we can overwrite the old method by this new one.

If δ belong to the framework-parameters Π, then the derivation of P must be postponed, until we have an instantiation of the framework parameters by framework composition (using another open or closed framework).

Example 7. Let $\mathcal{LIST}_1(Elem_1, \lhd_1) = \mu(\mathcal{LIST}(Elem, \lhd))$, where μ is a signature morphism renaming the symbols of $\mathcal{LIST}$. In $\mathcal{LIST}_1(Elem_1, \lhd_1)$ we can

---

[9] For instance, we have considered this in [10].

define:

$$X \triangleleft Y \leftrightarrow \exists B(X|B = Y) \vee$$
$$\exists I, a, A, b, B(X = I|a.A \wedge Y = I|b.A \wedge a \triangleleft_1 b \wedge \neg a = b)$$

We can prove that $\triangleleft$ is a partial ordering (by using the p-axioms). Therefore $\mathcal{LIST}[\mathcal{LIST}_1]$ satisfies the required proof obligation, and is a framework that inherits the sorting programs. Now we can develop programs to decide $\triangleleft$, or we can inherit them, if they had been derived in $\mathcal{F}_1$ before the composition.

This discussion shows the central rôle of frameworks in (reasoning about) the correctness of program composition. We believe that this use of frameworks is a new contribution to reasoning about modularity, reusability, and composition.

3.4 Objects

Classes introduced by frameworks in Section 3.1 can only be instantiated in their parameters, i.e. they are like *generic* classes in object-oriented programming, and as such they cannot be used directly to create instances called objects in object-oriented programming. Clearly, in order to implement our methodology as (part of) an object-oriented programming system, we need to have objects. To round off this paper, we make a tentative proposal for objects.

To introduce objects, we distinguish two kinds of frameworks: *adt*-frameworks and *obj*-frameworks. We use *adt*-frameworks to define the basic data types. They may be closed, like natural numbers, reals with a given precision, ASCII characters, and so on; or open, like lists with generic elements $\mathcal{LIST}(Elem)$. The ADTs defined by *adt*-frameworks are typically used (imported) by other frameworks.

On the other hand, we use *obj*-frameworks to define classes of objects. An *obj*-framework is open and the information needed to completely specify its open relations, which we will call *internal relations*, is stored in the objects. Objects are generated (and updated) at run-time, by supplying the missing information.

Example 8. An *obj*-framework looks like:

> **Framework** $\mathcal{SYM}$;
>
> INTERNAL: *ssym, fsym, rsym*;
> SORTS: *ssym, fsym, rsym*;
> FUNCTIONS: $\ldots : \rightarrow ssym$;
> $\ldots : \rightarrow fsym$;
> $=, \ldots : \rightarrow rsym$;

Framework $\mathcal{SIGN}$;

INTERNAL: *arity, kind*;

IMPORT: $\mathcal{LIST}(Elem = ssym, List = arity)[\mathcal{SYM}]$;

RELATIONS: *kind* : $(fsym, arity, ssym)$;

kind : $(rsym, arity)$;

I-AXIOMS: $\forall(\exists a, s\, kind(f, a, s))$

$\forall(kind(f, a, s_1) \wedge kind(f, a, s_2) \wedge \neg s_1 = s_2 \rightarrow false)$

$\forall r \exists a\, kind(r, a)$

$\forall A(kind(=, A) \leftrightarrow \exists s\, A = [s, s])$

The above is only a possible syntax to implement our ideas. $\mathcal{LIST}(Elem = ssym, List = arity)$ indicates the result of the signature morphism that renames *Elem* by *ssym* and *List* by *arity*. This *obj*-framework is a template for generating objects of class $\mathcal{SIGN}$. Except for those imported from lists, all the symbols are *internal*: they are like parameters, but the information on them will be held in the objects of the class. Moreover, part of the signature (indicated by ...) is left open and will be completed by the objects. Thus an object of this class will look like:

Object $\mathcal{PA\text{-}SIGN} : \mathcal{SIGN}$;

OBJ-SIGNATURE: $Nat \quad :\rightarrow ssym$;

$0, s, +, \cdot :\rightarrow fsym$;

OBJ-AXIOMS: $kind(0, A, S) \leftrightarrow A = nil \wedge S = Nat$

$kind(s, A, S) \leftrightarrow A = [Nat] \wedge S = Nat$

$kind(+, A, S) \leftrightarrow A = [Nat, Nat] \wedge S = Nat$

$kind(\cdot, A, S) \leftrightarrow A = [Nat, Nat] \wedge S = Nat$

We assume here the hypothesis of unique names, i.e. $\neg s = +, \neg + = \cdot$, and so on.[10] It is easy to see that the *obj*-axioms are the completion of a set of facts, that contain the information on the relation *kind*. The completion has the isoinitial model where the domains correspond to the constants, and the relations to the listed facts. We can also see that the intended model of this object satisfies the *i*-axioms.

This object can be composed with an open *class*-framework $\mathcal{AF}$, that contains the steadfast programs to decide if a given expression is an atomic formula of the signature stored in $\mathcal{PA\text{-}SIGN}$; in this way we obtain an object $\mathcal{PA\text{-}AF}$ to recognise the atomic formulas of $\mathcal{PA}$. Alternatively, the open *obj*-framework $\mathcal{SIGN}$ can be composed with $\mathcal{AF}$, and then we can build the object $\mathcal{PA\text{-}AF}$ exactly in the way shown before, since the internal open symbols are the same.

In an object, the internal information is supplied at run-time and is stored in its internal state. Thus it can be updated. For example, we can add new symbols to the signature of $\mathcal{PA}$, by storing them in the corresponding object.

Thus an *obj*-framework $\mathcal{F}(\text{INTERNAL} : \Pi)$ is an open framework with internal parameters Π, and an object is a closed instance of $\mathcal{F}$, that contains some pieces

---

[10] The problem of distinguishing e.g. $0 :\rightarrow fsym$ from $0 :\rightarrow Nat$ will be addressed below.

of internal information (lists of facts) that are generated and updated at run-time.

Adequacy of *obj*-frameworks is defined as we have done for open frameworks in Definition 2 (in Section 2.1). There is only the (obvious) difference that now the open symbols Π are the internal open symbols.

Finally, we also have to distinguish two kinds of methods: *class*-methods and *obj*-methods. *Class*-methods correspond to steadfast programs, as we have seen, e.g. steadfast open programs to recognise if an expression is a formula over an (open) signature. Note that it does not matter whether an open symbol is supplied as an external parameter or as an internal state. Therefore we can apply the same deductive synthesis approach, to derive class-methods both in *adt*-classes and in *obj*-classes.

Obj-methods allow us to create and update an object at run-time. Therefore they cannot be compared with steadfast programs. Rather, they correspond to a kind of parameter passing, and consequently we should verify that the *i*-axioms are satisfied by the actual parameters, i.e. by the information that is introduced in the object. In contrast to the case of framework composition, where the proof obligation on the *p*-axioms is tested at compile-time, here we have to endow *obj*-methods with programs to test at run-time that the updates give rise to intended models that still satisfy the *i*-axioms.

For example, updates could be done by using a mechanism like Prolog's *assert* and *retract*. Errors could be tested by suitable programs, with clauses like $error \leftarrow kind(f, a, s_1) \wedge kind(f, a, s_2) \wedge \neg s_1 = s_2$, and updates should be aborted when an error occurs. Moreover, if we allow the introduction of new symbols in the signature at object-level, we need to be able to distinguish between the object-level-signature and the framework-level-signature. We have yet to address these problems fully, and we intend to do so in future.

4 Related Work and Concluding Remarks

In this paper, we have made a preliminary proposal for a methodology for deductive synthesis of logic programs, that is object-oriented in the sense of the common view of object-oriented programming. Our motivation is not merely to jump on the 'object-oriented programming' bandwagon, but to borrow ideas from object-oriented programming for a methodology to construct quality software that is *correctly* reusable and extensible, and not only reliable but formally *correct* wrt specifications. Although it is good for constructing reusable and extensible software, current object-oriented programming technology does not support such formal program development. Our proposed methodology would hopefully be a first step towards this goal, which is of paramount importance in safety-critical applications in real-world software engineering.

To attack the correctness problem, our chief weapon is steadfastness. This is *a priori* correctness, which therefore guarantees correctness of program composition. It is thus the opposite of *a posteriori* correctness that is normally used in module systems based on type theories, where correctness of composition must be verified after composition.

Our notion of classes and inheritance is based on frameworks. In the terminology of conventional object-oriented programming, a steadfast logic program P in a framework $\mathcal{F}$ would be regarded as a *method* in the *class* $\mathcal{F}$. However, a framework captures much more than ADT definitions, as we already mentioned. In fact, a framework essentially characterises a family of classes, or a *generic* class, and in addition contains all the knowledge needed to reason about these classes and steadfastness. Consequently all that can be said and proved in a class can be said and proved in the framework.

Moreover, open frameworks can be composed with closed frameworks, giving rise to a hierarchy of frameworks. We believe such a hierarchy is a better semantic characterisation of type inheritance than the usual inheritance (and multiple inheritance) mechanisms in object-oriented programming which can be very unwieldy (see e.g. [3]).

Our methodology is similar in spirit to, but different in substance from, existing work on modular or object-oriented program construction. Basically, we have raised modularity and reusability to the semantic level. Our characterisation of object-oriented programming is different from that used in object-oriented logic programming, e.g. [11, 15], where the conventional notions of object-oriented programming are imported virtually wholesale, at the syntactic level.

Our characterisation of modularity and reusability is not only different from that in conventional object-oriented programming, but also from that in modular logic programming, e.g. [2, 4]. In the latter, composition is not performed in the context of a framework, and there is no notion of parametric correctness corresponding to steadfastness. Consequently, the notion of correct reusability is also missing there.

However, our work is only in its initial stage, and much more remains to be done. Details of the semantic issues involved need to be worked out, and we have not even begun to investigate the feasibility of implementing the methodology, although we do believe that some object-oriented programming language would provide a suitable vehicle.

Acknowledgements

We wish to thank Laurent Fribourg and Alberto Pettorossi for their insightful comments and constructive suggestions which have helped to improve this paper greatly.

References

1. A. Bertoni, G. Mauri and P. Miglioli. On the power of model theory in specifying abstract data types and in capturing their recursiveness. *Fundamenta Informaticae* VI(2):127–170, 1983.
2. A. Brogi, P. Mancarella, D. Pedreschi and F. Turini. Modular logic programming. *ACM TOPLAS* 16(4):1361-1398, 1994.

3. K.M. Bruce. A paradigmatic object-oriented programming language: Design, static typing and semantics. *J. Functional Programming* 4(2):127–206, 1994. Special issue: Type systems for object-oriented programming.

4. M. Bugliesi, E. Lamma and P. Mello. Modularity in logic programming. *J. Logic Programming* 19,20:443–502, 1994. Special issue: Ten years of logic programming.

5. C.C. Chang and H.J. Keisler. *Model Theory.* North-Holland, 1973.

6. Y. Deville and K.K. Lau. Logic program synthesis. *J. Logic Programming* 19,20:321–350, 1994. Special issue: Ten years of logic programming.

7. *J. Functional Programming* 4(2), 1994. Special issue: Type systems for object-oriented programming.

8. K.K. Lau and M. Ornaghi. On specification frameworks and deductive synthesis of logic programs. In L. Fribourg and F. Turini, editors, *Proc. LOPSTR 94 and META 94, Lecture Notes in Computer Science* 883, pages 104–121, Springer-Verlag, 1994.

9. K.K. Lau, M. Ornaghi and S.-Å. Tärnlund. The halting problem for deductive synthesis of logic programs. In P. van Hentenryck, editor, *Proc.* 11th *Int. Conf. on Logic Programming*, pages 665–683, MIT Press, 1994.

10. K.K. Lau, M. Ornaghi and S.-Å. Tärnlund. Steadfast logic programs. Submitted to *J. Logic Programming.*

11. F.G. McCabe. *L& O: Logic and Objects.* Prentice-Hall, 1992.

12. B. Meyer. *Object-oriented Software Construction.* Prentice Hall, 1988.

13. B. Meyer. *Eiffel the Language.* Prentice Hall, 1992.

14. P. Miglioli, U. Moscato and M. Ornaghi. Abstract parametric classes and abstract data types defined by classical and constructive logical methods. *J. Symb. Comp.* 18:41-81, 1994.

15. C.D.S. Moss. *Prolog++ The Power of Object-Oriented and Logic Programming.* Addison Wesley, 1994.

16. J. Palsberg and M.I. Schwartzbach. *Object-Oriented Type Systems.* Wiley, 1994.

17. M. Wirsing. Algebraic specification. In J. Van Leeuwen, editor, *Handbook of Theoretical Computer Science*, pages 675–788. Elsevier, 1990.

Logic Program Synthesis by Induction over Horn Clauses

Andrew J. Parkes
CIRL
1268 University of Oregon
Eugene, OR 97403-1269
USA
parkes@cs.uoregon.edu

Geraint A. Wiggins
Department of Artificial Intelligence
University of Edinburgh
80 South Bridge, Edinburgh EH1 1HN
Scotland
geraint@ai.ed.ac.uk

Abstract

We report on the implementation of a new induction scheme in the Whelk logic program synthesis and transformation system [5]. The scheme is based on work by Feferman [1], and allows constructive proof by induction over the minimal Herbrand model of a set of Horn Clauses. This is an important addition to the Whelk system, because it admits reasoning about and synthesis from "real" logic programs, whereas previously the system was limited to induction over recursive data structures.

The contribution of this work is practical, in the extension of the synthesis capability of the Whelk program synthesis system. Theoretically, it is closely related to an extension of [2] (reported in [3]), where a similar induction scheme is used to synthesise logic programs which embody functions.

Full details of the extension and its implementation may be found in [4].

References

1. S. Feferman. Finitary inductively presented logics. In *Logic Colloquium '88*, pages 191–220, Amsterdam, 1989. North-Holland.
2. L. Fribourg. Extracting logic programs from proofs that use extended Prolog execution and induction. In *Proceedings of Eighth International Conference on Logic Programming*, pages 685 – 699. MIT Press, June 1990. Extended version in [3].
3. J.-M. Jacquet, editor. *Constructing Logic Programs*. Wiley, 1993.
4. A. J. Parkes. Generator induction for relational proofs, logic programming and reasoning about database systems. MSc dissertation, Dept. of Artificial Intelligence, Edinburgh, 1994.
5. G. A. Wiggins. Synthesis and transformation of logic programs in the Whelk proof development system. In K. R. Apt, editor, *Proceedings of JICSLP-92*, pages 351–368. M.I.T. Press, Cambridge, MA, 1992.

Logic Program Transformation
through Generalization Schemata   [Extended Abstract]

Pierre Flener

Department of Computer Engineering
and Information Science
Bilkent University
TR–06533 Bilkent, Ankara, Turkey
Email: pf@cs.bilkent.edu.tr

Yves Deville

Department of Computing Science
and Engineering
Université Catholique de Louvain
B–1348 Louvain-la-Neuve, Belgium
Email: yde@info.ucl.ac.be

1 Introduction

Programs can be classified according to their construction methodologies, such as divide-and-conquer, top-down decomposition, global search, and so on, or any composition thereof. Informally, a *program schema* [2] is a template program with a fixed control and data flow, but without specific indications about the actual parameters or the actual computations, except that they must satisfy certain constraints. A program schema thus abstracts a whole family of particular programs that can be obtained by instantiating its place-holders to particular parameters or computations, using the specification, the program synthesized so far, and the constraints of the schema. It is therefore interesting to guide program construction by a schema that captures the essence of some methodology. This reflects the conjecture that experienced programmers actually instantiate schemata when programming, which schemata are summaries of their past programming experience.

Moreover, in contrast to traditional programming methodologies where program transformation sequentially follows program construction and is merely based on the syntax of the constructed program, these two phases can actually be interleaved in (semi-)automated program synthesis, based on information generated and exploited during the program construction process.

It would therefore be interesting to pre-compile transformation techniques at the schema-level: a *transformation schema* is a pair $\langle T_1, T_2 \rangle$ of program schemata, such that T_2 is a transformation of T_1, according to some transformation technique. Transformation at the program-level then reduces to (a) selecting a transformation schema $\langle T_1, T_2 \rangle$ such that T_1 covers the given program under some substitution σ, and (b) applying σ to T_2. This is similar to the work of Fuchs *et al.* [4] [also see this volume], except that they have a preliminary abstraction phase where the covering schema of the given program is discovered, whereas we here assume that this program was synthesized in a schema-guided fashion, so that the covering schema is already known.

It sometimes becomes "difficult," if not impossible, to follow the divide-and-conquer methodology. One can then generalize the initial specification and construct a (recursive) program from the generalized specification as well as express the initial problem as a particular case of the generalized one. Paradoxically, the new construction then becomes "easier," if not possible in the first place. As an additional and beneficial side-effect, programs for generalized problems are often more efficient, because they feature tail recursion and/or because the complexity could be reduced through loop merging..

2 Program Transformation by Structural Generalization

In *structural generalization* [1], one generalizes the structure (type) of some parameter. For instance, in *tupling generalization*, an integer parameter would be generalized into an integer-list parameter, and the intended relation would be generalized accordingly.

Example 1: Let flat (B, F) hold iff list F contains the elements of binary tree B as they are visited by a prefix traversal of B. We also say that F is the prefix representation of B. A corresponding "naive" divide-and-conquer logic program could be:

```
flat(void,[])
flat(btree(L,E,R),F) ← flat(L,U), flat(R,V),
    H=[E], append(U,V,I), append(H,I,F)
```

Tupling generalization yields: flats (Bs, F) holds iff list F is the concatenation of the prefix representations of the elements of binary tree list Bs. We obtain the program:

```
flat(B,F) ← flats([B],F)
flats([],[])
flats([void|Bs],F) ← flats(Bs,F)
flats([btree(L,E,R)|Bs],[E|TF]) ← flats([L,R|Bs],TF)
```

In contrast to the "naive" version above, this program has a linear time complexity, a better space complexity, and it can be made tail-recursive in the mode (in, out). ◆

Result 1: Suppose the specification of the initial problem is (where $\mathcal{R}$ is the intended relation, and $\mathcal{T}_1$, $\mathcal{T}_2$ are the types of its parameters):

$R(X,Y) \Leftrightarrow \mathcal{R}[X,Y]$, where $X \in \mathcal{T}_1$ and $Y \in \mathcal{T}_2$,

and that the initial program is covered by the following divide-and-conquer schema:

```
R(X,Y) ← Minimal(X), Solve(X,Y)                    (Schema 1)
R(X,Y) ← NonMinimal(X), Decompose(X,HX,TX₁,TX₂),
    R(TX₁,TY₁), R(TX₂,TY₂),
    Process(HX,HY), Compose(TY₁,TY₂,I), Compose(HY,I,Y)
```

where Compose/3 is associative and has some left/right-identity element e.

The *eureka*, that is, the formal specification of the tupling-generalized problem is [3]:

$Rs(Xs,Y) \Leftrightarrow (Xs=[] \wedge Y=e)$
$\vee (Xs=[X_1,X_2,...,X_n] \wedge R(X_i,Y_i) \wedge I_1=Y_1 \wedge \mathtt{Compose}(I_{i-1},Y_i,I_i) \wedge Y=I_n)$,
where $X \in$ list of $\mathcal{T}_1$ and $Y \in \mathcal{T}_2$.

and the new logic program is the corresponding instance of the following schema:

```
R(X,Y) ← Rs([X],Y)                                 (Schema 2)
Rs(Xs,Y) ← Xs=[], Y=e
Rs(Xs,Y) ← Xs=[X|TXs], Minimal(X),
    Rs(TXs,TY), Solve(X,HY), Compose(HY,TY,Y)
Rs(Xs,Y) ← Xs=[X|TXs], NonMinimal(X), Decompose(X,HX,TX₁,TX₂),
    Rs([TX₁,TX₂|TXs],TY), Process(HX,HY), Compose(HY,TY,Y)
```

If Solve (X,Y) converts X into a constant "size" Y and/or if Process (HX,HY) converts HX into a constant "size" HY, then some partial evaluation can be done, which often results in the disappearance of calls to Compose/3, if not in the possibility of making the recursive calls iterative ones. ◆

The pair ⟨Schema 1, Schema 2⟩ thus constitutes a first generalization schema. More generalization schemata must be pre-compiled, for different numbers of heads and tails of X, and for each ordering of composition of Y from HY and the TY [3].

3 Program Transformation by Descending Generalization

In *computational generalization* [1], one generalizes a state of computation in terms of "what has already been done" and "what remains to be done." If information about what has already been done is not needed, then it is called *descending generalization*.

Example 2: The "naive" logic program for the well-known `reverse(L,R)` is:

```
reverse([],[])
reverse([HL|TL],R) ← reverse(TL,TR), HR=[HL], append(TR,HR,R)
```

Descending generalization yields: `reverseDesc(L,R,A)` holds iff list R is the concatenation of list A to the end of the reverse of list L. We obtain the program:

```
reverse(L,R) ← reverseDesc(L,R,[])
reverseDesc([],R,R)
reverseDesc([HL|TL],R,A) ← reverseDesc(TL,R,[HL|A])
```

In contrast to the "naive" version above, this program has a linear time complexity, a better space complexity, and it can be made tail-recursive in the mode (in, out). ♦

Result 2: Suppose the initial problem exhibits a functional dependency from parameter X to parameter Y, and that the initial program is covered by the following schema:

```
R(X,Y) ← Minimal(X), Solve(X,Y)                          (Schema 3)
R(X,Y) ← NonMinimal(X), Decompose(X,HX,TX),
    R(TX,TY), Process(HX,HY), Compose(HY,TY,Y)
```

where `Compose/3` is associative with left-identity element e.

The *eureka* can be mechanically extracted [1] [3] from the initial program:

```
R-desc(X,Y,A) ⟺ ∃S R(X,S) ∧ Compose(A,S,Y)
```

and the new logic program is the corresponding instance of the following schema:

```
R(X,Y) ← R-desc(X,Y,e)                                   (Schema 4)
R-desc(X,Y,A) ← Minimal(X), Solve(X,S), Compose(A,S,Y)
R-desc(X,Y,A) ← NonMinimal(X), Decompose(X,HX,TX),
    Process(HX,HI), Compose(A,HI,NewA), R-desc(TX,Y,NewA)
```

If `Process(HX,HY)` converts HX into a constant "size" HY and/or if the intended relation behind R/2 maps the minimal form of parameter X into e, and e is also a right-identity element of `Compose/3`, then some partial evaluation can be done, which usually results in the disappearance of calls to `Compose/3`, if not in the possibility of making the recursive calls iterative ones. ♦

The pair ⟨`Schema 3`, `Schema 4`⟩ thus constitutes another generalization schema.

4 Conclusion

Both generalization techniques are very suitable for mechanical transformation: all operators of the generalized programs are operators of the initial programs. Given a divide-and-conquer program, a mere inspection of the properties of its solving, processing, and composition operators thus allows the detection of which kinds of generalization are possible, and to which optimizations they would lead. The *eureka* discoveries are compiled away, and the transformations can be completely automated.

References

[1] Y. Deville. *Logic Programming: Systematic Program Development*. Addison-Wesley, 1990.

[2] P. Flener. *Logic Program Synthesis from Incomplete Information*. Kluwer, 1995.

[3] P. Flener and Y. Deville. *Logic Program Transformation through Generalization Schemata*. TR BU-CEIS-95xx, Bilkent University, Ankara (Turkey), 1995.

[4] N.E. Fuchs and M.P.J. Fromherz. Schema-based transformations of logic programs. In Clement and Lau (eds), *Proc. of LOPSTR'91*, pp. 111–125. Springer-Verlag, 1992.

An Opportunistic Approach
for Logic Program Analysis and Optimisation
Using Enhanced Schema-Based Transformations*

Wamberto W. Vasconcelos** , Norbert E. Fuchs

Institut für Informatik

Universität Zürich

Switzerland

vascon@ifi.unizh.ch, fuchs@ifi.unizh.ch

Abstract. We propose an opportunistic approach for performing program analysis and optimisation: opportunities for improving a logic program are systematically attempted, either by examining its procedures in an isolated fashion, or by checking for conjunctions within clauses that can be used as joint specifications. Opportunities are represented as *enhanced schema-based transformations*, generic descriptions of inefficient programming constructs and of how these should be altered in order to confer a better computational behaviour on the program. The programming constructs are described in an abstract manner using an *enhanced schema language* which allows important features to be highlighted and irrelevant details to be disregarded.

1 Introduction

The clean declarative semantics of logic programs hides many performance issues which must be accounted for if the programs are to be executed using the currently available technology. These efficiency issues can be dealt with at an early stage, during the preparation of the program: standard logic programming constructs, also named *programming techniques*, which guarantee a good computational behaviour to those logic programs incorporating them, can be used. Prolog programming techniques have been extensively studied [Bowles *et al*, 94; O'Keefe, 90; Sterling & Shapiro, 94]; it has been advocated [Kirschenbaum *et al*, 94] that these standard practices should be explicitly taught as part of a discipline of methodical logic programming development; and logic programming environments have been implemented [Bowles *et al*, 94; Robertson, 91] incorporating them.

---

* This work was carried out within the European Human Capital and Mobility Scheme (contract No. CHRX-CT 93-00414/BBW 93.0268) while the first author was visiting the Institut für Informatik, Universität Zürich.

** PhD Student, Department of Artificial Intelligence, University of Edinburgh, Scotland, U.K., sponsored by the Brazilian National Research Council (CNPq, grant No. 201340/91-7), on leave from UECE/Ceará, Brazil.

A second approach addresses efficiency issues after the program has been devised, trying to optimise the existing code. This involves the analysis and subsequent transformation of a given, possibly inefficient, logic program into an equivalent version with better computational behaviour. An underlying assumption of this approach is that commonly occurring but computationally inefficient constructs in logic programs can be identified and eliminated, preferably in a fully automated way, thus relieving logic programmers of the extra burden of worrying about performance issues. A number of approaches for semi-automatic program transformation have been proposed [Fuchs & Fromherz, 91; Lakhotia & Sterling, 90; Nielson & Nielson, 90; Proietti & Pettorossi, 90].

A third option combines both previous approaches: individual predicates are devised using programming techniques and their interrelations are, whenever possible, improved by a program transformation system. Additional information concerning the intended use of each predicate can be collected via the program development tools and methods employed, thus making the transformation process easier and more sophisticated. This idea is pursued in [Flener, 95; Flener & Deville, 95], in which each procedure is devised by means of program templates employing divide-and-conquer algorithms. In [Vargas-Vera, 95; Vargas-Vera et al., 93] a similar idea is proposed, procedures being developed using Prolog programming techniques. In both approaches more sophisticated forms of program combination can be achieved by employing auxiliary information concerning the intended use of each procedure.

The work presented here fits into the second line of research above: we propose an approach for the systematic analysis of a program, detecting opportunities to improve its computational efficiency. These opportunities are generic descriptions of commonly occurring inefficient programming constructs and of how these should be changed in order to confer a better computational behaviour on the program. Changes to program constructs are depicted by means of transformations relating an inefficient programming construct described in a generic, schematic fashion to its modified, more efficient, version. A given program is systematically scanned and portions of its code are matched against the description of inefficient constructs of the transformations: if the matching occurs then the prescribed new version appropriately replaces the previous portions of code and further opportunities in the program are searched for. Each transformation is formulated so as to describe the programming constructs in an economic yet general fashion. We propose an enhanced version of Gegg-Harrison's schema language [Gegg-Harrison, 91] for this purpose, following the proposal in [Fuchs & Fromherz, 91].

In the next section we explain our enhanced schema language. In Section 3 we describe how enhanced program schemata are used to guide program transformations. In Section 4 we propose a realistic scenario in which transformations can be used to analyse and improve the computational performance of a program. In Section 5 we draw some conclusions and show directions for research.

2 Enhanced Program Schemata

An opportunity for improving a program is defined as a transformation mapping a common inefficient construct onto an equivalent version with better computational behaviour. The programming constructs are represented by means of *program schemata*, generic descriptions of a program in a suitable Horn-clause notation. A special schema language, an enhanced version of Gegg-Harrison's [Gegg-Harrison, 91] proposal, is used which enables the economic description of programs in an abstract fashion.

We provide a notational device which allows reference to arbitrary argument positions. It consists of adding the construct "#n", where n is the argument position, to the term being referred to. This circumvents the restriction of Gegg-Harrison's schema language of allowing only the representation of consecutive initial argument positions of procedures. Since we want program schemata to stand for generic descriptions of actual programs, we shall assume that our analysed programs are translated into an *explicit argument format*, in which subgoals of the form $p(t_1, \ldots, t_n)$ are replaced by $p(t_1\#1, \ldots, t_n\#n)$ and appropriately translated back into the conventional Prolog format after the analysis.

The adopted schema language allows the description of large classes of constructs sharing particular features, ignoring unimportant variations. The construct $t\#n$ represents the constraint that term t occupies position n in the subgoal; the symbol $\vec{A}_i$ stands for a possibly empty sequence of arguments; $\vec{G}_i$ represents a possibly empty sequence of *non-recursive* subgoals; $\overrightarrow{G_i}$ represents a possibly empty sequence of any sort of subgoals; $x\#1$ is $F(\vec{A}_n, y, \vec{A}_m)\#2$ represents a Prolog is subgoal in its explicit argument position format, such that the expression on the right-hand side has at least one reference to the variable symbol y: all references to y are economically represented by a single occurrence of that symbol.

The enhanced schema language also allows the abstract description of functors and their arguments, constants and system predicates which serve as tests. Constants are generically denoted as $ct(n)$ where n differentiates distinct constants in the same schema. Prolog tests, viz. $>$, $<$, $>$, *integer*/1, *ground*/1, *number*/1, and so on, are generically denoted by T_n where n differentiates distinct tests in a schema and may be omitted. Using these additional shorthands even larger classes of programs can be depicted by simple schemata. The schema below depicts those programs manipulating singly-recursive data structures, such that its termination occurs when a constant is found:

```
S(Ā₁,ct(_)#N,Ā₂):-
    Ḡ₁.
S(Ā₉,F(Ā₁₀,Xs,Ā₁₁)#N,Ā₁₂):-
    Ḡ₄,
    S(Ā₁₃,Xs#N,Ā₁₄),
    Ḡ₅.
```

Ordinary Prolog constructs can be used within program schemata, in which case they are considered as constraints, since they are specific syntactic patterns. A formal description of the enhanced schema language is presented in [Vasconcelos

& Fuchs, 95]. We use frames around schemata to improve their visualisation.

3 Enhanced Schema-Based Transformations of Logic Programs

[Fuchs & Fromherz, 91] have proposed the notion of schema-based program transformations, in which Gegg-Harrison's schema language is used to characterise an actual context whereby efficiency-improving alterations can be performed in a given program. These transformations can give logic programs a more procedural reading. A larger number of constructs can, however, be addressed if our enhanced schema language is used instead. For instance, in the following program

```
sum([],0).
sum([X|Xs],S):-
    sum(Xs,SXs),
    S is X + SXs.
dcount(0,[]).
dcount(C,[X|Xs]):-
    dcount(CXs,Xs),
    C is 1 + CXs.
p(L,S,C):- sum(L,S),dcount(C,L).
```

the same list L is being processed twice in the body of predicate p/3. The unusual definition of the dcount/2 predicate to count the elements of a list, with the inversion of the conventional argument order, puts this situation outside the scope of Fuchs and Fromherz's transformations. This is due to their adopting Gegg-Harrison's schema language, with its restriction of representing only sequences of consecutive initial argument positions. Our enhanced schema language, however, allows us to conveniently express such situations.

Schema-based transformations are standard syntactic manipulations of portions of a given program. Program schemata are used to depict both input programs and their improved output versions. The changes prescribed by the transformation comprise a complete sequence of transformation steps, involving the definition of new predicates (*eureka rules*), the order and choice of literals to apply unfold/fold rules, change of subgoals order, and any other relevant changes to the program. More formally, a schema-based transformation $\mathcal{T}$ is a quadruple of the form $\langle\langle G_1,\ldots,G_n\rangle,\langle S_1,\ldots,S_n\rangle,\langle H_1,\ldots,H_m\rangle,\langle T_1,\ldots,T_m\rangle\rangle$ where $\langle G_1,\ldots,G_n\rangle$ and $\langle H_1,\ldots,H_m\rangle$ are conjunctions of schematic subgoals, and $\langle S_1,\ldots,S_n\rangle$ and $\langle T_1,\ldots,T_m\rangle$ are respectively input and output program schemata. Such formalisation is to be understood as "given the conjunction of schematic subgoals $G_1,\ldots,G_n$, such that their definitions are respectively $S_1,\ldots,S_n$, then $G_1,\ldots,G_n$ can be replaced by $H_1,\ldots,H_m$ such that their definitions are respectively $T_1,\ldots,T_m$." The conjunction $G_1,\ldots,G_n$ provides, in a generic form, the context in which the transformation can take place; $S_1,\ldots,S_n$ and $T_1,\ldots,T_m$ are sequences of program schemata, describing, in an abstract fashion, the form the input and output procedures should have.

Given a schema-based transformation of the form above, the context of its successful application is a Prolog program Π with a clause C of the form $H:-\vec{I_1}, G_1, \ldots, G_n, \vec{I_2}$, where $G_i, i \geq 1$, are non-recursive subgoals, G_i being a call to procedure $\mathcal{P}_i$ of Π, $\vec{I_1}$ and $\vec{I_2}$ are (possibly empty) finite conjunctions of subgoals not relevant to the analysis, and there is a schema substitution Θ associating components of the program with the schema constructs such that $G_i \Theta = G_i$ and $S_i \Theta = \mathcal{P}_i$. [Vasconcelos & Fuchs, 95] describe a means to obtain schema substitutions for enhanced schemata.

The transformation below formalises, in a generic manner, those opportunities for efficiency improvements in which the same data structure is traversed twice in procedures being invoked:

$$\left\langle \left\langle \boxed{\begin{array}{l} \texttt{S1}(\vec{A_1},\texttt{L\#N},\vec{A_2}), \\ \texttt{S2}(\vec{A_3},\texttt{L\#M},\vec{A_4}) \end{array}} \right\rangle, \left\langle \boxed{\begin{array}{l} \texttt{S1}(\vec{A}_{11},\texttt{ct(1)\#N},\vec{A}_{12}):- \\ \quad \vec{G}_{11}. \\ \texttt{S1}(\vec{A}_{13},\texttt{G(X,Xs)\#N},\vec{A}_{14}):- \\ \quad \vec{G}_{12}, \\ \quad \texttt{S1}(\vec{A}_{15},\texttt{Xs\#N},\vec{A}_{16}) \\ \quad \vec{G}_{13}. \end{array}}, \boxed{\begin{array}{l} \texttt{S2}(\vec{A}_{21},\texttt{ct(1)\#M},\vec{A}_{22}):- \\ \quad \vec{G}_{21}. \\ \texttt{S2}(\vec{A}_{23},\texttt{G(Y,Ys)\#M},\vec{A}_{24}):- \\ \quad \vec{G}_{22}, \\ \quad \texttt{S2}(\vec{A}_{25},\texttt{Ys\#M},\vec{A}_{26}), \\ \quad \vec{G}_{23}. \end{array}} \right\rangle, \right.$$

$$\left. \left\langle \texttt{S1\_S2\_t1}(\vec{A_1},\vec{A_3},\texttt{L\#\_},\vec{A_2},\vec{A_4}) \right\rangle, \left\langle \boxed{\begin{array}{l} \texttt{S1\_S2\_t1}(\vec{A}_{11},\vec{A}_{21},\texttt{ct(1)\#\_},\vec{A}_{12},\vec{A}_{22}):- \\ \quad \vec{G}_{11}, \vec{G}_{21}. \\ \texttt{S1\_S2\_t1}(\vec{A}_{13},\vec{A}_{23},\texttt{G(X,Xs)\#\_},\vec{A}_{14},\vec{A}_{24}):- \\ \quad \texttt{Y} \Leftarrow \texttt{X}, \\ \quad \texttt{Ys} \Leftarrow \texttt{Xs}, \\ \quad \vec{G}_{12}, \vec{G}_{22}, \\ \quad \texttt{S1\_S2\_t1}(\vec{A}_{15},\vec{A}_{25},\texttt{Xs\#\_},\vec{A}_{16},\vec{A}_{26}), \\ \quad \vec{G}_{13}, \vec{G}_{23}. \end{array}} \right\rangle \right\rangle$$

Predicate variable symbols S1 and S2 abstract the actual predicate names and provide the name of the new, more efficient, combined procedure. A suffix "t1" is attached to the name of the new predicate, indicating the name of the transformation used. The "$x \Leftarrow t$" construct denotes the actual unification of the variable x with term t: it is not a syntactic addition to the output schema; it stands, instead, as a *command* to unify x with t within the clause it appears. Such unification commands are necessary because there might be prescribed substitutions by the transformation (in our example above the data structure G(Y,Ys) of the second procedure is to be replaced by G(X,Xs)) and all the references to the old variables must be updated with a reference to the new variables (in our example, there might be references to Y and Ys in $\vec{G}_{22}$ and/or $\vec{G}_{23}$ and these references must be replaced by appropriate references to X and Xs). The output schema does not show the precise position of the focused argument (an underscore symbol has been used) since the actual procedure will be translated back into the conventional Prolog form without the explicit argument positions. The transformation above is successfully matched by the conjunction comprising the body of p/3 of our previous example, since the definitions of sum/2 and dcount/2 match the input schemata. The matching itself also assigns the appropriate values to the abstract constructs of the output schema, thus defining the new predicate sum_dcount_t1/3:

```
sum_dcount_t1(0,[],0).
sum_dcount_t1(C,[X|Xs],S):-
    sum_dcount_t1(CXs,Xs,SXs),
    S is X + SXs,
    C is 1 + CXs.

p(L,S,C):- sum_dcount_t1(C,L,S).
```

Here the list is now processed only once in p/3 while its elements are summed and counted at the same time.

4 An Opportunistic Approach for Program Analysis and Optimisation

We have identified two kinds of opportunities for program optimisation, one concerning individual procedures and how they can be improved in an isolated manner, and the other concerning groups of procedures and how their joint usage can be optimised. Both alternatives can be appropriately described using our enhanced schema-based transformations and pursued in an opportunistic approach, consisting of analysing a program Π searching for opportunities to employ these enhanced schema-based transformations. Our framework aims at an *extended program* Π' such that if $\Pi \vdash G$ then $\Pi' \vdash G$, where "$\vdash$" is the logical implication symbol. We can say that Π is subsumed by Π' in the sense that the answers to queries posed to the former are still obtainable in the latter; however, new procedures may be introduced in Π', and hence some queries can be posed to Π' (and their answers would be appropriately obtained) which do not apply to Π.

4.1 Analysing Isolated Procedures

In our schema-based approach, an isolated procedure $\mathcal{P} \subseteq \Pi$ is analysed for possible improvements by being checked against the input schema **S** of some transformation $\mathcal{T}$. Let $\mathcal{T} = \langle \langle \mathbf{G} \rangle, \langle \mathbf{S} \rangle, \langle \mathbf{H} \rangle, \langle \mathbf{T} \rangle \rangle$ be an enhanced schema-based transformation such that $\mathbf{S}\Theta = \mathcal{P}$ and $\mathbf{T}\Theta = \mathcal{P}'$, where $\mathcal{P}'$ is the recommended transformed version of $\mathcal{P}$. $\mathcal{T}$ is suggesting improvements to be made to those procedures $\mathcal{P}$ matching the input schema **S**, or, alternatively, as a suggestion for the replacement of those procedures $\mathcal{P}$ by the procedure $\mathcal{P}'$ obtained after applying the substitution Θ to the output schema **T**. However, in order to carry out this replacement and properly extend Π, an additional clause must be introduced making the connection between the old procedure $\mathcal{P}$ to be removed and the newly obtained procedure $\mathcal{P}'$ to be inserted. This additional clause guarantees that queries posed to the new program Π' concerning the removed procedure $\mathcal{P}$ will be appropriately translated into queries concerning $\mathcal{P}'$.

Let H be the head goal of the clauses comprising $\mathcal{P}$ with fresh, uninstantiated variables, and H' the head goal of those clauses comprising $\mathcal{P}'$ also with fresh, uninstantiated variables. The *conversion clause* $C_{[\mathcal{P},\mathcal{P}']}$ between $\mathcal{P}$ and $\mathcal{P}'$, of the form $H :- H'$, is such that $\mathbf{G}\Theta^* = H$ and $\mathbf{H}\Theta^* = H'$ for some extension Θ^* of substitution Θ. $G\Theta$ is a subgoal of the form $p(t_1,\ldots,t_n)$ and $H\Theta$ is of the form $q(t'_1,\ldots,t'_m)$: if H is of the form $p(x_1,\ldots,x_n)$ and H' of the form $q(x'_1,\ldots,x'_m)$, then the extended schema transformation Θ^* can be obtained as the result of the set operation $\Theta^* = \Theta \cup \{x_i/t_i\} \cup \{x'_j/t'_j\}$, for every i and j, $1 \leq i \leq n$, $1 \leq j \leq m$. The final transformed program Π' is the result of the operation $\Pi' = (\Pi - \mathcal{P}) \cup \mathcal{P}' \cup C_{[\mathcal{P},\mathcal{P}']}$. Conversion clauses can be seen as initialisation calls [Sterling & Shapiro, 94; O'Keefe, 90] in which values are initially assigned to argument positions of a predicate being invoked.

If there is a program Π consisting solely of procedure dcount/2 shown above, then transformation $\mathcal{T}_{32}$ shown in the appendix can successfully be used to obtain the following more efficient procedure dcount_t3/3

```
dcount_t3(0,0,[]).
dcount_t3(Ac,C,[X|Xs]):-
    NAc is 1 + Ac,
    dcount_t3(NAc,C,Xs).
```

and in order to appropriately alter Π, by removing the inefficient procedure dcount/2 and inserting the new, more efficient procedure dcount_t3/3, we would also have to incorporate the conversion clause

```
dcount(C,L):-
    dcount_t3(0,C,L).
```

converting those queries previously answered via dcount/2 to queries now answered via dcount_t3/3. The new program Π' would thus be the more efficient procedure dcount_t3/3 and the conversion clause above. This new program subsumes the original one: the answers to queries posed to the initial dcount/2 procedure will still get the same answers, and additional queries to dcount_t3/3 can now be posed.

4.2 Analysing Combinations of Procedures

As shown in our first example, consecutive subgoals within the body of a clause may also provide a prospective opportunity for improvement to the performance of a program. In this case, a given program Π has its conjunctions, *i.e.* sequences of more than one subgoal in the body of one of its clauses, analysed by checking them and their respective procedures against the schema patterns of transformations. Both calling patterns and procedures are used in this analysis.

The context for this analysis is a clause $C \in \Pi$ of form $H:-\vec{I}_1, G_1, \ldots, G_n, \vec{I}_2$ where $G_i, i \geq 1$ are non-recursive subgoals, G_i being a call to procedure $\mathcal{P}_i \subseteq \Pi$, and $\vec{I}_j, j = 1,2$ are (possibly empty) finite sequences of subgoals. If there is a schema-based transformation $\mathcal{T} = \langle\langle G_1,\ldots,G_n\rangle, \langle S_1,\ldots,S_n\rangle, \langle H_1,\ldots, H_m\rangle, \langle T_1,\ldots,T_m\rangle\rangle$ and a schema substitution Θ such that $G_i\Theta = G_i$ and $S_i\Theta = \mathcal{P}_i, 1 \geq i \geq n$, then a *transformed clause* C' is obtained, of the form $H:-\vec{I}_1, G'_1,\ldots,G'_m, \vec{I}_2$ where $H_k\Theta = G'_k, 1 \geq k \geq m$. The transformed clause incorporates the changes suggested by the transformation, invoking new procedures $\mathcal{P}'_k$, such that $T_k\Theta = \mathcal{P}'_k, 1 \geq k \geq m$. The new transformed program incorporating these suggestions can be obtained by replacing clause C by its transformed version C' and inserting the new procedures $\mathcal{P}'_k$. This can be described by the set operation $\Pi' = (\Pi - \{C\}) \cup \{C'\} \cup \mathcal{P}'_1 \cup \ldots \cup \mathcal{P}'_m$. The procedures $\mathcal{P}_i, 1 \geq i \geq n$, previously employed by C are not altered since they may be used by other procedures and also because we are aiming at an extension of a program, which means that everything provable in Π, including queries to $\mathcal{P}_i, 1 \geq i \geq n$, must also be provable in Π'.

4.3 Systematic Search for Opportunities

The specific manners of dealing with isolated procedures and conjunctions are put together in the same framework to carry out opportunistic transformations in programs. The following simple Prolog code describes the policy of our opportunistic approach:

```
transform(Π,Π^F):-
    transform_predicate(Π,Π'),
    transform(Π',Π^F).
transform(Π,Π^F):-
    transform_conjunction(Π,Π'),
    transform(Π',Π^F).
transform(Π,Π).
```

Initially, attempts are made at transforming isolated procedures: transform_predicate/2 transforms one isolated procedure, obtaining a new version which replaces the chosen procedure in the program Π, together with its conversion clause. The newly obtained program Π' is then recursively used in further transformations. The second clause, if successful, chooses and transforms via transform_conjunction/2 a conjunction in Π, inserting a new combined procedure and appropriately replacing the occurrences of the chosen conjunction. The new transformed program Π' is recursively used in other transformations. When there are no more predicates or conjunctions to be transformed, then we can say that the program Π has reached its optimal state with respect to the available repertoire of transformations and that no more improvements can be done – the third clause caters for this possibility.

The order of clauses in the Prolog code above is such that initially all isolated procedures will be tested for prospective transformations. When there are no more procedures that can be isolatedly transformed (transform_predicate/2 fails), then their combinations, stated in the conjunctions of the program, will be analysed for possible transformations using the method explained above. The resulting program, after a new combined procedure is obtained and the conjunctions are altered, is tested again for any isolated predicate transformations. This process goes on until no more program transformations can be applied.

The ordering of our analysis, considering first isolated procedures and then their combinations, is based on the sort of alterations recommended by each program transformation of our repertoire. Those changes in isolated procedures recommended by our transformations involve the reordering of subgoals and the insertion of extra arguments: features like the relative ordering of arguments and the patterns of recursive data structures are not altered and these play an important role during the combination of procedures. In some cases this ordering is immaterial since the same final program (possibly with different names of predicates and variables, but similar structure) can be reached in any event.

The termination of the process above is only possible if the transformed program eventually converges to a form in which no further transformations can be applied to it. This convergence depends on the nature of the syntactic alterations prescribed by the available transformations. Each schema-based transformation should be designed bearing in mind the iterative framework within which they will be employed. In our repertoire an isolated procedure is altered by changing the order or removing some of its subgoals, and care was taken to ensure that each of them or their interaction would not lead to loops; conjunctions are always replaced by other smaller conjunctions, guaranteeing an eventual convergence of the program to a form in which no other conjunction-altering transformations can be applied.

4.4 Choosing the Best Transformation: Heuristics

For a given predicate or conjunction there might be more than one applicable transformation at one time. In order to solve this problem, [Fuchs & Fromherz, 91] adopt the intervention of a human user who chooses one of the prospective transformations and has it applied to the program. Since our system is aimed at analysing full programs and these can be of any size, asking a human user for assistance may not be a practical possibility. Fuchs and Fromherz, however, suggest that some form of heuristic could be incorporated into each transformation and be used as a means to automatically select the best candidate from a set of prospective schema-based program transformations. We have pursued this suggestion and incorporated simple heuristics to our enhanced schema-based program transformations.

The enhanced schema language and the realistic context in which to use it are more important than the specific program transformations shown here: these should be seen as examples and are not meant to be authoritative nor exhaustive. Following this line, we find of more importance not the particular heuristics assigned to our transformations, but the rationale used to do so. In this subsection we describe the method we used to assign heuristics to our program transformations: the purpose of this method is to aid humans in preparing their own program transformations.

In our approach opportunities to apply program transformations are continuously sought after. At one moment a given program may have more than one transformation applicable to one of its procedures or conjunctions: these transformations can be sequentially applied if they preserve the overall structure of the program, maintaining argument positions and their relative ordering, number of clauses, and so on. We suggest that transformations be assessed for their potential sequential use, maximising the number of transformations applicable to a given initial program. Our underlying assumption is that the more transformations a program has applied to it, the more efficient it will become.

The heuristics should allow the application of the largest number of transformations, delaying the use of those transformations that would prevent others from being employed. This interference is due to the extent and kind of the syntactic alterations performed by these transformations causing substantial changes to a procedure and preventing it from matching the schemata of other transformations. Heuristics should then be assigned to program transformations based on their interchangeability: the less dramatically a transformation alters a program, the better its heuristic should be, since other subsequent transformations will not be prevented from being used. We suggest a set of guidelines to analyse the syntactic changes of program transformations and establish our heuristics:

- Isolated procedure transformations which alter only the internal parts of a procedure, by changing the order of its subgoals (*e.g.* transformation $\mathcal{T}_{01}$, in our appendix) or replacing subgoals (*e.g.* $\mathcal{T}_{21}$) should be the first transformations to be applied. Their syntactic changes are localised and do not impair any further transformations in the resulting procedure.

- Isolated procedure transformations that insert extra arguments but maintain their relative ordering, as in the original procedure, and neither insert new clauses in the procedure nor change the ordering of its clauses should come next. The calls to the changed procedure are accordingly adapted, with the original arguments in their relative ordering extended by the additional inserted parameters: given that in our transformations only the relative ordering is used as a constraint, these changes do not prevent any further transformations from being applied.

- The program transformations which insert new clauses, remove arguments or alter the relative argument ordering should be the last ones to be used since they may prevent further transformations from being employed.

An interesting alternative to these heuristics is to enable our system to pursue all possible orderings in the application of transformations and select the longest path among them. Another altogether different approach would be to devise an evaluation function assessing the transformations carried out by judging the gain in efficiency in the resulting program. Such a function would assign values to the resulting programs, allowing the comparison of alternative options.

4.5 Choosing the Best Conjunction

In addition to the problem of having more than one applicable transformation to a given conjunction at a time, we also have to establish a method to pick up the best conjunction of a clause at each time, aiming at maximising number of applicable transformations.

We have defined a method to search for prospective conjunctions within a program. Given a program Π consisting of clauses $C_1, \ldots, C_n$, our analysis of each clause follows a top-down policy, analysing each clause at a time, and exhaustively attempting to apply one of the transformations of the available repertoire. In order to apply a transformation, our method must select from clause C_i

a subsequence of non-recursive subgoals. There might be, however, more than one of such subsequences and we must provide means to choose one of them. Our proposed solution to this problem is to analyse *all* possible subsequences, choosing the best transformation for each of them (see Section 4.4), and then choose among the set of possible conjunctions and their respective best transformation that conjunction which has the best heuristic value associated with its transformations.

Given a clause $p(\ldots) :\text{-} q_1(\ldots), q_2(\ldots), q_3(\ldots), \ldots$ then each of its prospective subsequences of subgoals must be analysed. Subsequences of size one are dealt with during the analysis of isolated procedures, and hence we concentrate our discussion on longer subsequences. Furthermore, recursive subgoals should not be allowed in subsequences: our implemented scanning mechanism skips any existing recursive subgoals in the clause. The clause above, assuming that all its subgoals are non-recursive, has candidate subsequences $\langle q_1(\ldots), q_2(\ldots)\rangle, \langle q_1(\ldots), q_2(\ldots), q_3(\ldots)\rangle, \ldots, \langle q_2(\ldots), q_3(\ldots)\rangle, \langle q_2(\ldots), q_3(\ldots), q_4(\ldots)\rangle, \ldots$, and so on. Our transformations only address sequences of *contiguous* subgoals, hence we need not consider subsequences such as $\langle q_1(\ldots), q_3(\ldots)\rangle, \langle q_1(\ldots), q_3(\ldots), q_4(\ldots)\rangle, \ldots$, and so on. The number of subsequences of subgoals with more than one element of a clause with n non-recursive subgoals is a polynomial function on n.

Let $\{\vec{G}_1, \ldots, \vec{G}_n\}$ be the set of subsequences of contiguous subgoals of a clause $C \in \Pi$, such that $\vec{G}_i$ is of the form $\langle q_j(\ldots), q_{j+1}(\ldots), \ldots\rangle$. Each $\vec{G}_i$ has a number of applicable enhanced schema-based transformations drawn from the available repertoire. The heuristic method described in the previous section can be used to select the best choice amongst those applicable transformations of each $\vec{G}_i$, thus obtaining a set of (best) applicable transformations $\{\mathcal{T}_1, \ldots, \mathcal{T}_n\}$ for $C \in \Pi$. The subgoals considered by these transformations might overlap, and hence the transformations may be mutually exclusive. If they do not overlap, then they can be pursued at different stages or even in parallel. If they are overlapping then we must devise a way to choose the best candidate for application.

Our proposed way to choose one element from a set of applicable transformations of a clause is a natural consequence of the heuristic method applied at the level of individual conjunctions. Since we associate with transformation a heuristic value, we can thus use the heuristic values of the best transformations $\{\mathcal{T}_1, \ldots, \mathcal{T}_n\}$ of $C \in \Pi$ to choose the best conjunction *and* its best transformation. Given that all possible conjunctions are considered and, for each of them, the best applicable transformation is obtained (via the heuristic method of Section 4.4), we can guarantee that among these best alternative transformations the best choice is that with the best heuristic value.

5 Conclusions and Directions of Research

We have proposed an opportunistic approach for performing program analysis and optimisation. In this framework two kinds of opportunities for program optimisation are systematically searched for, one concerning individual procedures and how they can be improved in an isolated manner, and the other concerning groups of procedures and how their joint usage can be optimised. These opportunities have been represented by enhanced schema-based program transformations, depicting, in a generic way, inefficient programming constructs and how they should be altered in order to confer a better computational behaviour to the program.

Our opportunistic approach matches the constructs of a program against the repertoire of program transformations: these are appropriately applied, always yielding extensions of the initial program, as long as there are opportunities to do so. The repertoire of program transformations has a decisive effect on the termination of this process: their syntactic modifications should ensure that the resulting program does not trigger any subsequence of those transformations applied so far. This constraint is, of course, added to the essential restriction that program transformations should preserve the meaning (*i.e.* set of logical consequences) and the termination status of the original program.

Our work extends previous research [Fuchs & Fromherz, 91] on using program schemata to guide program transformation. In order to address a larger class of constructs we have proposed some enhancements to the schema language used. We have additionally investigated their suggestion to associate heuristics with each transformation and use it as a means to automatically select the best candidate from a set of prospective schema-based program transformations. Since our intention is to encourage programmers to devise their own schema-based transformations, we have suggested guidelines to help them establish their own heuristics. These guidelines aim at maximising the number of transformations applicable to a given initial program, and the underlying assumption is that the more transformations a program has applied to it, the more efficient it should become.

We have introduced some useful enhanced schema-based program transformations which, once applied to a program, guarantee an improvement in its performance. It must be pointed out that our repertoire is by no means complete or exhaustive and providing such complete set of transformations is not our intention. Our main contributions are a language with which one can define program transformations and a context in which this should be used: these should be seen as tools that experienced programmers can use to devise their own strategies for program transformation and to make them available to the users of their program transformation systems.

OpTiS (**Op**portunistic **T**ransformation **S**ystem), a prototypical implementation of our approach, has been developed using LPA MacProlog32, adapting large portions of the system by Fuchs and Fromherz. The available schema-based transformations are those shown in the appendix. All those transformations available in the system of Fuchs and Fromherz can be translated into our proposed extended language in a straightforward way, or they can be extended to cover a larger number of constructs, for instance, by generalising functors and constants, inserting schema variables, and so on. Our repertoire is limited to singly-recursive procedures with two clauses, but as mentioned before, other special-purpose or more sophisticated transformations can be added on to it.

Non-syntactic additional constraints are sometimes necessary to properly describe a schema. It is not possible with our enhanced schema language to specify that a certain variable should or should not be found in a vector of goals or in a vector of arguments. Another interesting example of additional non-syntactic constraint is to state that a given vector of goals or arguments should or should not be empty. We suggest that a simple set-theoretical language be employed to cope with these issues, the schemata language being further augmented to accommodate it. According to this suggestion, schemata would consist of a syntactic part followed by a sequence of additional constraints using this set-theoretical language. For instance, the following augmented schema could be represented:

$$
\begin{array}{l}
S(\vec{A_1}, [] \# N, \vec{A_2}) :- \\
\quad \vec{G_1} . \\
S(\vec{A_3}, [X|Xs] \# N, \vec{A_4}) :- \\
\quad \vec{G_2} , \\
\quad S(\vec{A_5}, Xs \# N, \vec{A_6}) \\
\quad \vec{G_3} .
\end{array}
$$

$$\vec{G_2} \neq \emptyset \wedge \ ! \notin \vec{G_2} \wedge \vec{A_4} = \emptyset$$

The syntactic description of the procedure in the schema language remains unaltered, as shown in the upper rectangle, but it is complemented by a list of non-syntactic constraints, which in the example above consists of further specifying $\vec{G_2}$ as being a non-empty vector such that a cut ! subgoal is not found in it and that the vector of arguments $\vec{A_4}$ is empty.

A useful alternative framework for program development would combine programming techniques and program transformations. The use of programming techniques may provide us with programs whose individual procedures are optimally efficient but whose overall behaviour (*i.e.* inter-procedural relationships) can be improved. Subsequent program transformations could provide us with the desired overall efficiency. For instance, procedures sum/2 and dcount/2 of our first example could have been prepared by means of ready-made programming techniques, but their combined use in p/3 would still be an inefficient programming construct easily detectable by our program transformation system.

Acknowledgements: The first author would like to acknowledge the support from the Student Travel Fund (Department of Artificial Intelligence, University of Edinburgh) which partially sponsored his attendance to LoPSTr'95.

References

[Bowles *et al*, 94] A. Bowles, D. Robertson, W. Vasconcelos, M. Vargas-Vera, D. Bental. Applying Prolog Programming Techniques. *International Journal of Human-Computer Studies*, 41(3):329–350, September 1994.

[Flener, 95] P. Flener. *Logic Program Schemata: Synthesis and Analysis*. Technical Report BU-CEIS-9502, Bilkent University, Ankara, Turkey, 1995.

[Flener & Deville, 95] P. Flener, Y. Deville. Logic Program Transformation through Generalization Schemata. Extended abstract accepted for LoPSTr'95 (Utrecht, the Netherlands, 20-22 September, 1995)

[Fuchs & Fromherz, 91] N. E. Fuchs and M. P. J. Fromherz. Schema-Based Transformations of Logic Programs. In: *Proceedings of the Workshop in Logic Program Synthesis and Transformation (LoPSTr'91)*, Springer-Verlag, 1992.

[Gegg-Harrison, 91] T. S. Gegg-Harrison. Learning Prolog in a Schema-Based Environment. *Instructional Science*, 20:173–192, 1991.

[Kirschenbaum et al, 94] M. Kirschenbaum, S. Michaylov, and L. Sterling. *Skeletons and Techniques as a Normative Approach to Program Development in Logic-Based Languages*. OSU-CISRC-5/94-TR25, Dept. of Computer and Information Science, Ohio State University, Ohio, U.S.A., 1994.

[Lakhotia & Sterling, 90] A. Lakhotia and L. Sterling. How to Control Unfolding when Specialising Interpreters. In *The Practice of Prolog*, L. Sterling (Ed.), MIT Press, 1990.

[Nielson & Nielson, 90] H. R. Nielson and F. Nielson. Eureka Definitions for Free – Disagreement Points for Fold/Unfold Transformations. In *Proceedings of ESOP'90*, Lecture Notes in Computer Science 432, pp. 291–305, Springer-Verlag, 1990.

[O'Keefe, 90] R. A. O'Keefe. *The Craft of Prolog*. MIT Press, 1990.

[Proietti & Pettorossi, 90] M. Proietti and A. Pettorossi. Synthesis of Eureka Predicates for Developing Logic Programs. In *Proceedings of ESOP'90*, Lecture Notes in Computer Science 432, pp. 306–325, Springer-Verlag, 1990.

[Robertson, 91] D. Robertson. A Simple Prolog Techniques Editor for Novice Users. In *Proceedings of 3rd Annual Conference on Logic Programming*, Edinburgh, Scotland, April 1991. Springer-Verlag.

[Sterling & Shapiro, 94] L. Sterling and E. Y. Shapiro. *The Art of Prolog: Advanced Programming Techniques*. Second Edition. MIT Press, 1994.

[Vargas-Vera, 95] M. Vargas-Vera. *Using Prolog Techniques to Guide Program Composition*. PhD Thesis. University of Edinburgh. Edinburgh, Scotland, 1995.

[Vargas-Vera et al, 93] M. Vargas-Vera, D. Robertson, W. W. Vasconcelos. *Building Large-Scale Prolog Programs using a Techniques Editing System*. Technical Report 635. Department of Artificial Intelligence, University of Edinburgh. Edinburgh, Scotland, 1993.

[Vasconcelos & Fuchs, 95] W. W. Vasconcelos and N. E. Fuchs. Opportunistic Logic Program Analysis and Optimisation: Enhanced Schema-Based Transformations for Logic Programs and their Usage in an Opportunistic Framework for Program Analysis and Optimisation. Technical Report 95-24. Institut für Informatik, Universität Zürich, August 1995.

Appendix: Selected Schema-Based Program Transformations

In this section we list some selected schema-based program transformations offered by our system. We have only addressed procedures with two clauses, for the sake of simplicity. The additional number as the first component is the heuristic value assigned to the transformation. The empty set as a conjunction informs our system that the alterations prescribed by that transformation are confined to the procedure and no external adaptations (*e.g.* changing the order of parameters, inserting new arguments, and so on) have to be performed.

The first two transformations $\mathcal{T}_{01}$ and $\mathcal{T}_{02}$ change the order of a test predicate. Since our schema language does not support the representation of permutations, a transformation is devised for each focused clause. $\mathcal{T}_{01}$ focuses on the first clause:

$$
\langle\ 100, \emptyset, \langle\ \boxed{\begin{array}{l} \mathtt{S(\vec{A}_1):-} \\ \quad \vec{G}_1^*, \mathtt{P(\vec{A}_2, X\#_-, \vec{A}_3)}, \vec{G}_2^*, \\ \quad \mathtt{Q(\vec{A}_4)}, \vec{G}_3^*, \mathtt{T(\vec{A}_5, X\#_-, \vec{A}_6)}, \vec{G}_4^*. \\ \mathtt{S(\vec{A}_7):-}\ \vec{G}_5^*. \end{array}}\ \rangle, \emptyset, \langle\ \boxed{\begin{array}{l} \mathtt{S(\vec{A}_1):-} \\ \quad \vec{G}_1^*, \mathtt{P(\vec{A}_2, X\#_-, \vec{A}_3)}, \vec{G}_2^*, \\ \quad \mathtt{T(\vec{A}_5, X\#_-, \vec{A}_6)}, \mathtt{Q(\vec{A}_4)}, \vec{G}_3^*, \vec{G}_4^*. \\ \mathtt{S(\vec{A}_7):-}\ \vec{G}_5^*. \end{array}}\ \rangle\ \rangle
$$

$\mathcal{T}_{02}$, not shown here, focuses on the second clause, performing similar changes. Transformations $\mathcal{T}_{11}$ and $\mathcal{T}_{12}$ below change the ordering of an explicit instantiation, transferring it to a point before a subgoal. This simple alteration may save much computing time by constraining the execution of procedure P. Transformation $\mathcal{T}_{11}$ focuses on the first clause:

$$\left\langle\ 100,\emptyset,\left\langle\ \boxed{\begin{array}{l} S(\vec{A_1}):- \\ \quad \vec{G_1^*},P(\vec{A_2},X\#\_,\vec{A_3}),\vec{G_2^*}, \\ \quad X\#1\ =\ Y\#2,\vec{G_3^*}. \\ S(\vec{A_4}):-\ \vec{G_4^*}. \end{array}}\ \right\rangle,\emptyset,\left\langle\ \boxed{\begin{array}{l} S(\vec{A_1}):- \\ \quad \vec{G_1^*},X\#1\ =\ Y\#2, \\ \quad P(\vec{A_2},X\#\_,\vec{A_3}),\vec{G_2^*},\vec{G_3^*}. \\ S(\vec{A_4}):-\ \vec{G_4^*}. \end{array}}\ \right\rangle\ \right\rangle$$

Transformation $\mathcal{T}_{12}$, not shown here, focuses on the second clause. Transformations $\mathcal{T}_{21}$ and $\mathcal{T}_{22}$, not shown, remove spurious calls to the append/3 predicate, if the first argument is a singleton list [X]. Transformations $\mathcal{T}_{31}$ and $\mathcal{T}_{32}$ insert an accumulator pair in a procedure performing a non-tail-recursive arithmetic computation, thus making the procedure iterative. A generic description of a singly-recursive data-structure has been employed, thus imparting more expressiveness to the transformation. Different transformations have had to be provided, though, to address alternative relative orderings of argument positions. Transformation $\mathcal{T}_{31}$ describes procedures in which the data structure is an argument position situated to the left of the argument to which the arithmetic computation is assigned:

$$\left\langle\ 20,\langle S(\vec{A_1},L\#N,\vec{A_2},R\#M,\vec{A_3})\rangle,\left\langle \boxed{\begin{array}{l} S(\vec{A_4},ct(1)\#N,\vec{A_5},ct(2)\#M,\vec{A_6}):-\ \vec{G_1}. \\ S(\vec{A_7},G(X,Xs)\#N,\vec{A_8},Res\#M,\vec{A_9}):- \\ \quad \vec{G_2},S(\vec{A_{10}},Xs\#N,\vec{A_{11}},XsRes\#M,\vec{A_{12}}),\vec{G_3}, \\ \quad Res\#1\ is\ F(\vec{G_{13}},XsRes,\vec{G_{14}})\#2,\vec{G_4}. \end{array}}\right\rangle,\right.$$

$$\langle S\_t3(\vec{A_1},L\#N,\vec{A_2},ct(2)\#\_,R\#\_,\vec{A_3})\rangle,$$

$$\left.\left\langle \boxed{\begin{array}{l} S\_t3(\vec{A_4},ct(1)\#N,\vec{A_5},FAc\#\_,FAc\#\_,\vec{A_6}):-\ \vec{G_1}. \\ S\_t3(\vec{A_7},G(X,Xs)\#N,\vec{A_8},TAc\#\_,FAc\#\_,\vec{A_9}):- \\ \quad \vec{G_2},NAc\#1\ is\ F(\vec{G_{13}},TAc,\vec{G_{14}})\#2, \\ \quad S\_t3(\vec{A_{10}},Xs\#N,\vec{A_{11}},NAc\#\_,FAc\#\_,\vec{A_{12}}),\vec{G_3},\vec{G_4}. \end{array}}\right\rangle\ \right\rangle$$

Transformation $\mathcal{T}_{32}$, not shown, describes procedures in which the data structure is an argument position situated to the right of the argument to which the arithmetic computation is assigned.

Transformation $\mathcal{T}_4$ below is aimed at conjunctions: it joins two procedures manipulating the same singly-recursive data structure. The generic representation for the data structure ensures that $\mathcal{T}_4$ will be applied to any singly-recursive data structure with two clauses:

$$\left\langle\ 20,\left\langle\boxed{\begin{array}{l} S1(\vec{A_1},L\#N,\vec{A_2}), \\ S2(\vec{A_3},L\#M,\vec{A_4}) \end{array}}\right\rangle,\left\langle \boxed{\begin{array}{l} S1(\vec{A_{11}},ct(1)\#N,\vec{A_{12}}):- \\ \quad \vec{G_{11}}. \\ S1(\vec{A_{13}},G(X,Xs)\#N,\vec{A_{14}}):- \\ \quad \vec{G_{12}}, \\ \quad S1(\vec{A_{15}},Xs\#N,\vec{A_{16}}), \\ \quad \vec{G_{13}}. \end{array}},\ \boxed{\begin{array}{l} S2(\vec{A_{21}},ct(1)\#M,\vec{A_{22}}):- \\ \quad \vec{G_{21}}. \\ S2(\vec{A_{23}},G(Y,Ys)\#M,\vec{A_{24}}):- \\ \quad \vec{G_{22}}, \\ \quad S2(\vec{A_{25}},Ys\#M,\vec{A_{26}}), \\ \quad \vec{G_{23}}. \end{array}}\right\rangle,\right.$$

$$\left.\langle S1\_S2\_t4(\vec{A_1},\vec{A_3},L\#\_,\vec{A_2},\vec{A_4})\rangle,\left\langle \boxed{\begin{array}{l} S1\_S2\_t4(\vec{A_{11}},\vec{A_{21}},ct(1)\#\_,\vec{A_{12}},\vec{A_{22}}):- \\ \quad \vec{G_{11}},\ \vec{G_{21}}. \\ S1\_S2\_t4(\vec{A_{13}},\vec{A_{23}},G(X,Xs)\#\_,\vec{A_{14}},\vec{A_{24}}):- \\ \quad Y\ \Leftarrow\ X,\ Ys\ \Leftarrow\ Xs, \\ \quad \vec{G_{12}},\ \vec{G_{22}}, \\ \quad S1\_S2\_t4(\vec{A_{15}},\vec{A_{25}},Xs\#\_,\vec{A_{16}},\vec{A_{26}}), \\ \quad \vec{G_{13}},\ \vec{G_{23}}. \end{array}}\right\rangle\ \right\rangle$$

Solving Deductive Planning Problems Using Program Analysis and Transformation

D.A. de Waal* and M. Thielscher

FG Intellektik, FB Informatik, Technische Hochschule Darmstadt, Germany
{andre,mit}@intellektik.informatik.th-darmstadt.de

Abstract. Two general, problematic aspects of deductive planning, namely, detecting unsolvable planning problems and solving a certain kind of postdiction problem, are investigated. The work is based on a resource oriented approach to reasoning about actions and change using a logic programming paradigm. We show that ordinary resolution methods are insufficient for solving these problems and propose program analysis and transformation as a more promising and successful way to solve them.

1 Introduction

Understanding and modeling the ability of humans to reason about actions, change, and causality is one of the key issues in Artificial Intelligence and Cognitive Science. Since logic appears to play a fundamental role for intelligent behavior, many deductive methods for reasoning about change were developed and thoroughly investigated. It became apparent that a straightforward use of classical logic lacks the essential property that facts describing a world state may change in the course of time. To overcome this problem, the truth value of a particular fact (called *fluent* due to its dynamic nature) has to be associated with a particular state. This solution brings along the famous technical frame problem which captures the difficulty of expressing that the truth values of facts not affected by some action are not changed by the execution of this action.

Many deductive methods for reasoning about change are based on the ideas underlying the situation calculus [20,21]. Yet in recent years new deductive approaches have been developed which enable us to model situations, actions, and causality without the need to employ extra axioms due to the frame problem [1,19,14]. Instead of representing the atomic facts used to describe situations as fluents, these approaches take the facts as *resources*. Resources do not hold forever—they are consumed and produced by actions. Consequently, resources which are not affected by an action remain as they are and need not be updated.

In particular, the approach developed in [14] is based on logic programming with an associated equational theory. Although previous results illustrate the expressiveness of the equational logic programming approach (ELP, for short) in principle, the applicability of concrete proof strategies such as PROLOG has

---

* This author was supported by HCM Project: Compulog Group—Cooperation Group in Computational Logic under contract no. ERBCHBGCT930365.

not yet been assessed. A major difficulty is caused by the use of an underlying equational theory, which requires a non-standard unification procedure in conjunction with an extended resolution principle called *SLDE-resolution* [8,13]. In this paper, we follow an alternative direction and investigate a particular program where a unification algorithm for our special equational theory is integrated by means of additional program clauses while otherwise standard unification is used.

On the basis of this logic program, we illustrate two general classes of problems which deserve a successful treatment yet turn out to be unsolvable using ordinary resolution methods. First, non-terminating sequences of actions usually prevent us from deciding unsolvable planning problems. More precisely, a planning problem consists of an underlying set of action descriptions, a collection of initially available resources, and a goal specification (consisting of the resources we strive for). If no action sequence can be found that transforms the initial situation into a situation containing the goal, such a planning problem is called unsolvable; detecting this, however, is problematic as soon as infinite sequences of actions have to be considered. Second, we investigate a particular kind of so-called *postdiction* problem where we try to determine which resources can possibly be used to obtain a certain goal situation. Although our deductive planning approach can successfully model this problem in principle, it is not practical in any real implementation as there are possibly an infinite number of combinations of resources that may lead to one specific resource being produced. Moreover, since our logic program, and especially the encoding of the special unification algorithm, was not designed to reason backwards, it loops even in case of finite action sequences.

In this paper we propose elegant solutions to these two problems, detecting unsolvable planning problems and postdiction, based on logic program analysis and transformation. The solutions are based on the approach by de Waal and Gallagher [3,2]. In their approach a proof procedure for some logic is specialized with respect to a specific theorem proving problem. The result of the specialization process is an optimized proof procedure that can only prove formulas in the given theorem proving problem. One of the effects of the specialization may be that one or more infinitely failed deductions may be detected and are then deleted. It is this property that makes the developed specialization process so attractive for optimizing difficult planning problems.

In the context of this paper, the particular proof procedure and theorem proving problem is the logic program to model actions and change along with a set of action descriptions defining the various feasible actions, their conditions and their effects. The aim is to detect unsolvable planning problems and derive finite descriptions of a possible infinite number of resources. However, we have found that the procedure suggested in [2] is not precise enough for the optimization of this logic program and needs improvement. The first problem sketched above may be solved by refining the specialization procedures developed in [3,2]. Nonetheless it is not feasible to give an exact solution to the second problem as we pointed out earlier. An approximation of the resources needed is therefore computed.

The layout of the rest of the paper is as follows. In the next section we introduce deductive planning problems. Furthermore, we introduce two exemplary classes of problems we aim to solve with our improved analysis and transformation techniques. In Section 3 we give an improved specialization procedure that better exploits the approximation results than was proposed in [2]. In Section 4, this refined technique is applied to the exemplary problems discussed in Section 2. This paper concludes with a comparison with related work and a short discussion of how to further improve the proposed specialization method.

2 Deductive Planning Problems

2.1 The Equational Logic Programming Approach

The completely reified representation of situations is the distinguishing feature of the ELP-based approach [14]. To this end, the *resources* being available in a situation are treated as terms and are connected using a special binary function symbol, denoted by $\circ$ and written in infix notation. As an example, consider the term[2]

$$d \circ q \circ f \circ f \circ dm \tag{1}$$

which shall represent a situation where we possess a dollar (d), a quarter (q), two fünfziger $(f$—fifty pfennige), and one deutschmark (dm). Intuitively, the order of the various resources occurring in a situation should be irrelevant, which is why we employ a particular equational theory, viz

$$(X \circ Y) \circ Z =_{AC1} X \circ (Y \circ Z) \tag{2}$$

$$X \circ Y =_{AC1} Y \circ X \tag{3}$$

$$X \circ \emptyset =_{AC1} X \tag{4}$$

where $\emptyset$ is a special constant denoting a unit element for $\circ$. This equational theory, written AC1, will be used as the underlying theory of our equational logic program modeling actions and change.

Based on this representation, actions are defined in a STRIPS-like fashion [4, 16] by stating a collection of resources to be removed from along with a collection of resources to be added to the situation at hand. Such an action is applicable if all resources to be removed are contained in the current situation. For instance, a machine that changes two fünfziger into a deutschmark can be specified by an action with condition $f \circ f$ and effect dm. This action is applicable in (1) since two resources of type f are included; the result of applying this action is

---

[2] Throughout this paper, we use a PROLOG-like syntax, i.e., constants and predicates are in lower cases whereas variables are denoted by upper case letters. Moreover, free variables are implicitly assumed to be universally quantified and, as usual, the term $[h \mid t]$ denotes a list with head h and tail t.

computed by removing two fünfziger from and adding a deutschmark to (1), i.e., $dm \circ d \circ q \circ dm$ which is exactly the expected outcome.

In what follows, we describe an equational logic program that formalizes the above concepts. First of all, actions are described by means of unit clauses using the ternary predicate $action(c, a, e)$ where c and e are the condition and effect, respectively, and a is a symbol denoting the name of the action. E.g., our exemplary change action is encoded as

$$action(f \circ f, gdm, dm) \leftarrow \tag{5}$$

where gdm is meant as an abbreviation of $get\text{-}deutschmark$.

Next, we have to find a formalization of testing whether the resources contained in a term c, denoting the condition of some action, are each contained in a term s, denoting the situation at hand. This can be achieved by stating an AC1-unification problem of the form $c \circ Z =_{AC1} s$, where Z is a new variable. It is easy to see that if this problem is solvable, i.e., if a substitution θ can be found such that $(c \circ Z)\theta =_{AC1} s\theta$, then all subterms occurring in c are also contained in s. For instance, the unification problem $f \circ f \circ Z =_{AC1} d \circ q \circ f \circ f \circ dm$ is solvable by taking $\theta = \{Z \mapsto d \circ q \circ dm\}$. Moreover, a side effect of solving such a unification problem is that the variable Z becomes bound to exactly those resources which are obtained by removing the elements in c from s. Hence, to obtain the resulting situation, we finally have to add the effect e of the action under consideration to $Z\theta$, i.e., the term $e \circ Z\theta$ represents the intended outcome. The reader should note that no additional axioms are needed here for solving the technical frame problem since all resources which are not affected by performing an action are automatically available in the resulting situation (e.g., the resources $d \circ q \circ dm$ in our example above). By means of logic program clauses, the application of actions is encoded using the ternary predicate $causes(i, p, g)$ where i and g are situation terms (called *initial* and *goal* situation, respectively) and p (called *plan*) is a sequence of action names:

$$
\begin{aligned}
causes(I, [\,], I) &\leftarrow \\
causes(I, [A|P], G) &\leftarrow action(C, A, E), \\
& \quad C \circ Z =_{AC1} I, \\
& \quad causes(E \circ Z, P, G)
\end{aligned}
\tag{6}
$$

In words, the empty sequence of actions, $[\,]$, changes nothing while an action a followed by a sequence of actions p applied to i yields g if a is applied as described above and, afterwards, applying p to the resulting situation, $(E \circ Z)\theta$, yields g[3].

A major difficulty as regards practical implementations of this approach is caused by the underlying equational theory, which is assumed to be built into the unification procedure. In [10] we argued that the AC1-unification problems that

---

[3] For the sake of an appropriate treatment of equality subgoals, we implicitly add the clause $X =_{AC1} X$ encoding *reflexivity*. Note that each SLDE-step is intended to be performed with respect to our equational theory, AC1.

occur when computing with our program are of a special kind, and we proposed a unification algorithm designed for these particular cases. In the rest of this paper, we investigate a standard logic program where this algorithm is modeled by means of additional program clauses rather than by means of an extended unification procedure. To this end, terms using our special connection function, ∘, are represented as lists containing the available resources. For instance, (1) is encoded as $[d, q, f, f, dm]$. Furthermore, we introduce a new predicate acl_match to model AC1-matching problems of the form $s \circ V =_{AC1} t$ where t is variable-free while s might contain variables but not on the level of the binary function ∘:

$$
\begin{aligned}
&causes(I, [\,], I) \leftarrow \\
&causes(I, [A|P], G) \leftarrow action(C, A, E), acl\_match(C, I, Z), \\
&\qquad\qquad\qquad\qquad append(E, Z, S), causes(S, P, G) \\[6pt]
&acl\_match(S, T, Z) \leftarrow mult\_subset(S, T, Z) \\[6pt]
&mult\_subset([\,], T, T) \leftarrow \\
&mult\_subset([E|S], T, R) \leftarrow mult\_minus(T, E, T2), \\
&\qquad\qquad\qquad\qquad\qquad mult\_subset(S, T2, R) \\[6pt]
&mult\_minus([E|R], E, R) \leftarrow \\
&mult\_minus([E1|R1], E, [E1|R2]) \leftarrow mult\_minus(R1, E, R2)
\end{aligned}
$$

(7)

In words, $acl\_match(s, t, z)$ shall be true iff s represents a multiset[4] of resources that are all contained in t; furthermore, z contains all resources occurring in t but not in s. The definition of the corresponding predicate $mult\_subset$ is based on a predicate named $mult\_minus(s, e, t)$ with the intended meaning that removing an element e of the multiset corresponding to s yields a multiset corresponding to t. Finally, we need the standard $append$ predicate to model adding the effect of an action to the remaining resources after having removed the condition.

2.2 Unsolvable Planning Problems

In this and the following subsection, we use a combined change/vending machine as the exemplary action scenario. We have already considered the action of changing two fünfziger into a deutschmark; furthermore, the machine shall change a deutschmark into two fünfziger (action gf) and also a dollar into four quarters (action gq) and vice versa (action gd); finally, two fünfziger are the price for a can of lemonade (l; action gl). To summarize, the following clauses specify

---

[4] The reader should observe that the axioms (2),(3) and (4) essentially model the datastructure multiset.

our exemplary domain:

$$\begin{aligned}
action([dm], gf, [f, f]) &\leftarrow \\
action([f, f], gdm, [dm]) &\leftarrow \\
action([d], gq, [q, q, q, q]) &\leftarrow \\
action([q, q, q, q], gd, [d]) &\leftarrow \\
action([f, f], gl, [l]) &\leftarrow
\end{aligned}$$
(8)

Now, consider the following query, which is used to ask for a plan whose execution yields a can of lemonade given a dollar plus a quarter:

$$\leftarrow causes([q, d], P, G), acl\_match([l], G, Z). \tag{9}$$

If this query succeeds then the answer substitution for P is a sequence of actions transforming the initially available collection of resources, $[q, d]$, into a situation G which includes a can of lemonade (and possibly other resources, bound to Z). Note that this way of formalizing a planning problem enables us to specify goal situations only partially.

It seems obvious that (9) cannot succeed with respect to the program depicted in (7) given the action descriptions (8) since we need some unaccessible German money to buy lemonade. Hence, our exemplary planning problem is unsolvable. Our logic program, however, loops when faced with this query since it computes alternate changes of a dollar into four quarters and back into a dollar forever. Thus, simply using SLD-resolution does not suffice to detect this kind of insolubility. Correspondingly, there is no finite failure SLDE-tree for the query

$$\leftarrow causes(q \circ d, P, l \circ Z) \tag{10}$$

with respect to the equational logic program depicted in (6) given a collection of action descriptions corresponding to (8)[5].

One might argue that a loop checking mechanism, detecting identical or subsumed goals in the same branch of the search tree, solves this problem. This is not true as we now illustrate. Consider the changing machine being partly out of order in so far as it changes a dollar into four quarters as before, but now just three quarters into a dollar. Again, it is impossible to find a refutation for our query (9). Yet we can use the machine to produce more and more resources by alternately changing the dollar into four quarters and using three quarters to reproduce the dollar. No ordinary loop checking is applicable here because no two subgoals match during the infinite derivation.

In Section 4, we show how our program analysis and transformation techniques provide a more general way of tackling the insolubility problem in planning.

---

[5] The third argument in (10), $l \circ Z$, encodes what is expressed by the second literal in (9), namely the fact that the goal situation might contain other resources aside from the required lemonade.

2.3 The Postcondition Problem in Deductive Planning

Apart from solving temporal projection (prediction) and planning problems, the ELP based approach is also suitable for a certain kind of postdiction problems, as has been argued in [15]. Postdiction means given a goal situation, what can be deduced about the initial situation, i.e., which resources are needed to obtain a specific goal. For example, suppose we want to buy a can of lemonade, what do we need to achieve this goal? To answer this question, the query $\leftarrow causes(I, P, l)$ can be executed with respect to the equational logic program depicted in (6) and a set of action descriptions corresponding to (8). The simplest answer to our question is that already possessing the lemonade clearly is sufficient to obtain it; but two fünfziger as well as a deutschmark too can be used to achieve the goal.

Although the set of initial situations is limited, there is an infinite number of ways generating the resulting situation, l. Due to the infiniteness of the corresponding SLDE-tree, it seems difficult to infer that the resources needed to obtain a can of lemonade are a can of lemonade itself, fünfziger, or deutschmarks, whereas dollars and quarters are needless. Even worse, if we run our logic program (7) given the following query $\leftarrow causes(I, P, [l])$ then we first obtain the answer $I = [l], P = []$ as intended but then the program loops without providing us with additional solutions.

3 Specialization

Logic program transformation and analysis provide a wide variety of techniques that can be used for program specialization. These techniques include for instance: partial evaluation, type checking, mode analysis and termination analysis. However, it was realized in [3] that a combination of analysis and transformation techniques provides the best specialization potential. Such a combination based on partial evaluation and regular approximation was then further developed in [3,2]. They developed a problem specific optimization technique: a proof procedure for some logic is specialized with respect to a specific theorem proving problem. The theorem proving problem is normally a set of axioms and hypotheses of some theory and includes a specific formula that may or may not be a theorem of the given theory.

The partial evaluation step creates, amongst other specializations, renamed versions of definitions according to some criteria (e.g. a specialized version of each inference rule in the proof procedure is created with respect to each predicate symbol appearing in the axioms and hypotheses). The approximation step then computes a safe approximation of the partially evaluated program. As a last step, a simple decision procedure is used to delete clauses in the partially evaluated program based of information contained in the regular approximation. The result of the specialization process is an optimized proof procedure that only proves theorems (or disproves non-theorems) in the given theory. Alternatively, the result may be a table of analysis information about the behavior of the proof procedure on this theorem proving problem.

Two criticisms against these techniques are: they are too problem specific and they do not use all the derived analysis information effectively. The first point criticizes the use of a specific formula (theorem or non-theorem) as a goal in the analysis. The method in [2] computes a new approximation for each query we are interested in. If the analysis could be done generally just with respect to a set of axioms and hypotheses, the analysis information will hold for any theorem or non-theorem we wish to analyze with respect to. The second point criticizes the use of the decision procedure used in [2]:

"Does a definition for some predicate $p(\ldots)$ exist in P (the source program), but not in A (the approximation of P)? If the answer is yes, all clauses containing positive occurrences of $p(\ldots)$ in the body of a clause in P are useless and can be deleted."

This procedure ignores all of the information contained within the approximation definitions (it just tests for the existence of an approximation).

Our aim is to extend the developed techniques taking the above criticisms into account. We will therefore try to keep the goal or query as general as possible so that the analysis does not need to be redone for every query we wish to investigate. Furthermore, in addition to using the above decision procedure, we will make use of information in the approximation for predicates that do not get deleted using the above criterion. In the next section we develop such a procedure.

We assume the reader is familiar with the basic concepts used in logic programming [17]. A logic meta-programming paradigm as defined by Lloyd [12] is used to state our proof procedure and theorem proving problem in. However, type definitions are not given as our specialization method does not depend on them. A partial evaluator and a regular approximation procedure capable of specializing and approximating pure logic programs are also assumed. Complete descriptions of one such partial evaluator and regular approximation procedure can be found in [5,7].

3.1 An Improved Decision Procedure

In this section we show how approximate information derived through a regular approximation may be used to achieve useful specializations. The class of Regular Unary Logic Programs was defined by Yardeni and Shapiro [24]. It is attractive to represent approximations of programs as Regular Unary Logic (RUL) Programs, as regular languages have a number of decidable properties and can conveniently be analyzed and manipulated for the use in program specialization. Due to lack of space we refer the interested reader to [7] for definitions of canonical regular unary clause, canonical regular unary logic program and regular definition of predicates.

A RUL program can now be obtained from a regular definition of predicates by replacing each clause $p_i(x_{1i}, \ldots, x_{ni}) \leftarrow B$ by a clause

$$approx(p_i(x_{1i}, \ldots, x_{ni})) \leftarrow B$$

where *approx* is a unique predicate symbol not used elsewhere in the RUL program. In this case the functor p_i denotes the predicate p_i. The predicate $any(X)$ denotes any term in the Herbrand Universe of the program. A regular safe approximation can now be defined in terms of a regular definition of predicates.

Definition 1. regular safe approximation

Let P be a definite program and A a regular definition of predicates in P. Then A is a **regular safe approximation** of P if the least Herbrand model of P is contained in the least Herbrand model of A.

This definition states that all logical consequences of P are contained in A. We now define a useless clause, that is a clause that never contributes to any solution.

Definition 2. useless clause with respect to a computation

Let P be a definite program, G a definite goal, R a safe computation rule and $C \in P$ be a clause. Let T be an SLD-tree of $P \cup \{G\}$ via R. Then C is useless with respect to T if C is not used in any refutations in T.

The above definition is restricted to definite programs as this simplifies the presentation (see [2] for a definition regarding normal programs) and as definite logic programs are sufficient for representing our equational logic programs.

Given a RUL program A that is a regular safe approximation (called a safe approximation from now on) of a program P, we want to use the information present in A to further optimize program P, that is to detect and delete more useless clauses.

The regular approximation system described in [7] contains a decision procedure for regular languages that can be used to detect useless clauses. However, if this system is not used to compute the approximation, the user has to implement such a procedure. The following condition from [2,3] is adequate for detecting useless clauses.

If $A \cup \{G\}$ has a finitely failed SLD-tree then $P \cup \{G\}$ has no SLD-refutation.

A procedure implementing this condition is given in Figure 1. Note that only a subset of possibly failed SLD-trees are detected. The result of the given transformation is a specialized version of P with zero or more clauses deleted. Although the procedure as stated may be inefficient, it can be efficiently implemented as we can have the approximation output its result in the format required by *Step 4*. The original decision procedure will then still be valid and we only need to check *Step 4* which can be done efficiently using any of the currently available logic programming language implementations.

The following theorem states the result of the above specialization precisely.

Theorem 3. preservation of all finite computations

Let P be a definite logic program, $\leftarrow G$ a definite goal and A a regular approximation of P with respect to $\leftarrow G$. Let P' be the result of applying the transformation given in Figure 1 to P.

Given a definite logic program P, a definite goal $\leftarrow G$ and a regular approximation A of P with respect to the goal $\leftarrow G$, a procedure for deciding if a clause $p \in P$ is useless with respect to the goal $\leftarrow G$ is:

1. Identify the arguments x_i, $(1 \leq i \leq n)$ in every approximation definition $approx(p_j(x_1, \ldots, x_n))$ that is approximated by only a finite number of facts.
2. Delete the approximation definitions for all other arguments that were not identified in *Step 1* (only a unique variable in each such argument position will remain).
3. Unfold with respect to the definitions of arguments identified in *Step 1* (this gives us a finite number of facts $approx(p_j(\ldots, x_i, \ldots))$, with zero or more arguments x_i instantiated to a ground term).
4. Delete all clauses in P that have a literal that can not possibly unify with at least one literal $p_j(x_1, \ldots, x_n)$ contained in an approximation definition $approx(p_j(\ldots))$.

Fig. 1. Specialization Procedure Exploiting Approximation Information

1. *If $P \cup \{G\}$ has an SLD-refutation with computed answer θ, then $P' \cup \{G\} $ has an SLD-refutation with computed answer θ.*
2. *If $P \cup \{G\}$ has a finitely failed SLD-tree then $P' \cup \{G\}$ has a finitely failed SLD-tree.*

Proof.
The proof is similar to that given in [3].

Our experiments with equational logic programs (of which some are given in the following section) showed that the improved decision procedure strikes a good balance between precision and efficiency (which should be one of the aims of every specialization/approximation system).

3.2 Interpreting Analysis Results

In the previous section we used part of the derived approximation to further specialize our program. However, there are many cases in which we are only interested in getting a finite description of the success set of a program and not in individual answers. It is also impractical to try to collect an infinite number of solutions by any means other than by approximation. Furthermore, we might have procedures designed to be used only with some arguments instantiated and others uninstantiated. Changing the mode of an argument will most certainly lead to nonterminating behavior of our program. In such cases an approximation tool may be very useful as it will in finite time give us a finite description of the success set of a program. We argue that a regular approximation is a useful description that may in many cases also be very informative.

One of the most useful properties of the regular approximation derived by procedures such as [7,11], is that the concrete and abstract domains (see [18] for further details) share the same constants and function symbols (except for the variable X in $any(X)$ in the approximation representing any term in the Herbrand universe of a program). A direct interpretation of the information given in the approximation is therefore possible without referring to abstraction and concretization functions as is usually the case in abstract interpretation. A constant a occurring in our approximation indicates that this constant may possibly occur in one or more solutions of the source program. The same also holds for any function symbol f. However, the number of solutions containing these constants and functions can not be deduced from the approximation.

In the next section we give a planning example where just such an approximation allows us to infer very useful results not possible with any other method known to us.

4 Solving Deductive Planning Problems

Two example problems, all related to the lemonade dispensing machine described in the previous section are specialized and analyzed in this section. Our aim with the first problem is to illustrate how an unsolvable planning problem may be detected. With the second problem, we illustrate how an approximate solution to a postdiction problem may be computed.

The five action descriptions in Program 1 together with the meta-program described in Section 2.1 describe a lemonade dispensing machine. The resources that can be consumed and produced are given by the actions stated by the five clauses.

$$action([d], gc, [q, q, q, q]) \leftarrow \qquad \text{\% change dollar into 4 quarters}$$
$$action([q, q, q], gd, [d]) \leftarrow \qquad \text{\% change 3 quarters into dollar}$$
$$action([dm], gf, [f, f]) \leftarrow \qquad \text{\% change deutschmark into 2 fünfziger}$$
$$action([f, f], gdm, [dm]) \leftarrow \qquad \text{\% change 2 fünfziger into deutschmark}$$
$$action([f, f], gl, [l]) \leftarrow \qquad \text{\% change 2 fünfziger into a lemonade}$$

Program 1: Action Descriptions of a Lemonade Dispensing Machine

As a first problem, we want to get **ONLY** a can of lemonade from the machine using a dollar and a quarter. This can be expressed by the following query $\leftarrow causes([d, q], Plan, [l])$. Specialization of the above program with the technique described in [3,2] gives the specialized program in Program 2. Note that we now only approximate Program 2 with respect to the query $\leftarrow causes(Resources, Plan, [l])$ as we will have another instance of this query in our second example and want to keep the specialization as general as possible (we therefore will not need to approximate again for our second example). This is in keeping with our aim stated at the beginning of the previous section to keep the query we specialize with respect to as general as possible.

$causes(X1, [\,], X1) \leftarrow$
$causes(X1, [gc|X2], X3) \leftarrow mult\_minus\_1(X1, d, X4),$
$\quad causes([q, q, q, q|X4], X2, X3)$
$causes(X1, [gd|X2], X3) \leftarrow mult\_minus\_1(X1, q, X4),$
$\quad mult\_minus\_1(X4, q, X5), mult\_minus\_1(X5, q, X6),$
$\quad causes([d|X6], X2, X3)$
$causes(X1, [gf|X2], X3) \leftarrow mult\_minus\_1(X1, dm, X4),$
$\quad causes([f, f|X4], X2, X3)$
$causes(X1, [gdm|X2], X3) \leftarrow mult\_minus\_1(X1, f, X4),$
$\quad mult\_minus\_1(X4, f, X5), causes([dm|X5], X2, X3)$
$causes(X1, [gl|X2], X3) \leftarrow mult\_minus\_1(X1, f, X4),$
$\quad mult\_minus\_1(X4, f, X5), causes\_1(X5, X2, X3)$

$mult\_minus\_1([X1|X2], X1, X2) \leftarrow$
$mult\_minus\_1([X1|X2], X3, [X1|X4]) \leftarrow mult\_minus\_1(X2, X3, X4)$

$causes\_1(X1, [\,], [l|X1]) \leftarrow$
$causes\_1(X1, [gc|X2], X3) \leftarrow mult\_minus\_1(X1, d, X4),$
$\quad causes([q, q, q, q, l|X4], X2, X3)$
$causes\_1(X1, [gd|X2], X3) \leftarrow mult\_minus\_1(X1, q, X4),$
$\quad mult\_minus\_1(X4, q, X5), mult\_minus\_1(X5, q, X6),$
$\quad causes([d, l|X6], X2, X3)$
$causes\_1(X1, [gf|X2], X3) \leftarrow mult\_minus\_1(X1, dm, X4),$
$\quad causes([f, f, l|X4], X2, X3)$
$causes\_1(X1, [gdm|X2], X3) \leftarrow mult\_minus\_1(X1, f, X4),$
$\quad mult\_minus\_1(X4, f, X5), causes([dm, l|X5], X2, X3)$
$causes\_1(X1, [gl|X2], X3) \leftarrow mult\_minus\_1(X1, f, X4),$
$\quad mult\_minus\_1(X4, f, X5), causes\_1([l|X5], X2, X3)$

Program 2: Program Specialized with respect to $\leftarrow causes(Res, Plan, [l])$

A non-empty approximation is computed (no clauses may be deleted) and the query $\leftarrow causes([d, q], Plan, [l])$ still fails to terminate and we are unable to detect that we will never be able to obtain a can of lemonade from the machine. However, by incorporating the refinement of the improved decision procedure into Program 2, we get a finitely failed computation. The transformed approximation as described in the previous section taking part in the specialization is given in Program 3.

$approx(causes(X1, X2, X3)) \leftarrow$
$approx(mult\_minus\_1(X1, dm, X2)) \leftarrow$
$approx(mult\_minus\_1(X1, f, X2)) \leftarrow$
$approx(causes\_1\_ans([\,], [\,], X1)) \leftarrow$

Program 3: Approximation Information Derived from Program 2

The program after further specialization is given in Program 4. Seven clauses could be deleted.

$causes(X1, [], X1) \leftarrow$

$causes(X1, [gf|X2], X3) \leftarrow mult\_minus\_1(X1, dm, X4),$
$\qquad causes([f, f|X4], X2, X3)$

$causes(X1, [gdm|X2], X3) \leftarrow mult\_minus\_1(X1, f, X4),$
$\qquad mult\_minus\_1(X4, f, X5), causes\_1([dm|X5], X2, X3)$

$causes(X1, [gl|X2], X3) \leftarrow mult\_minus\_1(X1, f, X4),$
$\qquad mult\_minus\_1(X4, f, X5), causes\_1(X5, X2, X3)$

$mult\_minus\_1([X1|X2], X1, X2) \leftarrow$
$mult\_minus\_1([X1|X2], X3, [X1|X4]) \leftarrow mult\_minus\_1(X2, X3, X4)$

$causes\_1(X1, [], [l|X1]) \leftarrow$

Program 4: Program After Further Specialization

The query $\leftarrow causes([d, q], Plan, [l])$ now fails finitely. We have therefore proved that it is impossible to get only a can of lemonade with a dollar and a quarter.

As a second problem we want to deduce what resources are needed to get lemonade. This can be expressed by the query $\leftarrow causes(Resources, Plan, [l])$. Running this query using our original program ((7) with Program 1) only tells us that if we start with a can of lemonade, we have achieved our goal and then the program goes into an infinitely failed deduction. One of the reasons for this unsatisfactory result is that the procedure in (7) was designed to run "forward" and not "backward" as we are trying to do in this example. If the query was stated slightly more generally in that we only require a can of lemonade to be included in the result of the deduction (not to be the only result), there may also be an infinite number of combinations of resources that may lead to this goal situation. Obviously, it is impossible to run the procedure and an approximation of the resources is the best answer we can give. Applying our improved specialization method to this query yields the result that a combination of deutschmarks and fünfziger (we do not know how many of each) are needed to get lemonade. Part of the approximation result is given in Program 5.

$approx(causes(X1, X2, X3) \leftarrow t1(X1), t5(X2), t7(X3)$
$t1([X1|X2]) \leftarrow t2(X1), t3(X2)$
$t5([]) \leftarrow$
$t5([X1|X2]) \leftarrow t6(X1), t5(X2)$
$t7([X1|X2]) \leftarrow t8(X1), t9(X2)$
$t3([]) \leftarrow$
$t3([X1|X2]) \leftarrow t4(X1), t3(X2)$
$t8(l) \leftarrow$
$t9([]) \leftarrow$

$t6(gl) \leftarrow$	$t6(gf) \leftarrow$	$t6(gdm) \leftarrow$
$t2(l) \leftarrow$	$t2(f) \leftarrow$	$t2(dm) \leftarrow$
$t4(dm) \leftarrow$	$t4(f) \leftarrow$	

Program 5: Approximation of Resources

We detected that dollars and quarters play no role in getting a can of lemonade. This is a satisfactory result with enough precision to be useful. This indicates that there are some redundant states in our machine that can never lead to a successful purchase of only a can of lemonade.

5 Discussion

The specialization procedure proposed in Section 3.1 bears some resemblance to the *v-reduction* rule for the connection graph proof procedure proposed by Munch in [22]. This rule considers sets of constants which certain clause variables may be instantiated to due to resolution. Links in the connection graph may be deleted if it is found that the *value_sets* of two corresponding arguments in two connected literals have no elements in common. These *value_sets* can be regarded as an approximation of the possible values that an argument position may take. Information inside recursive structures (such as arguments to functions) are also ignored similarly to our approach where we use information represented by a finite number of facts.

The work on approximation in automated theorem proving by for instance Giunchiglia and Walsh [9] and Plaisted [23] may also be applicable to the optimization of planning problems. However, their viewpoint is that it is the object theory that needs changing and not the logic (they would therefore not approximate the proof procedure for solving planning problems, but concentrate on approximating the action descriptions). Our approximation does not make this distinction. Furthermore, our general approximation procedure, namely a regular approximation, is fixed. This makes our method easier to adapt to new domains as we do not have to develop a new approximation for each new domain we want to investigate.

The proposed method may obviously be further improved by also using information represented by parts of the approximation other than only that represented by facts. However, the decision procedure will then be more complicated and we may then not rely any more on only SLD-resolution to test failure in the approximation. When more complicated action descriptions containing variables in resources are analyzed, we may need to take advantage of all the useful specializations. However, the partial evaluation step may assist in overcoming some of the problems posed by more complicated resource descriptions as it can factor out common structure at argument level (see [6,5] for further details).

References

1. W. Bibel. A Deductive Solution for Plan Generation. *New Generation Computing*, 4:115–132, 1986.
2. D.A. de Waal. *Analysis and Transformation of Proof Procedures*. PhD thesis, University of Bristol, October 1994.
3. D.A. de Waal and J.P. Gallagher. The applicability of logic program analysis and transformation to theorem proving. In A. Bundy, editor, *Automated Deduction—CADE-12*, pages 207–221. Springer-Verlag, 1994.

4. R. Fikes and N. Nilsson. STRIPS: A New Approach to the Application of Theorem Proving to Problem Solving. *Artificial Intelligence Journal*, 2:189–208, 1971.

5. J. Gallagher. A system for specialising logic programs. Technical Report TR-91-32, University of Bristol, November 1991.

6. J. Gallagher and M. Bruynooghe. Some low-level source transformations for logic programs. In M. Bruynooghe, editor, *Proceedings of Meta90 Workshop on Meta Programming in Logic, Leuven, Belgium*, 1990.

7. J. Gallagher and D.A. de Waal. Fast and precise regular approximations of logic programs. In *Proceedings of the Eleventh International Conference on Logic Programming*, pages 599–613. MIT Press, 1994.

8. J. H. Gallier and S. Raatz. Extending SLD-Resolution to Equational Horn Clauses Using E-Unification. *Journal of Logic Programming*, 6:3–44, 1989.

9. F. Giunchiglia and T. Walsh. A Theory of Abstraction. *Artificial Intelligence Journal*, 56(2–3):323–390, October 1992.

10. G. Große, S. Hölldobler, J. Schneeberger, U. Sigmund and M. Thielscher. Equational Logic Programming, Actions and Change. In K. Apt, editor, *Proceedings of IJCSLP*, pages 177–191, Washington, 1992. The MIT Press.

11. P. Van Hentenryck, A. Cortesi, and B. Le Charlier. Type analysis of Prolog using type graphs. Technical report, Brown University, Department of Computer Science, December 1993.

12. P.M. Hill and J.W. Lloyd. Analysis of meta-programs. In *Meta-Programming in Logic Programming*, pages 23–52. The MIT Press, 1989.

13. S. Hölldobler. *Foundations of Equational Logic Programming*, volume 353 of *LNAI*. Springer-Verlag, 1989.

14. S. Hölldobler and J. Schneeberger. A New Deductive Approach to Planning. *New Generation Computing*, 8:225–244, 1990.

15. S. Hölldobler and M. Thielscher. Computing change and specificity with equational logic programs. *Annals of Mathematics and Artificial Intelligence*, 14(1):99-133, 1995.

16. V. Lifschitz. On the Semantics of STRIPS. In M. P. Georgeff and A. L. Lansky, editors, *Proceedings of the Workshop on Reasoning about Actions & Plans*. Morgan Kaufmann, 1986.

17. J.W. Lloyd. *Foundations of Logic Programming*. Springer-Verlag, 1987.

18. K. Marriott and H. Søndergaard. Bottom-up dataflow analysis of logic programs. *Journal of Logic Programming*, 13:181–204, 1992.

19. M. Masseron, C. Tollu, and J. Vauzielles. Generating Plans in Linear Logic I. Actions as Proofs. *Theoretical Computer Science*, 113:349–370, 1993.

20. J. McCarthy. Situations and Actions and Causal Laws. Stanford Artificial Intelligence Project, Memo 2, 1963.

21. J. McCarthy and P.J. Hayes. Some Philosophical Problems from the Standpoint of Artificial Intelligence. *Machine Intelligence*, 4:463–502, 1969.

22. K.H. Munch. A new reduction rule for the connection graph proof procedure. *Journal of Automated Reasoning*, 4:425–444, 1988.

23. D. Plaisted. Abstraction mappings in mechanical theorem proving. *Automated Deduction—CADE-5*, pages 264–280. Springer-Verlag, 1980.

24. E. Yardeni and E.Y. Shapiro. A type system for logic programs. *Journal of Logic Programming*, 10(2):125–154, 1990.

Towards a Complete Proof Procedure to Prove Properties of Normal Logic Programs under the Completion

Sophie Renault

Department of Artificial Intelligence
University of Edinburgh
email: renault@ai.ed.ac.uk

Abstract. Extended execution is an extension of SLDNF resolution which was shown useful for proving properties of logic programs. It was meant for definite programs and an extension to normal ones was proposed afterwards. The correctness of the extended framework has been shown and in this paper we investigate the question of its completeness. We give results at the propositional level and discuss a possible alternative to achieve completeness at the non propositional one.

1 Introduction

Extended execution is an extension of SLDNF resolution which was proposed by Kanamori and Seki [13] in the perspective of logic program verification, and which has been used later also for program synthesis [9]. Although it is an extension of SLDNF, it was meant for definite programs only, and the purpose of extension was to allow more general goals than just definite ones. In particular, it can deal with universal queries and thus might overcome some cases of incompleteness of the negation as failure rule due to the floundering problem [15]. More precisely, it has been proved sound and complete [11] wrt the standard completion semantics [5], for the class of definite programs and S-formulas which mainly consists of goals of the form $\forall \overline{x} \, (A(\overline{x}) \rightarrow \exists \overline{y} \, B(\overline{x}, \overline{y}))$, where A and B denote conjunctions of atoms. However, the restriction to definite programs and S-formulas is quite a strong limitation in practice. The use of negation in program construction is not only realistic but also convenient since it increases expressiveness. In order to overcome this limitation, an extension of the method to normal programs was proposed in [18]. The soundness of the resulting system was proved, but the question of its completeness remained to be investigated. It is the aim of the present paper, to address this problem. We focus on the propositional case for which we give several results. Proofs require intermediary definitions and lemmas, which make the main part of the paper quite technical, although we attempted to motivate every notion by an example. Note that, unlike several works on negation which use a three-valued logic, we adopt the classical (two-valued) one. We justify this choice in the conclusion.

In what follows, we use EE to refer to extended execution for the class of normal programs as was proposed in [18], i.e. to the extension (to normal programs) of the original system of Kanamori and Seki.

The paper is organized as follows: Section 2 provides some preliminaries. Section 3 briefly recalls the outline of EE and its motivation regarding verification. Section 4 gives for the propositional case some completeness results and details their proofs. Section 5 discusses the passage to the general case.

2 Preliminaries

We assume that the reader is familiar with the basic concepts of logic programming and we use the standard terminology of [15]. A *(normal) program* P is a set of *normal clauses*, $A \leftarrow W$ where A is an atom and W a conjunction of literals. If L is a literal, then $-L$ denotes the *complementary* literal. $Comp(P)$ denotes the usual Clark's completion definition [5], which consists of the completed definition of each predicate together with Clark's Equality Theory. $Comp(P) \models G$ means that G is a consequence of $Comp(P)$, i.e. G is *true* in every model of $Comp(P)$. In the paper, we sometimes use "G is valid in $Comp(P)$" as a synonym for it. $F[G \leftarrow H]$ (resp. $F(G \leftarrow H)$) denotes the formula obtained by replacing one (resp. every) occurrence of G by H in F.

3 Motivations of EE

3.1 General description

A proof of a goal G in EE is a sequence of steps that derive *true* from G. Goals are any first order closed (without free variables) formula in an appropriate normal form. In the propositional case, this normal form is a disjunction of literals. A goal is obtained from its predecessor by an application of the *replacement* rule, which merely replaces an atom by the right hand side of its completed definition, or the *simplification* rule, which removes two complementary literals. The resulting formula is systematically subject to some *normalization* rules. They aim at simplifying goals. They include rules for equalities. The normalization of a quantifier free formula amounts to its conjunctive normal form [21], and every member of the conjunction is considered as a new independent goal.

Roughly compared to SLDNF resolution, EE acts by unfolding the definitions of $Comp(P)$ instead of the clauses of P.

A formal description of EE and the proof of its soundness is given in [18]. The soundness is stated by the following theorem [18]:

Theorem 1. *Let P be a normal program and G be a goal. If there exists a proof for G by EE, then $Comp(P) \models G$.*

3.2 An example

Let G_0 be the goal $\exists x(r(x) \wedge \neg q(x))$, and P and $Comp(P)$ be as follows:

$$P = \begin{cases} r(a). \\ r(b) \leftarrow r(b). \\ r(b) \leftarrow q(a). \\ q(a) \leftarrow q(a). \end{cases}$$

$$Comp(P) = \begin{cases} \forall x \; (r(x) \; \leftrightarrow \; \underbrace{x = a \vee (x = b \wedge r(b)) \vee (x = b \wedge q(a))}_{def(r(x))}). \\ \forall x \; (q(x) \; \leftrightarrow \; \underbrace{x = a \wedge q(a)}_{def(q(x))}). \end{cases}$$

A replacement of $r(x)$ in G_0 yields, after normalization, the goals G_1, G_2, G_3, and G_4, where G_1 and G_3 are reduced to $true$. The proof of G_2 and G_4 is achieved by a replacement of $\neg q(b)$. Details of the proof are given in appendix.

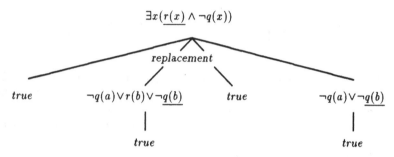

This example is borrowed from [1] where it is used to illustrate a case of incompleteness of SLDNF even in the case of definite programs and non floundering queries. Actually, there is no proof by SLDNF for the query $(\leftarrow r(x) \wedge \neg q(x))$. The inability of SLDNF to prove it comes from its attempt to instantiate x, but neither $(r(a) \wedge \neg q(a))$ nor $(r(b) \wedge \neg q(b))$ are consequences of $Comp(P)$. Only the disjunction $((r(a) \wedge \neg q(a)) \vee (r(b) \wedge \neg q(b))$ follows from $Comp(P)$. Hence, this example illustrates a case where EE overcomes a limitation of SLDNF.

3.3 Application to program verification

EE applies to verification by considering a goal as an expression of some (partial) specification S^P of a program P. Some examples are given in [13, 18]. S^P is a partial specification in the sense that it might either express a weak or a strong property of P. For example, a weak property of a sorting program $sort(l_1, l_2)$ could be: $\forall l_1 \; l_2 \; sort(l_1, l_2) \rightarrow ord(l_2)$, which would express that the second argument l_2 must be an ordered list. A stronger property could be: $\forall l_1 \; l_2 \; sort(l_1, l_2) \rightarrow subset(l_1, l_2) \wedge subset(l_2, l_1) \wedge ord(l_2)$, which would add the requirement that l_2 and l_1 contain exactly the same elements.

Note that EE applies naturally to the proof of program equivalence. For example, let $sort1$ and $sort2$ be two sorting programs, and let P be the union of their clauses. Then, equivalence between $sort1$ and $sort2$ could be established by providing a proof for the goal $\forall l_1 \; l_2 \; sort1(l_1, l_2) \leftrightarrow sort2(l_1, l_2)$.

Another interesting issue of EE regarding verification relies on the fact that the most popular model theoretic semantics for logic programs, like the well-founded semantics [10], use models of P which are also models of $Comp(P)$. As a result, a proof of S^P by EE implies that S^P is true in those particular models too.

4 Completeness in the propositional case

4.1 Some obstacles to completeness

Let P and $Comp(P)$ be as follows:

$$P = \begin{cases} p \leftarrow \neg p. \\ p \leftarrow q. \\ q \leftarrow q. \end{cases} \qquad Comp(P) = \begin{cases} p \leftrightarrow \neg p \vee q. \\ q \leftrightarrow q. \end{cases}$$

It is easy to see that $Comp(P)$ has a unique model $\{p, q\}$. Therefore $Comp(P) \models q$ and $Comp(P) \models p$. However, EE provides a proof for neither of the two goals p and q. For q, the only applicable rule is a replacement of q which yields the infinite derivation $q \rightarrow q \rightarrow q \rightarrow q \ldots$. For p, every attempt of a derivation is infinite too. In the figure below, boxes indicate that a cycle is introduced ($G \rightsquigarrow G'$ denotes that G' is the result of the normalization of G).

$$
\begin{array}{c}
\underline{p} \\
| \\
\boxed{\neg p \vee q} \\
| \\
((p \wedge \neg q) \vee q) \rightsquigarrow \quad \underline{p} \vee q \\
\qquad\qquad\qquad\qquad | \\
\qquad\qquad (\neg p \vee q \vee q) \rightsquigarrow \boxed{\neg p \vee q} \\
\qquad\qquad\qquad\qquad\qquad | \\
\qquad\qquad\qquad\qquad\qquad \vdots
\end{array}
$$

First obstacle: The incapability of EE to prove q comes from its inability to exploit the formula $(p \leftrightarrow \neg p \vee q)$. The particularity of this situation is that the validity of q in $Comp(P)$ depends on the definition of p, but p is not used to define q in P.

Second obstacle: Its incapability to prove p comes from the fact that the replacement rule exploits only partially the information contained in $Comp(P)$. Actually, the formula $(p \leftarrow \neg p \vee q)$ suffices to imply p (because p cannot be *false*), but the replacement of p by $(\neg p \vee q)$ is not powerful enough to detect the dependency between p and $\neg p$.

4.2 Removal of obstacles

This section introduces the notions that are used in the completeness results contained in Section 4.3.

Firstly, we introduce the notion of *weak replacement* to overcome the second obstacle pointed out in the above section. Intuitively, it amounts to keep track of the selected literals in the course of a derivation.

We use $def_{Comp(P)}(L)$ (or merely $def(L)$ when there is no ambiguity) to denote the right hand side (resp. the negation of the right hand side) of the completed definition of p, if $L = p$ (resp. $L = \neg p$). In the example of Section 4.1, we have $def(p) = \neg p \vee q$ and $def(\neg p) = p \wedge \neg q$. We recall that a propositional goal is a disjunction of literals (cf. Section 3.1).

Definition 2. Let G be a goal and L be a selected literal in G. The *weak replacement* is the rule that replaces L by $(L \vee def(L))$ in G.

In the remainder, "weak EE" will be used for EE where the weak replacement takes the place of the replacement rule.

Secondly, we introduce the notion of *weakening of goals* to overcome the first obstacle. Intuitively, this operation amounts to turning a goal G into an equivalent conjunction of two goals G' and G'' that use one new predicate. The proof of G is then replaced by the proof of G' and G''.

Definition 3. Let G be a goal and p be a predicate in P. The *weakening* of G by p is the set which consists of the two goals $(G \vee p)$ and $(G \vee \neg p)$.

The weakening of goals will ensure an interesting property regarding their validity in $Comp(P)$. It is expressed in Lemma 6 which uses the notions of *restriction* of programs and *strong validity* of goals, which we now define.

Definition 4. The *restriction of P to a goal G*, is the set of clauses in P that define the predicate symbols that occur in G. It is denoted $P|_G$.

To avoid possible confusion in the above definition, we stress the fact that the restriction is determined by looking only at the name of the predicates.

By extension, the weakening of G by $\{p_1, \ldots, p_n\}$ is the union of the weakening of each G_i by p_n, if G_i is a member of the weakening of G by $\{p_1, \ldots, p_{n-1}\}$. Furthermore, the *total weakening* of G is the weakening of G by Q, where Q is the set of predicates of P that do not occur in $P|_G$.

Finally, we define the notion of *strong validity* of a goal G. Intuitively, it means that the validity of G comes from the predicates that are used to define it.

Definition 5. G is *strongly valid* in $Comp(P)$ iff $Comp(P|_G) \models G$.

In the example of Section 4.1, we have $P|_q = \{q \leftarrow q\}$ and $P|_p = P$. Therefore, p is strongly valid in $Comp(P)$, since we already have $Comp(P) \models p$. However, q is not since $Comp(P|_q) \models q$ does not hold. The validity of q in $Comp(P)$ comes from the sole definition of p, whatever its own definition is.

Lemma 6. *Let P be a program and G be a valid goal in $Comp(P)$. Let $G_1, \ldots, G_k$ be the goals obtained after a total weakening of G. Then $G_1, \ldots, G_k$ are strongly valid goals in $Comp(P)$.*

Proof :

Every G_i is of the form $G \vee G'$ where G' contains an occurrence of every predicate in P that could not be introduced by a sequence of replacement from G. This means that $Comp(P|_{G_i}) = Comp(P)$. By construction, $\wedge_{i=1}^{k} G_i$ and G are logically equivalent, and therefore every G_i is strongly valid in $Comp(P|_{G_i})$, and then in $Comp(P)$. □

4.3 Some completeness results

This section provides three completeness results. The first one (Theorem 9) is the completeness of weak EE for the class of strongly valid goals. The second one (Corollary 10) is a generalization of Theorem 9 for unrestricted goals providing the condition of their weakening. The third one (Theorem 22) states the completeness of EE for the class of *call-consistent* programs.

The first result uses a *transformation τ* which merely removes a definition from $Comp(P)$.

Definition 7. *Let $Comp(P)$ be the completion of a program P and p a predicate in P. Then $Comp(P)\tau(p)$ is the set of formulas obtained from $Comp(P)$ by removing the definition of p.*

Lemma 8. *Let $G = (L_1 \vee \ldots \vee L_n)$ be a valid goal in $Comp(P)$. Then for every $L_i = p_i$ or $\neg p_i$ in G, we have $Comp(P)\tau(p_i) \models G[L_i \leftarrow L_i \vee def_{Comp(P)}(L_i)]$.*

Proof :

We suppose without loss of generality that $L_i = L_1$. We show that in every model of $Comp(P)\tau(p_1)$ in which $-L_1, -L_2, \ldots, -L_n$ are *true*, then $def_{Comp(P)}(L_1)$ is *true*, so that $G[L_i \leftarrow L_i \vee def_{Comp(P)}(L_i)]$ is *true* in every model of $Comp(P)\tau(p_1)$. By contradiction. If there exists a model of $Comp(P)\tau(p_1)$ in which $-L_1, -L_2, \ldots, -L_n$ and $\neg def_{Comp(P)}(L_1)$ are *true*, then it must also be a model of $Comp(P)$, since $Comp(P)$ equals to $Comp(P)\tau(p_1) \cup \{L_1 \leftrightarrow def_{Comp(P)}(L_1)\}$. Therefore, there would be a model of $Comp(P)$ in which $-L_1, -L_2, \ldots, -L_n$ are *true* which contracticts the hypothesis that $Comp(P) \models G$. □

Theorem 9. *Let P be a program and be G a goal. Then G is strongly valid in $Comp(P)$ iff there exists a proof of G by weak EE.*

Proof :

Let $p_1, \ldots, p_k$ be the relations that occur in $P|_G$. By definition of $P|_G$, these relations are exactly those that can be introduced by a sequence of replacements from G. Let us consider a weak derivation of G in which the selected literal in every goal uses a relation that has not already been selected in an ancestor goal.

At the k-th step (in the worst case), we obtain a goal G' which is a tautology. Actually, by Lemma 8, if $p_1, \ldots, p_k$ are the relations that occur in $P|_G$, we have $Comp(P|_G)\tau(p_1)\ldots\tau(p_k) \models G'$. Since $Comp(P|_G)\tau(p_1)\ldots\tau(p_k)$ is an empty set (by construction), G' must be a tautology. □

In the example of Section 4.1, we can easily verify that there exists a proof of p by weak EE.

The second result is the following corollary:

Corollary 10. *Let G be a goal and $G_1, \ldots, G_k$ the goals obtained by the total weakening of G. Then G is valid in $Comp(P)$ iff there exists a proof of every G_i by weak EE.*

Proof:
Immediate from Theorem 9 and Lemma 6. □

In the example of Section 4.1, we can easily verify that there exists a proof for q by weak EE after its total weakening. It amounts to the proof of the two goals $(q \vee p)$ and $(q \vee \neg p)$:

$$q \vee \underline{p} \qquad\qquad\qquad q \vee \underline{\neg p}$$
$$| \qquad\qquad\qquad\qquad |$$
$$q \vee p \vee \neg p \vee q \rightsquigarrow true \qquad q \vee \neg p \vee (p \wedge \neg q) \rightsquigarrow true$$

The third result says that the weakening of G which is required in Corollary 10, is unnecessary when P is a *call-consistent* program. It uses several intermediary definitions and lemmas. First, we recall a definition of call-consistency. Informally, call-consistency disallows self-recursion through an odd number of negative goals. We borrow a definition [6], based on the definition of *dependency graph*.

Definition 11. Let P be a program. The *dependency graph* of P, denoted by $G(P)$, is the directed graph defined by:

1. each predicate symbol in P is a node, and there are no other nodes.
2. there is an edge from q to p if there is a clause in P with q in the body and p in the head. The edge is marked positive (resp. negative) if q is in a positive (resp. negative) literal in the clause.

Let p and q be two predicate symbols in the program P and consider $G(P)$:

1. p *depends positively on* q iff either $p = q$ or in $G(P)$ all edges in the paths from q to p are marked positive.
2. p *depends negatively on* q iff in $G(p)$ there exists a path from q to p containing a negative edge.
3. p *depends evenly on* q iff in $G(P)$ there exists a path from q to p which contains an even number of negative edges.

4. *p depends oddly on q* iff in $G(P)$ there exists a path from q to p containing an odd number of negative edges.

Several subclasses of programs have been characterised by means of properties of their dependency graph.

Definition 12. A logic program P is

- *stratified* if no node in $G(P)$ depends negatively on itself.
- *strict* if there is no pair (p, q) of nodes in $G(P)$ such that p depends both evenly and oddly on q.
- *call-consistent* if no node in $G(P)$ depends oddly on itself.

Notice that call-consistency generalizes both strictness and stratification. These different classes of programs have been extensively used in the literature, since they have the nice property to ensure consistency of the completion, as stated in the following theorem [6]:

Theorem 13. *If P is call-consistent, then $Comp(P)$ is consistent.*

The program in Section 4.1 is not call-consistent since p depends oddly on its negation. The one made of the two clauses $\{p \leftarrow \neg q, \ q \leftarrow \neg p\}$ is on the contrary call-consistent (but not stratified) since p depends on itself through two negations.

The following lemma gives a property of goals in call-consistent programs.

Lemma 14. *Let P be a call-consistent program and $G = (L_1 \vee \ldots \vee L_n)$ be a valid goal in $Comp(P)$. Then:*
G is a tautology (there exists i and j, $1 \leq i, j \leq n$, such that $L_i = -L_j$), or there exists $L_i = p_i$ or $\neg p_i$ in G such that $\not\models (def(p_i) \leftrightarrow p_i)$.

Proof :
By contradiction. If every L_i $(1 \leq i \leq n)$ were such that $\models (def(p_i) \leftrightarrow p_i)$, then $Comp(P)$ would be $\{p_1 \leftrightarrow p_1, \ldots, p_n \leftrightarrow p_n, p_{n+1} \leftrightarrow F_{n+1}, \ldots, p_k \leftrightarrow F_k\}$. By replacing in $Comp(P)$ every L_i by *false* $(1 \leq i \leq n)$, we obtain a set $\mathcal{E}$ where the first n definitions are *true*. In the other definitions, if a right hand side has become *true*, (resp. *false*) for a corresponding left hand side p_j $(n+1 \leq j \leq k)$, then we go on replacing p_j by *true* (resp. *false*) in every other definition, and so on until we obtain a set of formulas of the form $\{p_{n+1} \leftrightarrow X_{n+1}, \ldots, p_k \leftrightarrow X_k\}$ where, for every X_i equals to *true* or *false*, p_i appears in no other X_j. This set can be partitioned into two sets $\mathcal{E}_1$ and $\mathcal{E}_2$. $\mathcal{E}_1$ contains every formulas of the form $(p_i \leftrightarrow X_i)$, where X_i is equal to *true* or *false*. $\mathcal{E}_1$ is consistent since the p_i's are all distinct. $\mathcal{E}_2$ contains formulas of the form $(p_i \leftrightarrow X_i)$ where X_i is a d.n.f. (disjunctive normal form) containing predicates in $\{p_{n+1}, \ldots, p_k\}$. $\mathcal{E}_2$ can therefore be seen as the completion of a program whose dependency graph is a subgraph of $G(P)$. By Theorem 13 $\mathcal{E}_2$ is consistent. $\mathcal{E}$, i.e. $Comp(P) \cup \{-L_1\} \cup \ldots \cup \{-L_n\}$ and finally $Comp(P) \cup \{\neg G\}$ is consistent which contradicts the hypothesis.

□

Lemma 15. *Let P be a call-consistent program, then for every predicate p in P, $Comp(P)\tau(p)$ is equivalent to the completion of a call-consistent program (which contains exactly the same predicates P does). $Comp(P)\tau(p)$ is therefore consistent.*

Proof :
$Comp(P)\tau(p)$ is equivalent to the completion of the program Q obtained from P by replacing the (possibly empty) packet of clauses associated to p by the unique clause $\{p \leftarrow p\}$. Actually, $Comp(Q)$ is equivalent to $Comp(P)\tau(p) \cup \{p \leftrightarrow p\}$ and then to $Comp(P)\tau(p)$. It follows that $G(Q)$ is a subgraph of $G(P)$. $\quad\square$

Now, we need the following lemma that states that there exists a proof by weak EE for every valid goal when P is call-consistent.

Lemma 16. *Let P be a call-consistent program and G a goal such that $Comp(P) \models G$. Then there exists a proof for G by weak EE.*

Proof :
We build a derivation for G by applying at every step G_i a (weak) replacement of a $L_i = p_i$ or $\neg p_i$ that satisfies the condition of Lemma 14 for some subset of $Comp(P)$ (initially $Comp(P)$) and G_i. It yields $G' = L_1 \vee \ldots \vee L_n \vee def(L_i)$ and, after normalization, the subgoals $G_{i1}, \ldots, G_{ik}$. By Lemma 8, for every G_{ij} ($1 \leq j \leq k$), we have $Comp(P)\tau(p_i) \models G_{ij}$, and by Lemma 15, $Comp(P)\tau(p_i)$ is equivalent to the completion of a call-consistent program (and therefore Lemma 14 applies again). Trivially, $Comp(P) \models G_{ij}$ since $Comp(P) \models (\wedge_{j=1}^{k} G_{ij}) \leftrightarrow G_i$. Eventually, every subgoal of G becomes *true*. The termination is ensured since at each step a definition of $Comp(P)$ is removed. $\quad\square$

The following corollary states that in the completion of call-consistent programs, valid goals and strongly valid goals are the same.

Corollary 17. *Let P be a call-consistent program and G be a goal. Then $Comp(P) \models G$ iff $Comp(P|_G) \models G$.*

Proof :
By Lemma 16 and Theorem 9. $\quad\square$

Lemma 18. *Let p be a predicate in P. Let $def(p)\!\downarrow$ and $def(\neg p)\!\downarrow$ be the c.n.f. (conjunctive normal forms) of $def(p)$ and $def(\neg p)$:*

$$def(p)\!\downarrow \ = W_1 \wedge \ldots \wedge W_n$$
$$def(\neg p)\!\downarrow \ = W_1' \wedge \ldots \wedge W_m'$$

Then for every pair (i, j) such that $1 \leq i \leq n$ and $1 \leq j \leq m$, W_i contains a complementary literal of a literal in W_j'.

Proof :
Immediate by construction of the c.n.f. of $def(p)$ and $def(\neg p)$. $\quad\square$

Corollary 19. *Let $def(p) \downarrow$ and $def(\neg p) \downarrow$ be defined as in Lemma 18. Then for every i and j ($1 \leq i \leq n$, $1 \leq j \leq m$), the formulas $(W_i \vee def(\neg p))$ and $(W'_j \vee def(p))$ are tautologies. In particular, $W_i \vee W'_j$ is a tautology.*

Lemma 20. *Let $G = (L_1 \vee \ldots \vee L_n)$ be a goal for which it exists a proof d_1 by EE of length k that uses a replacement of L_i ($1 \leq i \leq n$). Then it exists a proof d_2 for G by EE, of length $k' \leq k$, that starts with a replacement of L_i.*

Proof :
By induction on the length l of the derivation d_1. □

Lemma 21. *Let P be a call-consistent program. Let G be a subgoal and L be a literal in G. Then, if there exists a proof of $G[L \leftarrow L \vee def(L)]$ by EE, there exists a proof of G by EE.*

Proof :
By induction on the length l of the proof for $G[L \leftarrow L \vee def(L)]$, we show that there exists a proof for $G[L \leftarrow def(L)]$. This means that there exists a proof for G that starts by a replacement of L. □

Finally, we prove Theorem 22.

Theorem 22. *Let P be a call-consistent program and G be a goal. Then G is valid in $Comp(P)$ iff there exists a proof of G by EE.*

Proof :
Let G be $L_1 \vee \ldots \vee L_n$. By hypothesis, $Comp(P) \models G$. By Lemma 16 there exists a proof of G by weak EE. We reason by induction on its length l. Without loss of generality, let us assume that the derivation starts by the (weak) replacement of $L_1 = p_1$ or $\neg p_1$, and that $def(L_1) \downarrow = W_1 \wedge \ldots \wedge W_k$.

- If $l = 1$, it means that every subgoal obtained from G after the replacement are reduced to *true*. They have the form $G_j = (L_1 \vee W_j \vee L_2 \vee \ldots \vee L_n)$, ($1 \leq j \leq k$). G_j is reduced to *true* if $W_j = true$ or if G_j contains a pair of complementary literals. By definition of call-consistency, $-L_1$ does not occur in W_j. Therefore, for every j, $1 \leq j \leq k$, a pair of complementary literals occurs in $(W_j \vee L_2 \vee \ldots \vee L_n)$, which means that there exists a proof of G by EE (in one step) by a replacement of L_1.
- We assume that the property is true for $l = n$, i.e. that if there exists a proof of G with length n by weak EE, then there exists a proof of G by EE.
- Now, let us consider a proof of G of length $l = n + 1$. At the first step, the subgoals G_j, for $1 \leq j \leq k$, have the form $(L_1 \vee W_j \vee L_2 \vee \ldots \vee L_n)$. By induction hypothesis, there exists a proof of every G_j ($1 \leq j \leq k$) by EE. By Lemma 21, there exists a proof of $(L_1 \vee L_2 \vee \ldots \vee L_n)$, i.e. a proof of G by EE.

□

5 Towards completeness in the non propositional case

In the above section, we showed that a slight variation of EE, called "weak EE", was enough to achieve completeness at propositional level. We also showed that this weakening was unnecessary for a large class of programs which contains *call-consistent* programs. This is interesting, since EE roughly amounts to "unfolding + simplification" which is a simple and intuitive inference mechanism. Moreover, goals are handled in a human-oriented manner, unlike theorem provers based on classical resolution, which require formulas to be turned in a clausal form. This is one of the reasons that make EE attractive from a verification point of view. Because proofs are more understandable, we can imagine a possible interaction with users for their guidance, and a better intuition of how they could operate appropriate changes in programs and specifications.

5.1 No immediate generalization

Unfortunately, the results obtained in the propositional case cannot be immediately generalized. The following example illustrates a case of incompleteness due to a lack of instanciation of the variables in G. Let P and $Comp(P)$ be as follows:

$$P = \begin{cases} p(f(x)) \leftarrow p(x). \\ q(a). \end{cases} \qquad Comp(P) = \begin{cases} p(x) \leftrightarrow \exists y \ (x = f(y) \land p(y)). \\ q(x) \leftrightarrow x = a. \end{cases}$$

It is easy to see that $\neg p(a)$ is a consequence of $Comp(P)$. However, any attempt of proving $\exists x \neg p(x)$ yields the infinite derivation described below (normalization of goals is implicite):

$$
\begin{array}{ll}
G_0 : & \exists x \neg p(x) \\
& \mid \\
G_{10} : & \exists x (\forall y (x \neq f(y) \lor \neg p(y))) \\
& \mid \\
G_{110} : & \exists x (\forall y' (x \neq f(f(y')) \lor \neg p(y'))) \\
& \mid \\
G_{1110} : & \exists x (\forall y'' (x \neq f(f(f(y''))) \lor \neg p(y''))) \\
& \mid \\
& \cdots \qquad\qquad \cdots
\end{array}
$$

Note that the use of the weak replacement would not help to achieve the proof of G_0. The problem comes from the necessity to eliminate (instanciate) the variable x, but this instanciation cannot be done by means of a replacement (nor by a simplification).

Instead of adding new rules to EE which would break the simple idea of "unfolding + simplification", we have experimented with other proof systems, known to be complete for first-order logic, in order to see whether or not they would be adequate to prove consequences of $Comp(P)$. In particular, *nonclausal resolution* turned out to present interesting features, as it is discussed below.

5.2 Alternative via nonclausal resolution

Nonclausal (NC) resolution was introduced by Murray [16] as a generalization of
the resolution rule [19] to formulas that are more general that mere clauses. Actually, it deals with any quantifier-free formulas (i.e. formulas whose skolemized
form are universal formulas, but not necessarily a disjunction of literals). It reduces to clausal resolution when the formulas are restricted to being clauses. The
NC inference rule is as follows: Let F_1 and F_2 be two formulas such that a literal
L has a positive (resp. negative) occurrence in F_1 (resp. F_2), then applying the
NC-rule on F_1 and F_2 yields the new formula $F_1(L \leftarrow false) \vee F_2(L \leftarrow true)$,
where $F(L \leftarrow X)$ denotes the replacement of all occurrences of L by X in F.
Note that F_1 and F_2 might be the same formula when L occurs both positively
and negatively in it. The polarity of a literal is defined as usual, i.e. L is a positive (resp. negative) occurrence of G if it appears in G within an even number of
negation (explicitly, or implicitly in the left-hand-side of an implication). Note
that a same literal may have both positive and negative occurrences in a formula,
and in particular in equivalences.
The following is a proof of the inconsistency of $Comp(P) \cup \{\neg G\}$, where P is
the program used in Section 4.1, and G is p (on the left) or q (on the right).

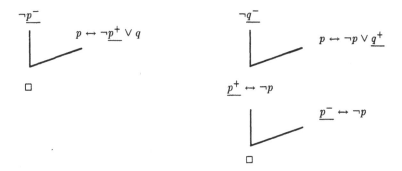

The main reasons why NC resolution must be regarded as an interesting technique to prove formulas of $Comp(P)$ rely on the following aspects:
- it avoids the cost of turning $Comp(P)$ into a clausal form. It only requires the
skolemization step (which is nearly immediate regarding the particular use of
quantifiers in the formulas of $Comp(P)$),
- the replacement rule of EE resembles a lot to the NC-resolution rule: In particular, when applied to the propositional case, where the formulas of $Comp(P)$
are directly applicable to NC-resolution (since they are quantifier free), we can
observe that EE is a restriction of NC-resolution. This restriction is to select
literals in the left-hand side of formulas of $Comp(P)$ only. This means that in
the propositional case, EE can be seen as a particular strategy to apply NC-
resolution.
The question of dealing with the axioms of the CET in this framework still
remains to be investigated.

6 Conclusion

In this paper we have investigated the completeness of EE which was proposed in [18] as a generalization to normal programs of an initial proof procedure by Kanamori and Seki [13], which in turn was proposed as an extension of SLDNF resolution. We have provided some completeness results at the propositional level, and suggested a possible solution to achieve completeness at the general level by exploiting its similarity with nonclausal resolution.

EE was shown of interest to the fields of verification [13, 12, 18] and synthesis [9] of logic programs. Regarding verification, we would like to emphasize the fact that EE applies naturally to prove properties wrt several canonical semantics which provide models of P which are also models of $Comp(P)$, like the well-founded semantics [10].

Because it is based on an extension of SLDNF, EE relates to the works that are explicitly devoted to extend the negation as failure rule, usually termed constructive negation (see [2] and [7] for a survey about those works). It is a fact that most of those approaches use a three-valued logic. The motivations of dealing with a three-valued framework come from Kleene, who suggested the use of an "undefined" truth value to capture the notion of infinite computations, i.e. of computations that fail to return an answer. Kunen [14] and Fitting [8] showed the relevance of this approach in the field of logic programming, and recent works on constructive negation widely refer to it. Since the three-valued semantics is weaker than the two-valued one, in the sense that two-valued models are a special case of three-valued models, it provides a more convenient framework to achieve completeness. As a result, most of the approaches for constructive negation achieve completeness for the three-valued completion [17, 4, 3, 20, 7]. Note that [20] presents a complete procedure which is also two-valued complete when the program is strict. It therefore would be interesting to study EE in three-valued logic. This would simplify the achievement of completeness at the propositional level, and its "lifting" to the general one. An illustration of that is to observe that, in the example of Section 4.1, neither p nor q is three-valued consequence of $Comp(P)$, since there exists a model of P in which p and q are both undefined. Nevertheless, although we agree on the naturalness of three-valued logic to provide a logical meaning of negation in SLDNF, we believe that it is too restrictive for verification concerns. Actually, it would be a too strong requirement for a specification to be consequence of the three-valued completion, and we do not have any practical example which would suggest that it might be of relevance. The properties that are used in [18] to illustrate the application of EE to verification are two-valued but not three-valued consequences of $Comp(P)$. Note that it is also the case for the example of Section 3.2. And above mentionned works on negation that refer to a three-valued logic do not pretend to address this problem, anyway.

7 Acknowledgments

This work was supported partly by an INRIA grant and partly by the Human Capital Mobility grant EC CHRX-CT93-00414. We would like to thank those who contributed to improve our earlier versions of this paper, and in particular anonymous referees for their corrections, suggestions and comments. Thanks also to Pierre Deransart and Gérard Ferrand for guidance, and to Laurent Fribourg for valuable discussions.

References

1. K. Apt. Introduction to Logic Programming. In J. Van Leeuven, editor, *Handbook of Theoretical Computer Science*. North Holland, 1990.
2. K. R. Apt and R. Bol. Logic Programming and Negation: A Survey. *Journal of Logic Programming*, 19,20:9–71, 1994.
3. A. Bottoni and G.Levi. Computing in the Completion. In *Atti dell Ottavo Convegno sulla Programmazione Logica (Gulp)*, pages 375–389. Mediterranean Press, 1993.
4. P. Bruscoli, F. Levi, G. Levi, and M. C. Meo. Intensional Negation in Constraint Logic Programs. In *Atti dell Ottavo Convegno sulla Programmazione Logica (Gulp)*, pages 359–373. Mediterranean Press, 1993.
5. K. L. Clark. Negation as Failure. In H. Gallaire and J. Minker, editors, *Logic and Databases*, pages 293–322. Plenum Press, New York, 1978.
6. A. Cortesi and G. Filé. Graph Properties for Normal Programs. *Theoretical Computer Science*, 107:277–303, 1993.
7. W. Drabent. What is Failure? An Approach to Constructive Negation. *Acta Informatica*, 32:27–59, 1995.
8. M. Fitting. A Kripke-Kleene Semantics for Logic Programs. *Journal of Logic Programming*, 2:295–312, 1985.
9. L. Fribourg. Extracting Logic Programs from Proofs that Use Extended Prolog Execution and Induction. In *Proceedings of the Seventh Int. Conference on Logic Programming, Jerusalem*, pages 685–699, 1990.
10. A. Van Gelder, K. A. Ross, and J. S. Schlipf. The Well-Founded Semantics for General Logic Programs. *Journal of the ACM*, 38(3):620–650, 1991.
11. T. Kanamori. Soundness and Completeness of Extended Execution for Proving Properties of Prolog Programs. Technical Report TR-175, ICOT, 1986.
12. T. Kanamori, H. Fujita, K. Horiuchi, and M. Maeji. ARGUS/V: a System for Verification of Prolog Programs. Technical Report TR-176, ICOT, 1986.
13. T. Kanamori and H. Seki. Verification of Logic Programs Using an Extension of Execution. In *Proceedings of the Third International Conference on Logic Programming, London*, pages 475–489, 1986.
14. K. Kunen. Negation in Logic Programming. *Journal of Logic Programming*, 4:289–308, 1987.
15. J. Lloyd. *Foundations of Logic Programming*. Springer-Verlag, Berlin, 1987.
16. N. V. Murray. Completely non-clausal theorem proving. *Journal of Artificial Intelligence*, 18:67–85, 1982.
17. D. Pedreschi R. Barbuti, P. Mancarella and F. Turini. A Transformational Approach to Negation in Logic Programming. *Journal of Logic Programming*, 8:201–228, 1990.

18. S. Renault. Generalizing Extended Execution for Normal Programs. In F. Turini and L. Fribourg, editors, *Proceedings of the Fourth International Workshops on Logic Program Synthesis and Transformation and Meta-Programming in Logic*, LNCS, pages 154–169. Springer-Verlag, 1994.

19. J. A. Robinson. A Machine Oriented Logic Based on the Resolution Principle. *Journal of the Association for Computing Machinery*, 12, 1965.

20. T. Sato and F. Motoyoshi. A Complete Top-down Interpreter for First Order Programs. In *Proceedings of the Int. Logic Programming Symposium, San Diego*, pages 35–53. MIT Press, 1991.

21. D. van Dalen. *Logic and Structure*. Springer Verlag, Berlin, second edition, 1987.

Appendix

We detail the proof of Section 3.2 and in particular the task performed during the normalization process. The normalization rules that are successively applied are concerned with: distributivity ($\wedge$), elimination of equalities, distributivity ($\vee$) and boolean simplification.

$$G : \exists x \ (\underline{r(x)} \wedge \neg q(x))$$

$$\vdots$$

$$G' : \exists x \ (\boxed{(x = a \ \vee \ (x = b \wedge r(b)) \ \vee \ (x = b \wedge q(a)))} \wedge \neg q(x))$$

$$\vdots$$

$$\exists x_1 \ (x_1 = a \wedge \neg q(x_1)) \vee \exists x_2 \ (x_2 = b \wedge r(b) \wedge \neg q(x_2)) \vee \exists x_3 \ (x_3 = b \wedge q(a) \wedge \neg q(x_3)))$$

$$\vdots$$

$$\neg q(a) \ \vee \ (r(b) \wedge \neg q(b)) \ \vee \ (q(a) \wedge \neg q(b))$$

$$\vdots$$

$$\underbrace{\neg q(a) \vee r(b) \vee q(a)}_{G'_{11}} \qquad \underbrace{\neg q(a) \vee \neg q(b) \vee q(a)}_{G'_{21}} \qquad \underbrace{\neg q(a) \vee r(b) \vee \neg q(b)}_{G'_{12}} \qquad \underbrace{\neg q(a) \vee \neg q(b) \vee \neg q(b)}_{G'_{22}}$$

$$\vdots$$

$$\underbrace{\neg q(a) \vee r(b) \vee \underline{\neg q(b)}}_{G_2} \qquad \underbrace{\neg q(a) \vee \underline{\neg q(b)}}_{G_4}$$

$$\vdots$$

$$\underbrace{\neg q(a) \vee r(b) \vee \boxed{\neg \ false}}_{G'_{21}} \qquad \underbrace{\neg q(a) \vee \boxed{\neg \ false}}_{G'_{41}}$$

$$\vdots$$

$$true$$

Termination of Logic Programs Using Semantic Unification

Thomas Arts and Hans Zantema

Utrecht University, Department of Computer Science,
P.O. Box 80.089, 3508 TB Utrecht, The Netherlands
e-mail: {thomas,hansz}@cs.ruu.nl

Abstract. We introduce a transformation of well-moded logic programs into constructor systems, a subclass of term rewrite systems, such that left-termination of the logic program follows from termination of the derived constructor system. Thereafter, we present a new technique to prove termination of constructor systems. In the technique semantic unification is used. Thus, surprisingly, semantic unification can be used for giving termination proofs for logic programs. Parts of the technique can be automated very easily. Other parts can be automated for subclasses of constructor systems. The technique is powerful enough to prove termination of some constructor systems that are not simply terminating, and therefore, the technique is suitable to prove termination of some difficult logic programs.

1 Introduction

Several approaches to prove termination of logic programs are proposed (for a survey see [SD93]). One of the approaches, introduced by Krishna Rao *et al.* [KKS91], is to transform the logic program into a term rewrite system (TRS) such that the termination property is preserved. More precisely, if the TRS terminates, then the original well-moded logic program is left-terminating, thus terminates for all well-moded goals. Other authors followed this approach and came up with transformations suitable for proving termination of a larger class of logic programs [GW92, CR93, AM93, AZ94, Mar94]. Most transformation algorithms transform the logic programs into constructor systems (CSs), a subclass of the TRSs. This paper describes a technique to prove termination of CSs. The technique is in particular suitable for, but not limited to, those CSs that are obtained from the transformation algorithm described in this paper. We mention that it is also possible to present the technique without the notion of constructor system, by a direct translation of well-moded logic programs into *dependency pairs*. However, in the latter approach the definition of the equational theory, needed for the semantic unification, would be very unnatural. Moreover, in the approach based on CSs we really use the CSs to construct/find an equational theory automatically [Art96, AZ95].

The following logic program is a typical example of a well-moded logic program for which the technique is applicable. As a leading example for this paper we have

Example 1.

$$append(nil, xs, xs)$$
$$append(cons(x, xs_1), xs_2, cons(x, ys)) \leftarrow append(xs_1, xs_2, ys)$$

$$split(xs, nil, xs)$$
$$split(cons(x, xs), cons(x, ys_1), ys_2) \quad \leftarrow split(xs, ys_1, ys_2)$$

$$perm(nil, nil)$$
$$perm(xs, cons(y, ys)) \qquad\qquad \leftarrow split(xs, ys_1, cons(y, ys_2)),$$
$$append(ys_1, ys_2, zs),$$
$$perm(zs, ys)$$

The modings are $append(in, in, out)$, $split(in, out, out)$ and $perm(in, out)$. By representing the lists by their length, which is a standard approach, termination of this logic program can be proved completely automatically by the technique presented in this paper. We describe an algorithm to transform well-moded logic programs into constructor systems such that termination of the logic program follows from termination of the obtained constructor system. Therefore, we concentrate on techniques to prove termination of constructor systems.

In Section 2 some definitions of term rewriting that are important in this paper and a brief description of semantic unification are presented. The transformation of a logic program into a TRS is described and explained in Section 3. In Section 4 the technique to prove termination of CSs is introduced and proved to be sound. We conclude in Section 5 with some remarks about the power of the introduced technique.

2 Preliminaries

In this section some definitions of term rewriting are summarised that are used in this paper. For a good survey in this area see [DJ90, Klo92]. Furthermore, we briefly describe semantic unification.

2.1 Term rewrite systems

Definition 1. A *term rewrite system* (TRS) is a pair $(\mathcal{F}, \mathcal{R})$ consisting of a signature $\mathcal{F}$, a set of function symbols, and a set $\mathcal{R}$ of rewrite rules between terms over this signature.

Constructor systems are a subclass of TRSs.

Definition 2. A *constructor system* is a TRS $(\mathcal{F}, \mathcal{R})$ with the property that $\mathcal{F}$ can be partitioned into disjoint sets $\mathcal{D}$ and $\mathcal{C}$ such that every left-hand side $f(t_1, \ldots, t_n)$ of a rewrite rule of $\mathcal{R}$ satisfies $f \in \mathcal{D}$ and $t_1, \ldots, t_n$ are terms without symbols of $\mathcal{D}$. Function symbols in $\mathcal{D}$ are called *defined symbols* and these in $\mathcal{C}$ *constructor symbols* or *constructors*.

Definition 3. A TRS R is called *terminating* if there exists no infinite reduction. Thus, if there exists no term with an infinite reduction in R.

In this paper we focus on automatically proving termination. Methods that are used to prove termination of TRSs automatically, are often based on a special kind of well-founded orders, the so called simplification orders. We introduce a stronger notion of termination, called *simple termination*. If a TRS is simple terminating, then it is terminating, but the converse thus not hold. A TRS that is not simply terminating can be terminating, but there is no simplification order to prove termination of such a TRS. Thus, methods based on simplification orders will always fail in proving termination of TRS that are not simply terminating.

Definition 4. For a set $\mathcal{F}$ of operation symbols $Emb(\mathcal{F})$ is defined to be the TRS consisting of all the rules $f(x_1, \ldots, x_n) \to x_i$ with $f \in \mathcal{F}$ and $i \in \{1, \ldots, n\}$. These rules are called the *embedding rules*.

Definition 5 [Zan94]. A TRS R over a set $\mathcal{F}$ of function symbols is called *simply terminating* if $R \cup Emb(\mathcal{F})$ is terminating.

A standard technique to prove termination of TRSs, of which several implementations exist, is the so called recursive path order (RPO). This technique is not applicable to all TRSs. For example it is not applicable to terminating TRSs that are not simply terminating. A direct consequence of the recursive path order (among others in [Der87, FZ94]) is the following theorem

Proposition 6. *Let $\rhd$ be a well-founded order on the signature of a TRS R. If for every rule $l \to r$ in R we have that $head(l) \rhd f$ for all function symbols f that occur in r, then R is terminating.*

2.2 Semantic unification

Syntactic unification theory is concerned with the problem whether for two given terms t_1 and t_2 the equation $t_1 = t_2$ can be solved 'syntactically', i.e. find a unifier σ such that $t_1^\sigma = t_2^\sigma$; this is a particular case of the problem to solve equations 'semantically', i.e. modulo some equational theory E (for this reason semantical unification is also called E-unification). More precisely, in the presence of an equational theory E, and given an equation $t_1 = t_2$, we want to find unifiers σ such that $t_1^\sigma =_E t_2^\sigma$. Narrowing is a technique to solve equations $t_1 = t_2$ in the presence of an equational theory E. We will not discuss the technique here, but refer to [Hul80, Klo92] for the basic principles of narrowing, and to [Sie89, Höl89, Han94] for surveys in the area.

What is important for this paper is that we need narrowing to find all possible unifiers σ that solve the equation, not just one solution. The set of all unifiers, or the complete set of E-unifiers, is recursively enumerable for any decidable theory E: just enumerate all substitutions and check if each one unifies the given terms, which is possible as E is decidable.

3 Transforming a logic program into a rewrite system

In the area of term rewrite systems, various techniques have been developed to prove termination of TRSs. Dealing with termination of logic programs, one could wonder whether the techniques for TRSs could be used for logic programs too. Since a logic program is not a TRS, there are two possible ways to use the techniques: transfer the theory of the technique to the area of logic programs and prove that the technique can also be applied to a logic program, or transform the logic program into a TRS, prove that the logic program is terminating if the TRS is terminating and apply the technique to the TRS. In the second approach, only once a transformation has to be developed and for this transformation a soundness proof has to be given, after that, all known and new techniques to prove termination of TRSs can be applied to logic programs. The first transformation was presented by Krishna Rao, et al. [KKS91] and as the other transformations it is applicable to well-moded logic programs. The concept of well-modedness is due to Dembinski and Maluszynski [DM85]. The definition of a well-moded program constrains the 'flow-of-data' through the clauses of the program. Some left-terminating well-moded logic programs are by the transformation transformed into TRSs that are not terminating. Hence, the technique was not successful for these logic programs. The transformation presented in [GW92] improves the former transformation such that a larger class of left-terminating well-moded logic programs correspond to terminating TRSs. The algorithm of [GW92] transforms well-moded logic programs into conditional rewrite systems. In [CR93] a two-step transformation was presented, which extended this algorithm with a second transformation of the resulting conditional rewrite system into a TRS. Our transformation is inspired by this two-step transformation. Independently, in [AM93] a transformation was presented to transform a well-moded logic program together with a goal into a TRS. We proved [AZ94] that for our transformation single-redex normalisation of the TRS is sufficient to conclude termination of the well-moded logic programs independent of the given well-moded goal, which is stronger than the other results. We also proved that the proposed transformation is complete with respect to the class of structural recursive programs, a subclass of the well-moded logic programs.

Example 2. The logic program

$$p(a,b) \qquad tc(x,y) \leftarrow p(x,y)$$
$$p(b,c) \qquad tc(x,z) \leftarrow p(x,y), tc(y,z)$$

with modes $p(in, out)$ and $tc(in, out)$ transforms, using the transformation of [KKS91] into the rewrite system

$$p(a) \rightarrow b \qquad tc(x) \rightarrow p(x)$$
$$p(b) \rightarrow c \qquad tc(x) \rightarrow tc(p(x))$$

Since there is an infinite reduction, $tc(a) \rightarrow tc(p(a)) \rightarrow tc(p(p(a))) \rightarrow \ldots$, this TRS is not terminating, although the logic program is left-terminating. Resolution with the goal $tc(a, x)$ and the logic program with the left-to-right selection rule, forces the predicate p to be evaluated before tc is evaluated. Reduction of the term $tc(a)$ and the rewrite system does not force the reduction of p to take place before the reduction of tc. This motivates a different transformation of logic programs into rewrite systems. The transformation that we propose forces the same evaluation order for rewriting terms as is used for resolving goals.

Our transformation algorithm introduces a new k-symbol for every atom in the body of a clause and a new function symbol $pout$ for every predicate symbol p. The intuition is that resolving a predicate $p(\mathbf{in}, \mathbf{out})$ corresponds to reduction of a term $p(\mathbf{in})$ to a term $pout(\mathbf{out})$. In the algorithm the literals are denoted in such a way that the first arguments are the in-positions and the last arguments are the out-positions. Furthermore, we write $p(t_1, \ldots, t_k, t_{k+1}, \ldots, t_{k+k'})$ to denote that $t_1, \ldots, t_k$ are the arguments on input positions and $t_{k+1}, \ldots, t_{k+k'}$ are the arguments on output positions. We write $var(t_1, \ldots, t_n)$ for the ordered sequence of all variables in the terms $t_1, \ldots, t_n$. For example if $x < y < z$, then $var(p(z), max(x, x, x), less(0, y))$ is the sequence x, y, z.

```
program Transform (P:in, R_P:out);
begin
    R_P := ∅; index := 0;
    for each clause B_0 ← B_1, ..., B_m ∈ P do
    begin
        Let B_0 be p_0(t_1, ..., t_k, t_{k+1}, ..., t_{k+k'});
        Out := p_0out(t_{k+1}, ..., t_{k+k'});
        if (m = 0)          /* Program clause without body */
        then R_P := R_P ∪ {p_0(t_1, ..., t_k) → Out};
        else                /* Program clause with body */
        begin
            for j = 1 to m do
            begin
                Let B_{j-1} be p_{j-1}(t_1, ..., t_k, t_{k+1}, ..., t_{k+k'});
                Let B_j be p_j(s_1, ..., s_l, s_{l+1}, ..., s_{l+l'});
                index := index + 1;
                Varold := Var;
                Var := var(t_1, ..., t_k);
                if (j = 1)
                then
                    R_P := R_P ∪ {p_0(t_1, ..., t_k) → k_{index}(Var, p_j(s_1, ..., s_l))};
                else
                    R_P := R_P ∪ {k_{index-1}(Var, p_{j-1}out(t_{k+1}, ..., t_{k+k'})) →
                              k_{index}(Varold, p_j(s_1, ..., s_l))};
            end
            R_P := R_P ∪ {k_{index}(Var, p_mout(s_{l+1}, ..., s_{l+l'})) → Out};
        end
    end
end
```

For details concerning the transformation algorithm and the proof of the following theorem we refer to [AZ94].

Theorem 7. *Let P be a well-moded logic program and R_P be the TRS obtained by the described transformation. If the TRS R_P is terminating, then the logic program P is left-terminating.*

Example 3. Transforming the logic program of Example 2 with our algorithm results in

$$
\begin{aligned}
p(a) &\rightarrow pout(b) \\
p(b) &\rightarrow pout(c) \\
tc(x) &\rightarrow k_1(p(x)) \\
k_1(pout(y)) &\rightarrow tcout(y) \\
tc(x) &\rightarrow k_2(p(x)) \\
k_2(pout(y)) &\rightarrow k_3(tc(y)) \\
k_3(tcout(z)) &\rightarrow tcout(z)
\end{aligned}
$$

Termination of the transformed logic program can automatically be proved by existing techniques developed to prove termination of TRSs.

Example 4. The transformation algorithm can be applied to mutual recursive logic programs as well. The resulting TRS will be mutual recursive, which need not be a problem for the existing techniques to prove termination of TRSs. For example, the following logic program [SD93, p. 245]

$$
\begin{aligned}
dis(x \vee y) &\leftarrow con(x), dis(y) \\
dis(x) &\leftarrow con(x) \\
con(x \wedge y) &\leftarrow dis(x), con(y) \\
con(x) &\leftarrow bool(x) \\
bool(true) & \\
bool(false) &
\end{aligned}
$$

transforms by our algorithm into a TRS that can automatically be proved terminating by existing techniques.

We are interested in termination of logic programs, and specially interested in *automatically* proving termination of logic programs. Since termination of logic programs, and even of well-moded logic programs, is in general undecidable, it is impossible to automatically prove termination of logic programs in general. However, automatically proving termination of subclasses of logic programs or TRSs is possible. Since the logic programs transform by our algorithm into TRSs of a very special structure, we developed a technique to prove termination of these TRSs and hence to prove termination of the associated logic programs. The technique enables automatically proving of termination for a subclass of all transformed logic programs.

4 Chains of dependency pairs, a technique to prove termination

In this section we present a new technique to prove termination of constructor systems. First we give a sketch of the technique and following the leading example, we give the formal definitions. Consider the following rewrite system $\{f(s(x)) \to k(x), k(x) \to f(x)\}$ Analysing the reason why there is no infinite reduction starting with a term of the form $f(s(t))$, with t in normal form, we find that this term is reduced by repeatedly using the two rewrite rules. Every time both rules have been used, the argument has decreased. Eventually this has to come to an end. This very informal observation is formalised in this section. As a leading example we consider the constructor system $\mathcal{R}_{perm}$,

$$
\begin{aligned}
append(nil, xs) &\to appout(xs) \\
append(cons(x, xs_1), xs_2) &\to k_1(x, append(xs_1, xs_2)) \\
k_1(x, appout(ys)) &\to appout(cons(x, ys)) \\
split(xs) &\to spout(nil, xs) \\
split(cons(x, xs)) &\to k_2(x, split(xs)) \\
k_2(x, spout(ys_1, ys_2)) &\to spout(cons(x, ys_1), ys_2)
\end{aligned}
$$

$$
\begin{aligned}
perm(nil) &\to permout(nil) \\
perm(xs) &\to k_3(split(xs)) \\
k_3(spout(ys_1, cons(y, ys_2))) &\to k_4(y, append(ys_1, ys_2)) \\
k_4(y, appout(zs)) &\to k_5(y, perm(zs)) \\
k_5(y, permout(ys)) &\to permout(cons(y, ys))
\end{aligned}
$$

which is obtained by applying the transformation as described in [AZ94] on the logic program of Example 1. The set of defined symbols of this constructor system is $\{append, k_1, split, k_2, perm, k_3, k_4, k_5\}$; all other function symbols are constructor symbols.

4.1 An equational theory

Consider the reduction of any term containing a subterm of the form $perm(xs^\sigma)$. This subterm allows the following reduction in $\mathcal{R}_{perm}$:

$$
\begin{array}{l}
perm(xs^\sigma) \to k_3(split(xs^\sigma)) \\
\qquad \downarrow_* \\
\quad k_3(spout(ys_1^\sigma, cons(y^\sigma, ys_2^\sigma))) \to k_4(y^\sigma, append(ys_1^\sigma, ys_2^\sigma)) \\
\qquad\qquad \downarrow_* \\
\qquad k_4(y^\sigma, appout(zs^\sigma)) \to k_5(y^\sigma, perm(zs^\sigma)) \\
\qquad\qquad\qquad \| \\
\qquad\qquad perm(ys^\sigma) \to k_3(split(ys^\sigma))
\end{array}
$$

By the knowledge of the behaviour of the logic program, we expect ys^σ to be less than xs^σ, in the sense that the list ys^σ is a list with one element less than the list xs^σ. Phrased differently, we observe that after every successive application of the rewrite rule $perm(xs) \rightarrow k_3(split(xs))$, the length of the list-argument has decreased.

The correctness of this observation depends on another implicit observation: we assume *append* and *split* to behave as they ought to do, i.e. we assume that splitting a list results in two lists of which the sum of the lengths equals the length of the original list. Thus, if $split(s)$ reduces to $spout(s_1, s_2)$, then $|s| = |s_1| + |s_2|$. There is an easy way to find out whether *append* and *split* do behave in the appropriate manner, just define an equational theory that strokes with the expected behaviour. In particular we would like to have

$$
\begin{aligned}
nil & = 0 \\
cons(x, xs) & = s(xs) \\
append(xs_1, xs_2) & = xs_1 + xs_2 \\
appout(xs) & = xs \\
split(ys) & = ys \\
spout(ys_1, ys_2) & = ys_1 + ys_2
\end{aligned}
$$

Thereafter we have to check that *the rewrite system is contained in this equational theory*, more precise, for every rewrite rule of $\mathcal{R}_{perm}$ the left-hand side and the right-hand side have to be equal in the equational theory. By adding two more equations, viz. $k_1(x, xs) = s(xs)$ and $k_2(x, xs) = s(xs)$, this demand is fulfilled. Now terms equal their reduct in the theory. In this particular case, the length of the list is not changed by applying the rewrite rules. Thus, by rewriting a term of the form $append(t_1, t_2)$ we obtain a term t_3 such that $append(t_1, t_2)$ and t_3 are equivalent in the theory.

Since the eventual aim is to automate the technique, it should be stressed that finding these equational theories can in general not be done automatically. In [Art96, AZ95] we show that for a subclass of CSs a kind of standard theories can be given.

In order to check whether $\mathcal{R}$ is contained in an equational theory E, one can perform E-unification. To perform as much as possible automatically, we want to have an effective method for this E-unification. Therefore, we demand that the equational theory can be described by a complete TRS $\mathcal{E}$, such that narrowing suffices to check whether $\mathcal{R}$ is contained in the equational theory. Note that, although many efficient narrowing strategies exist, finding all E-unifiers of a given equation is in general undecidable. We stress that we are only interested in normal E-unifiers (thus all terms are in normal form w.r.t. a rewrite system $\mathcal{E}$ that represents the theory); in the following we will always assume the E-unifiers to be normal. In practice the rewrite system $\mathcal{E}$ will be very uncomplicated and termination and confluence of this rewrite system can therefore be checked automatically. From now on we identify complete rewrite systems and the equational theory that is obtained by replacing the rewrite relations in the rewrite system by equalities.

The TRS $\mathcal{R}_{perm}$ is contained in the following complete TRS $\mathcal{E}$. We are not interested in the *perm* related function symbols and therefore just require that these function symbols equal a constant, 0 say. We add rewrite rules for addition to be able to compute with natural numbers. Thus, $\mathcal{E}$ is given by

$$
\begin{array}{llll}
nil & \rightarrow 0 & perm(xs) & \rightarrow 0 \\
cons(x, xs) & \rightarrow s(xs) & permout(xs) & \rightarrow 0 \\
append(xs_1, xs_2) & \rightarrow xs_1 + xs_2 & k_3(xs) & \rightarrow 0 \\
appout(xs) & \rightarrow xs & k_4(x, xs) & \rightarrow 0 \\
split(xs) & \rightarrow xs & k_5(x, xs) & \rightarrow 0 \\
spout(xs_1, xs_2) & \rightarrow xs_1 + xs_2 & 0 + y & \rightarrow y \\
k_1(x, xs) & \rightarrow s(xs) & s(x) + y & \rightarrow s(x + y) \\
k_2(x, xs) & \rightarrow s(xs) & &
\end{array}
$$

4.2 Chains of dependency pairs

We now abstract from the rewriting itself and concentrate on the possible rewrite rules that are concerned in the reduction of a term.

Definition 8. Let $(\mathcal{D}, \mathcal{C}, \mathcal{R})$ be a CS. If $f(t_1, \ldots, t_m) \rightarrow C[g(s_1, \ldots, s_n)]$ is a rewrite rule of $\mathcal{R}$, $f, g \in \mathcal{D}$, and C is a context then $\langle f(t_1, \ldots, t_m), g(s_1, \ldots, s_n)\rangle$ is called a *dependency pair* (of $\mathcal{R}$).

We say that two dependency pairs $\langle s_1, t_1 \rangle$ and $\langle s_2, t_2 \rangle$ are equivalent, notation $\langle s_1, t_1 \rangle \sim \langle s_2, t_2 \rangle$, if there exists a renaming τ such that $s_1^\tau \equiv s_2$ and $t_1^\tau \equiv t_2$. We are interested in dependency pairs up to equivalence and when useful, we may assume, without loss of generality, that two dependency pairs have disjoint sets of variables. For $\mathcal{R}_{perm}$, we have the following dependency pairs:

(1) $\langle append(cons(x, xs_1), xs_2), k_1(x, append(xs_1, xs_2))\rangle$
(2) $\langle append(cons(x, xs_1), xs_2), append(xs_1, xs_2)\rangle$
(3) $\langle split(cons(x, xs)), k_2(x, split(xs))\rangle$
(4) $\langle split(cons(x, xs)), split(xs)\rangle$
(5) $\langle perm(xs), k_3(split(xs))\rangle$
(6) $\langle perm(xs), split(xs)\rangle$
(7) $\langle k_3(spout(ys_1, cons(y, ys_2))), k_4(y, append(ys_1, ys_2))\rangle$
(8) $\langle k_3(spout(ys_1, cons(y, ys_2))), append(ys_1, ys_2)\rangle$
(9) $\langle k_4(y, appout(zs)), k_5(y, perm(zs))\rangle$
(10) $\langle k_4(y, appout(zs)), perm(zs)\rangle$

We can also define these dependency pairs directly from the logic program, but use this definition because we also need the constructor system $\mathcal{R}_{perm}$ to find the equational theory $\mathcal{E}$.

Definition 9. Let $\mathcal{E}$ be an equational theory, such that $\mathcal{R}$ is contained in $\mathcal{E}$. A sequence (finite or infinite) of dependency pairs is called a *chain* w.r.t. $\mathcal{E}$ if there exists an $\mathcal{E}$-unifier σ such that for all consecutive dependency pairs in the sequence $\langle s_i, t_i \rangle \langle s_{i+1}, t_{i+1} \rangle$

1. the root symbol of t_i equals the root symbol of s_{i+1}, and

2. the arguments of t_i^σ and s_{i+1}^σ are equivalent in $\mathcal{E}$; thus if $t_i = f(u_1, \ldots, u_k)$ and $s_{i+1} = f(v_1, \ldots, v_k)$, then $u_1^\sigma =_\mathcal{E} v_1^\sigma, \ldots, u_k^\sigma =_\mathcal{E} v_k^\sigma$

With Theorem 12 we prove that if there exists an equational theory $\mathcal{E}$ such that $\mathcal{R}$ is contained in $\mathcal{E}$, and no infinite chain w.r.t. $\mathcal{E}$ exists, then termination of the rewrite system is guaranteed. Hence for proving termination of $\mathcal{R}_{perm}$ it remains to show that no infinite chain w.r.t. $\mathcal{E}$, as given above, exists. Referring to the above numbering of dependency pairs, we note that the dependency pairs (1), (3), (6), (8) and (9) cannot occur in an infinite chain. The other dependency pairs (2), (4), (5), (7) and (10) can only occur in infinite chains of the form $(2)(2)(2)\ldots$, $(4)(4)(4)\ldots$, or $\ldots(5)(7)(10)(5)\ldots$. With narrowing we show that the first coordinate of the dependency pairs (2), (4) and (5) all decrease when they appear further on in the chain. In other words, there is a well-founded order $\sqsupset$, such that for all $\mathcal{E}$-unifiers σ of (2)(2), (4)(4) and (5)(7)(10)(5) the first coordinate of the first dependency pair is larger than the first coordinate of the last dependency pair. Therefore, no infinite chain exists. The chain

$$(2)(2) = \langle append(cons(x, xs_1), xs_2), append(xs_1, xs_2) \rangle$$
$$\langle append(cons(y, ys_1), ys_2), append(ys_1, ys_2) \rangle$$

has only $\mathcal{E}$-unifiers that are instances of $\tau = \{xs_1 = s(ys_1), xs_2 = ys_2\}$. (Recall that we only consider normal substitutions w.r.t. $\mathcal{E}$). Thus, $\sqsupset$ has to fulfil

$$s(xs_1) = s(s(ys_1)) \sqsupset s(ys_1) \qquad ys_2 = ys_2$$

The $\mathcal{E}$-unifiers of the chain

$$(5)(7)(10)(5) = \langle perm(xs), k_3(split(xs)) \rangle$$
$$\langle k_3(spout(ys_1, cons(y, ys_2))), k_4(y, append(ys_1, ys_2)) \rangle$$
$$\langle k_4(y, appout(zs)), perm(zs) \rangle$$
$$\langle perm(zs), k_3(split(zs)) \rangle$$

are all instances of $\sigma = \{xs = s(zs)\}$. Thus, $\sqsupset$ also has to fulfil $xs = s(zs) \sqsupset zs$. In the same way, the other chain results in $s(s(ys)) \sqsupset s(ys)$. All demands can be fulfilled by choosing $\sqsupset$ as the embedding order on the normal forms w.r.t. $\mathcal{E}$. Therefore, no infinite chain exists. We now prove that this ensures termination of the TRS $\mathcal{R}_{perm}$ and, by Theorem 7, termination of the logic program of Example 1. This depends on the theory of *semantic labelling*, which we therefore introduce first.

Semantic labelling

Semantic labelling is a technique to transform a TRS [Zan95]. If of a certain TRS, termination has to be proved, then the TRS can be transformed, using semantic labelling, into a TRS that might be easier to prove terminating. The transformation is sound and complete with respect to termination, hence termination of the TRS may be concluded from termination of the transformed TRS.

Since we are mainly interested in constructor systems, we describe semantic labelling in this section restricted to constructor systems. For a complete and more detailed description of the technique we refer to [Zan95]. For the reader who is already familiar with the technique, we remark that we perform a self-labelling on all defined symbols.

Let $\mathcal{R} = (\mathcal{D}, \mathcal{C}, R)$ be a CS, over a signature $\mathcal{F} = \mathcal{D} \cup \mathcal{C}$ and a set $\mathcal{V}$ of variable symbols, of which termination has to be proved. Let $\mathcal{E}$ be an $\mathcal{F}$-algebra consisting of a carrier set M and for every function symbol $f \in \mathcal{F}$ of arity n a function symbol $f_{\mathcal{E}} : M^n \to M$.

Definition 10. The term interpretation $[\![\,]\!]_\rho : \mathcal{T}(\mathcal{F}, \mathcal{V}) \to M$ for a valuation $\rho : \mathcal{V} \to M$ is defined inductively by

$$[\![x]\!]_\rho = \rho(x),$$
$$[\![f(t_1, \ldots, t_n)]\!]_\rho = f_{\mathcal{E}}([\![t_1]\!]_\rho, \ldots, [\![t_n]\!]_\rho)$$

for $x \in \mathcal{V}, f \in \mathcal{F}, t_1, \ldots, t_n \in \mathcal{T}(\mathcal{F}, \mathcal{V})$.

Semantic labelling can be applied to transform the CS $\mathcal{R}$ into a CS $\overline{\mathcal{R}} = (\overline{\mathcal{D}}, \mathcal{C}, \overline{R})$, whenever the following demand is fulfilled (recall that $\mathcal{F} = \mathcal{D} \cup \mathcal{C}$):

There exists an $\mathcal{F}$-algebra $\mathcal{E}$ consisting of a carrier set M and for every function symbol $f \in \mathcal{F}$ of arity n a function symbol $f_{\mathcal{E}} : M^n \to M$, such that $\mathcal{E}$ is a model for $\mathcal{R}$, i.e. $[\![l]\!]_\rho = [\![r]\!]_\rho$ for every rewrite rule $l \to r$ of R and for all valuations ρ.

One of the main difficulties in the technique is to find such a model. If this model $\mathcal{E}$ is given, then the semantic labelling transformation[1] is fixed by

- For every defined symbol $f \in \mathcal{D}$ of arity n we introduce a set of label symbols S_f consisting of all terms of the form $f(t_1, \ldots, t_n)$, where $t_1, \ldots, t_n$ are elements of M.
- A new set of defined symbols is defined by $\overline{\mathcal{D}} = \{f_s | f \in \mathcal{D}, s \in S_f\}$
- A new signature $\overline{\mathcal{F}}$ is defined by $\overline{\mathcal{D}} \cup \mathcal{C}$.

Note that $\overline{\mathcal{F}}$ can be infinite, even if $\mathcal{F}$ is finite. We define a labelling of terms $\text{lab} : \mathcal{T}(\mathcal{F}, \mathcal{V}) \times M^{\mathcal{V}} \to \mathcal{T}(\overline{\mathcal{F}}, \mathcal{V})$ inductively by

$$\text{lab}(x, \rho) = x,$$
$$\text{lab}(f(t_1, \ldots, t_n), \rho) = f_{f([\![t_1]\!]_\rho, \ldots, [\![t_n]\!]_\rho)}(\text{lab}(t_1, \rho), \ldots, \text{lab}(t_n, \rho))$$

for $x \in \mathcal{V}, \rho : \mathcal{V} \to M, f \in \mathcal{F}, t_1, \ldots, t_n \in \mathcal{T}(\mathcal{F}, \mathcal{V})$. We call $f([\![t_1]\!]_\rho, \ldots, [\![t_n]\!]_\rho)$ the label of the term $f(t_1, \ldots, t_n)$. Now $\overline{R}$ is defined to be the TRS over $\overline{\mathcal{F}}$ consisting of the rules $\text{lab}(l, \rho) \to \text{lab}(r, \rho)$ for all $\rho : \mathcal{V} \to M$ and all rules $l \to r$ of R. It is not hard to see that $\overline{R}$ is indeed a constructor system with $\overline{\mathcal{D}}$ as set of defined symbols and $\mathcal{C}$ as set of constructor symbols. The following proposition directly follows from the main result of semantic labelling (for a proof we refer to [Zan95]).

---

[1] We consider a special kind of semantic labelling, the general transformation is more complex and not fixed by a given model.

Proposition 11. *Let $\mathcal{E}$ be a model for a CS $\mathcal{R}$ and let $\overline{\mathcal{R}}$ be defined as above. Then $\mathcal{R}$ is terminating if and only if $\overline{\mathcal{R}}$ is terminating.*

Soundness of the technique

Theorem 12. *Let $(\mathcal{D}, \mathcal{C}, \mathcal{R})$ be a constructor system, and $\mathcal{E}$ a complete TRS such that $\mathcal{R}$ is contained in $\mathcal{E}$. If no infinite chain w.r.t. $\mathcal{E}$ exists, then $\mathcal{R}$ is terminating.*

We construct a labelling on $\mathcal{R}$ such that the elements in the dependency pairs correspond to the labels of the defined symbols of R. Thus, if

$$append(cons(x, xs_1), xs_2) \to k_1(x, append(xs_1, xs_2))$$

is a rewrite rule of $\mathcal{R}$ and $\mathcal{E}$ as given in 4.1 defines the model, then this rewrite rule is transformed by semantic labelling in all rewrite rules of the form

$$append_{append(s(m_1), m_2)}(cons(x, xs_1), xs_2) \to$$
$$k_{1,k_1(m, m_1+m_2)}(x, append_{append(m_1, m_2)}(xs_1, xs_2))$$

with $m, m_1, m_2 \in M$. The dependency pairs with the arguments interpreted in the equational theory, correspond to the labels of this rule

(1) $\langle append(s(m_1), m_2), k_1(m, m_1 + m_2) \rangle$
(2) $\langle append(s(m_1), m_2), append(m_1, m_2) \rangle$

The main observation is that if a term of the form $append_l(\ldots)$, where l is a label, has to be reduced, then it has to be reduced by a rewrite rule which exactly matches this label, i.e. a rewrite rule of the form $append_l(t) \to \ldots$.

Proof. We define an algebra $\mathcal{A}$ to consist of a carrier set $\mathcal{T}(\mathcal{F})$ and for every f in $\mathcal{D} \cup \mathcal{C}$ the interpretation $f_{\mathcal{A}}(x_1, \ldots, x_n) = f(x_1, \ldots, x_n) \!\downarrow_{\mathcal{E}}$. Since $\mathcal{E}$ is complete, this is well defined. By the semantic labelling, the transformed CS $\overline{\mathcal{R}}$ is hereby fixed. We will prove that the labelled constructor system $\overline{\mathcal{R}}$ is terminating. Hence by Proposition 11, $\mathcal{R}$ is terminating.

Define a relation $\rightsquigarrow$ on defined symbols, i.e. elements of $\overline{\mathcal{D}}$, of the labelled CS $\overline{\mathcal{R}}$ as follows: $f_l \rightsquigarrow g_m$ if $f_l(t_1, \ldots, t_n) \to C[g_m(s_1, \ldots, s_k)]$ is a rewrite rule of the labelled CS. With this relation a precedence $\triangleright$ is defined as the transitive closure of $\rightsquigarrow$ together with $\overline{\mathcal{D}} \triangleright \mathcal{C}$ (i.e. all constructor symbols are smaller than a defined symbol). If the precedence $\triangleright$ is well-founded, then termination of $\overline{\mathcal{R}}$ is proved by Proposition 6, since in that case the root symbol of the left-hand side of a rule is always larger than all symbols in the right-hand side of that rule. Hence, it suffices to prove well-foundedness of $\triangleright$. Assume $\triangleright$ is not well-founded, then there is an infinite sequence $d_{1, l_1} \rightsquigarrow d_{2, l_2} \rightsquigarrow d_{3, l_3} \rightsquigarrow \ldots$ of labelled defined symbols. Note that $d_{1, l_1} \rightsquigarrow d_{2, l_2}$ means that there is a rewrite rule in $\overline{\mathcal{R}}$ of the form $d_{1, l_1}(t_1) \to C[d_{2, l_2}(s_1)]$ and a ground substitution ρ such that $l_1 = d_1([t_1]_\rho)$ and $l_2 = d_2([s_1]_\rho)$. Thus,

- for every $d_{i,l_i} \leadsto d_{i+1,l_{i+1}}$ there is a rewrite rule in $\mathcal{R}$ of the form $d_i(t_i) \to C[d_{i+1}(s_i)]$ that defines a dependency pair $\langle d_i(t_i), d_{i+1}(s_i) \rangle$, and
- there exist ground substitutions ρ_i such that $l_i = d_i([\![t_i]\!]_{\rho_i})$ and $l_{i+1} = d_{i+1}([\![s_i]\!]_{\rho_i})$.

Hence there exist an infinite sequence of dependency pairs

$$\langle d_1(t_1), d_2(s_1) \rangle \langle d_2(t_2), d_3(s_2) \rangle \langle d_3(t_3), d_4(s_3) \rangle \cdots$$

together with an infinite sequence of ground substitutions $\rho_1, \rho_2, \rho_3, \ldots$, such that

$$l_1 = d_1([\![t_1]\!]_{\rho_1})$$
$$d_2([\![s_1]\!]_{\rho_1}) = l_2 = d_2([\![t_2]\!]_{\rho_2})$$
$$d_3([\![s_2]\!]_{\rho_2}) = l_3 = d_3([\![t_3]\!]_{\rho_3})$$
$$\vdots$$

Note also that all dependency pairs can be chosen in such a way that the variables of each pair are disjoint. Thus, there exists one infinite substitution $\rho = \rho_1 \circ \rho_2 \circ \rho_3 \circ \ldots$, which is a unifier that unifies all connected dependency pairs, hence

$$s_1{}^\rho =_\varepsilon t_2{}^\rho, s_2{}^\rho =_\varepsilon t_3{}^\rho, \ldots$$

Thus the infinite sequence of dependency pairs is an infinite chain. This contradicts the assumption that no infinite chain exists, hence $\triangleright$ is a well-founded order and therefore $\mathcal{R}$ is terminating. $\qquad\square$

5 Conclusions

The technique as described above, following the example rewrite system $\mathcal{R}_{perm}$, can be summarised as follows

1. Find a complete term rewrite system $\mathcal{E}$ such that $\mathcal{R}$ is contained in $\mathcal{E}$.
2. Compose all dependency pairs.
3. Form all chains, find all most general $\mathcal{E}$-unifiers of these chains.
4. Every most general $\mathcal{E}$-unifier σ for a chain $\langle s_1, t_1 \rangle \ldots \langle s'_1, t'_1 \rangle \ldots$ w.r.t. $\mathcal{E}$ determines a requirement $s_1^\sigma \sqsupseteq s'_1{}^\sigma$. Form a list of these requirements on the order $\sqsupseteq$.
5. Find a well-founded order, closed under substitution, that satisfies these requirements.

Example 5. In practise, finding the well-founded order demanded by the last step of the technique is equal to proving termination of a (different) TRS. Consider the following well-moded logic program, which termination proof is considered to be a hard problem for the existing techniques.

$right(tree(x, xs_1, xs_2), xs_2)$
$flat(niltree, nil)$
$flat(tree(x, niltree, xs), cons(x, ys)) \leftarrow right(tree(x, niltree, xs), zs),$
$\qquad\qquad\qquad\qquad\qquad\qquad flat(zs, ys)$
$flat(tree(x, tree(y, ys_1, ys_2), xs), zs) \leftarrow flat(tree(y, ys_1, tree(x, ys_2, xs)), zs)$

with modes $right(in, in, out)$ and $flat(in, out)$. Transforming this logic program into a constructor system results in

$$
\begin{aligned}
right(tree(x, xs_1, xs_2)) &\rightarrow rightout(xs_2) \\
flat(niltree) &\rightarrow flatout(nil) \\
flat(tree(x, niltree, xs)) &\rightarrow k_1(x, right(tree(x, niltree, xs))) \\
k_1(x, rightout(zs)) &\rightarrow k_2(x, flat(zs)) \\
k_2(x, flatout(ys)) &\rightarrow flatout(cons(x, ys)) \\
flat(tree(x, tree(y, ys_1, ys_2), xs)) &\rightarrow k_3(flat(tree(y, ys_1, tree(x, ys_2, xs)))) \\
k_3(flatout(zs)) &\rightarrow flatout(zs)
\end{aligned}
$$

This constructor system is not simply terminating and therefore termination of it cannot be proved by the standard techniques based on simplification orders. The technique with chains of dependency pairs succeeds in automatically proving termination of this CS. A complete TRS $\mathcal{E}$, in which this CS is contained, is automatically constructed using the heuristics as described in [Art96].

$$
\begin{aligned}
right(tree(x, xs_1, xs_2)) &\rightarrow rightout(xs_2) \\
flat(x) &\rightarrow C \\
flatout(x) &\rightarrow C \\
k_1(x, y) &\rightarrow C \\
k_2(x) &\rightarrow C
\end{aligned}
$$

The dependency pairs of the CS that are on a cycle are

$$
\begin{aligned}
&\langle flat(tree(x, niltree, xs)), k_1(x, right(tree(x, niltree, xs))) \rangle \\
&\langle k_1(x, rightout(zs)), flat(zs) \rangle \\
&\langle flat(tree(x, tree(y, ys_1, ys_2), xs)), flat(tree(y, ys_1, tree(x, ys_2, xs))) \rangle
\end{aligned}
$$

The $\mathcal{E}$-unifier for the first two dependency pairs demands $xs = zs$. Hence, the demands for the order $\sqsupseteq$ are

$$
\begin{aligned}
tree(x, niltree, xs) &\sqsupseteq xs \\
tree(x, tree(y, ys_1, ys_2), xs) &\sqsupseteq tree(y, ys_1, tree(x, ys_2, xs))
\end{aligned}
$$

If we are able to prove that the rewrite system

$$
\begin{aligned}
tree(x, niltree, xs) &\rightarrow xs \\
tree(x, tree(y, ys_1, ys_2), xs) &\rightarrow tree(y, ys_1, tree(x, ys_2, xs))
\end{aligned}
$$

is terminating, then $\sqsupseteq$ is a well-founded order, closed under substitution. Hence, no infinite chain of dependency pairs exists. Termination of the latter rewrite system can automatically be proved by existing standard techniques.

The presented new technique for proving termination of constructor systems is in particular suitable for those constructor systems that are obtained from the translation of logic programs. Since many parts of the technique can be automated, an implementation is in progress. Although many improvements can be carried out on the implementation part, we are now able to prove termination automatically of constructor systems that cannot be proved terminating automatically with existing standard methods and are therefore able to prove termination of some difficult logic programs.

References

[AM93] G. Aguzzi and U. Modigliani. Proving termination of logic programs by transforming them into equivalent term rewriting systems. *Proceedings of FST&TCS 13*, LNCS(761):114–124, December 1993.

[Art96] Thomas Arts. Termination by absence of infinite chains of dependency pairs. In *Proceedings of CAAP'96*, April 1996. Full version appeared as technical report UU-CS-1995-32, Utrecht University.

[AZ94] Thomas Arts and Hans Zantema. Termination of logic programs via labelled term rewrite systems. Technical Report UU-CS-1994-20, Utrecht University.

[AZ95] Thomas Arts and Hans Zantema. Termination of constructor systems using semantic unification. Technical Report UU-CS-1995-17, Utrecht University.

[CR93] Maher Chtourou and Michaël Rusinowitch. Méthode transformationnelle pour la preuve de terminaison des programmes logiques. Unpublished manuscript in French, 1993.

[Der87] N. Dershowitz. Termination of rewriting. *Journal of Symbolic Computation*, 3(1):69–116, 1987.

[DJ90] N. Dershowitz and J.-P. Jouannaud. Rewrite systems. In J. van Leeuwen, editor, *Handbook of Theoretical Computer Science*, volume B, pages 243–320. North-Holland, 1990.

[DM85] P. Dembinski and J. Maluszynski. And-parallelism with intelligent backtracking for annotated logic programs. *Proceedings of the International Symposium on Logic Programming*, pages 29–38, 1985.

[FZ94] Maria Ferreira and Hans Zantema. Syntactical analysis of total termination. *Proceedings of ALP'94*, LNCS(850):204–222, September 1994.

[GW92] Harald Ganzinger and Uwe Waldmann. Termination proofs of well-moded logic programs via conditional rewrite systems. *Proceedings of CTRS*, LNCS(656):430–437, July 1992.

[Han94] M. Hanus. The intergration of functions into logic programming: From theory to practice. *Journal of Logic Programming*, 19-20:583–628, 1994.

[Höl89] S. Hölldobler. *Foundations of Equational Logic Programming*, volume 353 of *LNAI*, 1989. Subseries of LNCS.

[Hul80] J.M. Hullot. Canonical forms and unification. *5th International Conference on Automated Deduction*, LNCS(87):318–334, 1980.

[KKS91] M.R.K. Krishna Rao, Deepak Kapur, and R.K. Shyamasundar. A transformational methodology for proving termination of logic programs. *Proceedings of CSL*, LNCS(626):213–226, 1991.

[Klo92] J.W. Klop. Term rewriting systems. In S. Abramsky, D.M. Gabbay, and T.S.E. Maibaum, editors, *Handbook of Logic in Computer Science*, volume 2, pages 1–116. Oxford University Press, New York, 1992.

[Mar94] Massimo Marchiori. Logic programs as term rewrite systems. *Proceedings of ALP'94*, LNCS(850):223–241, September 1994.

[SD93] Danny de Schreye and Stefaan Decorte. Termination of logic programs: The never-ending story. *Journal of Logic Programming*, 19,20:199-260, 1994.

[Sie89] J.H. Siekmann. Unification theory. *Journal of Symbolic Computation*, 7:207–274, 1989.

[Zan94] H. Zantema. Termination of term rewriting: interpretation and type elimination. *Journal of Symbolic Computation*, 17:23–50, 1994.

[Zan95] H. Zantema. Termination of term rewriting by semantic labelling. *Fundamenta Informaticae*, 24:89–105, 1995.

On the Mechanics of Metasystem Hierarchies in Program Transformation

Robert Glück*

DIKU, Department of Computer Science, University of Copenhagen,
Universitetsparken 1, DK-2100 Copenhagen Ø, Denmark
e-mail: glueck@diku.dk

Abstract. Self-applicable partial evaluators have been used for more than a decade for generating compilers and other program generators, but it seems hard to reason about the mechanics of hierarchies of program transformers and to describe applications that go beyond the 'classical' Futamura projections. This paper identifies and clarifies foundational issues involved in multi-level metasystem hierarchies. After studying the role of abstraction, encoding, and metasystem transition, the Futamura projections are reexamined and problems of their practical realization are discussed. Finally, preliminary results using a multi-level metaprogramming environment for self-application are reported. Connections between logic programming and metacomputation are made.

Keywords: program transformation, metacomputation, metasystem transition, self-application, program inversion, program specialization.

1 Introduction

Metasystem hierarchies have been used for more than a decade to generate compilers and other program generators. The best known example are the Futamura projections [8] which were the driving force behind the initial work on self-application of partial evaluators. This work identified binding-time analysis as a useful tool for attacking the fundamental problem of tracking unknown values and taming self-application [17]. Binding-time analysis and the mix-equations, a well-known formalization of the Futamura projections, have been useful tools for reasoning about the results of self-application [16].

On the other hand, more powerful specialization methods, such as supercompilation [25] or partial deduction [19], have not yet given satisfactory results for all three Futamura projections. It seems hard to reason about the mechanics of hierarchies of program transformers and to describe applications that go beyond the 'classical' Futamura projections, such as multiple self-application [9] or the specializer projections [10]. Indeed, they are just a special case of the more general principle of metasystem transition [23].

---

* Partially supported by an Erwin-Schrödinger-Fellowship of the Austrian Science Foundation (FWF) under grant J0780 & J0964 and by the DART project funded by the Danish Natural Sciences Research Council.

More generally, the field of metaprogramming is in need of an adequate formalism which can be used to formalize operations on programs in a uniform and language independent way. The lack of an adequate formalism has led to difficulties in describing, implementing and comparing metaprograms (*cf.* [14, 13, 18, 20, 5]). An 'interdisciplinary' approach, regardless of a particular language or transformation paradigm, may possibly generate new insights and developments. We argue that a clear understanding of the role of abstraction, encoding, and metasystem transition is necessary to achieve further progress in this direction. The intention of this paper is to establish a solid semantic foundation for hierarchies of metasystems and to achieve full formalization and clarity with minimal means.

We refer to any process of simulating, analyzing or transforming programs by means of programs as *metacomputation* ("programs as data objects"), a term that stresses the fact that this activity is one level higher than ordinary computation. Program specialization, composition, and inversion are examples of metacomputation; programs that carry out these tasks, are *metaprograms*. The step from a program to the application of a metaprogram to the encoded form of the program is a *metasystem transition* and repeated use of metasystem transition leads to a multi-level *metasystem hierarchy*.

$$\frac{metaprogram}{program} \qquad \frac{metacomputation}{computation}$$

The concepts and notations presented in this paper are clearly applicable to any semantics paradigm. Different operations over programs have been described using this formalism [12], with the results that they are seen to have deep similarities. On a more practical level, the insights obtained from using this formalism led to the development of a partial evaluator based on a multi-level metaprogramming environment. Moreover, connections between logic and functional languages can be made that allow to explain certain problems occurring in multi-level metasystem hierarchies in a consistent way. The formalization established here is based upon the ideas of Turchin [23, 24, 25, 27] and motivated by our work on self-application and metasystem transition [9, 10, 11, 12].

The outline of the paper is as follows. After developing a language for multi-level metasystem hierarchies (Section 2), we reexamine the mix-equations (Section 3) and discuss problems of their practical realization (Section 4). Finally, we report on preliminary results using a multi-level metaprogramming environment for self-application (Section 5). We assume that the reader is familiar with the basic concepts of self-application and partial evaluation, *e.g.* as presented in [16], Chapter II.

2 Metasystem Hierarchies Revisited

We shall start from first principles to make our discourse as clear and systematic as possible. We develop step-by-step three languages: an application language A, a metacomputation language B, and a metasystem transition language C. We study the role of abstraction and encoding, and redefine the Futamura projections using our formalism. Connections between logic programming and metacomputation are made as we develop the concepts. Certain features of the meta-notation in which the paper is written are explicitly marked as *Convention*: they are not part of the defined languages.

2.1 Computation

Programs and Data. We assume a fixed set of first-order *data* D to represent programs written in different languages, as well as their input and output. A suitable choice of D is the set of list data as defined by the grammar

$$D ::= K \mid [D^*]$$

where K is a set of constants (including numbers) and D^* a sequence of D-expressions. We use `typewriter` font for elements of D and enclose constants in quotes ' '; omitted for numbers. For instance, `['A' [1 2]]` is a list of two elements whose last element is also a list. Alternatively, we could have chosen symbol strings, constructor terms, or something else.

Convention. Capitalized names in `typewriter` font denote arbitrary elements of D, *e.g.* `DAT` $\in D$. They are free variables of the meta-notation. We use the same font both for concrete data and for variables denoting data to minimize notation.

Application. To express the application of programs to data we define an *application language* A by the grammar

$$A ::= K \mid [A^*] \mid <A\ A^*>$$

where the symbols $<, > \notin D$ denote the application of a program to its input. For instance, the intended meaning of the A-expression `<PGM X Y>` is the application of program `PGM` $\in D$ to the input `X, Y` $\in D$ (note that $D \subseteq A$).

We are not interested in a specific programming language for writing programs; there can be several versions of the application in the A-language, *e.g.* $<\ >_L, <\ >_S, <\ >_T$ using subscripts to indicate the programming language.

Example 1. Application in a logic language corresponds to a query with ground terms and the answer is '`Yes`' or '`No`'. In the concrete syntax of a logic language the application of `APPEND` to three ground terms is written as

$$\leftarrow \text{APPEND}([1\ 2], [3], [1\ 2\ 3])$$

and as an A-expression one would write

$$\text{<APPEND [1 2] [3] [1 2 3]>}$$

Computation. For every language L there is a computation mechanism that reduces A-expressions involving $<\ >_L$. We write

$$a \Rightarrow D$$

to denote the *computation* (reduction) of an expression $a \in A$ to $D \in D$. For instance, `<PGM X Y>` $\Rightarrow$ `OUT` is the computation of program `PGM` $\in D$ with input `X, Y` $\in D$ and output `OUT` $\in D$. The relation is undefined when a program goes into an infinite loop. Nested applications are reduced with a leftmost-innermost strategy. Computation of $D \in D$ is the trivial identity: `D` $\Rightarrow$ `D`.

Definition 1 (computational equivalence). Two A-expressions $a, b \in A$ are *computationally equivalent* if they can be reduced to identical D-expressions:

$$a = b \ \textit{iff} \ \forall \text{X} \in D : (a \Rightarrow \text{X} \ \textit{iff} \ b \Rightarrow \text{X})$$

2.2 Metacomputation

Abstraction. To represent sets of A-expressions, we define a *metacomputation language* B by the grammar

$$B ::= K \mid M \mid [B^*] \mid <B\ B^*>$$

where M is a set of metavariables. A *metavariable* $\mathtt{m} \in M$, $M \cap A = \emptyset$, is a placeholder that stands for an unspecified data element $\mathtt{D} \in D$. We use lowercase names in **typewriter** font to write elements of M, e.g. metavariable $\mathtt{dat} \in M$.

A B-expression b is an abstraction that represents the set of all A-expressions obtained by replacing metavariables $\mathtt{m} \in M$ by elements of D. We write $a \in b$ to denote that $a \in A$ is an element of the set represented by $b \in B$. We refer to a B-expression also as a *configuration*.

Example 2. The following B-expression represents a set of A-expressions:

`<APPEND [1 2] y    z>`	*abstraction*
`<APPEND [1 2] []   [1 2]>`	*concretization*
`<APPEND [1 2] [3]  [7 6 5]>`	
`...`	

An expression $b \in B$ is *ground* if it does not include metavariables; *non-ground* otherwise (hence, all expressions $a \in A$ are ground). An expression $b \in B$ is *passive* if it does not include an application `<>`; *active* otherwise. A passive, ground expression is a *data* expression.

Encoding. Expressions in the metacomputation language need to be represented as data in order to manipulate them by means of programs (ordinary computation cannot reduce B-expressions because metavariables are not in A). A *metacoding* [24] is an injective mapping $B \rightarrow D$ to encode B-expressions in D. The inverse mapping, a partial function, is called *demetacoding*. A metacoding in metacomputation corresponds to a Gödel numeration in logics where statements about a theory are encoded in the theory itself.

Convention. We write a horizontal line above an expression, $\bar{b}$, to denote the result of metacoding b. Repeated metacoding is well-defined because $D \subseteq B$ and we write $\bar{b}^n$ to denote the result of metacoding b n-times ($n \geq 0$).

Once an expression $b \in B$ is metacoded we have $\bar{b} \in D$ and, consequently, further metacoding is reduced to a mapping $D \rightarrow D$. We define $\mathtt{DN} \in D$ to be a program ('down') that computes the $\mathtt{N}$-th metacode for all $\mathtt{D} \in D$:

$$<\mathtt{DN\ N\ D}> \Rightarrow \bar{\mathtt{D}}^{\mathtt{N}}$$

We are not interested in a specific way of metacoding, but assume, for notational convenience, that metacoding is homomorphic with respect to the composition of expressions: $\overline{\circ(b_1 \ldots b_n)} = \star(\bar{b}_1 \ldots \bar{b}_n)$ where $\circ$ builds a B-expression with $b_1 \ldots b_n \in B$, and $\star$ a D-expression with their metacode $\bar{b}_1 \ldots \bar{b}_n \in D$. There is one $\circ$ for each way a B-expression can be built (`[]`, `<>`), and $\star$ is derived from $\circ$. We use this property to replace metacoded subexpressions by arbitrary expressions and take the liberty to interrupt the horizontal line above the enclosing operator $\circ$. For instance, if we replace $\bar{b}_1$ by b_0 in $\overline{\circ(b_1, b_2)} = \star(\bar{b}_1, \bar{b}_2)$, we write $\overline{\circ(}b_0, \bar{b}_2) = \star(b_0, \bar{b}_2)$.

Example 3. A straightforward metacode for B-expressions can be defined as

Expression	b	$\overline{b}$
Constant	k	$[\text{'K'}\ k]$
Metavariable	m	$[\text{'M'}\ \text{'m'}]$
List	$[b_1 \ldots b_n]$	$[\text{'L'}\ \overline{b_1} \ldots \overline{b_n}]$
Application	$\langle b_1 \ldots b_n \rangle$	$[\text{'A'}\ \overline{b_1} \ldots \overline{b_n}]$

where each syntactic entity is represented by a tagged list. We assume a unique naming relation that associates $m \in M$ with its image $\text{'m'} \in D$. With this metacode, any B-expression can be encoded as data. As example, consider the metacode of the B-expression (the metacode of program APPEND is not expanded):

$$\overline{\langle \text{APPEND}\ [1\ 2]\ y\ z\rangle} =$$
$$[\text{'A'}\ \overline{\text{APPEND}}\ [\text{'L'}\ [\text{'K'}\ 1]\ [\text{'K'}\ 2]]\ [\text{'M'}\ \text{'y'}]\ [\text{'M'}\ \text{'z'}]]$$

This metacoding enjoys the convenient property of being homomorphic. For instance, let the composition operators be $\circ = [\ldots]$ and $\star = [\text{'L'}\ \ldots]$, then

$$\overline{[1\ 2]} = [\text{'L'}\ [\text{'K'}\ 1]\ [\text{'K'}\ 2]] = [\text{'L'}\ \overline{1}\ \overline{2}]$$

To avoid writing concrete metacode when we replace a metacoded subexpression, *e.g.* $\overline{1}$ by 1, we interrupt the horizontal line above the enclosing syntactic entity:

$$\overline{[1\ \overline{2}]} = [\text{'L'}\ 1\ [\text{'K'}\ 2]] = [\text{'L'}\ 1\ \overline{2}]$$

Metacomputation. We refer to any process of simulating, analyzing or transforming programs by means of programs as *metacomputation*, a term that stresses the fact that this activity is one level higher than ordinary computation. We shall use this term in a general way, independent of a specific transformation paradigm. It follows from our notation that

$$\langle \text{MC}\ \overline{b}\rangle \Rightarrow D$$

denotes metacomputation on an expression $b \in B$ using a metaprogram $\text{MC} \in D$. The application of MC to the metacoded B-expression is an A-expression that can be reduced by ordinary computation (metacomputation is a certain class of computation). We should stress that this characterization of metacomputation says nothing about its concrete nature, excepts that it involves a metaprogram MC that operates on a metacoded configuration $\overline{b}$. Different metaprograms may perform different operations on a configuration, such as program specialization, program inversion, or program composition. Metacoding can be avoided in some cases, *e.g.* for source program $\text{PGM} \in D$ of a compiler.

Program inversion. The formulation of *interpretive inversion* is as follows. Let EQ be a program that tests the equality of two data elements. Given X, Z find an Y such that

$$\langle \text{EQ}\ \langle \text{PGM}\ X\ Y\rangle\ Z\rangle \Rightarrow \text{'True'}$$

In logic programming, one defines a predicate by a program PGM and solves the inversion problem for $Z = \text{'Yes'}$. We define an inverting interpreter SOLVE for this class of inversion problems. Let S and M be programming languages.

Definition 2 (inverting interpreter). An M-program **SOLVE** $\in D$ is an *inverting interpreter* if for every S-program **PGM** $\in D$ injective in its second argument, every input **X** $\in D$ and metavariable **y** $\in M$, there exists **Y** $\in D$ such that

$$\text{<SOLVE } \overline{\text{<PGM X y>}_S}\text{>}_M \Rightarrow \text{Y} \quad \text{and} \quad \text{<PGM X Y>}_S \Rightarrow \text{'Yes'}$$

Program **PGM** is injective in its second argument if for all **X, Y1, Y2** $\in D$: **<PGM X Y1>** = **<PGM X Y2>** implies that **Y1** and **Y2** are the same element of D. In general, when **PGM** is not injective, **SOLVE** must return a list of answers for **y**.[2] Sometimes we use **X1...Xn, y1...ym** instead of **X** and **y**.

Example 4. In the concrete syntax of the logic language Gödel [15] the application of **APPEND** to an unspecified second and third argument is written as

$$\leftarrow \text{APPEND([1 2],y,z)}$$

while in our framework we have to use a metaprogram, namely the inverting interpreter **SOLVE**, which takes the ground representation of the goal as input:

$$\text{<SOLVE } \overline{\text{<APPEND [1 2] y z>>}}$$

There is a close relation between queries in logic programming and *B*-expressions: logic variables play the same role as metavariables in program inversion (note that the latter are defined independently of a particular language or transformation paradigm). In other words, non-ground resolution can be seen as metacomputation. The definition of **PGM** may be perceived as non-procedural with respect to **SOLVE**, but its semantics is still defined in terms of computation. We find it useful to make a clear distinction between computation and metacomputation, and to view logic languages as operating on a metacomputation level, while viewing imperative and functional languages as operating on a computation level [25, 1, 12]. This allows us to clarify foundational issues involved in metasystem hierarchies and to identify general solutions, *e.g.* elevated metavariables (explained later).

Program specialization. We now define program specialization in terms of metacomputation. Let S, T and M be programming languages.

Definition 3 (program specializer). An M-program **SPEC** $\in D$ is an S→T-*specializer* if for every S-program **PGM** $\in D$, every input **X, Y** $\in D$ and metavariable **y** $\in M$, there exists **RES** $\in D$ such that

$$\text{<SPEC } \overline{\text{<PGM X y>}_S}\text{>}_M \Rightarrow \text{RES} \tag{1}$$

$$\text{<PGM X Y>}_S = \text{<RES Y>}_T \tag{2}$$

The last equation defines the correctness of the specializer in terms of computation. In a logic language the correctness is defined in terms of metacomputation, namely with respect to an inverse semantics of S and T:

$$\text{<SOLVE } \overline{\text{<PGM X p>}_S}\text{>}_M = \text{<SOLVE' } \overline{\text{<RES p>}_T}\text{>}_M \tag{3}$$

where $p \in B$ is a passive expression. Line (3) replaces line (2). Note that the formulation of specialization in line (1) is not affected by this change. Variations of the correctness condition can be formulated, *e.g.* whether the order of the answer substitutions is relevant, but we shall not consider this here.

---

[2] There are two types of inversion: either we are interested in an *existential* solution (one of the possible answers), or in a *universal* solution (all possible answers).

2.3   Metasystem Transition

Elevated metavariables. Having introduced the basic concepts of metacomputation, we now consider the use of multi-level metasystem hierarchies. During the construction of multi-level hierachies, we will frequently need to replace metacoded subexpressions by metavariables. The correct treatment of metacode is so essential in self-application [9], that we make elevated metavariables [27] an integral part of the MST-language. We define a *metasystem transition language* C by the grammar

$$C ::= K \mid M_{I\!N} \mid [C^*] \mid <C \; C^*>$$

where $M_{I\!N}$ is a set of elevated metavariables $\mathtt{m_H}$, $\mathtt{H} \in I\!N$. An *elevated metavariable* $\mathtt{m_H}$ ranges over data metacoded $\mathtt{H}$-times. We denote by $D^{\mathtt{H}}$ the set of metacode $\overline{D}^{\mathtt{H}}$ of all $\mathtt{D} \in D$ and write $dom(\mathtt{m_H}) = D^{\mathtt{H}}$ (note that $B \subseteq C$ with $M = M_0$).

A C-expression c is an abstraction that represents the set of all A-expressions obtained by replacing elevated metavariables $\mathtt{m_H}$ by elements of $D^{\mathtt{H}}$. We write $a \in c$ to denote that $a \in A$ is an element of the set represented by $c \in C$.

The terms ground, non-ground, configuration *etc.* carry over to C. Metacoding is easily extended to elevated metavariables, *e.g.* map $\mathtt{m_H}$ to $[\mathtt{'M'} \; \mathtt{'m'} \; \mathtt{H}]$ in Example 3.

Metasystem transition. The construction of each next level in a metasystem hierarchy, referred to as *metasystem transition* (MST) [23], is done in three steps [12]:

  (A) given an initial A-expression a,   ('computation')
  (B) define a C-expression c such that $a \in c$,   ('abstraction')
  (C) apply a metaprogram $\mathtt{MC}$ to the metacode $\overline{c}$.   ('metacomputation')

The expression obtained in the last step is again an A-expression and the same procedure can be repeated until the MST *degenerates* (the procedure comes to a fixed point when, after some MST is performed, no new system is produced [12]). Expressions obtained by MST are called *MST-formulas*. This definition says nothing about the goal of the MST, except that it is an abstraction of an A-expression a to a configuration c, followed by the application of a metaprogram $\mathtt{MC}$ to $\overline{c}$. [3]

Example 5. We now show two consecutive MSTs. Consider the A-expression of Example 1 as initial expression, define a C-expression by replacing the subexpressions $[3], [1 \; 2 \; 3] \in D^0$ by the metavariables $\mathtt{y_0, z_0} \in M_0$, and apply a program specializer $\mathtt{SPEC}$ to the metacoded C-expression. We have performed a transition from a one-level to a two-level metasystem hierarchy: the 1st MST.

  (A0)   `<APPEND [1 2] [3] [1 2 3]>`

  (B0)   `<APPEND [1 2] ` $\mathtt{y_0}$ ` ` $\mathtt{z_0}$ `>`

  (C1)   `<SPEC ` $\overline{\text{`<APPEND [1 2] } \mathtt{y_0} \; \mathtt{z_0}\text{>}}$ `>`

---

[3] Abstraction in the λ-calculus can be viewed as a rudimentary form of MST: steps (A,B), without $\mathtt{MC}$ in step (C). This enabled the development of powerful metaprogramming techniques in functional languages (higher-order programming).

We continue with the next MST. Take the A-expression (C1) as initial expression (A1), define a C-expression by replacing $\overline{\texttt{[1 2]}} \in D^1$ by a metavariable $\mathbf{x_1} \in M_1$, and apply a program specializer $\texttt{SPEC}'$ to its metacode: the 2nd MST. Note that it would be *wrong* to use a metacoded metavariable, *e.g.* $\overline{\mathbf{x_1}}$, instead of $\mathbf{x_1}$ in (B1) because then (A1) would not be an element of (B1) as required by MST-step (B).

$$\text{(A1)} \quad \texttt{<SPEC } \overline{\texttt{<APPEND [1 2] } y_0\ z_0\texttt{>>}}$$

$$\text{(B1)} \quad \texttt{<SPEC } \overline{\texttt{<APPEND } x_1\ y_0\ z_0\texttt{>>}}$$

$$\text{(C2)} \quad \texttt{<SPEC}' \texttt{ <SPEC } \overline{\texttt{<APPEND } x_1\ y_0\ z_0\texttt{>>>}}$$

Example 6. Why is elevation so essential? Assume that we want to define a configuration which describes the specialization of $\texttt{APPEND}$ with respect to its first argument, *i.e.* any $\overline{\texttt{D}} \in D^1$ instead of $\overline{\texttt{[1 2]}}$ in (A1). If we replace $\overline{\texttt{[1 2]}} \in D^1$ by a metavariable $\mathbf{x_0} \in M^0$ with zero elevation, we obtain a C-expression (B1') that does not only represent A-expressions of the intended form, but also expressions of the form (i) that do not specialize $\texttt{APPEND}$, and expressions of the form (ii) that do not include a correct metacode. Recall that a metavariable may be replaced by any element of its domain, *e.g.* $\overline{\mathbf{x_0}}$, $\overline{\texttt{[5]}} \in dom(\mathbf{x_0})$. In other words, we have not expressed what we meant and, hence, we can not expect to get the desired result (the generation of an 'APPEND compiler').

(B1')	$\texttt{<SPEC } \overline{\texttt{<APPEND } x_0}\texttt{ y z>>}$	*abstraction*
(i)	$\texttt{<SPEC } \overline{\texttt{<APPEND } x_0}\texttt{ y z>>}$	*concretization*
(ii)	$\texttt{<SPEC } \overline{\texttt{<APPEND [5]}}\texttt{ y z>>}$	

Finally note that we can always enforce the correct metacode using program $\texttt{DN}$. In fact, instead of using $\texttt{DN}$ we added $\texttt{H}$ as an elevation index to metavariables. In other words, the elevation information can either be expressed by an explicit elevation index, a primitive of the MST-language C, or by an expression involving program $\texttt{DN}$ (alternatively, we can write out parts of the concrete metacode, as shown in [9]). Practically speaking, an elevation index is often easier to handle than program $\texttt{DN}$, *e.g.* when generalizing two configurations during metacomputation.

$$m_H \equiv \texttt{<DN H } m_0\texttt{>}$$

Example 7. Consider a subexpression $\overline{\overline{\texttt{[8]}}}$ in some A-expression: either we replace it by an elevated metavariable m_2, or we demetacode it twice, apply program $\texttt{DN}$ to the result, and replace $\texttt{DN}$'s argument $\overline{\texttt{[8]}}$ by a metavariable m_0. The latter method is correct because

$$\overline{\overline{\texttt{[8]}}} = \texttt{<DN 2 } \overline{\texttt{[8]}}\texttt{>}$$

and we can chose any of the two expressions as initial expression for MST:

$$\text{(A)} \quad \ldots\ \overline{\overline{\texttt{[8]}}}\ \ldots \qquad \ldots \texttt{<DN 2 } \overline{\texttt{[8]}}\texttt{>}\ \ldots$$

$$\text{(B)} \quad \ldots m_2 \ldots \qquad \ldots \texttt{<DN 2 } \overline{m_0}\texttt{>}\ \ldots$$

$$\text{(C)} \quad \ldots \overline{m_2} \ldots \qquad \ldots \overline{\texttt{<DN 2 } m_0\texttt{>}}\ \ldots$$

2.4 Futamura Projections as MST

The *Futamura projections* (FMP) [8] are, in all probability, the first example of program transformation beyond a single metasystem level. Here we focus on their formalization as MST-formulas. We assume that the reader is familiar with the FMPs as we will not justify their interpretation here. Given a program specializer SPEC the FMPs define compilation, compiler generation, and compiler-generator generation for every $INT, PGM, DAT \in D$ and every $int_2, pgm_1, dat_0 \in M_{IN}$ where INT is an interpreter, PGM a program, and DAT its input data.

Definition 4 (interpreter). An M-program INT is an S-*interpreter* if for every S-program $PGM \in D$ and every $DAT \in D$ [4]

$$<PGM\ DAT>_S = <INT\ PGM\ DAT>_M$$

We speak of *self-application* if all program specializers are identical. In general, self-application of a program specializer SPEC requires $M \subseteq S$. For simplicity we assume that $S = T = M$; for multi-language specialization see [10].

(A0) `<INT PGM DAT> ⇒ OUT`	(computation)
(B0) `<INT PGM dat_0>`	(abstraction)
....	
(A1) `<SPEC' <INT PGM dat_0>> ⇒ TARGET`	(1st FMP)
(B1) `<SPEC' <INT pgm_1 dat_0>>`	(abstraction)
....	
(A2) `<SPEC'' <SPEC' <INT pgm_1 dat_0>>> ⇒ COMP`	(2nd FMP)
(B2) `<SPEC'' <SPEC' <int_2 pgm_1 dat_0>>>`	(abstraction)
....	
(A3) `<SPEC''' <SPEC'' <SPEC' <int_2 pgm_1 dat_0>>>> ⇒ COGEN`	(3rd FMP)

The initial expression is an A-expression (A0) that interprets a program $PGM \in D$ and its input $DAT \in D$ by means of an interpreter $INT \in D$.

1st FMP Define a C-expression (B0) by replacing DAT by dat_0 (elevation zero) in the A-expression (A0), and apply SPEC' to the metacoded C-expression (A1): the result is a compiled program TARGET (A1).

2nd FMP Define a C-expression (B1) by replacing $\overline{PGM}$ by pgm_1 (elevation one) in the 1st FMP (A1), and apply SPEC'' to the metacoded C-expression: the result is a compiler COMP (A2).

3rd FMP Define a C-expression (B2) by replacing $\overline{\overline{INT}}$ by int_2 (elevation two) in the 2nd FMP (A2), and apply SPEC''' to the metacoded C-expression: the result is a compiler generator COGEN (A3).

With Definition 3 we obtain the equations:

$$<TARGET\ DAT> = OUT, \quad <COMP\ PGM> = TARGET, \quad <COGEN\ DAT> = COMP$$

---

[4] Interpretation is an instance of metacomputation: $<PGM\ DAT>_S = <INT\ \overline{<PGM\ DAT>_S}>_M$. However, by definition an interpreter is only applied to non-nested, ground A-expressions which motivates and justifies the above, simplified definition.

Example 8. Make a thought experiment with (B1) to see why elevation and meta-coding are so essential in the FMPs: decrease the elevation of pgm_1 to pgm_0 and replace $\overline{dat_0}$ by a metavariable dat_0. We obtain a new configuration (B1″) and apply **SPEC″** to its metacode (A2″). The modification is correct because $(A1) \in (B1'')$ as required by MST-step (B).

$$(A2'') \quad \texttt{<SPEC'' <SPEC' } \overline{\texttt{<INT } pgm_0 \ dat_0\texttt{>}}\texttt{>>} \Rightarrow \texttt{CRAZY}$$

However, the new MST-formula (A2″) does *not* specify the generation of a compiler **COMP** as the 2nd FMP (A2), but of a program, called **CRAZY** in [16], Sect. 7. The generated 'compiler' is much more general than necessary. To see this, take (B1″) and replace pgm_0 by $x_0 \in dom(pgm_0)$, and dat_0 by $\overline{DAT} \in dom(dat_0)$: we obtain an *A*-expression which specializes **INT** when given data, but not the source program.

$$(A1'') \quad \texttt{<SPEC' } \overline{\texttt{<INT } x_0 \ DAT\texttt{>}}\texttt{>} \Rightarrow \texttt{CRAZYTARGET}$$

Two-dimensional notation. A hierarchy of metasystems can be visualized using a *2-dimensional notation*: (i) an expression is moved down one line down for each metacoding; (ii) the elevation of a metavariable m_H is shown by a bullet • located H lines below the metavariable (and we omit its elevation index). Such an MST-formula is also called an *MST-scheme*. This notation was introduced by Turchin; in a published form it appeared first in [9].

Example 9. The 3rd FMP (A3) shows the expressive power of the two-dimensional notation: the metasystem levels to which metavariables belong can be seen immediatley.

```
<SPEC'''_____> ⇒ COGEN
       <SPEC''_____ int _____>
             <SPEC'_  |  pgm ____>
                   <  •   •  dat>
```

Example 10. Assume that we split the input of a program into two components and replace each by a metavariable. As illustrated below, we have three possibilities in the next MST: (a) both metavariables are metacoded (the input is treated as unspecified on the lower level), (b) both metavariables are elevated (the input is treated as specified on the lower level), (c) a combination of the two cases (the input is treated as partly specified/unspecified on the lower level). The FMPs make use case (a), the specializer projections [10] make use of case (c). In the context of a logic language, case (c) can be used to express the situation where the input of a program will either be a ground term or a logic variable (one could also introduce different metavariable types for the same purpose as in [18]).

```
(a) ____ ____        (b) dat1 dat2       (c) dat1 ____
    dat1 dat2             •    •              •    dat2
```

Larger perspectives. The application of metasystem hierarchies in program transformation is not limited to the three Futamura projections. Program specialization is one possibility. What a program on the level $n + 1$ does with a program on the level n may vary: it can be program inversion, program composition, or another program transformation, or a combination of transformers. Several interesting applications have been identified, *e.g.* [25, 1, 12].

3   The Mix-Equations Reexamined

In this section we establish the relation between the MST-formulas and the *mix-equations* [17, 16], the 'classical' formalization of the Futamura projections. We identify the corresponding metacomputation language and show that it imposes certain limitations on the formalism. Elevation is present, but implicit in the concrete metacoding.

Mix application language. Define subset B' of language B as

$$B' ::= <D \ \{D \mid M\}^*>$$

and require that no metavariable $m \in M$ occurs more than once in a B'-expression (this is rather restrictive because repeated metavariables are essential in supercompilation or partial deduction, *e.g.* in unification). Note that B' does not provide nested applications either; necessary to express program composition.

Mix metacode. Define a metacoding that accumulates the metacode of a B'-expression in two separate lists: a list of tags ('S/D-classification') and a list of data ('static input'). The metacode of $<>$ can be omitted since every B'-expression includes exactly one application. Virtually all mix-style partial evaluators use this metacode where data is marked as *static* (known) and a metavariable as *dynamic* (unknown). We shall write 'SD' as shorthand for ['S' 'D'], *etc.*

Expression	b	tag	val
Data	d	'S'	d
Metavariable	m	'D'	–

Definition 5 (mix partial evaluator). [5] An M-program MIX $\in D$ is an S→T-*mix partial evaluator* if for every S-program PGM $\in D$, every X, Y $\in D$ and S/D-classification 'SD' $\in D$, there exists RES $\in D$ such that

$$\text{<MIX PGM 'SD' [X]>}_M \Rightarrow \text{RES}$$

$$\text{<PGM X Y>}_S = \text{<RES Y>}_T$$

Mix-equations. We assume S = T = M for the source-, target- and metalanguage, and let MIX' = MIX'' = MIX''' for self-application.

- The 1st FMP defines the specialization of an interpreter using MIX'. This amounts to compilation. The first argument of INT is data PGM while the second argument is a metavariable. Thus the S/D-classification is 'SD'.

$$\text{<MIX' INT 'SD' [PGM]>} \Rightarrow \text{TARGET}$$

- The 2nd FMP defines the specialization of MIX' by MIX''. The result is a compiler COMP. The first argument of MIX' is data INT, the second argument is data 'SD' and the third argument becomes a metavariable. Thus the S/D-classification is 'SSD'.

$$\text{<MIX'' MIX' 'SSD' [INT 'SD']>} \Rightarrow \text{COMP}$$

---

[5] Compare with Definition 3.

– The 3rd FMP defines the specialization of MIX″ with respect to MIX′ using MIX‴. The result is a compiler generator COGEN. The first argument of MIX″ is data MIX′, the second argument is data 'SSD' and the third argument becomes a metavariable. Thus the S/D-classification is 'SD'. Note that INT and the SD-classification 'SSD' become dynamic (COGEN expects a program INT and its S/D-classification as input).

$$\text{<MIX‴ MIX″ 'SSD' [MIX′ 'SSD']>} \Rightarrow \text{COGEN}$$

Binding-time analysis. The mix-equations suggest that tags and data can be manipulated independently. Indeed, offline partial evaluation approximates the flow of metacode tags in a preprocessing phase, called *binding-time analysis* and annotates all operations in a source program with 'SD'-tags (depending on whether they will operate on data D or metavariables M). This separation of the specialization process granted the first successful self-application of a partial evaluator [17] as it ensured the proper flow of metacode tags in self-application. An *offline* partial evaluator MIX is defined as a two-stage process

    (i)   <BTA PGM 'SD'> ⇒ PGMSD

    (ii)   <SP PGMSD X>   ⇒ RES

The main problem in self-application is to reduce as many operations on metacode tags as possible. We can distinguish between two extreme cases: (i) all operations on metacode tags can be computed at transformation time (as in offline partial evaluation), or (ii) all metacode operations are delayed until runtime of the generated program. Case (i) led to the 'mix criterion' requiring that successful self-application must be able to remove all operations on metacode tags (more precisely, in the 2nd FMP).

Conclusion. Two approximations limit the power of offline mix partial evaluation: (i) the restriction in the metacomputation language B' (no repeated metavariables), and (ii) the binding-time analysis (approximates the flow of tags independently of data). While granting the first successful self-application, these two approximations impose fundamental limitations on the method: offline partial evaluation is strictly weaker than partial deduction and supercompilation, two *online* methods that make use of the full metacomputation language.

    The mix-equations *do* involve (a specific way of) metacoding. Elevation is present, but hidden in the concrete metacoding (via a combination of static/dynamic tags). The mix-equations are frequently abbreviated, *e.g.* the 3rd FMP to <MIX‴ MIX″ MIX′>, which makes it impossible to define other MST-formulas, such as the specializer projections. The formalism presented in Section 2 takes the opposite approach: all underlying assumptions are made explicit.

4   Constructive Problems of Metasystem Hierarchies

We discuss four categories of problems involved in metasystem hierarchies and conclude each with a summary of solutions known for program specialization. We distinguish between two constructive problems (*computation time, space consumption*), and the time at which these problems occur (*transformation time, generator time*). For instance, in the 2nd FMP the transformation time is the 'compiler generation time', and the generator time is the 'compilation time'.

Transformation time.

1. **Computation time.** The run time of the transformation is affected by (i) the height of the metasystem hierarchy and (ii) the actual transformations (and analyses) performed at each level. Generally speaking: the higher the hierarchy and the more sophisticated the transformations at each level, the slower the overall transformation. Assume that t is the run-time of a program p, then $t * k^n$ is the time required to run p on a tower of n self-interpreters where k is the factor of their interpretive overhead. Since most non-trivial, self-applicable specializers incorporate a self-interpreter for evaluating static expressions, the run-time of multiple self-application grows exponentially with the number of self-application levels.

   Solutions. Different approaches have been employed to improve the performance of self-application: *action trees* [6], an off-line method that compiles the information obtained by the binding-time analysis into directives for the partial evaluator; *freezer* [26] in supercompilation, an on-line method that allows the evaluation of metacoded expressions by the underlying implementation; the *"cogen approach"* [4] fixes an MST-scheme two self-applications; the *"multi-cogen approach"* [11] is an effective solution for multiple self-application; *incremental self-application* [9] for 'step-wise' self-application.

2. **Space consumption.** This representation problem is caused by repeated metacoding. An example is the notorious encoding problem well-known from self-application of partial evaluators for typed languages [16]: types in source programs need to be mapped into an universal type in the partial evaluator. A straightforward, additive encodings (as in Example 3) leads to an exponential growth in the number of metacodings.

   Solutions. Choosing a more effective metacoding may reduce the metacode explosion to logarithmic cost, as with the external metacode; fixing the metasystem hierarchy to a certain MST-scheme, *e.g.* to multiple self-application of a partial evaluator, as in the (multi-)cogen approach.

Generator time.

1. **Computation time.** The run-time of the generated program depends on the operations inherited from the metasystem hierarchy, *e.g.* metacode operations.

   Solutions. The binding-time analysis is an effective solution for partial evaluation because all metacode operations are computed at transformation time.

2. **Space consumption.** The size of the generated programs is affected by the number of transformation operations left in the generated program. Consider the case of multiple self-application in partial evaluation [9]: each level of self-application adds one more layer of code generation to the generated generating extension: code is generated that generates code-generating code that generates code-generating code *etc.*

   Solutions. Since the binding-time analysis of offline partial evaluation aims at removing all operations on metacode, the resulting generators are much smaller, than those generators incorporating these operations. Another solution is to parameterize code generation, as in the multi-cogen approach [11].

5 A Case Study: Starmix

In this section we report on preliminary results with an implementation based on some of concepts put forward in the previous sections. A main goal is to design a *multi-level metaprogramming environment* that makes program transformation via metasystem hierarchies practical. The ultimate goal is to provide a metaprogramming environment not biased towards a particular form of metacomputation. At the present stage of our work, however, we have program specialization in mind. In particular, we applied some of these principles to the design of a fully self-applicable online partial evaluator that fullfills the 'mix criterion'. The system is implemented in the functional language Scheme. Here we can only briefly review the system, as space is limited. Similar methods can be used in other languages.

Structure. The system consists of two components: (1) a metainterpreter *mint* that implements a so-called internal metacode [27] and provides, beside the standard Scheme procedures, additional operations on the metacode ('Scheme*'), (2) a self-applicable partial evaluator *peval* that uses the metacode operations provided by the metainterpreter. The concrete representation of metavariables in the metainterpreter is hidden from the partial evaluator (and can be changed without affecting the working of the partial evaluator). Ultimately all Scheme* operations could be provided by the underlying Scheme implementation, instead of using a metainterpreter *mint*.

Metainterpreter. We realized an internal metacode in the metainterpreter. In fact, the metainterpreter extends the standard S-expressions with additional metavariables ('Data*'). Their representation is entirely hidden in the metainterpreter. Beside the conventional Scheme procedures (CAR, CDR, *etc.*), the following set of metaprogramming procedures is provided: creation of metavariables (MVAR), test for metavariables (MVAR?), and conversion of the internal representation into a valid Scheme* expression (UPCODE). The semantics of the operations is defined in Appendix A. Other operations can be provided in a similar way.

Metacoding. The metacode makes use of level numbers and, thus, avoids the exponential growth of straightforward, additive encodings (as in Example 3). In fact, we can distinguish between two encodings: the first encoding to represent *B*-expressions as S-expressions, and a second encoding to metacode S-expressions. The latter is defined in Appendix A.

Partial evaluation. Self-application runs on the metainterpreter and the partial evaluator makes use of the procedures provided by the metainterpreter, in particular operating on the metacode.

Results. A prototype has been constructed, that gives sensible and efficient results on programs including the 'classical' examples of a Turing machine interpreter (with a dynamic tape) and the Norma interpreter (with dynamic input y). The system fulfills the 'mix criterion' for multiple self-application.

While multiple self-application is space efficient, the specialization time is slow compared to existing program specializers because multiple self-application runs on a metainterpreter which in turn runs on a Scheme interpreter (and the present implementation of the partial evaluator and the metainterpreter has not been tuned for speed). As with other programs that are specialized, binding-time improvements were necessary in the partial evaluator to ensure sufficient flow of 'static' values and thereby avoid 'overly general' program generators. Technically speaking, we could make use of our own 'medicine' and specialize the metainpreter with respect to the partial evaluator to remove the interpretive overhead and to 'inline' the metacode procedures.

6   Related Work

The idea of encoding expressions as data that can be manipulated as objects can be traced back to Gödel who used natural numbers for representing expressions in a first order language (Gödel numbering) to prove the well-known completeness and incompleteness theorems and is a standard method in mathematical logics. In computer science, especially in the area of logic programming, the encoding of programs has been studied under various names, *e.g. naming relation* [28, 2]. Representing and reasoning about object level theories is an important field in logic and artificial intelligence and has led to the development of logic languages that facilitate metaprogramming (*e.g.* the logic languages Gödel [15] and Reflective Prolog [7] provide a built-in ground representation). The reader is referred to the surveys on metaprogramming [2, 13] and for metaprogramming techniques to the textbook [22].

The reader may be surprised that we have not discussed non-ground and ground representation, as is customary in the field of metaprogramming. Firstly, non-ground representation is not as expressive as ground representation [13, 18, 20], although it can be advantageous in certain cases to speed-up metacomputation [5]. Secondly, using non-ground representation in multi-level metasystem hierarchies is risky at best because levels are easily confused in multi-level hierarchies (this problem has been addressed in [14, 21]). Thirdly, logic variables and unification, as provided by the underlying logic system, on which a non-ground representation relies, lack the notion of elevation which, as argued above, is essential for the correct treatment of metavariables in a metasystem hierarchy. In conclusion, what is needed is an efficient and powerful multi-level metaprogramming environment with a clean semantic foundation instead of a 'patched-up' solution.

A multilevel metalogic programming language has been suggested in [3], an approach similar to our multi-level metaprogramming environment, but directed towards the hierarchical organization of knowledge (*e.g.* for legal reasoning) and allowing deductions on different metalevels. Type systems may be added to facilitate declarative metaprogramming in a multi-level metaprogramming environment (similar to [14, 15]).

Acknowledgments. This work could not have been carried out without the pioneering work of Valentin Turchin. We are grateful for many stimulating discussions. It is a pleasure to acknowledge many useful discussions with Andrei Klimov on related topics. Neil Jones and Bern Martens gave valuable feedback on an earlier version of the paper. Thanks are also due to Anders Bondorf, John Hatcliff, Jesper Jørgensen, Laura Lafave, Michael Leuschel, Kristian Nielsen, Sergei Romanenko, and the anonymous referees for constructive comments. It is a pleasure to acknowledge the presentation and discussion of this paper at LoPSTr'95.

References

1. Sergei M. Abramov. Metacomputation and logic programming. *Programmirovanie*, (3):31–44, 1991. (In Russian).
2. Jonas Barklund. Metaprogramming in logic. Technical Report 80, Uppsala University, Dept. of Computing Science, 1994. To be published in *Encyclopedia of Computer Science and Technology*, Marcell Dekker, New York.
3. Jonas Barklund, Katrin Boberg, and Pierangelo Dell'Acqua. A basis for a multilevel metalogic programming language. In L. Fribourg and F. Turini, editors, *Logic Program Synthesis and Transformation – Meta-Programming in Logic. Proceedings*, volume 883 of *Lecture Notes in Computer Science*, pages 262–275. Springer-Verlag, 1994.
4. Lars Birkedal and Morten Welinder. Hand-writing program generator generators. In M. Hermenegildo and J. Penjam, editors, *Programming Language Implementation and Logic Programming. Proceedings*, volume 844 of *Lecture Notes in Computer Science*, pages 198–214. Springer-Verlag, 1994.
5. Antony F. Bowers and Corin A. Gurr. Towards fast and declarative metaprogramming. In K. Apt and F. Turini, editors, *Meta-Logics and Logic Programming*, Logic Programming, pages 137–166. MIT Press, 1995.
6. Charles Consel and Olivier Danvy. From interpreting to compiling binding times. In N. D. Jones, editor, *ESOP '90*, volume 432 of *Lecture Notes in Computer Science*, pages 88–105. Springer-Verlag, 1990.
7. Stefania Costantini and Gaetano Lanzarone. A metalogic programming language. In G. Levi and M. Martelli, editors, *Proceedings Sixth International Conference on Logic Programming*, pages 218–233. MIT Press, 1989.
8. Yoshihiko Futamura. Partial evaluation of computing process – an approach to a compiler-compiler. *Systems, Computers, Controls*, 2(5):45–50, 1971.
9. Robert Glück. Towards multiple self-application. In *Proceedings of the Symposium on Partial Evaluation and Semantics-Based Program Manipulation*, pages 309–320. ACM Press, 1991.
10. Robert Glück. On the generation of specializers. *Journal of Functional Programming*, 4(4):499–514, 1994.
11. Robert Glück and Jesper Jørgensen. Efficient multi-level generating extensions for program specialization. In S.D. Swierstra and M. Hermenegildo, editors, *Programming Languages: Implementations, Logics and Programs (PLILP'95)*, volume 982 of *Lecture Notes in Computer Science*, pages 259–278. Springer-Verlag, 1995.
12. Robert Glück and Andrei V. Klimov. Metasystem transition schemes in computer science and mathematics. *World Futures: the Journal of General Evolution*, 45:213–243, 1995.
13. Patricia Hill and John Gallagher. Meta-programming in logic programming. Technical Report 94.22, School of Computer Studies, University of Leeds, 1994. To be published in *Handbook of Logic in Artificial Intelligence and Logic Programming*, Vol. V. Oxford University Press.

14. Patricia Hill and John W. Lloyd. Analysis of meta-programs. In H. D. Abramson and M. H. Rogers, editors, *Meta-Programming in Logic Programming. Proceedings Meta'88*, pages 23–52. MIT Press, 1989.
15. Patricia Hill and John W. Lloyd. *The Gödel Programming Language*. MIT Press, Cambridge, Massachusetts, 1994.
16. Neil D. Jones, Carsten K. Gomard, and Peter Sestoft. *Partial Evaluation and Automatic Program Generation*. Prentice-Hall, 1993.
17. Neil D. Jones, Peter Sestoft, and Harald Søndergaard. An experiment in partial evaluation: the generation of a compiler generator. In J.-P. Jouannaud, editor, *Rewriting Techniques and Applications*, volume 202 of *Lecture Notes in Computer Science*, pages 124–140. Springer-Verlag, 1985.
18. Michael Leuschel and Bern Martens. Partial deduction of the ground representation and its application to integrity checking. In J.W. Lloyd, editor, *Logic Programming: Proceedings of the 1995 International Symposium*, Logic Programming, pages 495–509. MIT Press, 1995.
19. John W. Lloyd and J. C. Shepherdson. Partial evaluation in logic programming. *Journal of Logic Programming*, 11(3–4):217–242, 1991.
20. Bern Martens and Danny De Schreye. Two semantics for definite meta-programs, using the non-ground representation. In K. Apt and F. Turini, editors, *Meta-Logics and Logic Programming*, Logic Programming, pages 57–81. MIT Press, Cambridge, Massachusetts, 1995.
21. Bern Martens and Danny De Schreye. Why untyped non-ground meta-programming is not (much of) a problem. *Journal of Logic Programming*, 22(1):47–99, 1995.
22. Leon Sterling and Ehud Shapiro. *The Art of Prolog*. MIT Press, Cambridge, Massachusetts, 1986.
23. Valentin F. Turchin. *The Phenomenon of Science*. Columbia University Press, New York, 1977.
24. Valentin F. Turchin. The language Refal, the theory of compilation and metasystem analysis. Courant Computer Science Report 20, Courant Institute of Mathematical Sciences, New York University, 1980.
25. Valentin F. Turchin. The concept of a supercompiler. *Transactions on Programming Languages and Systems*, 8(3):292–325, 1986.
26. Valentin F. Turchin. *Refal-5, Programming Guide and Reference Manual*. New England Publishing Co., Holyoke, Massachusetts, 1989.
27. Valentin F. Turchin and Andrei P. Nemytykh. Metavariables: their implementation and use in program transformation. Technical Report CSc. TR 95-012, City College of the City University of New York, 1995.
28. Frank van Harmelen. Definable naming relations in meta-level systems. In A. Pettorossi, editor, *Meta-Programming in Logic. Proceedings*, volume 649 of *Lecture Notes in Computer Science*, pages 89–104. Springer-Verlag, 1992.

A Metainterpreter

A.1 Internal Metacode: Data*

Metavariables and data are represented as S-expressions in Scheme*. Lists are marked with tag L, while metavariables are marked with a degree d (the number of metacodings). We omitted a degree for data, since generalization of data does not take place in folding and we never need to determine its degree (bias towards mix partial evaluation).

Expression	b	s
Atom	k	k
Metavariable	m_h	$(d\ m\ h)$
List	$[b_1 \ldots b_n]$	$(L\ s_1 \ldots s_n)$

Metacoding in Data* is straightforward, once an expression is represented in the internal metacode. The space required for the representation of the metacode grows logarithmically in the number of metacodings.

Expression	s	$\overline{s}$
Atom	k	k
Metavariable	$(i\ m\ h)$	$(i+1\ h\ m)$
List	$(L\ s_1 \ldots s_n)$	$(L\ \overline{s_1} \ldots \overline{s_n})$

The function *upcode* converts Data* into a Scheme* expression. This is used when data* has to be converted in code (*e.g.* lifting).

Expression	s	$\underline{s}$
Atom	k	$(L\ \text{QUOTE}\ k)$
Metavariable	$(i\ m\ h)$	$(L\ \text{MVAR}\ \underline{i}\ \underline{h}\ \underline{m})$
List	$(L\ s_1 \ldots s_n)$	$(L\ \text{LIST}\ \underline{s_1} \ldots \underline{s_n})$

A.2 Semantics: Scheme*

The metacode operations and a few Scheme operations are shown (the remaining operations are implemented similar to CAR, CDR, *etc.*).

$$\{MVAR\} \quad \frac{\Gamma \vdash e_1 \hookrightarrow d \quad \Gamma \vdash e_2 \hookrightarrow h \quad \Gamma \vdash e_3 \hookrightarrow m}{\Gamma \vdash (\text{MVAR}\ e_1\ e_2\ e_3) \hookrightarrow (\text{M}\ d\ h\ m)}$$

$$\{MVAR?\} \quad \frac{\Gamma \vdash e_1 \hookrightarrow d \quad \Gamma \vdash e_2 \hookrightarrow (\text{M}\ d'\ h\ m) \quad isEqual(d, d') = t}{\Gamma \vdash (\text{MVAR?}\ e_1\ e_2) \hookrightarrow t}$$

$$\{UPCODE\} \quad \frac{\Gamma \vdash e \hookrightarrow a \quad upcode(a) = a'}{\Gamma \vdash (\text{UPCODE}\ e) \hookrightarrow a'}$$

$$\{CAR\} \quad \frac{\Gamma \vdash e \hookrightarrow (L\ a.b)}{\Gamma \vdash (\text{CAR}\ e) \hookrightarrow a}$$

$$\{CDR\} \quad \frac{\Gamma \vdash e \hookrightarrow (L\ a.b)}{\Gamma \vdash (\text{CDR}\ e) \hookrightarrow (L\ b)}$$

$$\{LIST\} \quad \frac{\Gamma \vdash e_1 \hookrightarrow a_1 \ldots \Gamma \vdash e_n \hookrightarrow a_n}{\Gamma \vdash (\text{LIST}\ e_1 \ldots e_n) \hookrightarrow (L\ a_1 \ldots a_n)}$$

Efficient Translation of Lazy Functional Logic Programs into Prolog

Michael Hanus

Informatik II, RWTH Aachen
D-52056 Aachen, Germany
`hanus@informatik.rwth-aachen.de`

Abstract. In this paper, we present a high-level implementation of lazy functional logic programs by transforming them into Prolog programs. The transformation is controlled by generalized definitional trees which specify the narrowing strategy to be implemented. Since we consider a sophisticated narrowing strategy, a direct mapping of functions into predicates is not possible. Therefore, we present new techniques to reduce the interpretational overhead of the generated Prolog code. This leads to a portable and efficient implementation of functional logic programs.

1 Introduction

In recent years, a lot of proposals have been made to amalgamate functional and logic programming languages [15]. Functional logic languages with a sound and complete operational semantics are based on *narrowing*, a combination of the reduction principle of functional languages and the resolution principle of logic languages. Narrowing, originally introduced in automated theorem proving [26], is used to *solve* equations by finding appropriate values for variables occurring in arguments of functions. A *narrowing step* instantiates some variables in a goal and applies a reduction step to a redex of the instantiated goal. The instantiation of goal variables is usually computed by unifying a subterm of the goal with the left-hand side of some rule.

Example 1. Consider the following rules defining the addition and comparison of natural numbers which are represented by terms built from 0 and s:

$$
\begin{array}{ll}
0 + y \;\rightarrow\; y & (R_1) \\
s(x) + y \;\rightarrow\; s(x + y) & (R_2)
\end{array}
\qquad
\begin{array}{lll}
0 \le x & \rightarrow\; true & (R_3) \\
s(x) \le 0 & \rightarrow\; false & (R_4) \\
s(x) \le s(y) & \rightarrow\; x \le y & (R_5)
\end{array}
$$

The equation $x + y \le 0 \approx true$ can be solved by a narrowing step with rule R_1 followed by a narrowing step with rule R_3 so that x and y are instantiated to 0 and the instantiated equation is reduced to the trivial equation $true \approx true$:

$$ x + y \le 0 \approx true \;\leadsto_{\{x \mapsto 0\}}\; y \le 0 \approx true \;\leadsto_{\{y \mapsto 0\}}\; true \approx true $$

Hence we have found the solution $\{x \mapsto 0, y \mapsto 0\}$ to the given equation. □

Similarly to functional languages, we have to fix the selection of positions for the next narrowing step in order to reduce the search space. Eager functional logic languages like ALF [12], eager-BABEL [18], or SLOG [8] apply narrowing steps at innermost positions. To ensure completeness, they require a terminating set of rewrite rules which prohibit the application of typical functional programming techniques like infinite data structures. Therefore, we are interested in lazy narrowing strategies [22, 25] where narrowing steps are applied at outermost positions in general and at an inner position only if it is demanded and contributes to some later narrowing step at an outer position. Although such a lazy strategy can avoid useless computation steps, it has been shown that this is not generally true if one does not take care of a controlled instantiation of logical variables [4]. However, for the class of inductively sequential programs, which covers typical functional programs, there is a strategy, called *needed narrowing* [4], which is optimal w.r.t. the length of the narrowing derivations and the number of computed solutions. Inductively sequential programs do not allow overlapping left-hand sides of the rewrite rules. However, in some applications, particularly in logic programming, such overlapping rules are useful. Unfortunately, overlapping rules may lead to nonterminating computations w.r.t. lazy narrowing strategies [11]. This can be avoided if lazy narrowing is combined with simplification between narrowing steps [14]. Therefore, we obtain a good lazy narrowing strategy if we apply needed narrowing on inductively sequential programs and integrate simplification for the remaining programs.

In this paper, we consider the high-level implementation of such a sophisticated narrowing strategy. To avoid a complex direct implementation based on a new abstract machine (see [15] for a survey on these implementation techniques), we follow the proposals presented in [2, 6, 17, 19]. We translate lazy functional logic programs into Prolog programs and obtain by this simple transformation a portable and efficient implementation of our narrowing strategy. The translation of eager narrowing strategies into Prolog is straightforward by flattening nested function calls [5]. However, the translation of lazy narrowing strategies is a challenging task, in particular, if narrowing is interleaved with simplification. Our solution is the first Prolog implementation of a lazy narrowing strategy which comprises simplification. Nevertheless, we obtain a better run-time behavior w.r.t. previous work since we apply partial evaluation techniques to the translated program.

In the next section, we recall basic notions and introduce our narrowing strategy. In Section 3, we present the translation of inductively sequential programs, whereas Section 4 contains the translation of arbitrary functional logic programs. Optimizations obtained by partial evaluation and the implementation of sharing are discussed in Sections 5 and 6, respectively. Finally, we discuss the efficiency of our translation techniques by means of some benchmarks.

2 Lazy Narrowing Strategies

We assume familiarity with basic notions of term rewriting [7]. We consider a *many-sorted signature* partitioned into a set $\mathcal{C}$ of constructors and a set $\mathcal{F}$ of functions. We write $c/n \in \mathcal{C}$ and $f/n \in \mathcal{F}$ for n-ary constructor and function symbols, respectively. The set of *terms* and *constructor terms* with variables from

$\mathcal{X}$ are denoted by $\mathcal{T}(\mathcal{C} \cup \mathcal{F}, \mathcal{X})$ and $\mathcal{T}(\mathcal{C}, \mathcal{X})$. $Var(t)$ denotes the set of variables occurring in a term t. A *pattern* is a term of the form $f(t_1, \ldots, t_n)$ where $f/n \in \mathcal{F}$ and $t_1, \ldots, t_n \in \mathcal{T}(\mathcal{C}, \mathcal{X})$. A *head normal form* is a variable or a term of the form $c(t_1, \ldots, t_n)$ with $c/n \in \mathcal{C}$. A *position* p in a term t is represented by a sequence of natural numbers, $t|_p$ denotes the *subterm* of t at position p, and $t[s]_p$ denotes the result of *replacing the subterm* $t|_p$ by the term s (see [7] for details).

A *term rewriting system* $\mathcal{R}$ is a set of *rewrite rules* $l \to r$ where l is a pattern and $Var(r) \subseteq Var(l)$. l and r are called left-hand side and right-hand side, respectively.[1] A rewrite rule is called a *variant* of another rule if it is obtained by a unique replacement of variables by other variables.

Narrowing is a method to compute solutions to an equation $s \approx t$. $t \leadsto_\sigma t'$ is a narrowing step if there are a nonvariable position p in t (i.e., $t|_p \notin \mathcal{X}$), a variant $l \to r$ of a rewrite rule of $\mathcal{R}$ with $Var(t) \cap Var(l) = \emptyset$, and a unifier[2] σ of $t|_p$ and l with $t' := \sigma(t[r]_p)$.[3] Since narrowing applies rewrite rules only in one direction, additional restrictions are necessary for the completeness of narrowing, i.e., we require the confluence of $\mathcal{R}$. This can be ensured by the following condition: if $l_1 \to r_1$ and $l_2 \to r_2$ are variants of rewrite rules and σ is a unifier for l_1 and l_2, then $\sigma(r_1) = \sigma(r_2)$ (*weak orthogonality*).

Since we do not require terminating term rewriting systems, normal forms may not exist. Therefore, we define the validity of an equation as a *strict equality* on terms [10, 22] by the following rules, where $\wedge$ is assumed to be a right-associative infix symbol.

$$c \approx c \to true \qquad\qquad\qquad \forall c/0 \in \mathcal{C}$$
$$c(x_1, \ldots, x_n) \approx c(y_1, \ldots, y_n) \to (x_1 \approx y_1) \wedge \cdots \wedge (x_n \approx y_n) \quad \forall c/n \in \mathcal{C}$$
$$true \wedge x \to x$$

A solution of an *equation* $t_1 \approx t_2$ is computed by narrowing it to *true* with these rules. Since this simple narrowing procedure (enumerating all narrowing derivations) is very inefficient, several authors have proposed restrictions on the admissible narrowing derivations (see [15] for a detailed survey). We are interested in *lazy narrowing* [21, 25] which is influenced by the idea of lazy evaluation in functional programming languages. Lazy narrowing steps are only applied at outermost positions with the exception that arguments are evaluated by narrowing to their head normal form if their values are required for an outermost narrowing step. Since the notion of "required arguments" depends on the rule to be applied

---

[1] In this paper, we consider only unconditional rewrite rules for the sake of simplicity. Nevertheless, the presented implementation techniques can be extended to conditional rules (e.g., as done in [19]) and completeness results for the conditional case can be found in [16].

[2] In most papers, narrowing is defined with most general unifiers. As shown in [4], an optimal narrowing strategy which avoids superfluous steps can only be obtained if the restriction to mgu's is dropped. Therefore, we consider arbitrary unifiers. However, only a small subset of these unifiers are computed by our narrowing strategy.

[3] Since the instantiation of the variables in the rule $l \to r$ by σ is not relevant for the computed solution of a narrowing derivation, we omit this part of σ in the example derivations in this paper.

and leaves some freedom, different lazy narrowing strategies have been proposed [4, 17, 19, 21, 22]. We will specify our narrowing strategy by the use of definitional trees, a concept introduced by Antoy [3] to define efficient normalization strategies.

$\mathcal{T}$ is called *generalized definitional tree* with pattern π iff one of the following cases holds:

$\mathcal{T} = rule(\pi \to r)$, where $\pi \to r$ is a variant of a rule in $\mathcal{R}$.

$\mathcal{T} = branch(\pi, o, \mathcal{T}_1, \ldots, \mathcal{T}_k)$, where π is a pattern, o is an occurrence of a variable in π, $c_1, \ldots, c_k$ are different constructors of the sort of $\pi|_o$ ($k > 0$), and, for $i = 1, \ldots, k$, $\mathcal{T}_i$ is a generalized definitional tree with pattern $\pi[c_i(x_1, \ldots, x_n)]_o$, where n is the arity of c_i and $x_1, \ldots, x_n$ are new distinct variables.

$\mathcal{T} = or(\mathcal{T}_1, \ldots, \mathcal{T}_k)$, where $\mathcal{T}_1, \ldots, \mathcal{T}_k$ are generalized definitional trees with pattern π.

A *generalized definitional tree* of an n-ary function f is a generalized definitional tree $\mathcal{T}$ with pattern $f(x_1, \ldots, x_n)$, where $x_1, \ldots, x_n$ are distinct variables, such that for each rule $l \to r$ with $l = f(t_1, \ldots, t_n)$ there is a node $rule(l' \to r')$ in $\mathcal{T}$ with l variant of l'. A *definitional tree* is a generalized definitional tree without *or*-nodes.[4] For instance, the definitional tree of the function $\leq$ in Example 1 is

$$branch(x \leq y, 1, rule(\mathbf{0} \leq y \to true),$$
$$branch(s(x_1) \leq y, 2, rule(s(x_1) \leq \mathbf{0} \to false),$$
$$rule(s(x_1) \leq s(y_1) \to x_1 \leq y_1)))$$

A function f is called *inductively sequential* if there exists a definitional tree of f such that each *rule* node corresponds to exactly one rule of $\mathcal{R}$. We denote this property by $f/n \in IS(\mathcal{R})$. The term rewriting system $\mathcal{R}$ is called inductively sequential if each function defined by $\mathcal{R}$ is inductively sequential.

A generalized definitional tree defines a strategy to apply narrowing steps.[5] To narrow a term t, we consider the generalized definitional tree $\mathcal{T}$ of the outermost function symbol of t (note that, by definition of strict equality, the outermost symbol is always a function if we narrow equations):

$\mathcal{T} = rule(\pi \to r)$: Apply rule $\pi \to r$ to t (note that t is always an instance of π).

$\mathcal{T} = branch(\pi, o, \mathcal{T}_1, \ldots, \mathcal{T}_k)$: Consider the subterm $t|_o$.
1. If $t|_o$ has a function symbol at the top, we narrow this subterm (to a head normal form) by recursively applying our strategy to $t|_o$.
2. If $t|_o$ has a constructor symbol at the top, we narrow t with $\mathcal{T}_j$, where the pattern of $\mathcal{T}_j$ unifies with t, otherwise (if no pattern unifies) we fail.
3. If $t|_o$ is a variable, we nondeterministically select a subtree $\mathcal{T}_j$, unify t with the pattern of $\mathcal{T}_j$ (i.e., $t|_o$ is instantiated to the constructor of the pattern of $\mathcal{T}_j$ at position o), and narrow this instance of t with $\mathcal{T}_j$.

$\mathcal{T} = or(\mathcal{T}_1, \ldots, \mathcal{T}_k)$: Nondeterministically select a subtree $\mathcal{T}_j$ and proceed narrowing t with $\mathcal{T}_j$.

---

[4] This corresponds to Antoy's notion [3] except that we ignore *exempt* nodes.

[5] Due to lack of space, we omit a precise definition which can be found in [4] for inductively sequential systems and in [19] for generalized definitional trees.

For definitional trees (i.e., without *or* nodes), this strategy is called *needed narrowing* [4] which is the currently best narrowing strategy due to its optimality w.r.t. the length of derivations (if terms are shared, compare Section 6) and the number of computed solutions. For instance, the rewrite system of Example 1 is inductively sequential and the successful derivation is a needed narrowing derivation. There is only one further needed narrowing derivation for this goal, which is not successful:

$$x + y \leq 0 \approx true \leadsto_{\{x \mapsto s(x_1)\}} s(x_1 + y) \leq 0 \approx true \leadsto_{\{\}} false \approx true$$

Note that the equivalent Prolog program obtained by flattening [5] has an infinite search space, since the first literal of the goal "add(X,Y,Z),leq(Z,0,true)" has infinitely many solutions (which can be avoided by additional delay declarations [23]; however, this may cause the loss of completeness).

We consider generalized definitional trees as a part of the program since they specify the concrete evaluation strategy (like when/wait declarations in Prolog systems). However, the user can also omit the trees since there are various methods to construct them (e.g., [19]).

3 Translation of Inductively Sequential Programs

In this section, we assume that $\mathcal{R}$ is inductively sequential. For this class of programs, it is shown in [4] that needed narrowing, i.e., narrowing with definitional trees, is an optimal strategy. To implement this strategy, we define three kinds of predicates in Prolog:

1. A === B is satisfied if A and B are strictly equal, i.e., A and B are reducible to a same ground constructor term. This predicate is implemented by repeated narrowing of A and B to head normal forms and comparing the outermost constructors (note that lazy narrowing reduces terms to head normal form and not to normal form).
2. hnf(T,H) is satisfied if H is a head normal form of T. If T is not in head normal form, T is narrowed using the strategy described above.
3. $f_p(t_1, \ldots, t_n, H)$ is satisfied if H is a head normal form of $f(t_1, \ldots, t_n)$, where the subterms of $f(t_1, \ldots, t_n)$ at the positions in the set p are already in head normal form.

The clauses to define strict equality are straightforward:

```
A === B :- hnf(A,HA), hnf(B,HB), seq(HA,HB).
seq(c(X₁,...,Xₙ),c(Y₁,...,Yₙ)) :- X₁===Y₁,...,Xₙ===Yₙ.    ∀c/n ∈ C
```

The clauses to define hnf are also a straightforward translation of the definition of head normal form:

```
hnf(T,T) :- var(T), !.
hnf(f(X₁,...,Xₙ),H) :- !, f∅(X₁,...,Xₙ,H).    ∀f/n ∈ F
hnf(T,T).    % T is constructor-headed due to the previous clauses.
```

The definition of the clauses for the predicates $f_p(X_1, \ldots, X_n, H)$ is slightly more complicated but also an obvious translation of our previously described strategy.

We specify the generation of these clauses by a translation function *trans* which takes a definitional tree $\mathcal{T}$ with pattern π and a set p of already evaluated positions of π as input and yields a set of Prolog clauses. Each function f is translated by $trans(\mathcal{T}, \emptyset)$ if $\mathcal{T}$ is a definitional tree of f.

$trans(rule(f(t_1, \ldots, t_n) \to r), p) \quad :=$

$\boxed{f_p(t_1, \ldots, t_n, \text{H}) \ :\text{-}\ \text{hnf}(r, \text{H}).}$

$trans(branch(\pi, o, \mathcal{T}_1, \ldots, \mathcal{T}_k), p) \quad :=$

$\boxed{f_p(t_1, \ldots, t_n, \text{H}) \ :\text{-}\ \text{hnf}(x, \text{Y}),\ f_{p \cup \{o\}}(t'_1, \ldots, t'_n, \text{H}).}$

$trans(\mathcal{T}_1, p \cup \{o\})$

$\ldots$

$trans(\mathcal{T}_k, p \cup \{o\})$

where $\pi = f(t_1, \ldots, t_n)$, $\pi|_o = x$, $\pi[\text{Y}]_o = f(t'_1, \ldots, t'_n)$

In these and all subsequent translation schemes, all unspecified variables occurring in the rules are new (here: H and Y are new variables). It is obvious that this translation scheme implements the narrowing strategy described above. To distinguish the different predicates corresponding to different nodes of $\mathcal{T}$, the predicate names are indexed by p. A *rule* node is translated into a clause which applies this rule by computing the head normal form of the right-hand side. For a *branch* node, the requested subterm is evaluated to head normal form followed by a call to the predicate corresponding to the immediate subtrees.

If we translate all rules of Example 1 by this scheme (the generated clauses are shown in Appendix A), we can compute solutions to the equation $z + s(0) \approx s(s(0))$ by proving the Prolog goal "?- Z+s(0)===s(s(0))."

4 Translation of Lazy Narrowing with Simplification

Inductively sequential systems do not allow *or* nodes in the definitional trees, in particular, overlapping rules are not permitted. Nevertheless, overlapping rules sometimes occur in programs written in a logic programming style. Therefore, we consider in this section a term rewriting system $\mathcal{R}$ which may not be inductively sequential. Our translation scheme could be simply extended to such programs by defining the following additional rule to translate *or* nodes:

$trans(or(\mathcal{T}_1, \ldots, \mathcal{T}_k), p) \quad :=$
$\qquad trans(\mathcal{T}_1, p) \ \cdots \ trans(\mathcal{T}_k, p)$

This means that the different alternatives represented by an *or* node are translated into alternative clauses (this is identical to the translation scheme in [19]), and we obtain the behavior of (simple) lazy narrowing [21, 22, 25]. However, in the presence of overlapping rules, simple lazy narrowing has a high risk to run into infinite loops by selecting the "wrong" rule and evaluating the "wrong" argument to head normal form.

Example 2. Consider the following rules defining arithmetic operations:

$$
\begin{array}{llll}
0 * x \ \to \ 0 & (R_1) & \qquad one(0) \ \to \ s(0) & (R_3) \\
x * 0 \ \to \ 0 & (R_2) & \qquad one(s(x)) \ \to \ one(x) & (R_4)
\end{array}
$$

To compute a solution to the equation $one(x) * 0 \approx 0$, we could choose rule R_1 to evaluate the left-hand side. Rule R_1 demands the evaluation of $one(x)$ to a head normal form. Unfortunately, there are infinitely many possibilities to evaluate $one(x)$, in particular, there is an infinite derivation using R_4 in each step:

$$one(x) * 0 \approx 0 \rightsquigarrow_{\{x \mapsto s(x_1)\}} one(x_1) * 0 \approx 0 \rightsquigarrow_{\{x_1 \mapsto s(x_2)\}} \cdots$$

This infinite loop can be avoided if the goal is *simplified* before a narrowing step is performed. Simplification is similar to narrowing but does not instantiate goal variables and is, therefore, a deterministic evaluation process. Since the term $one(x) * 0$ can be simplified to 0 by rule R_2, *lazy narrowing with simplification* [14] has a finite search space in this example. □

Lazy narrowing with simplification reduces the search space and is sound and complete if the set of rules used for simplification is terminating [14]. Moreover, simplification must be performed with the same strategy as narrowing (of course, without instantiating goal variables). Thus, we can define a similar translation scheme for simplification and call the predicates performing simplification before each narrowing step. However, simplification has no effect for inductively sequential systems due to the optimality of needed narrowing (see [14] for more details). Therefore, simplification should be applied only if a function $f/n \notin IS(\mathcal{R})$ occurs at run time. This leads to the following implementation scheme:

1. We generate the narrowing scheme of Section 3 for inductively sequential functions.
2. We generate a simplification scheme similar to the narrowing scheme. However, there are some important differences since simplification always succeeds and returns a simplified term which is not necessarily in head normal form.

The clauses of the predicate hnf are defined by the following modified scheme:

```
hnf(T,T) :- var(T), !.
hnf(f(X₁,...,Xₙ),H) :- !, f∅(X₁,...,Xₙ,H).    ∀f/n ∈ IS(R)
hnf(f(X₁,...,Xₙ),H) :- !, simp(f(X₁,...,Xₙ),T),
                          nstep(T,R,_), hnf(R,H).  ∀f/n ∉ IS(R)
hnf(T,T).
```

simp simplifies a term using the same strategy as narrowing, and nstep performs a single narrowing step on the simplified term. Due to the similarity of the strategies for simplification and narrowing, we implement simplification by a scheme similar to narrowing presented above. Thus, the predicate simp corresponds to the predicate hnf but with the difference that simp does not fail and always returns a simplified term (which may not be in head normal form if simplication rules are not applicable due to the insufficient instantiation of variables).

```
simp(T,T) :- var(T), !.
simp(f(X₁,...,Xₙ),T) :- !, simp_{f,∅}(X₁,...,Xₙ,T).  ∀f/n ∈ F
simp(T,T).
```

simp is called if a term T should be reduced to head normal form in order to apply a simplification step. The following translation scheme is similar to *trans*. It generates for each generalized definitional tree of a function f the clauses for simplifying a function call $f(\cdots)$:

$$simptrans(rule(f(t_1,\ldots,t_n) \to r),p) \quad :=$$

> $\text{simp}_{f,p}(t_1,\ldots,t_n,\text{R}) \;:\text{- } !, \; \text{simp}(r,\text{R}).$

$$simptrans(branch(\pi,o,T_1,\ldots,T_k),p) \quad :=$$

> $\text{simp}_{f,p}(t_1,\ldots,t_n,\text{R}) \;:\text{- } !, \; \text{simp}(x,\text{Y}),$
> $\quad (\text{nonvar}(\text{Y}) \; \text{->} \; \text{simp}_{f,p\cup\{o\}}(t'_1,\ldots,t'_n,\text{R}) \; ; \; \text{R}=f(t'_1,\ldots,t'_n) \;).$

$$simptrans(T_1,p \cup \{o\})$$

$$\ldots$$

$$simptrans(T_k,p \cup \{o\})$$

> $\text{simp}_{f,p\cup\{o\}}(t_1,\ldots,t_n,f(t_1,\ldots,t_n)).$

where $\pi = f(t_1,\ldots,t_n)$, $\pi|_o = x$, $\pi[\text{Y}]_o = f(t'_1,\ldots,t'_n)$

The cuts in the generated rules emphasize the deterministic behavior of the simplification process. The final clause generated for each *branch* node is necessary to return the current term instead of causing a failure if no simplification rule is applicable. The condition nonvar(Y) in the translation of *branch* nodes is necessary to ensure that the goal variable Y is not instantiated in subsequent simplification rules (recall that this is the basic difference between simplification and narrowing). If Y is an unbound variable, then no simplification rules of the subtrees $T_1,\ldots,T_k$ are applicable. Hence, the simplified term $f(t'_1,\ldots,t'_n)$ is returned instead of applying further simplification rules.

Additionally, a node $or(T_1,\ldots,T_k)$ is processed by *simptrans*[6] by translating each T_j into separate Prolog predicates. However, the translation scheme for T_j is slightly changed for $j = 1,\ldots,k-1$. Instead of constructing the term $f(t_1,\ldots,t_n)$ if no rule is applicable, the simplification predicates corresponding to the generalized definitional tree T_{j+1} are called since T_{j+1} may contain alternative simplification rules (see Appendix B for the translation of the overlapping *-rules of Example 2).

The predicate nstep is responsible to perform a *single* narrowing step. For this purpose, an additional argument C is used which is instantiated iff a narrowing step has been applied. Therefore, we generate the clauses

```
nstep(T,T,C) :- var(T), !.
nstep(f(X_1,...,X_n),T,C) :- !, f_step_∅(X_1,...,X_n,T,C).   ∀f/n ∈ F
nstep(T,T,C).   % T is constructor-headed due to the previous clauses.
```

and clauses for each generalized definitional tree by the following scheme, which is a slightly modified translation scheme for narrowing rules:

$$steptrans(rule(f(t_1,\ldots,t_n) \to r),p) \quad :=$$

> $f\text{\_step}_p(t_1,\ldots,t_n,r,\text{step}).$ % *instantiate control variable to* step

$$steptrans(branch(\pi,o,T_1,\ldots,T_k),p) \quad :=$$

> $f\text{\_step}_p(t_1,\ldots,t_n,\text{R},\text{C}) \;:\text{- } \text{nstep}(x,\text{Y},\text{C}),$
> $\quad (\text{var}(\text{C}) \; \text{->} \; f\text{\_step}_{p\cup\{o\}}(t'_1,\ldots,t'_n,\text{R},\text{C}) \; ; \; \text{R}=f(t'_1,\ldots,t'_n) \;).$

$$steptrans(T_1,p \cup \{o\})$$

$$\ldots$$

---

[6] Due to space limitations, we do not show the formal definition.

$$steptrans(\mathcal{T}_k, p \cup \{o\})$$
$$\textbf{where } \pi = f(t_1, \ldots, t_n), \ \pi|_o = x, \ \pi[\mathtt{Y}]_o = f(t'_1, \ldots, t'_n)$$
$$steptrans(or(\mathcal{T}_1, \ldots, \mathcal{T}_k), p) \quad :=$$
$$steptrans(\mathcal{T}_1, p)$$
$$\cdots$$
$$steptrans(\mathcal{T}_k, p)$$

Due to the condition `var(C)->`$\cdots$ in clauses corresponding to branch nodes, the predicate f_step_p may not return a head normal form but performs only one narrowing step. All clauses generated by our scheme for Example 2 are shown in Appendix B. The size of the translated programs is approximately doubled in comparison to the translation without the simplification scheme. This is due to the fact that each rule can be applied in a "narrowing mode" and a "simplification mode" which requires different implementations.

Since the rewrite rules are separately translated into clauses for narrowing and simplification, we can also choose different rewrite rules for narrowing and simplification. Actually, the programmer has to specify a terminating subset of $\mathcal{R}$ which is used for simplification in order to ensure completeness (see [14]). Moreover, it has been argued in [8] that it is sensible to use additionally inductive consequences or CWA-valid rules for simplification. All this is supported by our separate translation of narrowing and simplification rules.

5   Optimization by Partial Evaluation

It is not surprising that our general translation scheme contains many opportunities for optimization. Therefore, we add the following useful optimizations which are standard in the partial evaluation of logic programs [9]:

Delete redundant constructors: In a generalized definitional tree, the patterns of subtrees are instances of the patterns of ancestor nodes. Therefore, the generated clauses often contain redundant constructors, i.e., there are predicates p where all calls to p are of the form $p(\ldots, c(t), \ldots)$ and all left-hand sides have the same structure. In this case, we delete c.

Swap arguments for better indexing: Most Prolog implementations use first argument indexing [1]. In order to provide a portable *and* efficient implementation, we swap arguments so that the case distinction in left-hand sides is always made on the first argument (note that the *branch* nodes in a tree clearly indicate the indexed argument).

Unfold deterministic literals: The translation scheme for lazy narrowing with simplification often generates chains of predicate calls where at most one clause is applicable (see, for instance, predicates `hnf`, `simp`, `nstep`). To improve the execution time of the generated code, we unfold such deterministic predicate calls.

The optimized clauses corresponding to Example 1 can be found in Appendix C.

6 Implementation of Sharing

It is well-known that lazy evaluation strategies require the sharing of terms in order to avoid potential reevaluations of identical expressions. For instance, consider the rule

$$double(x) \rightarrow x + x$$

and the term $double(t)$ which is immediately rewritten to $t + t$. Thus, without sharing, t is evaluated twice. To avoid this problem, we have to share the result of evaluating t among the different occurrences of t. This can be implemented in Prolog by representing each function call $f(t_1, \ldots, t_n)$ by the term $f(S, t_1, \ldots, t_n, H)$ where S is an unbound variable until the call $f(t_1, \ldots, t_n)$ will be evaluated (to the head normal form H).[7] Therefore, we only have to change the definition of the predicates which triggers the computation of a head normal form (e.g., hnf in Section 3) so that a term $f(S, \ldots, H)$ will be evaluated to the head normal form H only if S is an unbound variable, otherwise H already contains the result. Thus, the new definition of hnf to implement sharing is

```
hnf(T,T) :- var(T), !.
hnf(f(S,X_1,...,X_n,H),H) :- !, (var(S) -> S=eval, f_0(X_1,...,X_n,H)
                             ; true ).      ∀f/n ∈ F
hnf(T,T).
```

7 Experimental Results

We have implemented the translation scheme as a compiler from lazy functional logic programs into Prolog. If all functions are inductively sequential, the scheme of Section 3 is used, otherwise the scheme presented in Section 4.

First we consider inductively sequential programs. The following table contains a comparison of our translation method w.r.t. the methods proposed in [2, 6, 17, 19]. Remember that natural numbers are implemented by $0/s$-terms. The translated programs are executed with Sicstus-Prolog 2.1 on a Sparc-10. The run times are in seconds for computing the first solution (an entry "?" denotes a run time of more than 1000 seconds).

Goal:	[2]	[6]	[17]	[19]	trans	sharing	Babel	direct
$10000 \le 10000 + 10000 \approx true$	0.39	6.1	0.7	0.32	0.25	0.39	0.16	0.10
$1000 \le x + x \approx true$	3.2	86.6	?	2.7	1.9	1.8	4.3	1.2
$400 + x \le (x + 200) + x \approx true$	4.8	?	?	2.2	1.7	2.3	4.1	0.6
$2000 \le 1000 + (x + x) \approx true$	3.3	83.1	?	2.7	1.9	1.8	4.2	5.3
$double(double(one(100000))) \approx x$	2.8	36.1	2.9	3.5	2.8	0.9	0.35	0.17

The column *trans* contains the execution times of our translation scheme (with the optimizations of Section 5) and column *sharing* the timings of our scheme

---

[7] This is nearly identical to the technique proposed in [6]. Jiménez-Martin et al. [17] proposed a similar technique, but it does not really implement sharing since they omitted the evaluation flag S.

with sharing (Section 6). In many cases sharing has no advantage but causes an overhead (note that [2, 19] do not implement sharing). Since [6, 17] are based on narrowing strategies different from needed narrowing, the results clearly show the superiority of the needed narrowing strategy. [2] uses only one predicate to implement all rewrite rules, and Loogen et al. [19] do not perform any optimizations on the generated clauses. This explains the worse execution times in comparison to our approach.

The column "Babel" shows the execution time of needed narrowing implemented in the functional logic language Babel based on the compilation into a low-level abstract machine [11]. It is interesting to note that our high-level implementation is faster for typical search problems. The column *direct* shows the run times of a direct definition of the predicates in Prolog which is often more efficient since term structures with nested functions calls are not generated (note that *direct* corresponds to a call-by-value strategy which can be implemented more efficiently). However, there is also an example where needed narrowing is much faster since it avoids the superfluous computation of some subterms. Moreover, needed narrowing allows the computation with infinite data structures and may terminate where logic programs have an infinite search space (see, for instance, Example 1). In order to make a fair comparison between our implementation of needed narrowing and Prolog, we have omitted such examples.

The direct implementation has a good behavior on this example since current Prolog implementations are tailored towards the efficient implementation of "functional-like" programs. However, there is an interesting class of programs, namely "generate-and-test" programs, where it has been shown that narrowing with simplification can dramatically reduce the search space [8, 13]. A typical example for such programs is the "permutation sort" program, where a list is sorted by enumerating all permutations and checking whether they are sorted. In the Prolog version of this program [27, p. 55], *all* permutations are enumerated and checked. However, if we execute the same program by lazy narrowing with simplification (in this case predicates are considered as Boolean functions, see [8, p. 182]), then the simplification process cuts some parts of the search space so that not all permutations are completely enumerated. Therefore, we obtain the following execution times in seconds to sort the list $[n, \ldots, 2, 1]$ for different values of n:

Length n	Prolog	Lazy	Lazy+Simp
5	0.01	0.06	0.06
6	0.05	0.4	0.2
7	0.4	2.8	0.4
8	3.0	22.9	1.0
9	27.3	212.2	2.1
10	281.3	2188.2	4.7

The column "Lazy+Simp" contains the execution times for lazy narrowing with simplification implemented as shown in this paper, the column "Lazy" the times for pure lazy narrowing without simplification (implemented as proposed in the beginning of Section 4), and the column "Prolog" the times for the direct implementation of permutation sort in Prolog. The search spaces of "Prolog" and "Lazy" are essentially the same. However, the last column shows that the overhead of the lazy narrowing implementation can be compensated by the search space reduction due to the simplification process.

8 Conclusions

We have presented a high-level implementation of lazy functional logic languages by a transformation into Prolog. For the operational semantics, we have considered needed narrowing for inductively sequential programs and lazy narrowing with simplification for programs with overlapping left-hand sides. We have introduced generalized definitional trees in order to specify the concrete narrowing strategy. We have shown that generalized definitional trees are also useful to specify and implement the transformation of functional logic programs into Prolog. Our implementation of needed narrowing is faster compared to previous approaches, whereas the implementation of lazy narrowing with simplification is a completely new approach. We have demonstrated the advanced operational behavior of the latter strategy in comparison to Prolog for a typical class of logic programs.

Our transformation yields a portable and efficient implementation of lazy functional logic programs. Since the transformation is strongly based on the formal definition of a narrowing strategy for which soundness and completeness results are known [4, 14], the implementation is also sound and complete (modulo incompleteness problems of Prolog implementations due to the backtracking strategy). This is in contrast to other, possibly more efficient implementations of functional logic programs in Prolog with coroutining [20, 24] that do not enjoy completeness due to floundering (i.e., unevaluable delayed literals).

References

1. H. Aït-Kaci. *Warren's Abstract Machine*. MIT Press, 1991.

2. S. Antoy. Non-Determinism and Lazy Evaluation in Logic Programming. In *Proc. Int. Workshop on Logic Program Synthesis and Transformation (LOPSTR'91)*, pp. 318–331. Springer Workshops in Computing, 1991.

3. S. Antoy. Definitional Trees. In *Proc. of the 3rd Int. Conference on Algebraic and Logic Programming*, pp. 143–157. Springer LNCS 632, 1992.

4. S. Antoy, R. Echahed, and M. Hanus. A Needed Narrowing Strategy. In *Proc. 21st ACM Symp. on Principles of Programming Languages*, pp. 268–279, Portland, 1994.

5. P.G. Bosco, E. Giovannetti, and C. Moiso. Narrowing vs. SLD-Resolution. *Theoretical Computer Science 59*, pp. 3–23, 1988.

6. P.H. Cheong and L. Fribourg. Implementation of Narrowing: The Prolog-Based Approach. In *Logic programming languages: constraints, functions, and objects*, pp. 1–20. MIT Press, 1993.

7. N. Dershowitz and J.-P. Jouannaud. Rewrite Systems. In J. van Leeuwen, editor, *Handbook of Theoretical Computer Science, Vol. B*, pp. 243–320. Elsevier, 1990.

8. L. Fribourg. SLOG: A Logic Programming Language Interpreter Based on Clausal Superposition and Rewriting. In *Proc. IEEE Int. Symposium on Logic Programming*, pp. 172–184, Boston, 1985.

9. J.P. Gallagher. Tutorial on Specialisation of Logic Programs. In *Proceedings of the ACM SIGPLAN Symposium on Partial Evaluation and Semantics Based Program Manipulation (PEPM'93)*, pp. 88–98. ACM Press, 1993.

10. E. Giovannetti, G. Levi, C. Moiso, and C. Palamidessi. Kernel LEAF: A Logic plus Functional Language. *Journal of Computer and System Sciences*, Vol. 42, No. 2, pp. 139–185, 1991.

11. W. Hans, R. Loogen, and S. Winkler. On the Interaction of Lazy Evaluation and Backtracking. In *Proc. of the 4th Int. Symposium on Programming Language Implementation and Logic Programming*, pp. 355–369. Springer LNCS 631, 1992.

12. M. Hanus. Compiling Logic Programs with Equality. In *Proc. of the 2nd Int. Workshop on Programming Language Implementation and Logic Programming*, pp. 387–401. Springer LNCS 456, 1990.

13. M. Hanus. Improving Control of Logic Programs by Using Functional Logic Languages. In *Proc. of the 4th International Symposium on Programming Language Implementation and Logic Programming*, pp. 1–23. Springer LNCS 631, 1992.

14. M. Hanus. Combining Lazy Narrowing and Simplification. In *Proc. of the 6th International Symposium on Programming Language Implementation and Logic Programming*, pp. 370–384. Springer LNCS 844, 1994.

15. M. Hanus. The Integration of Functions into Logic Programming: From Theory to Practice. *Journal of Logic Programming*, Vol. 19&20, pp. 583–628, 1994.

16. M. Hanus. On Extra Variables in (Equational) Logic Programming. In *Proc. International Conference on Logic Programming*, pp. 665–679. MIT Press, 1995.

17. J.A. Jiménez-Martin, J. Marino-Carballo, and J.J. Moreno-Navarro. Efficient Compilation of Lazy Narrowing into Prolog. In *Proc. Int. Workshop on Logic Program Synthesis and Transformation (LOPSTR'92)*, pp. 253–270. Springer, 1992

18. H. Kuchen, R. Loogen, J.J. Moreno-Navarro, and M. Rodríguez-Artalejo. Graph-based Implementation of a Functional Logic Language. In *Proc. ESOP 90*, pp. 271–290. Springer LNCS 432, 1990.

19. R. Loogen, F. Lopez Fraguas, and M. Rodríguez Artalejo. A Demand Driven Computation Strategy for Lazy Narrowing. In *Proc. of the 5th Int. Symp. on Programming Language Implementation and Logic Programming*, pp. 184–200. Springer LNCS 714, 1993.

20. T. Mogensen. Personal Communication. 1995

21. J.J. Moreno-Navarro, H. Kuchen, R. Loogen, and M. Rodríguez-Artalejo. Lazy Narrowing in a Graph Machine. In *Proc. Second International Conference on Algebraic and Logic Programming*, pp. 298–317. Springer LNCS 463, 1990.

22. J.J. Moreno-Navarro and M. Rodríguez-Artalejo. Logic Programming with Functions and Predicates: The Language BABEL. *Journal of Logic Programming*, Vol. 12, pp. 191–223, 1992.

23. L. Naish. *Negation and Control in Prolog*. Springer LNCS 238, 1987.

24. L. Naish. Adding equations to NU-Prolog. In *Proc. of the 3rd Int. Symposium on Programming Language Implementation and Logic Programming*, pp. 15–26. Springer LNCS 528, 1991.

25. U.S. Reddy. Narrowing as the Operational Semantics of Functional Languages. In *Proc. IEEE Int. Symposium on Logic Programming*, pp. 138–151, Boston, 1985.

26. J.R. Slagle. Automated Theorem-Proving for Theories with Simplifiers, Commutativity, and Associativity. *Journal of the ACM*, Vol. 21, No. 4, pp. 622–642, 1974.

27. L. Sterling and E. Shapiro. *The Art of Prolog*. MIT Press, 1986.

A Generated Prolog Clauses for Example 1

The program of Example 1 is inductively sequential where both functions have a unique definitional tree. Therefore, our transformation scheme of Section 3 generates the following Prolog program.

```
A===B :- hnf(A,HA), hnf(B,HB), seq(HA,HB).
seq(0,0).
seq(s(A),s(B)) :- A===B.
seq(false,false).
seq(true,true).

hnf(T,T) :- var(T), !.
hnf(A+B,H) :- !, +(A,B,H).
hnf(leq(A,B),H) :- !, leq(A,B,H).
hnf(T,T).

+(A,B,R) :- hnf(A,HA), '+_1'(HA,B,R).
'+_1'(0,B,R) :- hnf(B,R).
'+_1'(s(A),B,R) :- hnf(s(A+B),R).

leq(A,B,R) :- hnf(A,HA), leq_1(HA,B,R).
leq_1(0,B,R) :- hnf(true,R).
leq_1(s(A),B,R) :- hnf(B,HB), leq_1_2(s(A),HB,R).
leq_1_2(s(A),0,R) :- hnf(false,R).
leq_1_2(s(A),s(B),R) :- hnf(leq(A,B),R).
```

B Generated Prolog Clauses for Example 2

Since the program of Example 2 is not inductively sequential, we have to translate it by the transformation scheme of Section 4 which yields the following Prolog program.

```
A===B :- hnf(A,HA), hnf(B,HB), seq(HA,HB).
seq(0,0).
seq(s(A),s(B)) :- A===B.

hnf(T,T) :- var(T), !.
hnf(A*B,H) :- !, simp(A*B,T), nstep(T,R,_), hnf(R,H).
hnf(one(A),H) :- !, one(A,H).
hnf(T,T).

one(A,R) :- hnf(A,HA), one_1(HA,R).
one_1(0,R) :- hnf(s(0),R).
one_1(s(A),R) :- hnf(one(A),R).

simp(T,T) :- var(T), !.
simp(A*B,T) :- !, 'simp_*'(A,B,T).
simp(one(A),T) :- !, simp_one(A,T).
simp(T,T).

'simp_*'(A,B,R) :- !, simp(A,SA),
    (nonvar(SA) -> 'simp_*_1'(SA,B,R) ; 'simp_*_or'(SA,B,R)).
'simp_*_1'(0,A,R) :- !, simp(0,R). % first alternative of *
'simp_*_1'(A,B,R) :- 'simp_*_or'(A,B,R).
```

```
'simp_*_or'(A,B,R) :- !, simp(B,SB),
    (nonvar(SB) -> 'simp_*_or_2'(A,SB,R) ; R=A*SB).
'simp_*_or_2'(A,0,R) :- !, simp(0,R). % second alternative of *
'simp_*_or_2'(A,B,A*B).

simp_one(A,R) :- !, simp(A,SA),
    (nonvar(SA) -> simp_one_1(SA,R) ; R=one(SA)).
simp_one_1(0,R) :- !, simp(s(0),R).
simp_one_1(s(A),R) :- !, simp(one(A),R).
simp_one_1(A,one(A)).

nstep(T,T,C) :- var(T), !.
nstep(A*B,T,C) :- !, '*_step'(A,B,T,C).
nstep(one(A),T,C) :- !, one_step(A,T,C).
nstep(T,T,C).

'*_step'(A,B,R,C) :- nstep(A,NA,C),
    (var(C) -> '*_step_1'(NA,B,R,C) ; R=NA*B).
'*_step'(A,B,R,C) :- nstep(B,NB,C),
    (var(C) -> '*_step_2'(A,NB,R,C) ; R=A*NB).
'*_step_1'(0,A,0,step).
'*_step_2'(A,0,0,step).

one_step(A,R,C) :- nstep(A,NA,C),
    (var(C) -> one_step_1(NA,R,C) ; R=one(NA)).
one_step_1(0,s(0),step).
one_step_1(s(A),one(A),step).
```

C Optimized Prolog Program for Example 1

If we apply the optimization techniques discussed in Section 5 to the program of Appendix A, we obtain the following optimized Prolog program (where superfluous clauses are deleted).

```
A===B :- hnf(A,HA), hnf(B,HB), seq(HA,HB).
seq(0,0).
seq(s(A),s(B)) :- hnf(A,HA), hnf(B,HB), seq(HA,HB).
seq(false,false).
seq(true,true).

hnf(T,T) :- var(T), !.
hnf(A+B,H) :- !, hnf(A,HA), '+_1'(HA,B,H).
hnf(leq(A,B),H) :- !, hnf(A,HA), leq_1(HA,B,H).
hnf(T,T).

'+_1'(0,B,R) :- hnf(B,R).
'+_1'(s(A),B,s(A+B)).

leq_1(0,B,true).
leq_1(s(A),B,R) :- hnf(B,HB), leq_1s_2(HB,A,R).
leq_1s_2(0,A,false).
leq_1s_2(s(B),A,R) :- hnf(A,HA), leq_1(HA,B,R).
```

Author Index

Lecture Notes in Computer Science

For information about Vols. 1–975

please contact your bookseller or Springer-Verlag

Vol. 1011: T. Furuhashi (Ed.), Advances in Fuzzy Logic, Neural Networks and Genetic Algorithms. Proceedings, 1994. (Subseries LNAI).

Vol. 1012: M. Bartošek, J. Staudek, J. Wiedermann (Eds.), SOFSEM '95: Theory and Practice of Informatics. Proceedings, 1995. XI, 499 pages. 1995.

Vol. 1013: T W. Ling, A.O. Mendelzon, L. Vieille (Eds.), Deductive and Object-Oriented Databases. Proceedings, 1995. XIV, 557 pages. 1995.

Vol. 1014: A.P. del Pobil, M.A. Serna, Spatial Representation and Motion Planning. XII, 242 pages. 1995.

Vol. 1015: B. Blumenthal, J. Gornostaev, C. Unger (Eds.), Human-Computer Interaction. Proceedings, 1995. VIII, 203 pages. 1995.

VOL. 1016: R. Cipolla, Active Visual Inference of Surface Shape. XII, 194 pages. 1995.

Vol. 1017: M. Nagl (Ed.), Graph-Theoretic Concepts in Computer Science. Proceedings, 1995. XI, 406 pages. 1995.

Vol. 1018: T.D.C. Little, R. Gusella (Eds.), Network and Operating Systems Support for Digital Audio and Video. Proceedings, 1995. XI, 357 pages. 1995.

Vol. 1019: E. Brinksma, W.R. Cleaveland, K.G. Larsen, T. Margaria, B. Steffen (Eds.), Tools and Algorithms for the Construction and Analysis of Systems. Selected Papers, 1995. VII, 291 pages. 1995.

Vol. 1020: I.D. Watson (Ed.), Progress in Case-Based Reasoning. Proceedings, 1995. VIII, 209 pages. 1995. (Subseries LNAI).

Vol. 1021: M.P. Papazoglou (Ed.), OOER '95: Object-Oriented and Entity-Relationship Modeling. Proceedings, 1995. XVII, 451 pages. 1995.

Vol. 1022: P.H. Hartel, R. Plasmeijer (Eds.), Functional Programming Languages in Education. Proceedings, 1995. X, 309 pages. 1995.

Vol. 1023: K. Kanchanasut, J.-J. Lévy (Eds.), Algorithms, Concurrency ar d Knowlwdge. Proceedings, 1995. X, 410 pages. 1995.

Vol. 1024: R.T. Chin, H.H.S. Ip, A.C. Naiman, T.-C. Pong (Eds.), Image Analysis Applications and Computer Graphics. Proceedings, 1995. XVI, 533 pages. 1995.

Vol. 1025: C. Boyd (Ed.), Cryptography and Coding. Proceedings, 1995. IX, 291 pages. 1995.

Vol. 1026: P.S. Thiagarajan (Ed.), Foundations of Software Technology and Theoretical Computer Science. Proceedings, 1995. XII, 515 pages. 1995.

Vol. 1027: F.J. Brandenburg (Ed.), Graph Drawing. Proceedings, 1995. XII, 526 pages. 1996.

Vol. 1028: N.R. Adam, Y. Yesha (Eds.), Electronic Commerce. X, 155 pages. 1996.

Vol. 1029: E. Dawson, J. Golić (Eds.), Cryptography: Policy and Algcrithms. Proceedings, 1995. XI, 327 pages. 1996.

Vol. 1030: F. Pichler, R. Moreno-Díaz, R. Albrecht (Eds.), Computer Aided Systems Theory - EUROCAST '95. Proceedings, 1995. XII, 539 pages. 1996.

Vol.1031: M. Toussaint (Ed.), Ada in Europe. Proceedings, 1995. XI, 455 pages. 1996.

Vol. 1032: P. Godefroid, Partial-Order Methods for the Verification of Concurrent Systems. IV, 143 pages. 1996.

Vol. 1033: C.-H. Huang, P. Sadayappan, U. Banerjee, D. Gelernter, A. Nicolau, D. Padua (Eds.), Languages and Compilers for Parallel Computing. Proceedings, 1995. XIII, 597 pages. 1996.

Vol. 1034: G. Kuper, M. Wallace (Eds.), Constraint Databases and Applications. Proceedings, 1995. VII, 185 pages. 1996.

Vol. 1035: S.Z. Li, D.P. Mital, E.K. Teoh, H. Wang (Eds.), Recent Developments in Computer Vision. Proceedings, 1995. XI, 604 pages. 1996.

Vol. 1036: G. Adorni, M. Zock (Eds.), Trends in Natural Language Generation - An Artificial Intelligence Perspective. Proceedings, 1993. IX, 382 pages. 1996. (Subseries LNAI).

Vol. 1037: M. Wooldridge, J.P. Müller, M. Tambe (Eds.), Intelligent Agents II. Proceedings, 1995. XVI, 437 pages. 1996. (Subseries LNAI).

Vol. 1038: W: Van de Velde, J.W. Perram (Eds.), Agents Breaking Away. Proceedings, 1996. XIV, 232 pages. 1996. (Subseries LNAI).

Vol. 1039: D. Gollmann (Ed.), Fast Software Encryption. Proceedings, 1996. X, 219 pages. 1996.

Vol. 1040: S. Wermter, E. Riloff, G. Scheler (Eds.), Connectionist, Statistical, and Symbolic Approaches to Learning for Natural Language Processing. Proceedings, 1995. IX, 468 pages. 1996. (Subseries LNAI).

Vol. 1041: J. Dongarra, K. Madsen, J. Waśniewski (Eds.), Applied Parallel Computing. Proceedings, 1995. XII, 562 pages. 1996.

Vol. 1042: G. Weiß, S. Sen (Eds.), Adaption and Learning in Multi-Agent Systems. Proceedings, 1995. X, 238 pages. 1996. (Subseries LNAI).

Vol. 1043: F. Moller, G. Birtwistle (Eds.), Logics for Concurrency. XI, 266 pages. 1996.

Vol. 1044: B. Plattner (Ed.), Broadband Communications. Proceedings, 1996. XIV, 359 pages. 1996.

Vol. 1045: B. Butscher, E. Moeller, H. Pusch (Eds.), Interactive Distributed Multimedia Systems and Services. Proceedings, 1996. XI, 333 pages. 1996.

Vol. 1046: C. Puech, R. Reischuk (Eds.), STACS 96. Proceedings, 1996. XII, 690 pages. 1996.

Vol. 1047: E. Hajnicz, Time Structures. IX, 244 pages. 1996. (Subseries LNAI).

Vol. 1048: M. Proietti (Ed.), Logic Program Syynthesis and Transformation. Proceedings, 1995. X, 267 pages. 1996.

Vol. 1049: K. Futatsugi, S. Matsuoka (Eds.), Object Technologies for Advanced Software. Proceedings, 1996. X, 309 pages. 1996.

Vol. 1050: R. Dyckhoff, H. Herre, P. Schroeder-Heister (Eds.), Extensions of Logic Programming. Proceedings, 1996. VII, 318 pages. 1996. (Subseries LNAI).

Vol. 1051: M.-C. Gaudel, J. Woodcock (Eds.), FME '96: Industrial Benefit of Formal Methods. Proceedings, 1996. XII, 704 pages. 1996.